AF560810

ASIAN ECONOMIC INTEGRATION

ASIAN ECONOMIC INTEGRATION

Edited by

ANIL KUMAR THAKUR

and

ADESH SHARMA

Foreword by

PROFESSOR PULIN B. NAYAK

Director

Delhi School of Economics

Published on behalf of

THE INDIAN ECONOMIC ASSOCIATION

DEEP & DEEP PUBLICATIONS PVT. LTD.

F-159, Rajouri Garden, New Delhi-110027

ASIAN ECONOMIC INTEGRATION

ISBN 978-81-8450-058-5

Typeset by ASHISH TECHNOGRAPHICS,
3190, Mohindra Park, Shakur Basti, Delhi-110034.

Printed in India at NEW ELEGANT PRINTERS,
A-49/1, Maya Puri, Phase-I, New Delhi-110064.

Published by DEEP & DEEP PUBLICATIONS PVT. LTD.
F-159, Rajouri Garden, New Delhi-110027.
Phones: 25435369, 25440916
E-mail: ddpbooks@yahoo.co.in • ddpubs@gmail.com
Showroom:
2/13, Ansari Road, Daryaganj, New Delhi-110002 • Telefax: 23245122

Contents

Foreword

The continent of Asia is today at a momentous stage in its long and hoary history. China and India are today among the fastest growing major economies of the world. China has achieved a sustained growth rate of around 9 to 10 per cent over the past quarter century. India has recorded a growth rate of upwards of 8.5 per cent in the last four years, with the growth rate during 2006-07 being around 9.2 per cent. China and India together account for about 38 per cent of the world population and about 20 per cent of the global economy in terms of purchasing power parity. Some of the countries of East Asia today comprise the richest part of the world outside the old industrial centres of Western Europe and North America. Many of these countries have recorded spectacular improvements in human development indicators in terms of education and health status in recent years.

Yet it is also true that there are large tracts of Asia which are among the most underdeveloped parts of the world. Asia is home to the bulk of the world's poor and the deprived. The case for purposive economic and social policy to bring about rapid and equitable development has never been stronger than at present.

It is against this backdrop that the case for greater economic integration amongst Asian countries assumes significance. Indeed, this would also seem to be the imperative of the day. The European Economic Community was founded in 1957, and following the Maastricht Treaty the European Union came into being in 1993. The EU today is a powerful and growing political economic force in the world today bound by a common currency. Similar economic groupings have come-up in the context of the America as well. Even though the theoretical case for classical free trade in the tradition of Smith and Ricardo continues to dominate the intellectual discourse of academic economists, the politics of world trade and development have followed a course that has led to the mushrooming growth of regional trading blocks.

Regional trading blocks or customs unions are a classic instance of the theory of the second best at work. In his pioneering contribution on the customs union Jacob Viner in 1950 had analytically distinguished the trade creating and trade diverting effects of such trade groupings. While it is possible to argue that the members within a union might gain from such a move, the implication on world welfare need not necessarily be unambiguously positive.

Yet the case for Asian economic integration has never been stronger. Being the largest continent Asia possibly displays the widest diversity amongst its countries. But there are large geographic regions that share a common culture and history. It is one of the paradoxes of modern day globalisation characterised by the internet and jet travel that while individual countries in Asia would seem to have become closer to the US or countries in Western Europe, oftentimes the links with immediate neighbours within Asia are fraught with political and strategic differences. It goes without saying that the shedding of historical baggage and stinking cooperatively for a new resurgent Asia can only bring positive benefits to all members. Many crucial issues need to be considered carefully. For example, should we go in for a common currency? What are the pros and cons?

The editors of this volume, Dr. Anil Kumar Thakur and Dr. Adesh Sharma deserve our thanks for putting together this very useful volume which looks into the issues pertaining to the idea of Asian economic integration from various possible perspectives. I am personally grateful to Adesh for so very kindly asking me to contribute these few words. The contributors are all well known academicians and policy-makers in their own right. I have no doubt that this volume will set the agenda for all subsequent serious deliberations on the question of Asian economic integration in the coming years.

PROFESSOR PULIN B. NAYAK
Director
Delhi School of Economics

Preface

The essence of economic integration among Asian countries is getting prominence through various economic cooperation initiatives. While these initiatives, emerged from existing trade pacts, are limited to largely trade in goods and investment flows, some of them do go beyond and attempt to delve into deeper cooperation by way of encompassing issues, such as government regulations, trade facilitation, customs, procedures, etc. Currently, such kind of numerous pacts are already in place in Asia with the primary aim of harnessing greater benefits from trade liberalization amongst Asian countries. The efficacy of economic cooperation will come to the fore when the deeper cooperation measures will truly be in effect; which would, in due course, initiate the process of economic integration. At this point of time, economic integration is lagged far behind. Very often, economic integration is misinterpreted as economic cooperation, where as, economic integration should be distinguished as a step further from cooperation. A careful look reveals that in order to foster the process of economic integration certain measures like common harmonized framework across various of pacts, definite cohesive instruments like common currency, etc. are required. Moreover, the existing regional integration initiatives bear testimony to the fact that despite diverse economic situations and interests of countries from all across Asia are attempting to explore the possibility of an increased economic cooperation in the region.

Issues and concerns around economic integration are not restricted to trade integration alone. They also encompass broader and often interlinked issues like monetary integration, foreign exchange reserves, labour mobility and monetary reform. The real challenge, however, lies in setting out an appropriate road map to achieve the diverse objectives that might come under the umbrella of an economic integration initiative. As far as Asian Economic Integration is concerned, various alternative road maps have been suggested to achieve this goal. These, among others, include the idea of creating a new Asian Economic Institution with the aim of bringing financial stability and economic progress in the region.

In the backdrop of increasing tendencies towards regional integration in Asia, the present volume makes a timely attempt to capture the essence and urgency of Asian Economic Integration. The research papers included in this volume attempt to study, in depth, the recent proliferation of regional and bilateral agreements and various nuances of the existing regional agreements amongst Asian countries on the basis of theoretical analysis as well as empirical evidences. It brings to the fore issues such as, commodity-level integration, factor-level integration, financial integration, etc.

Importantly, some of the papers highlight the crucial roles that some of the more powerful and faster growing economies like China, Japan, South Korea and India, assume in the whole process of regional integration in Asia. The book raises fundamental questions, such as how far Asian countries are from an effective economic integration; what steps are required to be undertaken for achieving this goal; what kind of learning the Asian countries might have from the EU's experiences regarding the possibility of creating a common currency union; and so on. India, being a crucial player in the region, this volume focuses specifically on India and critically examines diverse issues from an Indian perspective.

We hope this volume would go a long way in articulating the debates and discussions around the issue and would facilitate more informed policy-making in this part of the world.

ANIL KUMAR THAKUR
ADESH SHARMA

Abbreviations

A

AB	Accreditation Board
ADB	Asian Development Bank
AFAS	ASEAN Framework Agreement on Services
ANCERTA	Australia-New Zealand Closer Economic Relations Trade Agreement
APEC	Asia-Pacific Economic Cooperation
APTA	Asia Pacific Trade Agreement
ARF	ASEAN Regional Forum
ASEAN	Association of South East Asian Nations
ASEM	Asia-Europe Meeting
ASSOCHAM	Associated Chambers of Commerce and Industry of India
AUSFTA	Australia-US Free Trade Agreement

B

B2B	Business to Business
BIMSTEC	Bay of Bengal Initiative for Multi-sectoral Technical and Economic Co-operation
BoP	Balance of Payment
BPM	Balance of Payments Manual, IMF
BPO	Business Process Outsourcing

C

CAGR	Compounded Annual Growth Rate
CARICOM	Caribbean Community
CCI	Communications Commission of India

CECA	Comprehensive Economic Cooperation Agreement
CEPA	Comprehensive Economic Partnership Agreement
CII	Confederation of Indian Industry
CAP	Certified Public Accountant
CSO	Central Statistical Organisation, India
CTS	(WTO) Council for Trade in Services

D

DTAA	Double Tax Avoidance Agreement
DWP	Doha Work Programme

E

EAC	East Asian Community
EC	European Community
ECNR	Emigration Check Not Required
EDI	Electronic Data Interchange
EEA	European Economic Area
EHEA	European Higher Education Area
EMS	European Monetary System
ENT	Economic Needs Test
ESCAP	(UN) Economic and Social Commission for Asia and the Pacific
ESM	Emergency Safeguard Measure
EU	European Union
EXIM	Export Import

F

FDI	Foreign Direct Investment
FEMA	Foreign Exchange Management Act
FICCI	Federation of Indian Chambers of Commerce and Industry
FIPB	Foreign Investment Promotion Board
FTA	Free Trade Agreement
FTSE	Financial Times Stock Exchange
FY	Financial Year

G

3G	Third Generation
GATS	General Agreement on Trade in Services
GATT	General Agreement on Tariffs and Trade
GCC	Gulf Cooperation Council
GDP	Gross Domestic Product
GER	Gross Enrolment Ratio (related to education)
GP	Government Procurement
GSM	Global System for Mobile Communications

I

ICESCR	International Covenant on Economic, Social and Cultural Rights
ICSID	International Centre for Settlement of Investment Disputes
ICT	Informational and Communications Technologies
IFAC	International Federation of Accountants
IERS	International Financing Reporting Standards
ILO	International Labour Organization
IMF	International Monetary Fund
IPA	Investment Promotion Agency
IRDA	Insurance Regulatory and Development Authority
ISCECA	India-Singapore Comprehensive Economic Cooperation Agreement
ISCO	(ILO's) International Standard Classification of Occupations
ISIC	International Standard Industrial Classification (UN)
ISP	Internet Service Provider
ISRO	Indian Space Research Organisation
IT	Information Technology
ITES	IT-Enabled Services

J

JETCO	(UK-India) Joint Economic Trade Committee
JSEPA	Japan-Singapore Economic Partnership Corporation
JV	Joint Venture

L

LLP	Limited Liability Partnership

M

MA	Market Access
MERCOSUR	Mercado Comun del Sur (Southern Common Market)
MFN	Most Favoured Nation
MNC	Multinational Corporation
MOIA	Ministry of Overseas Indian Affairs, Govt of India
MRA	Mutual Recognition Agreement
MTS	Multilateral Trading System

N

NAFTA	North American Free Trade Agreement
NAMA	Non-Agricultural Market Access
NASSCOM	National Association of Software and Services Companies
NBA	National Board of Accreditation
NCLEX-RN	National Council Licensure Examination
NCMH	National Commission on Macro-economics and Health, India
NGBT	Negotiating Group on Basic Telecommunications (WTO)
NRI	Non-Resident Indians
NT	National Treatment

O

OCA	Optimum Currency Area

OECD	Organisation for Economic Co-operation and Development
OFDI	Outward Foreign Direct Investment
OPA	Optimum Currency Areas
OTC	Over the Counter

P

PCI	Per Capita Income
PCO	Public Call Office
PR	Permanent Resident
PTAs	Preferential Trade Agreements

R

RBI	Reserve Bank of India
RCA	Revealed Comparative Advantage
RoO	Rules of Origin
RTAs	Regional Trade Agreements

S

S&DT	Special and Differential Treatment
SAARC	South Asian Association for Regional Cooperation
SACODL	SAARC Consortium of Open and Distance Learning
SACU	Southern Africa Customs Union
SADC	Southern African Development Community
SAFTA	Singapore-Australia Free Trade Agreement
SAFTA	South Asian Free Trade Agreement
SAPTA	South Asian Preferential Trade Agreement
SCO	Shangai Cooperation Organisation
SEBI	Securities and Exchange Board of India
SEZ	Special Economic Zone
SIA	Secretariat for Industrial Assistance
SIDBI	Small Industries Development Bank of India
S-O Act	Sarbanes-Oxley Act
SPV	Service Provider Visa

T

TDSAT	Telecom Disputes Settlement and Appellate Tribunal
TNC	Transnational Corporation

U

UAE	United Arab Emirates
UASL	Unified Access Service Licence
UNCTAD	United Nations Conference on Trade and Development
UNDP	United Nations Development Programme
UNESCO	United Nations Educational, Scientific and Cultural Organization

W

WHO	World Health Organization
WPDR	Working Party on Domestic Regulation (WTO)
WPPS	Working Party on Professional Services (WTO)
WTO	World Trade Organization

List of Contributors

Indernath Mukherji, Professor of Economics, Jawaharlal Nehru University, New Delhi.

Debesh Bhowmik, International Institute for Development Studies, Kolkata.

Davinder Kumar Madaan, Professor of Economics, Department of Management, Lovely Professional University, Phagwara, Punjab.

Paramjit Nanda, Reader, Punjab School of Economics, Guru Nanak Dev University, Amritsar.

P.S. Raikhy, Professor, Punjab School of Economics, Guru Nanak Dev University, Amritsar.

Smriti Mukherjee, Gokhale Institute of Politics and Economics, Pune.

D.R. Albal, Professor and Head, Department of Studies in Economics, Karnatak University K.R.C.P.G. Centre, Belgaum.

H.H. Uliveppa, Reader and Local Head, Department of Studies in Sociology, Karnatak University, K.R.C.P.G. Centre, Belgaum.

M.N. Siddalingappanavar, Doctoral Scholar, Department of Studies in Economics, Karnatak University, K.R.C.P.G. Centre, Belgaum.

Amalesh Banerjee, Rabindra Bharati University, 110-B, N.S.C. Bose Road, Kolkata.

Krishan K. Kaushik, ICDEO, H.P. University, Red Roof, Shimla-171004, Himachal Pradesh.

Kurt K. Klein, Department of Economics, The University of Lethbridge, 4401 University Orive Lethbridge, Alberta T1K3M4, Canada.

V.N. Attri, Professor and Chairman, Department of Economics, Kurukshetra University, Kurukshetra.

Shrawan Kumar Singh, Formerly Professor of Economics, IGNOU, Jagan Institute of Management Studies, New Delhi.

Priyanka Gaur, Department of Economics, University of Allahabad.

Puspa Tarafdar, Reader in Economics (ex.), Sarojini Naidu College for Women, Kolkata.

Readingstar John Nongbri, Research Scholar, Department of Economics, North Eastern Hill University, Shillong.

M.S. Sidhu, Senior Economist (Marketing), Department of Economics, Punjab Agricultural University, Ludhiana.

Lavleen Kaur, Department of Economics, Punjab Agricultural University, Ludhiana.

Pashupati Ray, A.S. College, Deoghar.

Chandrima Sikdar, Faculty, ICFAI Business School, IBS Campus, Old Delhi Jaipur Road, Dundahera, Gurgaon-122016, Haryana.

Sita Ram Singh, University Professor of Economics and Principal, A.N. College, Patna, Bihar.

Mohan Prasad Shrivastava, University Professor, Deptt. of Economics, M.U., Bodh Gaya, Bihar.

S.P. Saha, Head, Deptt. of Commerce, JMPDL Mahila College, Madhubani, L.N.M. University, Darbhanga, Bihar.

Vinod Kumar Choudhary, Lecturer in Rural Economics, MLSM College, Darbhanga, Bihar.

Dev Raj, Professor (IB) and Examinations Controller, EMPI Business School, New Delhi.

Introduction and Overview

Anil Kumar Thakur and Adesh Sharma

Asian economic integration has long been a dream of the region. This will allow Asian countries to hedge and protect against adverse domestic, regional and international shocks and induce a more efficient allocation of resources. The Asian governments have embarked on various initiatives for institutional cooperation to support market-driven integration. Various challenges and open questions arise from these developments:

(i) How far the Asian countries are prepared to go in their endeavors towards regional integration?
(ii) How far Asia satisfies the economic feasibility criteria of framing an Asian currency union?
(iii) Does Europe's experience provide any guide to get a common currency in Asia too?

In common parlance, Economic Integration is the process by which barriers of goods, services and capital are reduced, allowing the freer play of market forces. It refers to reducing barriers among countries to transactions and to movements of goods, capital, and labour, including harmonization of laws, regulations, and standards.

General trend towards regionalism, of the world, like the formation of NAFTA, APEC, EU, etc. A strong regionalism has emerged in weak workability of WTO, currency and financial crises in Asian countries in 1990s, and physical deepening of economic integration in the Asian region through increased intra-regional trade, capital transaction, and strong human networks, are some crucial reasons for the emergence of Asian Economic Integration.

The Asian countries will have to take certain precautions to ensure that Asian Economic Integration becomes a successful mission:

(i) To ensure not to repeat the 1990's crises in future;
(ii) To nurture Asian Bond Markets;
(iii) To stabilize the exchange rates of the regional currencies;
(iv) To finalise altogether an East Asian or ASEAN—Wide social infrastructure;
(v) To reduce income disparities among the member-countries;
(vi) To protect the business environment in the region;
(vii) To fight against the terrorists; and
(viii) To further cooperates on energy-saving and conservation efforts.

If the tenth anniversary of the currency-led Asian economic crisis went by largely unnoticed, it was not just because most of the affected countries bounced back within a comparatively short time. Many of them had also learnt the right lessons from the traumatic experience and are once again on a high growth path as a part of the larger Asia-Pacific region that is leading the global economy. Most experts had written of the Asian economic success story at the start of the currency crises. It was on July 2, 1997, that the Thai Baht came under attack from speculator, having lost the confidence of international investors and banks. Trying in vain to defend the currency that was then rigidly tied to the dollar, the Thai authorities helplessly watched their reserves evaporate. The currency crisis was only the starting point, and it inevitably set off a devastating chain reaction across the economy. As several East and South-East Asian nations were pursuing similar economic policies and were inextricably linked to one another, the contagion spread quickly across most of Asia. India and China were considerably less affected by the contagion. Both were following what was then regarded as an insular policy regime. There are still lessons to be learnt from the great Asian crisis.

Some of the key macro-economic issues are still being debated in India and elsewhere although the context has changed. For instance, in the 1990s most of the East and South-East Asian countries ran huge currency account deficits in the region of 7 to 8 per cent of the GDP and capital flows of other countries that once bridged the deficit reversed at the first sign of a crisis. Also, most of those governments had encouraged their large corporates to go in for short-term loans from abroad. The unwillingness of the lenders to roll over the loans caused widespread bankruptcy. Aggravating the crisis was the fact that most currencies of the region were rigidly tied to the dollar. All countries in the region now have "a managed float" and invariably run a current account surplus and there is a much better system of financial sector regulation. Another lesson, probably too well learnt, is to build-up foreign exchange reserves as an insurance. Today the debate is not over the need for such reserves but the appropriate size for each country. Many Asian countries, with China in the fore-front, have built-up huge reserves whose deployment had major consequences for the global economy. There are policy dilemmas in India and other countries in dealing with the huge dollar inflows. It is clear that in many policy areas the impact of the Asian crisis will continue to be felt for a long time.

This book is a collection of chapters on various dimensions of Asian Economic Integration. It aims to provide an understanding of the trade and investment opportunities and constraints that the countries of this region and particularly India is facing, and the role of unilateral liberalisation and reforms as well as multilateral and other negotiations in tapping opportunities and overcoming constraints. Each chapter provides a global as well as indigenous overview of the concerned issue or sector. Each chapter outlines recent trends in terms of trade and investment flows, takes stock of the existing domestic and external policy environment, and highlights relevant external and domestic barriers. Most chapters also discuss-related developments in multilateral as well as bilateral and other fore and outlines strategies and reforms required for further economic integration.

Prof. Indernath Mukherjee in his paper, "Asian Economic Integration" highlights that in recent years, Asian governments have begun to develop more formalized institutions to deepen the process of economic integration. He analysed the need for this was more explicitly noted by Asian policy-makers in the wake of the financial crisis of 1997-98, which called for the need for greater economic cooperation and coordination to better address the challenges to globalization.

In the next paper, i.e. "The Road Map of Economic Integration of an Asian Block: JACEAS", Debesh Bhowmik's endeavour to study the feasibility of the track and monetary integration of the Japan, ASEAN, China, East Asia and SAARC (JACEAS) shows that the welfare gain from Asian Free Trade to Asian Countries (US $ 170.87 bn) are comparatively better than that of the welfare gain from global trade liberalization (US $ 197.9 bn) in 2025. The share of intra-Asian Trade in global trade would increase. The creation of new Asian Economic Institution could bring enhanced financial stability and economic progress for Asian region as well as the whole world.

The paper, "Towards an Asian Trade Bloc: Role of East Asia, ASEAN and SAARC" by Davinder Kumar Madaan shows that broader regional integration in Asia has the potential of generating billions of dollars of new output and put Asia on a fastest growth path. A trade liberalization in the framework of an RTA among ASEAN, China, India, Japan and South Korea (ASEAN+4) could produce efficiency gains worth US $ 147 billion. Thus, the formation of Asian Trade Bloc could facilitate the exploitation of substantial gains. However, the success of this bloc would depend upon the mutual trust among all the member countries.

Paramjit Nanda and P.S. Raikhy in their paper, "Regional Blocs, Trade Flows and Revealed Comparative Advantages: Case for Asian Economic Integration" attempt to study complementarities in production and trade among JACIK, Pan-Asia and EAECI members. The formation of proposed Asian Economic Regional groups (JACIK, Pan-Asia and EAECI) would facilitate fuller exploitation of the region's resources by increasing intra-regional trade. Though Pan-Asia had high share in world's population and GDP, but EAECI has high share in world's trade and EDI, indicating that India will gain if it becomes member of Pan-Asia and/or EAECI.

The paper, written by Smriti Mukherjee titled "Trade Integration in South Asia: Problems and Prospects", analyses the extent to which SAARC fulfils the condition of a successful regional group and at the same time contribute to faster economic growth. She observed one interesting fact that the pattern of regional trade that emerges is that since the mid-nineties intra-regional trade share is increasing for most of the members. She discusses the spate of economic reforms sweeping through the countries might have directly contributed to the phenomenon. She argues unless upgrading of economic status for Bhutan, Nepal and Maldives dynamic centre of trade.

H.H. Uliveppa, D.R. Albal and M.N. Siddalingappanavar in their paper, "Asian Economic Integration: A Strategic Relevance of Broad Approach", examine the strategic relevance of possible approaches and assess the possibilities/feasibilities for regional cooperation in Asia. They opined the welding together of two or more unstable economies makes the taste of achieving stability and growth more difficult. They noted monetary imbalance and inconvertibility in these countries is not very compatible with a regional free trade policy. Furthermore, most of the countries in Asia swear by the ideals of Socialism/Religion and resort to severe governmental restrictions and controls, which necessarily implies that their customs union should be accompanied not only by the integration of their national economic programmes but also methods of intervention. They argued unless this is achieved, no regional co-operation will succeed.

Amalesh Banerjee, in "Agenda for Asian Economic Integration: Problems and Prospects" analyses that Asian countries have experienced diverse level of economic growth, which has not eliminate their hunger and poverty. He discussed integration of finance capital and monetary integration alone can hardly enhance welfare of Asian people.

He focused pro-poor development strategy based on democratic values is the right agenda for Asian development. He examine India is better suited for leadership in Asian integration than China. Although her market socialism has produced better result both in respect of economic growth and human development. He concluded to fulfil this historic task of Asian integration leadership, India must make rapid growth both in respect of physical achievement as well as human welfare.

"Asian Economic Integration: Issues and Challenges", by Krishan K. Kaushik and Kurt K. Klein highlights various challenges and open questions on Asian Economic Integration. They noted that the deepening of Asian Economic Integration have two major challenges: designing the ancillary thresholds for business regulation, that are the needed props to making an Asian single market sustainable and steering the political-diplomatic mechanisms that help Asia transition from a traditional development regime of national economic polities and priorities to a regime of regionally well managed economic interdependence. They concluded that Regional developments in Asia should be driven by its own political dynamics and unique historical background. They argued, why should this not be a basis for greater monetary integration, if that is what the people of Asia desire?

V.N. Attri in his paper, "Asian Economic Integration: An Emerging Sub-Paradigm in Regional Groupings" analyses the major developments in Economics of Regional Grouping at theoretical as well as empirical level in terms of theory of paradigm shift(s) propounded by Kuhn's theory of paradigm-shift and Lakatosian alternative approach known as Methodology of Scientific Research Programme (MSRP) since the publication of Viner's theory of custom unions (1950). He made deep study of the major developments of classical, Neoclassical, Keynesian, and post-Keynesian Economics, and felt that a synthesis of the first two approaches, i.e. classical and neo-classical gives a better insight for analysis of Regional Groupings. He observed that the process of Global Economic Integration seems to be a panacea for the contemporary economic problems being faced by the developed as well as developing countries. Thus he concluded that the theory of paradigms given by Kuhn and the Lakatosian approach known as MSRP, explains emergence of sub-paradigm in regional groupings, known as Asian Economic Integration.

Paper entitled "Asian Regional Financial Integration: An Analysis of a Possible Road Map", by Shrawan Kumar Singh highlights that Asia has come a long way in opening its financial system and clearly understands how it can benefit from deeper financial integration. It examines the combination of favourable economic conditions and a clear commitment to integration can provide a fitting environment in which the policy debate can flourish—and Asia's financial integration can continue to advance. Singh concludes, Regional integration can be achieved, step-by-step, through strengthening various co-operation channels under a long-term vision of "Integrated Asia".

Priyanka Gaur, in her paper attempts to answer a policy question, Can South Asia Create a Common Currency? And concludes that the region is not suitable for a currency union (CU) for this time, greater economic integration will reduce the cost of monetary cooperation. Thus, the complexity of this issue highlights the need for comprehensive and integrated plan regarding monetary cooperation in SA including the necessary preconditions. In the interim, activity of SAARC FINANCE may be considered the start for greater monetary cooperation in the region. SAARC FINANCE may also be able to begin preliminary work for developing a comprehensive and integrated road map toward greater cooperation, which would not be inconsistent with the broad objective organisation. At last, she recognises that a single SAARC currency would symbolize a major step towards the realization of the dream of peaceful stable and integrated South Asia.

Puspa Tarafdar in her paper "Exchange Rate Regimes and Monetary Policy for Asian Countries" focuses on issues arising from rapid increase in the foreign exchange reserves in Asia consequent on heavy capital inflows. The stock of foreign exchange reserve exceeded US $1,800 billion including Japan at the end of 2003 which constitute half of total global reserves. Against this background this paper seeks to examine the issues relating to exchange rate regimes in Asia namely exchange rate policies, monetary policies and policies regarding financial flows.

Readingstar John Nongbri in his paper, "Integration of the North Eastern Region with the Neighbouring Countries in Trade and Commerce: Look East Policy Implicates" analyses the prospect of trade and economic integration between the North East and the Neighbouring Countries and suggests that NER's economy requires lots of self-integration before its integration with the NC including Bangladesh, Myanmar, China, Bhutan, Nepal and the South East Asian Countries takes place Partial or Sectoral integration will be better given preference than complete integration for the moment as intelligent trade relation is very likely to be better than fully open trade. Indian policy-makers (more importantly the local political leadership of north-eastern region) should carefully consider creation of a strong foundation for an internationally Competitive Sector to sustain trade and development.

M.S. Sidhu, Lavleen Kaur and Pashupati Ray in their paper "India's Regional Trading with the SAARC Countries: Some Issues", examine India's regional trading with the SAARC countries in the recent years. Findings of their study show that the share of India's exports to the SAARC countries was about six per cent in her total exports to all over the world. During the year 2003-04, India's imports from the SAARC countries were to the extent of about US $ 0.64 billion. India's base of agricultural and industrial sector is strong as compared to other SAARC countries. Therefore, our dependency on South-Asia is less as far as imports are concerned.

Chandrima Sikdar's paper titled "Free Trade between India and the European Union-15: A General Equilibrium Approach" attempts to study bilateral free trade between India and the EU-15 by constructing a competitive benchmark based only on the fundamentals of the two economies: endowments, preferences and technologies. A linear programme along with an input-output framework helps to determine endogenously the direction of trade taking place between the countries in a perfectly competitive world characterized by free trade. The empirical implementation of the model developed in this paper considers trade in fourteen sectors consistent with input-output tables of the two economies.

Sita Ram Singh and Mohan Prasad Shrivastava in their paper, "An Economic Overview of Asian Integration with Special Reference to Indo-Korean Economic Alliance", advocate that Asian economic integration specially among the economic giants like India, China, Korea and Japan is the need of hour to meet the global challenges; maintain sustainable development; create massive job opportunities and to become economic superpower by competing European and American Mission. The paper, aims at to make an economic overview of Asian Economic Integration under various economic challenges and opportunities particularly with reference to Indo-Korean Economic Relation. Both Asian nations—India and Korea have emerged as the global leader. So Indian shall be quite happy if Korean economy comes forward in promoting its heavy investment with Indian collaboration in our country in different fields in meeting the basic challenges of poverty alleviation, eradication of unemployment and correction of imbalances. We must take lesson from the trend of economic supremacy of China, Japan, Korea and Thailand and should make every effort to Asian economic integration in eco-friendly system. The paper concludes that India's global integration has to be a two-way process, encompassing movement of people with some caveats, trade in a free and equitable manner and financial integration on a specially sequenced basis.

The paper "With Special Reference to Indo-Nepal Trade Relation" by S.P. Saha and V.K. Choudhary shows that there are tremendous opportunities for boosting India's export to, as well as, import from, among members of SAARC in general and between India and Nepal in particular. For this purpose, new initiatives would be required in order to enable us to take advantage of the expanding unified Indo-Nepal Trade Market. They suggest that India should act as a "Big Brother" not as a "Big Bully" in SAARC.

Prof. Dev Raj in his paper, "Asian Economic Integration: Issues, Challenges and Future Prospects Thereof", has discussed integration with various dimensions, limitations and suggestions. He stands with an opinion that The Asian Economic Integration is taking shape indeed, but slowly. In the course of process of integration, there will be occurring many disputes and conflicts with clashing economic interests amongst the Asian countries. But the Integration may provide a dynamic plateform for democratic exchange and peaceful negotiations within the framework of International Laws for the Common good. In this process of integration, the national interests can find a higher gratification and fulfilment in the international integration and cooperation and can increase synergetic efficiency of all the Asian countries and globe as a whole.

Developing Asian Economic Integration is a home to nearly two-thirds of the world's poor people. Asian Economic Integration can be a powerful tool to help all the countries to sustain high levels of economic and employment growth, to spread the benefits of growth more equitably, and to realise the dream of an Asian region free from poverty.

References

Bayoumi, T. and Eichorgreen, B. (1994), One Money or Many?, "Analyzing the Prospects for Monetary Unification in Various Parts of the World", *Princeton Studies in International Finance*, No. 76.

Jones, E. and Plummer, G.M. (2004), "EU-Asia: Links and Lessons", *Journal of Asian Economics*, Vol. 14, pp. 826-40.

Mohanty, S.K.; Rohit, Sanjib and Roy Saikat, S. (2004), "Towards Formation of Close Economic Cooperation among Asian Countries", Discussion Paper No. 78, Research and Information System for the Non-Aligned and other Developing Countries, New Delhi.

Saxena, S.C. (2005), "Can South Asia adopt a Common Currency?", *Journal of Asian Economics*, Vol. 16, pp. 635-59.

Srinivasan, G. (April 11, 2006), "India Moves Ahead in Merchandise Exports", *Hindu Business Line*.

www.aseansec.org

Asian Economic Integration

INDERNATH MUKHERJI

TYPOLOGIES OF REGIONAL INTEGRATION

Article 1 of General Agreement on Trade and Tariffs (GATT) established in 1947-48 laid down the Most Favoured Nation (MFN) principle of non-discrimination as the cornerstone of the multilateral trading system (MTS). Noting however that a number of Members (notably the EU) were contemplating to set-up regional arrangements and with a view to attracting maximum participation, a number of exceptions to the MFN principle were permitted.[1] Little did the founding members realize that in the years to follow, this principle would indeed become an exception!

In economic theory, the degrees of regional economic integration have been classified. These are generally classified under five categories beginning with the loosest one to the most comprehensive. These are

1. Preferential Trade Agreements (PTAs) in which members of the PTA impose a preferential tariff or lower customs duty on the product originating from the member countries;

2. Free Trade Agreements (FTAs) is a special case of PTAs where all tariff and non-tariff barriers are abolished and free access is allowed to the products of member countries. Under both PTA and FTA, member countries are free to set their level of trade restrictions with non-members. Rules of origin between the members of PTA and FTA are agreed to ensure that genuine products of partners are allowed preferential or free access.
3. Customs Unions (CUs) move beyond a free trade area by establishing a common external tariff on all trade between members and non-members.
4. Common Markets (CMs) deepen a customs union by providing free flow of factors of production such as labour and capital in addition to the flow of goods.
5. Under Economic Unions (EUs) members share common currency and macro-economic policy.

Although Article XXIV stipulates a number of conditions[2] for the working of RTAs, in practice, a majority of them have not been adequately scrutinized or monitored.[3] Thus many as 129 of the notifications for new RTAs were issued under Article XXIV representing Free Trade Agreements and 6 notifications under the same Article representing Customs Unions; 21 notifications were issued under Enabling Clause and 43 under GATS Article V.[4]

TRENDS AND CHARACTERISTICS OF RTAs: A GLOBAL PERSPECTIVE

Currently all WTO Members have notified participation in one or more RTAs.[5] The surge in RTAs has continued unabated since the early 1990s and by July 2005 a total of 330 had been notified to WTO and its predecessor GATT. Of these, 206 were notified after WTO was created in January 2005 and as of 15 September 2006, 211 RTAs were in force. Several others are in force, even though not notified. Quite a number of earlier RTAs have ceased to exist but have reappeared under new nomenclature reflecting deeper integration.

The decade of the 1990s is widely seen as a decade of globalization. This was however accompanied by an even more marked move towards regionalization in the different parts of the world led by led by Single European Market by European Union (EU) in 1992 and North American Free Trade Agreement (NAFTA) in 1994. These RTAs pursued deeper type of integration covering preferential free trade agreements complemented by strong rules of origin. It is interesting to note that many of these arrangements include subjects under the 'Singapore Issues' (trade facilitation, investment, government procurement, and competition), thereby considerably enlarging its scope.[6]

MOTIVATIONS FOR RTAs

The sluggish progress in multilateral trade negotiations under the Doha Development Agenda (2001), appears to have accelerated further the urge to forge RTAs.[7] Under RTA with limited members, decisions can be taken faster in contrast to the multilateral level where decisions have to be arrived at by consensus and need to be sufficiently flexible to accommodate the concern countries at different levels of development.

Countries participating in RTAs seek to secure sufficient access to large regional markets and benefit from economies of scale. Access to large markets permits opportunities to even smaller countries to attract more domestic and foreign investment.

A regional agreement can also help with region specific issues such as environment, border controls, transit, migration or development of trans-boundary infrastructure.

A regional agreement can reinforce internal regulatory or structural reforms thorough external treaty obligations and visible political commitments.[8]

We must not also lose sight of the fact that notwithstanding the end of the cold war, RTAs are being embraced by most WTO members, not merely to serve their economic interest, but as a part of their wider foreign policy and security objectives.[9]

Finally, the domino or snowballing effect of RTAs, particularly for late entrants to regionalism need special mention. Non-members, feeling insecure of being isolated and marginalized, realize that they are left with no other alternative but to follow suit either by joining other such arrangements, or by initiating new arrangements so as to retain their competitiveness in regional and global markets. Thus both proactive as well as reactive strategies have been at work in explaining the recent surge in RTAs. The proactive strategy ensures that by being early movers in a regional grouping, members intend to either pre-empt the entry of other members, or consolidate their own positions before they do. The reactive strategy is intended to neutralize or partially neutralize the competitive disadvantage arising from a competitor member countries' first mover advantage.[10]

ASIAN REGIONALISM

The first attempt to promote Asian regionalism was made when the Bangkok Agreement, was signed in July 1975 under the auspices of United Nations Economic and Social Council for Asia and the Pacific (ESCAP).

The original signatories to the Agreement were Bangladesh, India, Lao People's Democratic Republic, the Republic of Korea and Sri Lanka. In an important recent event, China formally became a member of the Bangkok Agreement in 2001. China's accession has major implications for trade in Asia Pacific Region.[11] All developing Member Countries of ESCAP are eligible to accede to the Agreement.

The Bangkok Agreement is essentially a preferential trading arrangement designed to liberalize and expand trade progressively in the ESCAP region through such measures as the relaxation of tariff and non-tariff barriers and trade-related economic cooperation.

Recognizing that the international trading system has evolved substantially since the Agreement came into force in the mid-1970s, the Participating States of Bangkok Agreement have recently launched a process of revitalization, one of them being the elevation of its formal structure to the Ministerial level.

The First Session of the Ministerial Council was held on 2 November, 2005 during which the name of the Bangkok

Agreement was changed to Asia Pacific Trade Agreement (APTA), in keeping with its new role. The Ministerial Declaration announced the change in the text of APTA to take into account the global development that has taken place in recent years. It mentioned the conclusion of Third Round concessions, which would be put in place with effect from 1 September, 2006, upon completion of internal procedures of all Participating States. The Declaration also expressed the hope of exploring the possibilities of APTA to evolve into a common framework mechanism for all regional trade arrangements in the region. However since the scope of the Agreement has been limited to trade in goods only, and lacks mechanisms for deeper integration, its impact on trade in the region has been quite limited.

In South-East Asia, the Association of South East Asian Nations (ASEAN) was set-up in 1976. Its original signatories included Indonesia, Malaysia, Philippines, Singapore, Thailand and Brunei. Later it was joined by Vietnam, Laos, Myanmar, and Cambodia.

The Association's real integration however started only in the early 1990s. ASEAN Free Trade Area (AFTA) was launched in 1992 in response to the challenges of the European and North American economic integration organizations EC and NAFTA. Until the year 2001, AFTA was the only ten- member RTA operating in South East and East Asian region.

However following the Asian financial crisis adversely impacting on ASEAN countries, and given impasse at the WTO Ministerial Meeting in 1999, highly trade-dependent country of ASEAN, viz. Singapore, embarked on bilateralism by free trade agreement in goods and services with New Zealand in 2001. In November of the same year, it followed-up by a signing similar agreement with Japan and with Australia in 2003. In January 2004, it again signed a very comprehensive free trade and services agreement with the US and with Korea in 2006. Earlier in 2003 Singapore had signed a free trade and services agreement with EFTA.

Taking serious note of Singapore's shift towards bilateralism, Thailand followed the bandwagon of bilateralism by signing a free trade and services agreement with Australia and New Zealand in 2005. Korea too signed one with EFTA in September 2006.

From the foregoing trends it is clear that bilateralism has dominated RTAs in South-East and East Asian region in recent years. These RTAs are very comprehensive, with no exceptions to tariff elimination, and including facilitation of trade in goods and services, investments, government procurement and intellectual property protection representing all the features of WTO-Plus provisions and all elements of deeper New-Age Regionalism.

In South Asia, South Asian Association for Regional Cooperation (SAARC) was set-up in 1985. The Association made slow progress in regional integration. Until the Agreement on South Asian Preferential Trading Arrangement (SAPTA) could be launched in December 2005. It was not until the twelfth SAARC Summit held in Islamabad in 2004 that a draft Framework Treaty for South Asian Free Trade Agreement (SAFTA) could be enacted. The Agreement entered into force on 1st July, 2006 upon completion of formalities, including ratification by all Contracting States and issuance of a notification thereof by the SAARC Secretariat.

The Trade Liberation Programme under SAFTA appears to be slow and protracted since it will be not until end of 2015 that customs tariffs in the region would be brought down between 0-5 per cent (with products under the Sensitive List exempted). The above features of the Framework Agreement on SAFTA clearly reveals its slow and protracted process which envisages 0-5 per cent tariffs for all contracting states by end of 2015. Nor any time limit is specified for the elimination of non-tariff barriers. Given the faster pace of liberalization at the multilateral level, as also the proliferation of bilateral trade agreements referred to above, the relevance of SAFTA is likely to be considerably eroded.

The Bay of Bengal Investment for Multisectoral Technical and Economic Cooperation (BIMSTEC), an international organization was formed in Bangkok, Thailand on 6 June, 1997. Its original signatories included India, Bangladesh, Sri Lanka and Thailand. Three more countries, viz. Myanmar, Nepal and Bhutan acceded subsequently making this a group of five members from South Asia and two from South-East Asia.

The seven nation grouping have endorsed a plan for a free trade pact by 2017 (with the more developed countries—Sri Lanka, India and Thailand attaining it by 2012).

This grouping is significant because it seeks to promote deeper integration by including not only trade in goods, but also in services. It also seeks to promote sectoral cooperation in transport, investment, energy and tourism. Besides the composition of the members demonstrates the first attempt to link-up the two sub-regions in Asia—viz. South with South East Asia.[12]

In West Asia the Gulf Cooperation Council (GCC) members including Bahrain, Kuwait, Oman, Qatar, Saudi Arabia and United Arab Emirates (UAE) ratified a Charter in 1981 that called for the establishment of Cooperation Council for the Arab States.

The basic objectives of the Cooperation Council as enshrined in the Charter is to effect coordination and integration between Member States; to deepen and strengthen existing relations; to formulate similar regulations in various fields including economic and financial affairs, commerce, customs and communication, education and culture; to stimulate scientific and technological progress and to encourage cooperation by private sector through joint ventures.[13]

With effect from March 1983, the Intra-GCC Free Trade Area was launched whereby all GCC national products were exempted from customs duties and the other charges. The customs union came into force in January 2003.[14] The same year formal adoption of the US dollar as intermediate peg was accepted. In 2004 the Member States agreed 'in principle' on key convergence criteria. They envisaged a common market by 2007 and a unified currency by 2010.

In the early 1990s, five Central Asian countries, viz. Kazakhstan, Azerbaijan, Kyrgystan, Uzbekistan and Turkmenistan, became independent from Soviet Union. In order to reduce their economic dependence on Russia, Kazakhstan, Azerbaijan, Kyrgystan, and Uzbekistan formed the Central Asian Economic Community. This started the process of Central Asian regional economic integration. In

2000, the four countries signed development strategies for the integration of Central Asian Economic Community countries, and decided upon its four stages, that is, free trade area, a customs union, a monetary union, and a single labour market.

The Shangai Cooperation Organisation (SCO) founded in 2001 has become the bridge for cooperation between Central Asia and China. SCO is composed of four central Asian states, Russia and China. It was a security cooperation organization at first, but is progressing towards economic integration. In September 2003, SCO adopted a plan for multilateral economic and trade cooperation, and set out its objectives. They include realizing goods trade, services trade and investment liberalization by 2020. In July 2005, India, Pakistan and Iran were accepted as observers. SCO is likely to become an important organization for Asian economic integration in future.[15]

TOWARDS AN ASIAN ECONOMIC COMMUNITY

Unlike North America and Europe, which enforced two mega region-wide trading agreements through NAFTA and EU, there has been no pan-Asian efforts towards regionalism, until recently.

The emergence of a larger economic community is reflected in is the growth in intra-regional trade. While still at a modest level in Central and South Asia, intra-regional trade in East Asia has risen from 43 per cent of total trade in early 1990s to 55 per cent in 2005. This is higher than the 46% figure for NAFTA and only modestly lower than the 62 per cent figure for the EU-15 countries.[16]

Intraregional investment in this region is also substantial. Since 1980, FDI inflows into East Asia (including Japan) have more than quadrupled, reaching 21 per cent as a share of world FDI in 2004. Over the same period, the share of East Asian FDI outflows increased from 5 per cent to 14 per cent of the world total. Intra-regional FDI flows accounted for much of this increase.[17]

The Asian region has been an engine of growth in recent years, growing more rapidly than any other region in the world.

The integration processes mentioned above have been largely market-driven, through the establishment of global and regional supply chains and production networks created largely by Japanese investment in the region. However, in recent years, Asian governments have begun to develop more formalized institutions to deepen the process of economic integration. The need for this was more explicitly noted by Asian policy-makers in the wake of the financial crisis of 1997-98, which called for the need for greater economic cooperation and coordination to better address the challenges to globalization.

In December 1997, when East Asia was still suffering from financial crisis, Association of South-East Asian Nations (ASEAN), China, Japan and Korea held the first Summit in Kuala Lumpur to discuss strategies to combat the crisis and regional cooperation. Since then, East Asian leaders, meeting every year, developed from an informal to formal mechanism that has been institutionalized into 10+3 cooperation framework. The objective of 10+3 cooperation is to establish an East Asian Free Trade Area, and further, an East Asian Community. Thus 10+3 has become the main mechanism to promote East Asian economic integration. At the same time there, are 10+1 mechanisms that is, regional-bilateral mechanisms such as ASEAN+China, ASEAN+Japan, and ASEAN+ Korea and more recently, ASEAN+India. India has signed Framework Agreement on Comprehensive Economic Cooperation with ASEAN and negotiating issues of implementation.

Besides, there is trilateral cooperation among China, Japan and Korea. In 2003 the three countries met during ASEAN+3 Summit held in Bali, Indonesia in October 2003, leaders of the three countries signed 'The joint Declaration of China, Japan and South Korea on Promoting Tripartite Cooperation' which suggested establishing an FTA of the three countries in North-East Asia. The three countries pledged to make concerted efforts to press ahead with Asian regional cooperation in various forms. They agreed to step-up the process of implementing the measures put forward in the Final Report of the East Asia Study Group, promote the 10+3 cooperation in the direction of East Asia cooperation, and support ASEAN's key role in this process. They further agreed to enhance cooperation within such mechanisms as ASEAN Regional Forum (ARF), Asia-Pacific Economic Cooperation (APEC) and Asia-Europe Meeting (ASEM).

As per the decision taken at the ASEAN+3 Summit held in conjunction with ASEAN Summit in Laos in November 2004, an East Asian block was formed in Kuala Lumpur in December 2004 with the objective to launch the process of forming an East Asian Community (EAC) by combining the ASEAN–10, Japan, China, India and Republic of Korea and Australia and New Zealand. The first EAC so conceived, was held in December 14, 2005 at Kuala Lumpur, Malaysia.

The EAC could form a formidable block in the Asia-Pacific region, being roughly the size of the EU in terms of income, and bigger than NAFTA in terms of trade. It accounts for half of the world's population, and holds foreign exchange reserves exceeding those of the EU and NAFTA put together!

Following the Asian financial crisis adversely impacting on ASEAN countries, and given impasse at the WTO Ministerial Meeting in 1999, highly trade-dependent country of ASEAN, viz. Singapore, embarked on bilateralism by free trade agreement in goods and services with New Zealand in 2001. In November of the same year, it followed-up by a signing similar agreement with Japan and with Australia in 2003. In January 2004 it again signed a very comprehensive free trade and services agreement with the US and with Korea in 2006. Earlier in 2003, Singapore had signed a free trade and services agreement with EFTA.

Taking serious note of Singapore's shift towards bilateralism, Thailand followed the bandwagon of bilateralism by signing a free trade and services agreement with Australia and New Zealand in 2005. Korea too signed one with EFTA in September 2006.

As of September 2006 there were 183 FTAs of which 38 were plurilateral (trade blocks) and 145 bilateral. Of the 183 FTAs, 46 were at the proposal stage, 54 under negotiations, 30 had been signed and 53 under implementation.

Of the 38 plurilateral FTAs, only 9 had been notified.

Of the 29 that had not been notified, 5 were under implementation, 3 had been signed, 15 under negotiation and 6 were at the proposal stage.

Again of the 38 plurilateral FTAs, the largest number-14, related to non-Asian Block + Asian country, 9 related to cross-regional Block, 8 related to Asian Block, 5 to Asian Block and Asian country, and 2 to non-Asian Block and Asian block.

Of the 145 bilateral FTAs, 24 were within the sub-region, 39 were across the sub-region, and 82 were with non-Asian countries.

From the foregoing trends it is clear that bilateralism has dominated RTAs in South-East and East Asian region in recent years. These RTAs are very comprehensive, with no exceptions to tariff elimination, and including facilitation of trade in goods and services, investments, government procurement and intellectual property protection representing all the features of WTO—Plus provisions and all elements of deeper New Age Regionalism. The above characteristics of RTAs further reflect the wider geographical spread since more of them appear to be located beyond Asian region rather than within.[18] Thus no longer are RTAs confined to 'natural trading partners' but extend far beyond their geographical confines.

The Asian countries are also pursuing the deepening of monetary and financial cooperation. With ADB support, ASEAN+ 3 (China, Japan and Korea) Finance Ministers have been working together to develop and deepen regional bond markets and ensure financial stability through regional economic surveillance and regional reserve pooling. At their meeting at Hyderabad in May 2005, the ASEAN+3 Finance Ministers agreed to explore further options for multilateralising the Chiang Mai Initiative—the network of bilateral swap and repurchase arrangements—and for strengthening the regional economic surveillance.[19]

The Asian Bond markets Initiative, under the aegis of ASEAN+3, focuses on developing the financial market infrastructure conducive to efficient local currency bond markets. Developing efficient domestic bond markets will ensure that more of Asia's savings be invested in the region, providing the resources developing Asian countries need in order to meet their massive private investment needs, particularly in physical infrastructure and human capital.[20]

In view of the attempts already made at Asian regional integration, Kumar[21] has suggested that in the initial phase AEC could include five blocks to constitute a core grouping, viz. Japan, ASEAN, China, India and Korea (JACIK). Once the process of integration is consolidated and some gains of integration are visible, AEC could be thrown open to other economies of the region.

Some countries of the region have surplus resources in sectors such as construction and IT while others have large unmet demands in these areas. In such a scenario, Kumar argues 'regional pump priming or regional Keyenesism could be quite effective in reviving demand for utilizing the excess capacity'.[22]

RTAs AND DEVELOPMENT

Theoretically, a free trade regime extending globally is the first best choice for achieving maximum global welfare from trade. However, if for various reasons trade liberalization is initiated at the regional level, this is often considered to be the second best option. Regional trade liberalization would result in increased competition, efficiency and acquisition of new technology through widening of the market and increased specialization. The net welfare implications would however, depend on the initial conditions and the nature of regional trade liberalization.

The classical trade theory framework was provided by Jacob Viner (1950). Viner introduced the concept of 'trade creation' and 'trade diversion'. According to him 'trade creation' takes place when there is a movement of factors of production from high domestic cost to a low cost domestic source of one or more partner countries. 'Trade diversion' takes place when there is a movement of factors of production from low cost extra-regional producers to high cost regional producers.

The change in welfare due to preferences granted to members would depend upon whether the most efficient in the world is a part of the group or outside it. If it is a part of the group, the economic integration would be welfare promoting. However even if the most efficient producer is outside the group, then forming of regional blocks could result in trade diversion or trade creation depending on the initial conditions. Consider for instance that prior to the formation of a block, the tariff was prohibitive and the country met the entire demand of the product from domestic supplies. However, when the tariff rates are reduced preferentially, some participating member states may become competitive enough to enter the regional market, thereby replacing the erstwhile high cost domestic producers. Thus in any preferential trading arrangement the impact on a member state will depend on its initial tariff. For the grouping as a whole, some members may suffer welfare losses while others may experience welfare gains and the net welfare of the grouping will depend on the balance of the two forces.

Drawing from both theoretical and empirical studies, the welfare creating impact of RTAs depends on the following key factors:

(a) the larger the pre-RTA tariff and non-tariff barriers (NTBs), the more likely that the trade creating effect will dominate;
(b) the greater the demand for each country's goods by the partner country, the greater the scope for specialization;
(c) the greater the elasticity of demand for regional products and the greater their supply elasticity, the greater the possibility of trade creation;
(d) the greater the level of intra-regional trade among partners and greater the share of such trade liberalized, the greater the possibility of trade creation;
(e) the lower the external tariff after the formation of the grouping, the lesser the trade diversion; and
(f) the more restrictive the rules of origin, the greater the possibility of trade diversion.

The above indicated principles need to be taken into

account when Asian countries are liberalizing their trade and investment policies. In order to minimize trade diversion, they need to lower their MFN tariff rates and NTBs while they similarly liberalize their trade restrictions within the region. They should further, try to liberalize 'substantially all trade.' While safeguarding their domestic industries from deflected trade, they should try not to impose unduly restrictive rules of origin that tend to divert trade. They should ensure adequate domestic reforms, permitting competition among stakeholders so that opening-up of their economies do not unduly hurt their interests. Not least, there should be as much as feasible, public ownership of reforms so that their acceptability is rationalized.

As aptly stated by Kumar, the sub-regional attempts at regional cooperation initiated such as those under the framework of SAARC and ASEAN are unlikely to exploit the full potential of regional economic integration in Asia. At the pan-Asian level the diversities of levels of economic development and capabilities are quite wide, thus providing for more extensive and mutually beneficial trade.[23] By bringing the major countries in a single block, and increasing their economic interdependence, the Community can promote peace and stability in the region.

Notes and References

1. The exceptions relate to (I) paragraphs 4 to 10 of Article XXIV that provide for the formation and operation of customs unions and free trade areas covering trade in goods; (ii) the Enabling Clause (under 1979 Decision on Differential and More Favourable Treatment, Reciprocity and Fuller Participation of Developing Countries—providing for preferential trade arrangements in goods between developing country Members); and (iii) Article V of General Agreement on Trade in Services (GATS) for both developed and developing countries. For other non-generalized preferential schemes, for example non-reciprocal agreements involving developing and developed countries require Members to seek a waiver from WTO rules. Such agreements require the approval of three-quarters of WTO Members. Examples of such agreements include: US-Caribbean Economic Recovery Act, EC-ACP Partnership Agreement, Generalized Scheme of Preferences, etc.
2. Generally the conditions stipulate that RTAs, while reducing or eliminating trade barriers among Members, should not raise the

same against non-members; secondly they need to cover 'substantially all trade'; and finally, all RTAs must specify a time plan or schedule (generally not exceeding ten years) by which to phase out all trade barriers.

3. Even though all RTAs are subject to an examination process of WTO, out of 211 notifications (including 12 Accessions) issued till 15 September 2006, Reports have been adopted only on 20 of them; for 33 cases examination is not requested; for 65 factual examination has not started; 17 are under factual examination; for 16 factual examination has been concluded and for 7 consultations have taken place on the draft report. (http://www.wto.org)
4. http;/www.wto.org.
5. On 15 August 2004, Mongolia signed a Trade and Facilitation Agreement with the United States, a precursor to a Bilateral Trade Agreement. Prior to this, Mongolia was the only country that had not signed or participated in any RTA.
6. These four subjects were originally included under the DDA. Since there was no consensus on this issue, the Members agreed on 1 August, 2004 to proceed with the negotiations in only one subject, trade facilitation. The other three were dropped from the Doha Agenda. (http://www.wto.org).
7. The emergence of NAFTA is a good illustration of this. The US, earlier a strong votary of multilateralism, felt the need for a course correction. It felt that should the Uruguay Round fail, an alternative would be in place to go ahead to further the liberal agenda. Further, the steps initiated by NAFTA that went far beyond the WTO provisions, could be used as a bargaining chip to urge similar advances at the multilateral level.
8. Locking such reforms clearly motivated agreements between the EU and countries in Central and Eastern Europe.
9. To illustrate, in mid 1980s, MERCOSUR (the treaty between Argentina, Brazil, Paraguay and Uruguay to form a common market) was formed with a political agenda—quite apart from the economic one, of containing the military hostility between Argentina and Brazil.
10. To illustrate, China entered into a preferential trading arrangement with ASEAN in July 2003. India followed by signing a similar agreement with ASEAN in 2003 to offset its competitive disadvantage.
11. Papua New Guinea accessed to the Agreement in December 1993, though the Agreement has yet to be ratified by the Government of Papua New Guinea. Pakistan notified its intension to accede to the Agreement in February 1998, and is in the process of accession.
12. http://en.wikipedia.org
13. http://www.gcc.sg.org
14. Secretary General, The Customs Union of the GCC member States, January 2003
15. Paper on 'Asian Economic Integration: Perspectives from a Chinese

Scholar', presented by Lu Jianren at International Workshop on 'Preferential Trading Agreements in Asia: Towards an Asian Economic Community', Indian Council for Research in International Economic Research, New Delhi, March 30, 2006.

16. Speech, Haruhiko, President, Asian Development Bank at the Jehu Summer Forum—International Management Institute, 28 July, 2006.(http://www.adb.org/Documents/Speeches/2006.
17. *Ibid.*
18. These figures relating to the number of bilateral and plurilateral PTAs are based on data provided by Asian Development Bank's Asian Integration Unit (http://www.adb.org).
19. *Op. cit.*, n. 13.
20. *Ibid.*
21. Nagesh Kumar, RIS Policy Briefs: 'Relevance of Asian Economic Community, May, 2003.
22. *Ibid.*
23. Nagesh Kumar, *op. cit.*, n. 21.

The Road Map of Economic Integration of an Asian Block: JACEAS

DEBESH BHOWMIK

INTRODUCTION

China's soft landing in W.T.O. reshuffled world's regionalism in the multilateral framework of international trade. China became the second largest economy and second largest recipient of foreign direct investment and foreign exchange reserves. Chinese talk with SAARC and ASEAN nations enthused Asian trade to a greater extent. Japan reentered as surplus economy since 1980s and became dominant since 1990s. Japan's initiative of free trade with ASEAN and East Asia and dynamic Miyazawa Plan have emerged a new path of Asian integration. East Asian's desire to create a new monetary institution through monetary integration is showing Asia's new institutional identity in the global economy. Above all, SAARC and ASEAN targets of achieving free trade areas have been alarming to other regional blocs. Regional surveillance process through Asian

Monetary Fund has stepped forward for marching ahead through economic co-operation among Asian countries who would create a third major economic bloc which would alter the global balance of power. It may create a dollar or yen dominated bloc consisting of Japan, East Asia, and ASEAN or may be the Yuan dominated bloc consisting of China, ASEAN and SAARC respectively in the regimes of global dollarisation or dedollarisation process. But, if the realisation of Asian Monetary Fund be a threat to unilateralism of U.S.A. or a threat to the autonomy of I.M.F. then, the Asian bloc must emerge consisting of Japan, ASEAN, China, East Asia, and SAARC which will be the world's biggest regional bloc namely JACEAS, through dynamic process of economic integration.

In this paper, we will endeavour to study the feasibility of the trade and monetary integration of the JACEAS with special emphasis on the verification of the OCA criteria and convergence analysis.

PROSPECTS OF JACEAS

The rosy prospect of macro-economic fundamentals of the JACEAS is undoubtedly marvellous. Presently, its GDP is more than 20 per cent of the world's income which is greater than EU. The average growth rate of GDP of SAARC +ASEAN+East Asia during 1980-2000 and 2000-07 were found 6.875 per cent and 6.265 per cent respectively in comparison to 3.85 per cent and 1.72 per cent of Japan. Again, the average per capita GDP growth rate of SAARC+ASEAN+East Asia during 1980-2000 and 2000-07 were calculated as 4.95 per cent and 4.98 per cent respectively compared to 1.86 per cent for Japan during 2000-07. The export growth of the above region during 1960-2000 and 2000-07 were observed as 12.975 per cent and 14.744 per cent respectively which are greater than EU and NAFTA.

It's volume of export is 23.0 per cent of the world export which is more than NAFTA. Its export of services as per cent of world total services is mounting from 6.8 per cent in 1980 to 14.6 per cent in 2002 and 19.27 per cent in 2004 and service import as per cent of world total is also increasing from 6.9 per cent in 1980 to 15.2 per cent in 2002 and 22.32 per cent in 2004. The Intra-Asian export share in total South-South export of merchandise trade increased from 56 per cent in 1980 to 77.9 per cent in 2003. The region showed positive trade balance from negative trade balance as per cent of import, i.e. -19.7 per cent in 1970 to 6.6 per cent in 2002 and 28.92 per cent in 2004. In 2007, total trade balance will reach to 186974 million dollar. The industrial growth of this bloc during 2001-07 would show a high rate of 14.64 per cent where manufacturing growth rate of chemicals was 16.1 per cent, machinery and transport 14.4 per cent, electronics 19.6 per cent and other manufacturing 11.1 per cent respectively during 1980-2001. This Asian bloc has accumulated 1864757 million dollar of international reserves in 2005 which is greater than NAFTA and EU. (ADO-2006, UNCTAD-2004: Development and Globalisation, TAD-2005).

TOWARDS TRADE INTEGRATION

Trade integration in Asian Community creates serious attention towards free trade areas. AFTA and SAFTA have been already established. Except Japan and China, East Asia is a free trade area. Therefore, JACEAS may be a free trade area in the offing. The ADO (2006) reports that Asian Free Trade Area will start in 2007 and will be completed in 2025. This assumed that all bilateral tariff, tariff equivalent NTBs and export subsidies between the assumed hub and all Asian spokes will be eliminated over period 2007-2025.

Under the regime of multilateralism of WTO, Asian countries persue bilateralism as a competitive strategy for broad based trade liberalisation, although open regionalism is now on a strong upswing. This policy acts as a catalyst for deeper integration in Asia. Therefore, intraregional trade shares in blocs in Asia grew rapidly compared to EU and NAFTA. Even, intra trade share in East Asia including Japan has committed more than 50 per cent which is greater than NAFTA. In 1985, the shares of ASEAN and SAARC were 20.3 per cent and 4.8 per cent repectively which increased to 24.0 per cent and 4.9 per cent respectively in 2003. Table 1 explains it in detail.

TABLE 1

Intra Regional Trade Shares (%)

	1980	*1985*	*1990*	*1995*	*2000*	*2003*
East Asia (including Japan)	34.7	40.2	45.6	55.5	54.0	54.0
Developing East Asia	21.6	29.1	36.4	43.7	43.4	44.1
NIEs	7.7	10.7	14.3	18.1	16.4	16.1
ASEAN	18.0	20.3	18.9	24.1	25.7	24.0
SAARC	5.2	4.8	3.2	4.4	3.8	4.9
NAFTA	33.8	38.7	37.9	43.2	48.7	46.0
EU-15	52.4	52.5	58.6	56.8	62.2	64.4

Source: A.D.O.—2006.

From the trade trends during 1975-2001, it was found that East Asia and ASEAN shares of global exports expanded more than double. East Asia presently originates about the same share of global exports of NAFTA. Asian bloc as a whole (like JACEAS) comprises equal global export share to the share of EU. Intra regional exports expressed as a share of world trade experienced as even sharper expansion rising more than six fold during 1975-2001. To note that intra trade share as per centage of world trade of East Asia and ASEAN is greater than that of NAFTA and closer to EU. (Table 2). The value of intra ASEAN trade catapulted from 27365 million dollar in 1990 to 125531 million dollar (22.0 per cent of total exports) in 2004, and the value of intra SAARC trade increased from 863 million dollar in 1990 to 5919 million dollar (5.3 per cent of total exports) in 2004.

The growth of multinational enterprises and foreign direct investment has, in recent decades provided a boost to Asian trade, both intra regional and inter regional. Additional trade and production resulting from the lowering trade cost, liberalization of trade, and emergence of international production sharing have provided Asia with a new source of income and employment gains. The net flows of foreign direct investment in East Asia, South East Asia and South Asia was 10205 million dollar in 1992 which increased tremendously to 85035 trillion dollar in 2004, on the other hand, the net flow of foreign direct investment of Japan was

TABLE 2

Regional Exports Shares of World Trade (%)

	1975	*1980*	*1995*	*2001*
East Asia	5.4	9.4	16.3	18.7
ASEAN	2.7	3.6	6.0	6.3
EU-15	39.2	36.0	36.9	34.3
Japan	5.9	9.6	9.3	7.0
NAFTA	18.0	17.8	18.0	19.0
SAARC	0.7	0.8	1.0	1.1
East Asia intra-Trade	1.0	2.2	6.1	6.5
East Asia-Japan Trade	1.4	1.8	8.3	2.3
East Asia-China Trade	-	0.3	0.8	1.3
NAFTA intra-Trade	6.7	8.1	7.7	10.1
EU intra-Trade	24.1	21.1	22.7	20.2
ASEAN intra-Trade	0.3	0.6	1.3	1.2

Source: Francis Ng and Alexander Yeats (2003).

14634 million dollar in 1992 which increased to 23135 million dollar in 2004. The East Asian and ASEAN inflows of foreign direct investment became approximately doubled than that of their outflows during 1992-2004. Most of the foreign direct investment inflows of the developing Asia come from Japan, China followed by EU and USA. Hence intra Asian foreign direct investment flows predominate the Asia's trade since the last decade. (Table 3).

TABLE 3

Foreign Direct Investment of JACEAS

	Inflows (million dollar)				*Outflows (million dollar)*			
	1992	*1997*	*2002*	*2004*	*1992*	*1997*	*2002*	*2004*
EA+								
ASEAN+								
SAARC	27683	82411	86317	170372	17478	50157	42611	85337
Japan	2756	3224	9239	7816	17390	25993	32281	30951

Source: ADO—2006, UNCTAD—2004, EA includes China.

During the course of liberalization in WTO, for the prospect of regional free trade in Asia, 23 bilateral and regional free trade agreements were made including 120 preferential tariff agreements which will step-up to 240 in 2007. Asian Free Trade Areas also enable China to confirm its commitment to trade liberalization and acquire negotiating experience before defining a leadership role in WTO. It uses free trade area such as ASEAN-China free trade area proposed by "Zhu Rongi" in 2000. In 2002, China and ASEAN countries concluded a framework for the free trade area which includes an agreement to remove tariffs on all goods by 2015. Already, the region allowed to cut weighted tariff as per cent of partners from 7.8 per cent in 1993-95 to 3.7 per cent in 2001. In case of MFN unweighted tariff as per cent for all products, the bloc cut from 36.2 per cent in 1984-87 to 29.5 per cent in 1991-93 to 12.6 per cent in 2000-01 and MFN weighted tariff as per cent for all products was cut from 24.0 per cent to 14.5 per cent and to 9.8 per cent during the specified period respectively. Therefore, trade integration allows the region a trade cost reduction amounting to 673.45 billion dollar, i.e. 3.72 per cent of GDP in 2005 which implied a direct efficiency gain of 1.32 per cent of GDP.

Serious attention is drawn towards the vision of Asian Economic Integration in 2020, where trade integration clearly emphasises on the role of open regionalism for the soft landing of China in WTO and how China and Japan would dominate to form the free trade area within a bloc namely JACEAS (or JACIK). It was estimated that by 2020, China sustains and even increases its structural trade surplus with the rest of the world, while at the same time developing a structural deficit of about equal magnitude with rest of the East Asia and South Asia. Even, the estimated growth rates during 2000-2025 in real GDP, exports and imports and bilateral trade flows ensure that the regional free trade areas benefit most free trade Asian members. Chinese gain is much less in relative terms than either ASEAN in AFTA or rest of East and South East Asia under global trade liberalization. (Table 4). In the Table 5 below, it was shown that the welfare gain from Asian free trade to Asian countries are comparatively better than that of the welfare gain from global

TABLE 4

Growth Rates (%) and Bilateral Trade Flows of ASEAN+3

	Growth rate 2000-20			*Bilateral Trade flows % change in 2020*						
	GDP	*Exp*	*Imp*	*China*	*Japan*	*NIE*	*ASEAN*	*USA*	*EU*	*ROW*
China	7.1	6.27	5.85	0	21	33	27	-8	-9	-8
Japan	2.2	2.37	3.15	2	0	39	40	-2	-2	-2
NIE	4.34	4.04	4.21	3	50	31	43	0	-1	-2
ASEAN	4.75	4.46	4.25	4	49	35	26	5	4	0
USA	2.62	3.07	2.94	5	-4	-11	-9	1	1	1
EU	2.52	2.37	2.6	4	-2	-10	-11	1	0	0
ROW	3.65	3.69	3.4	5	-9	-10	-8	1	0	1

Source: David Ronald Holst, Iwan Aziz and Li-Gang Lin (2003).

TABLE 5

Welfare Gain in 2025

	Welfare gain from global trade liberalisation in 2025		*Welfare gain from Asian free trade base line in 2025*	
	Income ($ billion)	*% of GDP*	*Income ($ billion)*	*% of GDP*
Asia incl. Japan	194.92	1.08	170.87	0.95
Japan	42.12	0.65	37.69	0.59
Developing Asia	152.8	1.31	133.18	1.14
China	12.22	0.22	5.93	0.11
India	19.48	1.04	21.44	1.15
US	9.56	0.05	10.58	0.05
EU-15	82.70	0.61	23.30	0.17
World	341.44	0.53	228.56	0.35

Source: ADO—2006.

trade liberalisation in 2025. The pay off from trade liberalization is associated with both static gain resulting from a reallocation of reserves (trade creation) and dynamic gain from additional capital accumulation. There are also gains that accrue from scale and variety effects that are important when markets are imperfectly competitive. In spite of over all gain, Asian free trade will deteriorate terms of trade of India and China since their major shares went to outside Asia. The Asian Development Outlook (2006) asserted that in terms of direction of trade, Asian free trade would increase regional integration on some traditional measures. The share of intra Asian trade in global trade in 2025 rises to 19.3 per cent compared to 15.3 per cent in 2005. But the measure of trade intensity suggests that the intensity of trade within Asia would decline marginally (Table 6).

TABLE 6

Trade Intensity Index within Asian Free Trade 2025

	Intra Asia	*Intra EA*	*Intra ASEAN*	*Intra SAARC*	*EA-ASEAN ASEAN*	*EA-SAARC SAARC*	*ASEAN SAARC*
2005	1.67	1.7	3.05	1.71	1.58	0.7	1.58
2025	1.60	1.65	2.83	1.22	1.58	0.75	1.51

Source: ADO—2006.

TOWARDS MONETARY INTEGRATION

Monetary integration is one of the important steps towards economic integration. There are several pre-requisites reform measures of monetary integration which are banking and financial sector reform, capital market reform, fiscal reform and external sector reform respectively. Numerous policies are needed to implement for such reform of which the important are current and capital account convertibility of national currency to international currency, exchange rate stability and price stability, the profitability of public sector banks, deregulation of interest rate respectively for banking and financial sector reform. Free mobility of capital and other equities and derivative trading are the steps of reform for capital market development. Strong external sector stability is necessary to acquire foreign trade sector reform, so that the sector may boost the growth rate of national income. The following are the areas of convergence criteria for success of monetary integration, namely, (i) inflation or price convergence, (ii) fiscal convergence, (iii) interest rate convergence, (iv) debt/GDP convergence.

Since JACEAS bloc did not fix any convergence criteria for monetary integration to issue a single currency for a targeted year because the bloc did not start yet. Therefore, let us examine whether the bloc satisfy the hypothesis of convergence.

In the Table 7, the values of the coefficient â, i.e. the coefficient of semi-log linear trend line of inflation rate, debt/GDP ratio, the FD/GDP ratio of the member countries of JACEAS for 1990-2005, and the coefficient of variations of inter countries during the period of those variables along with initial values have been arranged. According to Salai-i-Martin (1996), the â and ó convergence hypothesis were verified for the JACEAS bloc during the specified period.

It was found that inflation or price convergence was achieved for the bloc because â and ó convergence were satisfied. The linear relationship between â and the average of five year initial values of inflation rates among 21 members of JACEAS was estimated as,

$$\beta = -0.0308 - 0.00228 \text{ inf}$$
$$(-0.0022) \quad (-3.168),$$

$R^2 = 0.343$, inf=inflation rate,
β = growth rate during the period (t)

where the coefficient was found significant and was declining. To test s convergence, the trend value of coefficient of variation of intercountries inflation rate during the period of 1990-2006 is stated below,

$$\text{Log(c.v.)} = 5.0981 - 0.0306 \text{ t}$$
$$(19.271) \quad (-1.1859), \quad R^2=0.0857,$$

c.v.= coefficient of variation,
t = time

TABLE 7A

Price, Fiscal, Interest Rate and Debt Convergence (b) of JACEAS during 1990-05

	Interest convergence		Price convergence		Fiscal convergence		Debt convergence	
	β	A_0	β	A_0	β	A_0	β	A_0
Japan	-0.335	3.45	0.144	2.02				
China	-0.4178	7.8	-0.108	10.34	-0.00748	-2.67	-0.014	17.0
Hong Kong	-0.04107	4.58	-0.1354	10.1	-0.0355	2.0	0.0555	17.64
Korea	-0.38035	6.2	-0.067	7.02	0.1619	-0.34	0.062	14.64
Teipei China			-0.0843	3.84	0.00832	-2.26	0.0504	10.45
Afghanistan								
Bangladesh	-0.2776	7.8	-0.00295	4.42	0.0044	1.28	-0.0231	42.1
Bhutan			-0.1487	11.3	0.14367	-2.578	0.0481	39.7
India	-0.4919	11.6	-0.0714	10.26	-0.022	-6.535	-0.0444	32.78
Maldives			-0.137	11.74	-0.1296	-13.74	0.00258	39.28
Nepal	-0.45	11.8	-0.0826	11.74	-0.0903	-7.46	0.0069	51.02
Pakistan	0.6136	11.0	-0.052	10.3	-0.06201	-7.34	-0.0049	50.06
Sri Lanka	0.4181	16.6	-0.0457	13.04	0.00215	-8.0	-0.0221	70.7
Cambodia			-0.276	103.36	-0.0086	-4.42	-0.0333	104.12
Indonesia	-0.2647	14.41	-0.00313	8.58	0.044	-0.42	0.0283	67.64
Lao PDR	-0.0579	26.22	-0.0189	14.4	-0.00549	-5.74	-0.0117	168.22
Malaysia			-0.0543	3.7	0.0635	-0.64	0.0371	38.52
Myanmar	0.1571	11.0	0.039	25.54				
Philippines	-0.1564	12.0	-0.0518	10.84	0.0644	-1.46	0.01348	65.76
Singapore			-0.0878	2.9	-0.0783	12.72	0.0636	10.56
Thailand	-0.5045	10.5	-0.0727	4.8	-0.3366	3.26	0.0327	39.88
Vietnam			0.01829	4.26	-0.0075	-3.9	-0.1813	248.72

Source: ADO—2006, IFS-1998, 2004, Calculated by author, where â = growth rate, A_0= 5 year average of initial values.

TABLE 7B

Convergence (σ) of Jaceas From 1990 to 2005

	Interest Convergence Intercountry c.v. (%)	*Price Convergence Intercountry c.v. (%)*	*Fiscal Convergence Intercountry c.v. (%)*	*Debt Convergence Intercountry c.v. (%)*
1990	33.648	189.54	178.177	128.573
1991	35.112	192.611	206.859	103.302
1992	47.22	151.969	225.949	102.459
1993	60.301	178.646	267.1536	100.0
1994	67.256	85.125	383.797	73.204
1995	66.462	73.713	394.565	67.753
1996	66.459	54.985	216.837	63.241
1997	51.307	97.986	335.111	63.032
1998	80.019	154.141	107.917	79.006
1999	81.524	257.496	121.608	70.045
2000	81.979	194.434	145.696	68.739
2001	116.663	142.154	115.951	64.315
2002	89.906	234.789	120.517	64.504
2003	94.460	183.214	115.452	59.905
2004	91.949	73.46	157.068	
2005		67.649	96.362	
2006		51.348		

Source: ADO—2006, IFS—1998, 2004, Calculated by author.

Its coefficient is insignificant but it is declining.

Secondly, it was verified that there is no b and s convergence in the interest rate (central bank's discount rate) in the JACEAS bloc during 1990-2005. The linear relationship between b and average of 5 year initial values of interest rate was calculated as,

$$\beta = -0.3412+0.0167\ r$$
$$(-1.641)\quad(0.992)$$

$R^2 = 0.0758$,
r = interest rate

where the coefficient was found insignificant and was increasing.

Again, the trend line of coefficient of variations of inter countries interest rate during 1990-2004 was estimated below,

$$\text{Log(c.v.)} = 3.633 + 0.0715\ t$$
$$(0.49)\quad(3.5249)$$

$R^2 = 0.47$

Its coefficient was found insignificant and was increasing. Therefore, no convergence in interest rate was found in the bloc.

Thirdly, for fiscal convergence, we have verified the b and s convergence hypothesis for JACEAS during 1990-2005. The linearity between the â and the average of 5 year initial values of fiscal deficit as percent of GDP for the member countries was estimated as,

$$b = -0.008656 + 0.000135\ FD$$
$$(-0.316)\quad(0.0286)$$

$R^2 = 0.000045$
FD = fiscal deficit as per cent of GDP
where the coefficient was found insignificant and was increasing. So β convergence was not satisfied. Again, the trend line of the coefficient of variation of intercountry fiscal deficit as per cent of GDP during 1990-2005 was estimated as,

$$\text{Log(c.v.)} = 5.7338 - 0.06408\ t$$
$$(29.96)\quad(-3.240)$$

$R^2 = 0.428$

where the coefficient was found significant and was decreasing. Hence, the s convergence was achieved by the JACEAS bloc during the survey period.

Fourthly, we verified the foreign debt as per cent of GDP convergence where b and s convergence were satisfied since,

$$b = 0.04865 - 0.000761\ D$$
$$(4.309)\quad(-5.573)$$

$R^2 = 0.646$

D = external debt as per cent of GDP was estimated through the average of 5 year values of external debt as per cent of GDP and the trend values of â of the member countries during 1990-2005. The coefficient was found significant and was declining over time.

Again, the trend line of coefficient of variation of intercountry external debt as per cent of GDP during 1990-2005 was calculated as,

$$\text{Log (c.v.)} = \underset{(60.235)}{4.7003} - \underset{(-5.2)}{0.00476}\ t$$

$R^2 = 0.692$

where the coefficient was significant and was decreasing over time. Therefore, the convergence hypothesis were achieved in the JACEAS bloc in inflation rate, fiscal deficit as per cent of GDP, external debt as per cent of GDP and except in interest rate during the period 1990-2005.

Hence, it is urgent to fix-up the convergence criteria for the JACEAS bloc for a common currency as laid down by the EU. And the bloc should implement the policy of deregulation of interest rate to achieve convergence criteria very soon.

VERIFICATION OF OCA CRITERIA FOR JACEAS

To justify the Optimum Currency Area criteria we have to satisfy (i) openness, (ii) labour mobility and (iii) pattern of shocks analysis that would guarantee the implementation of single currency in the JACEAS.

Openness

The degree of openness are very low in three giant economies such as Japan, China and India. Japan reached 10.73 per cent in 2004 from 8.75 per cent in 1990. China's degree of openness is the lowest, i.e. 4.22 per cent in 2004. On the contrary, India reached 12.9 per cent in 2004 from

2.41 per cent in 1990. Their progress of openness are very slow in the regime of liberalization. In the regional level, the NIEs average degree of openness was 43.94 per cent in 1990 (excluding Japan) which augmented to 64.13 per cent in 2004. The SAARC's progress is too little than the ASEAN and NIEs, i.e., from 16.66 per cent in 1990 to 24.94 per cent in 2004. The magnificient achievement in liberalization was happened to ASEAN whose average value of degree of openness was 50.38 per cent in 1990 which stepped up to 66.12 per cent in 2004. In the Asian community the more open economies are Singapore and Hong Kong followed by Malaysia, Vietnam etc. In the SAARC region, Maldives and Sri Lanka are more open than other economies. In the ASEAN, Singapore followed by Malaysia, Vietnam, Thailand, Philippines are being increasingly liberalised very soon.

But these evidences of degree of openness of JACEAS community are not sufficient for achieving optimum currency area criteria since the average degree of openness of the JACEAS community as a whole increased from 35.39 per cent in 1990 to 48.54 per cent in 2004. On the other hand, there are reasonable progress for trade integration that should be increased very soon since these degree of openness are much lower than EU and NAFTA. (Table 8).

Labour Mobility

Labour mobility is very low across the members of JACEAS because the degree of labour mobility has no impact in SAARC for activising RTA in WTO but it can affect ASEAN on the basis of GATS Mode-4 model. In this context, it has full labour mobility in the EU. But, NIEs have medium labour mobility among the members.

Patterns of Shocks

Eichengreen and Bayoumi (1999) verified the OCA criteria for East Asia where they showed that East Asia satisfied OCA criteria for a single currency and the region has not been facing any patterns of shocks like growth rate of output, nominal exchange rate with US dollar, and money supply as per cent of GDP, on the other hand, East Asia showed convergence of inflation rate, interest rate, fiscal

TABLE 8

Degree of Openness of Jaceas (1990–2004/05)

	1990	1995	2000	2004-05
Japan	0.0875	0.0756	0.1047	0.1073
China	0.0311	0.0240	0.0267	0.0422
Hong Kong	1.09118	1.2931	1.2538	1.6108
Korea	0.2556	0.2515	0.3251	0.3518
Teipei, China	0.3801	0.4055	0.4673	0.5607
Average	*0.3515*	*0.4099*	*0.4355*	*0.5131*
Bangladesh	0.0860	0.1199	0.1414	0.1574
Bhutan	0.2640	0.3802	0.3199	0.2896
India	0.0741	0.1066	0.1141	0.129
Maldives	–	0.3981	0.3722	0.4225
Nepal	0.1177	0.1936	0.2161	0.1993
Pakistan	0.1688	0.1714	0.1391	0.1603
Sri Lanka	0.2865	0.3527	0.4329	0.3879
Average	*0.1661*	*0.2460*	*0.2497*	*0.2494*
Cambodia	–	0.3137	0.4872	0.5867
Indonesia	0.2076	0.2128	0.2897	0.2138
Lao PDR	0.1538	0.2596	0.2514	0.1891
Malaysia	0.6666	0.8525	0.9975	0.9840
Philippines	0.2395	0.3098	0.4734	0.4836
Singapore	1.5325	1.4451	1.4724	1.6071
Thailand	0.3284	0.3786	0.5350	0.5901
Vietnam	0.3983	0.3280	0.4831	0.6357
Average	*0.5038*	*0.5125*	*0.6237*	*0.6612*
Grand average	*0.3404*	*0.3894*	*0.4363*	*0.4745*

Source: ADO—2006, IFS—1998, 2004, Calculated by author, Degree of openness=[(exports+imports)/2]/GDP.

deficit and external debt as percentage of GDP criteria. They also verified the OCA criteria for ASEAN where there is a little demand shocks but the bloc satisfies the convergence criteria. Therefore, the ASEAN fixed the target 2020 to issue a single currency for the region. I (2004) have verified that SAARC did not satisfy the OCA criteria as well as convergence criteria during 1980-2000.

Now, in this paper, I have showed that the JACEAS bloc has been facing asymmetric shocks in nominal exchange rate with US dollar, in growth rate of GDP and in money supply as per cent of GDP during the period from 1990 to 2006.

Firstly, from the analysis of the correlation matrix of regression errors of nominal exchange rates of member nations of JACEAS with US dollar during 1990-2006, we found that there are 126 minus sign coefficients in the correlation matrix in which 33 are found significant whereas, there are 274 plus sign coefficients in which 104 are significant. Therefore, nominal exchange rate with US dollar are not suitable for OCA criteria to start with a single currency.

Secondly, the correlation matrix of the regression errors of the money supply as per cent of GDP of the member countries of JACEAS bloc from 1990 to 2005 showed that the bloc faced 302 minus sign coefficients in which 93 are significant and also faced 198 plus sign coefficients in which 71 are found significant. Hence, the asymmetric shock of money supply as per cent of GDP rules out the possibility of OCA criteria.

Thirdly, the correlation matrix of the regression errors of the GDP growth rate of the members of JACEAS bloc during 1990-2006 verified that it encountered with 211 plus sign coefficients in which only 11 are significant and chased with 230 minus sign coefficients in which 26 are found significant. Therefore, GDP growth rate also ruled out the possibility of emerging a single currency for the bloc at present. (Table 9).

SOME LESSONS

Last 60 years, regional integration focused on trade integration. After 1980, regional integration stressed on monetary integration. Bela Balassa (1961) developed the sequence of PTA followed by free trade area, custom union, common market and economic union respectively. Viner (1950) explained trade creation and trade diversion effect showing welfare gain in free trade area. The latest wave in trade liberalisation started in the regionalism. Modern Monetary integration led by Mundell (1961), Mackinon (1963),

TABLE 9

Patterns of Shocks during 1990-2005

	No. of symmetric shocks	*Significant cases*	*No. of asymmetric shocks*	*Significant cases*	*Correlation Matrix*
GDP growth rate	211 +sign	11	230 -sign	26	21×21
Money supply % of GDP	302 +sign	93	198 -sign	71	20×20
Nominal Exchange rate with US $	274 +sign	104	126 -sign	33	20×20

Source: ADO—2006, IFS—1998, 2004, Calculated by author.

Krugman (1993), Barro (2002), Grauwe . (2000) showed common currency criteria, i.e. OCA for issuing a single currency for a region, resulting from reducing transaction cost and lesser disturbance in exchange rate changes. East Asia stepped towards monetary integration after 1997, without trade integration. The common transmission mechanism, open capital account, transparent monetary policy and international institutionalized monetary policy of the preconditioned were achieved by East Asia during the development process of CMI believing that common currency stimulates trade by reducing current account constraint. Even, Eichengreen and Bayoumi (1999) showed green signal for a common currency to East Asia having a good index of OCA with a low demand and supply shock than in EU.

Remind that creation of a common currency would take place at the last stage of full economic integration in any region or a group of countries. To pave the way for success of full economic integration through CMI, East Asia and ASEAN+4, should monitor surveillance process in different phases if they (Japan and China) opposed the idea of linking CMI with IMF programme for setting-up Asian surveillance coordination unit where CMI goes beyond the supplementary role to the IMF and seeks independent conditionality and maintain monetary integration coordinating exchange rate mechanism under regional surveillance. Since AMF ignores any Yen, Yuan or Dollar bloc domination, the Asian monetary system needs a new Asian monetary unit following Williamson's (2000) proposal of either soft margin or monitoring band of unit through managed floating with reserve intervention implementing various phases of monetary integration process stage by stage towards issuing a single currency for an Asian bloc.

CONCLUDING REMARKS

If CMI be the optimum foundation for Asian Economic Integration then AMF will be the final goal for Asian institutional identity and East Asian monetary integration will lead in the process of integration through Japanese domination and dollarisation will be the win-win policy to have an acceptance of IMF surveillance mechanism. Or, if dynamic economic integration succeeds, then trade integration combined with monetary integration will prevail and Chinese domination may predominate the Asian bloc under dedollarisation process without the evolution of AMF. Because, Korea, Japan, Philippines, Singapore and Hong Kong desire to include USA in the East Asian Regional Institute under surveillance mechanism of IMF but other nations denied it. Therefore, CMI may not be realised since there are several economic and political barriers to Asian Economic Integration, such as,

(i) Divergence of per capita income,
(ii) Economic rivalry among East Asian partners,
(iii) Co-operation of exchange rate mechanism uniformly rejected,
(iv) China and Japan are competitive not cooperative. They are historically enemies as England and France, Argentina and Brazil, etc.,
(v) Hong Kong and Singapore are vying to become the financial hub in East Asia,
(vi) Korea and Taiwan compete in global market,
(vii) Vietnam and Myanmer are trying to maintain highly authoritarian region even while they embrace market economies,
(viii) It is a threat to USA if Asian bloc sets-up AMF,

(ix) Time is needed for the causality among institution, geography of trade and economic integration,

(x) Monetary integration without trade integration may jeopardize the evolution of AMF,

(xi) IMF surveillance will chase against the evolution of AMF.

Thus, C.F. Bergsten (2000) puts it that the creation of new Asian Economic Institution could bring numerous positive results for the world as whole as well as for Asian itself. Financial Stability and economic progress could be enhanced. Also, he reminds that the new Asian challenge could be one of the defining elements of the world of early 21st century. It is imperative that Americans, Europeans and others, as well as Asians, begin to think hard about it now and work together to orient it in constructive direction that will enable the Asians to achieve their legitimate goal without disrupting security and stability around the globe.

REFERENCES

Ahmed, Syed Norman (2004), "Asian Integration: Prospects for India's Merchandise Trade", *The Indian Economic Journal*, Vol. 52, No. 1-2, pp. 131-37.

Akhtar, S.M. Jawed (2004/05), "Formation of Currency Union in SAARC Countries:Issues and Prospects", *The Indian Economic Journal*, Vol. 52, No. 3-4, pp. 125-132.

Alesina, Alberto and Barro Robert J., (2002), "Currency Unions", *Quarterly Journal of Economics* 117(2), pp. 409-36.

Asian Development Bank, (2005, 2006), A.D.O., 2005, 2006, www.adb.org

ASEAN, (2005), ASEAN Statistical Year Book—2003, www.aseansec.org

Balassa, Bela, (1961), "Theory of Economic Integration", Richard D., Irwin, Homewood-IL

Bergsten, C.F. (2000), "The New Asian Challenge", Institute for International Economics, March.

Bergsten, C.F. and Perk Yung Chul (2002), "Towards Creating a Regional Monetary Arrangement in East Asia." *ADB, Institute Research Paper Series No. 50*, December.

Bhowmik, Debesh, (1992), "A Plan for a New Asian Bloc", *Economic Studies*, Vol. 30, No. 3, pp. 209-212.

——(1997), "Prospect of Asia-Pacific Economies—A View from Indo-Asia-Pacific Trade", *International Journal of Development Planning Literature*, Vol. 12, Nos. 3 and 4, July-October, pp. 191-216.

——(1998), "Regional Trading Blocs and International Money", 80th *Conference Volume, IEA,* Bangalore, pp. 372-384.

——(1998), "Economic Cooperation among SAARC: A Plan for a Common Currency", *The Indian Economic Journal,* 45(1): pp. 138-45.

——(2004), "Globalisation, International Trade and Financial Integration", 24th *BEA Conference Volume,* Kolkata, p. 74

——and Barma Binita, (2004), "On Asian Economic Community: A Study", 87th *IEA Conference Volume,* Varanasi, pp. 809-814.

Bird, Graham and Rajan Ramkishen S., (2002), "The Evolving Asian Financial Architecture." *Essays in International Economics,* No. 226, February, Princeton University.

Carrer, Celine and Schiff Maurice, (2003), "On the Geography of Trade: Distance is Alive and Well", *World Bank Seminar Paper,* December.

Clarete, Ramon, Edmonds Christopher and Wallack Jessica Seddon (2002), "Asian Regionalism and its Affects on Trade in the 1980s and 1990s." *ERD, WP,* No. 30, ADB, November.

Das, Debendra Kumar and Bhowmik Debesh (2004), "Steps Towards Monetary Integration of SAARC", Unpublished paper.

De Grauwe, Paul (2000), "The Economics of Monetary Union." OUP.UK

Eichengreen, Barry (2004), "Real and Pseudo Preconditions for an Asian Monetary Union", *ADB Conference Paper,* July, Manila.

Eichengreen B. and Bayoumi T. (1999), "Is Asia Optimum Currency Area? Can it Become One?" In S. Collignon, J. Pisani-Ferry and Y.C. Park, eds. *Exchange Rate Policies in Emerging Asian Countries,* London, Routledge.

Fabella, Raul (2002), "Monetary Cooperation in East Asia: A Survey", *ERD, WP* No. 13, ADB, May.

Goldstein, Morris and Lardy Nicholas R. (2005), "China's Role in the Revived BrettonWoods System: A case of Mistaken Identity", *Institute for International Economics, WP-2,* March.

——(2004), "What Kind of Landing for the Chinese Economy?", *PB-7, Institute for International Economics,* November.

Holst, David Ronald, Azis Iwan and Liu Li-Gang (2003), "Regionalism and Globalisation: East and South East Asian Trade Related in the Wake of China's WTO Accession." *ADBI, DP,* January.

Hufbaner,Gary Clyde and Wong Yee (2005), "Prospect for Regional Free Trade in Asia", *WP-05-12,* October, *Institute for International Economics.*

I.M.F., (2005), "World Economic Outlook-(2005)", Global Development Finance (2005), www.imf.org

Ize, Alain and Yeyati Eduardo Levy (2005), "Financial Dedollarisation: Is it for Real?" *IMF, WP*-30, September.

Krugman, Paul (1993), "What do We Need to Know about the International Monetary System?", *Essays in International Economics,* No. 190, July.

McKinnon, Ronald (1963), "Optimum Currency Areas", *AER*-513, pp. 717-25.

——(2004), "East Asian Dollar Standard", *China Economic Review* 15, pp. 325-30.

Mundell, Robert (1961), "Theory of Optimum Currency Area", *AER*-51, pp. 657-65.

Ng, Francis and Yeats Alexander (2003), "Major Trade Trend in East Asia", *World Bank Policy Research Working Paper*-3084, June.

Park, Yung Chul (2001), "The East Asian Dilema: Restructuring Out or Growing Out?" *Essays in International Economics*, No. 223, August.

Pomfret, Richard (2004), "Sequencing Trade and Monetary Integration: Issues and Applications to Asia, *WP-14, University of Adelaide*, December.

Salai-i-Martin, X. (1996), "Regional Cohesion: Evidence and Theories of Regional Growth and Convergence", *European Economic Review*, Vol. 40, pp. 1325-52.

UNCTAD (2004), "Handbook of Statistics 2003", www.unctad.org

——(2004), "Development and Globalisation", www.unctad.org

——(2004), "Trade and Development Report-2004", www.unctad.org

——(2005, 2006), "World Investment Report-2005, 2006", www.unctad.org

——(2005), "Trade and Development Report-2005", www.unctad.org

Viner, Jacob (1950), "The Customs Union Issue, Carnegie Endowment for International Peace", NewYork.

Williamson, John (2000), "Exchange Rate Regime for East Asia, Reviving the Intermediate Option." In *Policy Analyses in International Economics* 60, Institute for International Economics.

Williamson, John (2005), "A Currency Basket for East Asia, Not Just", China, *Institute for International Economics, PB-05-1*, August.

W.T.O. (2005), "Annual Report—2005", www.wto.org

World Bank (2005, 2006), "World Development Report—2005, 2006", www.worldbank.org

Towards an Asian Trade Bloc

Role of East Asia, ASEAN and SAARC

Davinder Kumar Madaan

The Asian region comprises more than 4 billion people (60 per cent of the world population), living in 51 different countries. It is the largest and most populous continent, covering 29.8 per cent of land area. It is rich in natural resources, such as petroleum and iron. There is a huge disparity in wealth in Asia, with Japan being the world's second largest economy, and North Korea being one of the poorest. 28 countries of Asia are the members of World Trade Organization (WTO). Further, 11 Asian countries are in the process of accession to WTO.

The strategic access to markets has become an important factor of competitiveness. It is pushing countries all over the world to set-up Free Trade Areas (FTAs) and Regional Trade Arrangements (RTAs) to get preferential access to markets. The countries, which are not members of the RTAs, suffer from trade diversion and lack of access to these areas. There are about 290 RTAs in force—six times as many as two decades ago. About a third of global trade takes place between countries which have some form of reciprocal

RTA.[1] The manifestations of these RTAs are EU (European Union, 1957), ASEAN (Association of South East Asian Nations, 1967), NAFTA (North American Free Trade Area, 1994), APEC (Asia Pacific Economic Cooperation, 1989), SAARC (South Asian Association for Regional Cooperation, 1985), etc. The emergence of these RTAs is an attempt of these countries to operate in the global market with their increased economic strength. WTO has made important exceptions to regional trade bloc from the principle of non-discrimination. It provides Most Favoured Nation (MFN)[2] treatment to all its 149 member countries, and has allowed 100 per cent discrimination under Free Trade Area (FTA)[3] and Customs Union (CU)[4] along with the reduced concessional arrangement for the developing countries under tariff and subsidy reduction programmes.[5]

The formation of Asian Trade Bloc (ATB) would be a trend towards speeding-up Asian regional economic integration. The proposed ATB would be comprised of East Asia (China, Japan, South Korea, Australia and New Zealand), ASEAN-10, and SAARC-7. It would cover 24 economies, having more than half of the world's population, nearly a quarter of world output and trade, and two-thirds of global foreign exchange reserves. It would be larger than the EU-25 in terms of population, having trade higher than NAFTA and foreign exchange reserves greater than those of EU and NAFTA put together. In fact, the sub regional blocs like ASEAN and SAARC could not exploit the full trade potentials due to their limited complementarities, and much larger trade with East Asia than their intra-bloc trade. RIS studies conducted in computable general equilibrium (CGE) model framework have shown that a trade liberalization in the framework of an RTA among ASEAN, China, India, Japan and South Korea (ASEAN+4) could produce efficiency gains worth US $ 147 billion.[6]

India has to play an important role in formation of such Asian Trade Bloc. As a part of the look-east policy, India has consciously integrated its economy with East Asia since the early 1990s. It has taken steps to evolve FTAs with ASEAN, Thailand and Singapore, and is part of SAARC and BIMSTEC (Bangladesh, Bhutan, India, Myanmar, Nepal, Sri Lanka and

TABLE 1

Key Economic Indicators of Asian Countries During 2005

Sl. No.	Country	Area ('000, KM²)	Population Mid Year (million)	Growth of Population (per cent)	Gross Income (GNI) GNI (US $)	Per Capita National (US $, mn)	Growth of GDP (per cent)	Exports Total (US $, mn)	Imports Total (US $, mn)
1	2	3	4	5	6	7	8	9	10
	East Asia	*18086.3*	*1516*	*0.7*	*8977253*	*5922*	*4.7*	*2057946*	*1891382*
1.	Australia	7741.2	20.5	1.2	654645	32220	3.0	106499	119172
2.	China, People Rep.	9598.1	1307.6	0.6	2263825	1740	9.9	762338	660218
3.	Hong Kong, China*	1.1	6.9	0.7	192118	27670	7.3	289509	299967
4.	Macao, China*	0.03	0.5	0.6	7075	14150	2.1	2476	3913
5.	Japan	377.9	128.1	0.0	4988209	38980	2.8	591318	512733
6.	Korea, Rep. of	99.3	48.3	0.5	764684	15830	4.0	284077	269145
7.	New Zealand	268.7	4.1	1.0	106697	25960	4.0	21728	26234
	ASEAN	*4480.1*	*559*	*1.7*	*888553*	*1590*	*6.7*	*667246*	*601588*
1.	Brunei Darussalam	5.8	0.4	2.6	6840	23600	3.6	4967	1672
2.	Cambodia	181	13.8	1.9	5340	380	8.4	2856.6	4095
3.	Indonesia	1904.6	219.9	1.3	282158	1280	5.6	92909	64377
4.	Lao PDR	236.8	5.6	1.4	2618	440	7.2	693.3	1283
5.	Malaysia	329.8	26.1	2.2	125847	4960	5.3	161484	126796
6.	Myanmar	676.6	55.4	2.0	9196	166	12.2	3648.4	3616
7.	Philippines	300	85.2	2.1	108333	1300	5.1	52441	51839
8.	Singapore	0.7	4.4	1.6	119606	27490	6.4	207338	189745

9. Thailand	513.1	64.8	0.8	176937	2750	4.5	110107	118191
10. Vietnam	331.7	83.1	1.4	51678	620	8.4	30801	39976
SAARC	*4487.5*	*1444*	*1.8*	*998159*	*691*	*4.8*	*130394*	*192295*
1. Bangladesh	144	137.0	1.4	66242	470	5.8	8988	14291
2. Bhutan	47	0.8	2.4	799	870	5.8	186	411
3. India	3287.3	1107.0	1.7	793017	720	8.4	99764	139300
4. Maldives	0.3	0.3	1.6	787	2390	-2.9	135	818
5. Nepal	147.2	25.3	2.3	7275	270	2.8	652	1937
6. Pakistan	796.1	154.0	2.0	107284	690	7.8	14149	25640
7. Sri Lanka	65.6	19.7	1.3	22755	1160	6.0	6520	9899
*ASIA***	*27054*	*3519*	*1.4*	*10863965*	*3088*	*5.4*	*2855585*	*2685266*
World	*133941*	*6464.8*	*1.2*	*44983338*	*6987*	*4.0*	*10393000*	*10741000*
Asian Share in World (%)	*20.2*	*54.4*		*24.2*			*27.5*	*25.0*

* Hong Kong and Macao became a Special Administrative Regions of People's Republic of China w.e.f. July 1, 1997 and December 20, 1999 respectively

** ASIA includes only above cited countries.

Source: ADB, Key Economic Indicators, 2006 and UNESCAP, Statistical Indicators for Asia and Pacific, 2006.

Thailand). India and Japan have proposed free trade grouping in East Asia, combining the 16 countries that participated in the East Asia Summit (EAS),[7] a new forum launched in December 2005 in Kuala Lumpur. Thus, Asia seems to be getting ready to exploit the fruits of trade integration. India along with East Asia, ASEAN, and SAARC need to work together to make it happen. This paper is an attempt to analyze the role of East Asia, ASEAN and SAARC in forming an Asian Trade Bloc with the help of some statistical evidence. East Asian economies covered in this study are Australia, People's Republic of China, Hong Kong—China, Macao-China, Japan, Republic of Korea, and New Zealand.

Firstly, it is worthwhile to give some brief introduction of ASEAN and SAARC. ASEAN was established on 8th August, 1967 with the signing of Bangkok Declaration by five member countries, namely, Indonesia, Malaysia, Philippines, Singapore, and Thailand. Five more members joined it later, namely, Brunei Darussalam (January 1984), Vietnam (July 1995), Laos, PDR (July 1997), Myanmar (July 1997), and Cambodia (April 1999). ASEAN was formed to accelerate economic progress and to increase the stability of the South East Asian region. The permanent Secretariat of ASEAN was established in Jakarta (Indonesia). At the onset of ASEAN financial crisis of 1997-99, the meeting of ASEAN+3 (China, Japan and Korea—three major economies of East Asia) was held in November 1999, which agreed to strengthen regional unity, and establishment of an East Asian common market and currency.[8] On 1st January 2002, ASEAN Free Trade Area (AFTA) was formally come into operation among original six signatories (Brunei, Indonesia, Malaysia, Philippines, Singapore and Thailand).[9] It was agreed that original six members and new members of ASEAN would achieve the elimination of all tariffs by 2015 and 2018 respectively. Further, in November 2002, ASEAN leaders agreed to transform ASEAN into an ASEAN Economic Community (AEC) by 2020.[10]

SAARC consists of seven countries, viz., Bangladesh, Bhutan, India, Maldives, Nepal, Pakistan and Sri Lanka. It was established on 8th December 1985 after about four and a half years of its background work. Trade is one of the priority areas of economic cooperation among the SAARC countries. In spite of various commonalities of the SAARC countries, the intra-regional SAARC trade was 2.8 per cent of their global trade during 1985, which, however, picked-up to 4.9 per cent during 2005. The implicit idea behind the establishment of SAARC was to carry out regional co-operation to the highest stage of economic integration among these seven SAARC countries.[11] Though the pace is very slow, SAARC, since its inception, is heading towards that end. It has succeeded in establishing SAARC Preferential Trading Arrangement (SAPTA) in December 1995, and now, replaced it with SAARC Free Trade Area (SAFTA) from 1st January 2006. However, SAFTA will lead to free trade area in the region only on 1st January 2016.

KEY ECONOMIC INDICATORS OF ASIAN TRADE BLOC

Asian countries are the developing countries of the world except Australia, Japan, and New Zealand. Table 1 depicts some key economic indicators of these countries during 2005. It can be seen from this table that China has very largest area as well as population, whereas Maldives has very smallest area as well as population of this region.

The population of SAARC is more than two and half times that of ASEAN with almost equivalent area. However, seven East Asian economies have more than twice the combined area of ASEAN and SAARC with less population. The annual growth of population among Asian countries ranges between 2.6 per cent in case of Brunei Darussalam and neutral growth of Japan. ASEAN Gross National Income (GNI) stood at US $ 888.6 billion (bn), which was less than that of SAARC (US $ 998.2 bn), and East Asia (US $ 8977.3 bn). The highest GNI among Asian countries was of Japan (US $ 4988.2 bn), followed by China (US $ 2263.8 bn) and India (US $ 793 bn). Maldives had the least GNI (US $ 787 million) among Asian countries during 2005. Further, the per capita GNI of East Asia was US $ 5922, which was more than that of ASEAN (US $ 1590) and SAARC (US $ 691) during this period. The highest per capita GNI among Asian countries was of Japan (US $ 38980), followed by Australia

(US $ 32220), Hong Kong (US $ 27670) and Singapore (US $ 27490). Myanmar had the least per capita GNI (US $ 166), followed by Nepal (US $ 270) and Cambodia (US $ 380) among Asian countries during this period. Hence a large gap of inequality exists among Asian countries. However, the growth of Gross Domestic Product (GDP) in 2005 for ASEAN nations was 6.7 per cent, which was more than SAARC (4.8 per cent) and East Asia (4.7 per cent). The highest growth of GDP among Asian countries was of Myanmar (12.2 per cent), followed by China (9.9 per cent) and India, Cambodia and Vietnam (8.4 per cent). However, Maldives had minus 2.9 per cent growth of GDP. Trade is the major priority area of Asian countries. The exports of East Asia in 2005 stood at US $ 2057.9 bn, which was more than that of ASEAN (US $ 667.2 bn) and SAARC (US $ 130.4 bn). China was the major exporter of Asia with its exports worth US $ 762.3 bn, followed by Japan (US $ 591.3 bn), Hong Kong (US $ 289.5 bn) and South Korea (US $ 284.1 bn). Maldives was the least exporter of Asia with its exports worth US $ 135 million. The imports of East Asia in 2005 stood at US $ 1891.4 bn, which was more than that of ASEAN (US $ 601.6 bn) and SAARC (US $ 192.3 bn). The major importer was China (US $ 660.2 bn), followed by Japan (US $ 512.7 bn), Hong Kong (US $ 300 bn), and South Korea (US $ 269.1 bn). Bhutan was the least importer of Asia with its imports worth US $ 411 million only in 2005. Asian balance of trade was favourable in 2005 with US $ 285.6 bn worth of exports and US $ 268.5 bn worth of its imports. Only SAARC had unfavourable balance of trade during this period.

It is very interesting to note from Table 1 that the proposed Asian Trade Bloc comprises 3.5 bn of world population (54.4 per cent of the world) with 20.2 per cent of the world's area, 24.2 per cent of world's GNI and 26.2 per cent of the world trade. It would be comparable with EU-25 and NAFTA in the world.

ROLE OF ASIAN TRADE BLOC IN GLOBAL TRADE

The global trade volume of Asian Trade Bloc has increased more than twice during the post-WTO period (1995-

2005). The exports of ATB increased tremendously from US $ 1190 bn in 1995 to US $ 2855.6 bn in 2005. On the other hand, imports of ATB increased from US $ 1432 bn in 1995 to US $ 2685.3 bn in 2005. Further, unfavourable balance of trade of ATB during 1995-2001 became favourable from 2002 onwards. Moreover, the growth of ATB's trade was slightly more than that of the world.

It is relevant to discuss the share of Asian Trade Bloc in the global trade during post-WTO period. Table 2 shows this scenario in terms of exports, imports and total trade. It can be seen from this table that East Asia controlled 16.2 per cent of the global exports in 1995, which increased to 19.8 per cent in 2005. ASEAN had 6.4 per cent share in global exports in 1995 and 2005. Further, SAARC accounted for 0.9 per cent in the global exports during 1995, which increased to and 1.3 per cent during 2005. Overall, the share of Asian Trade Bloc in the global exports increased from 23.5 per cent in 1995 to 27.5 per cent in 2005. In terms of global imports, East Asia had 19.6 per cent share during 1995, which diminished to 17.6 per cent during 2005. Hence the dependence of East Asia on world imports decreased over the period. Further, share of ASEAN in the global imports also diminished from 7.1 per cent in 1995 to 5.6 per cent in 2005. But this share for SAARC increased from 1.1 per cent in 1995 to 1.8 per cent in 2005. Overall, the share of Asian Trade Bloc in the global imports decreased from 27.9 per cent in 1995 to 25 per cent in 2005. However, the share of East Asia in the total global trade increased from 17.9 per cent in 1995 to 18.7 per cent in 2005. SAARC's share also raised from 1 per cent in 1995 to 1.5 per cent in 2005. But this share for ASEAN decreased from 6.7 per cent in 1995 to 6 per cent in 2005.

On the whole, the share of Asian Trade Bloc in the world trade increased from 25.7 per cent in 1995 to 26.2 per cent 2005. East Asia had the major share in it. Further, SAARC and ASEAN were the marginal players in the world trade.

TRADE DEPENDENCE AMONG ASIAN COUNTRIES

The trade dependence among Asian countries is very much high. This can be judged from the position of intra-Asia trade. For this purpose, the share of trade among Asian Trade Bloc in its global trade has been traced out. Table 3 shows the intra-Asia trade during 2005. It is revealed in this table that ASEAN had the major share in intra-Asia trade, which was 56.5 per cent for exports, 59.3 per cent for imports and 57.8 per cent for total trade. Further, Intra-ASEAN trade was 22.8 per cent during 2005. East Asia had also significant shares of 49.1 per cent for intra-Asia exports, 49.8 per cent for intra-Asia imports, and 49.4 per cent in total intra-Asia trade during this period. However, SAARC accounted for 29.1 per cent in intra-Asia exports, 32.3 per cent in intra-Asia imports and 31 per cent in the total intra-Asia trade. But intra-SAARC trade was very much marginal. It was 5.1 per cent for exports, and 4.6 per cent for imports.

Overall, Asian Trade Bloc had 50.3 per cent intra-Asia trade, which is very much significant in view of the 4.9 per cent share of intra-SAARC and 22.8 per cent of the intra-ASEAN during 2005.

It may be noted that all the major Asian economies have been pursuing bilateral FTAs, which strengthened the process for the formation of Asian Trade Bloc.[12] The ASEAN's FTAs with its full dialogue partners, namely China, India, Japan, and South Korea; a trilateral FTA among Japan, China and South Korea; Japan-Australia FTA; under study ASEAN-Korea FTA; SAFTA, and Asian Cooperation Dialogue (ACD) forum of 28 countries, are some of the manifestations. But these FTAs are sub-optimal and could not reap the substantial gains of regional economic integration. Therefore, there is a need for building Asian Trade Bloc, involving all sub-regional and bilateral FTAs. The complementarities between Asian countries are obvious from the fact that the share of intra-regional trade was 50.3 per cent of their global trade during 2005. Studies have shown that broader regional integration in Asia has the potential of generating billions of dollars of new output and put Asia on a high growth path. Further, it has been shown that Asian economic integration will benefit the rest of the world, as it implies trade creation rather than trade diversion. Hence, it is a case of win-win for Asia, as well as the world economy.[13]

CONCLUDING REMARKS

Asian countries have emerged as the fastest growing economies of the world. These countries have a lot of complementarities. East Asia has the significant share in the world output and trade. The sub-regional blocs like ASEAN and SAARC could not exploit the full trade potentials due to their limited complementarities, and lower intra-regional trade. Further, all major economies of Asia have already pursuing bilateral FTAs. Therefore, the role of East Asia, ASEAN and SAARC is very much important for building broader Asian Trade Bloc. In 2005, the Asian Trade Bloc comprised of 3.5 billion of world population (54.4 per cent of the world) with 20.2 per cent of the world's area, 24.2 per cent of world's GNI and 26.2 per cent of the world trade. The growth of intra-Asia trade has been more than the global Asian trade during the post WTO period. The complementarities between Asian countries are obvious from the fact that the share of intra-regional trade was 50.3 per cent of their global trade during 2005. Studies have shown that broader regional integration in Asia has the potential of generating billions of dollars of new output and put Asia on a fastest growth path. A trade liberalization in the framework of an RTA among ASEAN, China, India, Japan and South Korea (ASEAN+4) could produce efficiency gains worth US $ 147 billion. Thus, the formation of Asian Trade Bloc could facilitate the exploitation of substantial gains. However, the success of this bloc would depend upon the mutual trust among all the member countries.

NOTES AND REFERENCES

1. World Bank, 2005, *Global Economic Prospects*.
2. MFN clause states that a country agrees not to give better treatment in international trade to any single nation than it gives to all the contracting parties of GATT/WTO.
3. Under FTA, all trade restrictions within the participating countries are abolished, but each participant is free to maintain any sort of external tariffs with the non-participating countries.
4. CU involves not only unrestricted free trade within the participating countries but also common external tariffs with the non-participating countries.

5. Goyal Arun. (ed.), *WTO in the New Millennium: Commentary, Case Law, Legal Texts*, Bombay, MVIRDC World Trade Centre, 2000).
6. Mohanty, S.K.; Pohit, Sanjib and Roy Saikat, S. (2004), "Towards Formation of Close Economic Cooperation among Asian Countries", *Discussion Paper No. 78, Research and Information System for the Non-Aligned and Other Developing Countries (RIS),* New Delhi.
7. The EAS is better known as the ASEAN+3, India, Australia and New Zealand. While the ASEAN consists of 10 South East Asian countries, the 'Plus-Three' countries are the ASEAN's long-standing dialogue partners—China, Japan and Korea, Republic of.
8. Kesavapany, K., (2003), "ASEAN's Contribution to the Building of an Asian Economic Community", *Discussion Paper No. 50, Research and Information System for the Non-Aligned and Other Developing Countries (RIS),* New Delhi, p.13.
9. ASEAN Secretariat (2004), *www.aseansec.org.*
10. Europa, (2004), *The Europa World Year Book 2003,* Europa Publications, London, 44th Edition, pp. 146-53.
11. Madaan, D.K., (ed), *SAARC: "Origin, Development and Programmes",* (New Delhi, Deep & Deep Publications, 1997), p. 224.
12. Asher, M.G. and Sen, Rahul (2005), "India-East Asia Integration: A Win-Win for Asia", Discussion Paper No. 91, *Research and Information System for the Non-Aligned and Other Developing Countries (RIS),* New Delhi.
13. Kumar, Nagesh (2005), "Towards a Broader Asian Economic Community: The Agenda for the East Asian Summit", *Discussion Paper No. 100, Research and Information System for the Non-Aligned and Other Developing Countries (RIS),* New Delhi.

Regional Blocs, Trade Flows and Revealed Comparative Advantages

Case for Asian Economic Integration

PARAMJIT NANDA AND P.S. RAIKHY

Globalisation could sustain a higher rate of growth of the world economies by improving allocation of resources, by narrowing down the differences in prices of goods and services and factors of production and hence removing disparities in per capita income between different economies. But in recent years, globalisation has been paralleled by contradictory developments, i.e. rise in trade protectionism and formation of more regional trading arrangements (RTAs). They have arisen as a reaction of failure of the international economic system in removing trade balances between countries and regions and also lack of confidence in WTO. Even WTO recognises regional trading arrangements 'as half way house on the path leading to full benefits of trade liberalisation and wider markets' and realises complementarities between regional and multilateral integration in the sense that constitution of RTAs may act as positive force for multilateral system. Now-a-days, nearly all of WTO members (149) have notified participation in one or more RTAs. At present, 250 RTAs have been notified to GATT/WTO and number might approach to 300 shortly. Of 250 RTAs, 124 were notified during GATT period, while 130 have been notified after 1995 indicating rapid surge in RTAs after WTO formation. Despite this proliferation, WTO recognises only NAFTA and EU, MERCOUSER, ASEAN and COMESA as best RTAs. These regional associations are shaping patterns of location of production and competitive advantage. In Asia, regional attempts like SAARC, EAEC, Bangkok agreements, etc. have been unable to exploit the potential of regional economic cooperation. India is member of SAARC only. However, with the possible inclusion of India as a member of Asian Economic Community (Japan, ASEAN, China, India, Korea) (JACIK Countries), Pan-Asia (JACIK + Australia and New Zealand) and EAECI (Brunei, China, Hong Kong China, Indonesia, Japan, Korea, Malaysia, Philippines, Singapore, Taiwan China and India), India may become member of more RTAs, playing more significant role in the regional groupings and shaping world trading system.

Against this backdrop, the present paper is an attempt to study complementarities in production and trade among JACIK, Pan-Asia and EAECI members. Accordingly, the paper has been divided into three sections. Section I builds a case for formation of Asian Economic Community by comparing three blocs (JACIK, Pan-Asia and EAECI), Section II examines trade flows among members of these blocs by examining intra-bloc trade shares, Section III analyses pattern of trade of countries by estimating Revealed Comparative Advantage (RCA) index (at the 3 digit SITC level) for 67 export items and 52 import items. These trade items have been selected from top ten traded commodities of each member of these blocs.

DATA BASE AND METHODOLOGY

Data for the study have been taken from UN, UNCTAD, World Bank and IMF publications for the year 1995, 2002, and 2004.

Revealed comparative advantage (RCA) index of

members of these blocs have been calculated at 3 digit SITC level for top 10 export items in the following manner:

$$RCA_{ij} = \frac{X_j / X_i}{X_{jw} / X_w}$$

where

RCA_{ij} = Revealed comparative advantage of commodity j for country i.
X_{ij} = Export of commodity j in country i.
X_{jw} = Exports of commodity j of the world.
X_w = Total exports of the world.

I

Various attempts at regional integration in Asia include Association of South East Asian Nations (ASEAN), Gulf Cooperation Council (GCC), Economic Cooperation Organisation (ECO), the South Asian Association for Regional Cooperation (SAARC), the Arab Common Market (ACM), Arab Magherb Union (AMU), Greater Arab Free Trade Area (GAFTA), East Asian Economic Caucus (EAEC) and Bangkok Agreement.

These efforts of promoting regional cooperation in Asia have not succeeded in exploiting the full potential of the regional economic integration across Asia due to limited complementarities at the sub-regional levels and consequently failed to promote intra-regional trade as compared to EU and NAFTA. Table 1 reflects the fact that trade ratios of Asian blocs are very low as compared to NAFTA and EU in world exports, intra-group and intra-regional exports. Share of EU in world exports is even higher than Asia as a whole. In a globalised economy, in order to maximise the benefits from trade liberalisation and to remain competitive in Asia, ASEAN would require broader integration of their economies to exploit complementarities fully. As compared to EU and NAFTA, an Asia-wide economic forum does not exist, though it is badly needed. In the initial stage, Asian Economic Community may consist of JACIK (Japan, ASEAN, China,

TABLE 1

Intra-Group Trade of Different Regional and Trade Groups

Economic Groupings	*As an age of World's Exports*				*Intra-trade of Groups as a Percentage of Regional Groups of each Group*				*Intra-trade of Groups as a Percentage of Total Exports of each Group*			
	1990	*1995*	*2000*	*2004*	*1990*	*1995*	*2000*	*2004*	*1990*	*1995*	*2000*	*2004*
ASEAN	4.1	6.1	6.7	6.1	34.00	42.00	39.1	35.8	19.0	24.6	23.0	22.0
Bangkok Agreement	3.5	4.6	5.2	5.1	3.2	12.7	15.8	22.2	1.6	6.8	8.0	11.0
ECO	1.1	1.2	1.3	1.5	11.1	25.5	18.2	20.6	3.2	7.9	5.6	6.4
GCC	2.5	2.0	2.6	2.5	14.6	12.1	7.5	7.2	8.0	6.8	4.9	4.6
MSG	–	–	–	–	0.8	1.2	2.4	3.6	0.3	0.4	0.6	0.8
SAARC	0.8	0.9	1.0	1.1	10.8	12.5	12.3	12.7	3.2	4.4	4.1	5.3
EAEC	20.9	26.1	26.0	25.4	–	–	–	–	39.7	47.9	46.6	49.4
NAFTA	16.2	16.8	19.0	15.5	88.7	87.3	91.0	91.0	41.4	46.2	55.7	55.2
EU	44.0	39.7	35.9	38.7	89.0	90.6	91.7	90.6	67.1	66.1	67.2	67.0

Source: UN: *UNCTAD Handbook of Trade Statistics*, 2005 and World Bank: *World Development Indicators*, 2005.

India and Korea) or Pan-Asia (JACIK + Australia and New Zealand). Further, because of higher export share of EAEC in the bloc, India may consider pursuing for membership of EAEC so as to change it to EAECI. Formation of these blocs will be comparable to EU and NAFTA in terms of GDP, exports, international reserves and population (Table 2). Selected indicators given in the Table show the significance of proposed regional trade grouping, JACIK (and Pan-Asia) group accounts for 48 (49) per cent of world's population, 21 (22) per cent of GDP, 21 (22) per cent of world's exports and 18 (18) per cent of world's imports. EAEC (and EAECI) group accounts for 29 (46) per cent of world's population, 20 (22) per cent of world's GDP, 25 (25) per cent of world exports and 21 (22) per cent of world's imports. All countries except Cambodia, Lao PDR, Vietnam, Australia and New Zealand have current account surplus. Openness index (trade to GDP ratio ranges from 6.88 per cent in Myanmar to 277 per cent in Singapore. External debt to income ratio is lowest for EAECI (25 per cent) than for JACIK and Pan Asia. Within EAECI, debt-income ratio is lowest for China and India. Regarding official development assistance (ODA, $ per capita) countries like Indonesia and Cambodia have been receiving higher level of ODA per capita, while China and India have been receiving less ODA per capita. JACIK and Pan-Asia countries received 14 per cent and 16 per cent of World's FDI respectively while EAEC and EAECI have received 15 per cent and 16 per cent of World's FDI respectively. Share of FDI to GDP in JACIK, Pan-Asia, EAEC and EAECI is respectively 2.10, 2.11, 2.69 and 2.53 per cent only, indicating flow of most of FDI between developed nations. FDI to GDP ratio is highest in Singapore (12.5 per cent) and lowest in Philippines (0.9 per cent).

Comparison of different blocs of Asia suggests that Pan Asia, had high share in world's population and GDP; while EAECI had high share in World's exports, imports, FDI and FDI to GDP ratio, indicating that India will gain if it becomes member of Pan-Asia and/or of EAEC. The success of each bloc will depend on increased intra-regional trade and realisation of complementarities in production and trade.

TABLE 2

Selected Indicators of JACIK, Pan-Asia, EAECI Countries (2003)

Country	*Population in Million*	*GDP ($ b)*	*External debt ($ b)*	*External debt as a percentage of GNI*	*Foreign exchange reserves ($ b)*	*ODA per capita*	*FDI ($ b)*	*FDI as a percentage of GDP*	*Exports ($ b)*	*Imports ($ b)*	*Current Balance ($ b)*	*Trade to GDP Ratio*	*GDP per Capita ($)*
1	*2*	*3*	*4*	*5*	*6*	*7*	*8*	*9*	*10*	*11*	*12*	*13*	*14*
JACIK	3065	7654	326.99	35.21		–	82.52	2.10	1604	1428.06	–	–	–
		(48.64)	(21.13)					(14.40)		(21.15)	(18.40)		
Japan	128	4301					6.23	.0	471	382	172.05	18.87	33819
ASEAN													
Brunei	0.358	4.62	–	–	–	–	–	–	4.5	1.54	–	130.84	12920
Cambodia	13	4	3.13	70	0.815	38	0.87	2.1	1.69	–	-0.125	67.25	278
Indonesia	215	208	134.38	82	34	8	-0.05	-0.03	60.95	32	7.25	51.13	944
Lao PDR	6	2	2.84	91	0.208	53	0.019	0.9	0.37	0.52	-0.008	44.50	361
Malaysia	25	103	49.07	56	44	4	2.33	2.4	99	81	13.381	182.43	4227
Myanmar	49	58.07	7.31	–	0.55	3	0.163	1	2	2	0.050	6.88	1174
Philippines	82	80	62.66	80	13.65	9	0.319	0.4	36	39	2.080	91.71	1005
Singapore	4	91	–	–	95.74	2	114.40	12.5	144	128	28.18	277.82	21195
Thailand	62	142	51.79	41	41.07	-16	1.94	1.4	80	76	7.090	109.85	2273
Vietnam	81	39	15.81	39	6.22	22	1.45	3.7	20	25	-0.604	51.76	2273
China	1288	1417	193.56	15	408	1	53.50	3.8	437	413	45.87	252.77	1100

India	1064	600	113.46	19	98	1	4.26	0.7	55	70	6.85	20.74	555
Korea	48	605	–	–	155	-10	0.8	0.5	193	178	27.613	65.99	11059
Pan-Asia	3090	8255.6 (49.03)	326.99 (22.79)	30.81	–	–	91.75	2.11 (16.01)	1691.5	1428.06 (22.32)	– (18.40)	–	–
Australia	20	522	–	–	–	–	6.8	1.3	71	–	-40	33.63	26525
New Zealand	5	79	–	–	–	–	2.43	3.1	16	–	-6.19	50.25	19350
EAEC	1881.95	7394.62 (29.86)	497.51 (20.41)	26	–	–	89.31	2.69 (15.58)	1897.35	1690.54 (25.03)	– (21.79)	–	
Hong Kong China	7	157	–	–	118	1	13.5	8.6	228	233	16.35	67.62	22618
Taiwan China	22.6	286	–	–	206	–	–	–	143.9	127.36	–	94.71	12669
EAECI	2945.95	7994.62 (46.75)	610.97 (22.07)	25.66	–	–	93.57	2.53 (16.32)	1952.35	1745.54 (25.76)	– (22.49)	–	
World	6301	36214	–	–	–	12	573	1.5	7578	7758	–	–	5747

Note: Figures in the parenthesis are percentages of world.

Source: UN: *UNCTAD Handbook of Trade Statistics*, 2005 and World Bank: *World Development Indicators*, 2005.

II

Regional Interdependence: Intra–ASEAN, JACIK, Pan-Asia, EAEC and EAECI Exports

Regional interdependence, measured in terms of intra-bloc export share given in Table 3 show that intra-ASEAN, intra-JACIK, intra Pan-Asia, intra-EAEC and intra-EAECI export share range between 6.29 per cent for Hong Kong to 39.31 per cent for Myanmar; 13.11 per cent for Cambodia to 57.22 per cent for Myanmar; 13.22 per cent for Cambodia to

TABLE 3

Intra-Regional Exports of ASEAN, JACIK, Pan-Asia, EAEC and EAECI Countries (Percent) (2002)

Country	*ASEAN*	*JACIK*	*Pan-Asia*	*EAEC*	*EAECI*
JACIK					
Japan	13.38	30.27	32.6	3.52	35.69
ASEAN					
Brunei	9.22	55.89	66.34	56.07	56.07
Cambodia	7.77	13.11	13.22	11.94	11.94
Indonesia	13.37	52.96	56.58	51.93	54.2
Lao PDR	38.75	42.50	42.57	25.46	25.46
Malaysia	26.00	42.51	45.10	50.87	52.75
Myanmar	39.31	57.22	57.61	50.47	57.94
Philippines	15.70	38.65	39.71	44.75	45.00
Singapore	27.17	46.06	49.08	50.72	52.83
Thailand	19.71	42.01	44.65	43.58	44.18
Vietnam	13.33	37.43	45.07	37.10	37.41
China	7.23	14.21	15.79	30.33	31.20
India	7.13	17.21	18.38	21.05	21.05
Korea	11.39	36.31	37.94	40.15	41.01
Pan-Asia					
Australia	12.2	45.18	54.64	48.57	50.57
New Zealand	7.82	28.97	49.31	29.88	30.50
EAEC					
Hong Kong China	6.29	53.65	54.99	52.32	53.04
Taiwan China	—	—	—	—	—

Source: UN, Statistical Year Book for Asia and Pacific, 2004.

66.34 per cent for Brunei; 11.94 per cent for Cambodia to 56.07 for Brunei respectively (only small variations in EAECI export share for all countries as compared to EAEC export share). Of 17 countries considered, 5 countries, namely Cambodia, Brunei, India, New Zealand, Hong Kong have single digit intra-Asean export share. All countries experienced an increase in intra-JACIK and intra Pan-Asia export share over time, indicating gains as a result of widening of regional integration. Countries, namely Malaysia, Philippines, Singapore, Korea and Japan have also experienced an increase in intra-EAEC export share as compared to Pan-Asia export share, indicating increasing gains from trade as a member of EAEC and these countries will further gain from EAECI (except Japan). India's intra-EAEC export share has increased as compared to intra-Pan Asia, indicating potentialities of gains from trade, if it becomes the member of EAEC. With the formation of EAECI, countries namely Australia, New Zealand, Hong Kong, Indonesia and China will also gain. Most spectacular increase in gain will occur to Hong Kong, Brunei, New Zealand, Korea and Indonesia.

Direction/Destination of Intra-Trade (ASEAN, JACIK, Pan-Asia, EAEC and EAECI)

Destination of exports of different Asian Regional Groups given in Table 4 shows that exports are concentrated to mainly four markets; Japan, Singapore, China and Hong Kong China. Japan accounted for highest share in exports of Brunei (share being 40 per cent). Philippines (15.04 per cent), Thailand (14.52 per cent), Vietnam (14.63 per cent), Australia (18.56 per cent) and Indonesia (21.07 per cent) in 2002. Lao PDR accounted for largest share in exports of Thailand and Vietnam (share being 21.46 per cent and 16.95 per cent respectively); for Malaysia, Singapore constituted 17.08 per cent share; for Myanmar, Thailand constituted 31.64 per cent share; for New Zealand, Australia constituted 20 per cent share; for Korea and Hong Kong China, China constituted largest export market with share being 14.70 per cent and 39.33 per cent respectively. Heavy dependence of countries on one or two markets indicates lack of market diversification,

TABLE 4

Direction of Exports of JACIK, Pan-Asia and EAECI (2002) (Share Matrix of Exports)

Country	*Japan*	*Brunei*	*Cambodia*	*Indonesia*	*Lao PDR*	*Malaysia*	*Myanmar*	*Philippines*	*Singapore*	*Thailand*	*Vietnam*	*China*	*India*	*Korea*	*Australia*	*New Zealand*	*Hong Kong China*
JACIK																	
Japan	—	0.07	0.01	1.49	0.00	2.64	0.02	2.02	3.40	3.17	0.51	9.59	0.44	6.86	1.99	0.34	6.10
ASEAN																	
Brunei	40.37	—	0.00	0.84	0.00	3.63	0.00	0.62	4.11	0.00	0.00	6.30	0.00	0.00	8.81	1.64	0.20
Cambodia	3.91	0.00	—	0.00	0.00	1.05	0.00	0.10	4.40	0.58	1.52	1.28	0.00	0.15	0.09	0.02	0.47
Indonesia	21.07	0.05	0.12	—	0.00	3.55	0.09	1.36	9.35	2.14	0.68	5.07	2.27	7.18	3.36	0.26	2.17
Lao PDR	1.54	0.00	0.00	0.04	—	0.08	0.00	0.00	0.11	21.46	16.95	2.21	0.00	0.02	0.07	0.00	0.00
Malaysia	11.27	0.27	0.05	1.92	0.00	—	0.25	1.42	17.08	4.25	0.71	5.62	1.88	3.36	2.25	0.34	5.68
Myanmar	3.81	0.01	0.00	1.08	0.00	2.65	—	0.06	3.70	31.64	0.14	4.73	7.43	1.94	0.37	0.02	0.82
Philippines	15.04	0.00	0.02	0.58	0.00	4.68	0.01	—	7.02	3.07	0.29	3.86	0.25	3.80	1.01	0.05	6.70
Singapore	7.14	0.36	0.28	0.00	0.02	17.43	0.41	2.42	—	4.56	1.66	5.48	2.11	4.16	2.69	0.33	9.17
Thailand	14.52	0.05	0.74	2.44	0.58	4.11	0.46	1.85	8.06	—	1.37	5.16	0.60	2.02	2.38	0.29	5.37
Vietnam	14.63	0.01	1.00	1.49	0.44	1.89	0.03	1.62	5.42	1.39	—	6.44	0.31	2.72	7.45	0.19	1.49
China	1.40	0.00	0.07	1.05	0.01	1.52	0.22	0.62	2.13	0.90	0.66	—	0.82	4.76	1.40	0.18	17.95
India	3.75	0.00	0.00	1.14	0.01	1.15	0.11	0.77	2.08	1.39	4.24	4.09	—	2.24	0.01	0.16	4.49
Korea	9.37	0.01	0.07	1.94	0.00	1.99	0.08	1.82	2.61	1.44	1.38	14.70	0.85	—	1.44	0.19	6.28
Pan-Asia (JACIK +Australia + NewZealand)																	
Australia	18.56	0.04	0.01	2.56	0.01	1.91	0.01	0.96	4.14	2.09	0.41	7.00	2.07	8.35	—	6.46	2.96
New Zealand	11.51	0.01	0.00	1.47	0.00	1.93	0.05	1.5	1.25	1.16	0.41	4.63	0.62	4.39	20.34	—	2.03
EAEC																	
Hong Kong China	5.36	0.02	0.16	0.43	0.00	0.99	0.03	1.15	2.02	1.07	0.38	39.33	0.72	1.95	1.20	0.14	—

Source: UN: *Statistical Year Book for Asia and Pacific*, 2004.

thereby leading to low intra-Asian exports as compared to NAFTA and EU. The intra-Asian exports can be increased by market diversification instead of market concentration.

III

COMPLEMENTARITIES IN TRADE

1. Trade Structure

Complementarities in trade measured in terms of export structure of countries of Asian Regional Groups given in Table 5 show that export basket of most of countries is dominated by manufactures (except Brunei, Indonesia, Myanmar, Australia, New Zealand and Vietnam). In Japan, Korea, Cambodia, China, Hong Kong China and Taiwan China, manufactures accounted for more than 90 per cent of total exports during pre as well as post-WTO period. In Brunei, fuels constitute 96 per cent of exports in 1995. Other countries experiencing high share in fuels include Indonesia, Vietnam, and Australia (in ores and minerals also). Export structure of Myanmar, Vietnam and New Zealand is dominated by all food items (Myanmar and New Zealand in agricultural raw material also). Almost similar export structure at section level continued in 2004 also. At sub-division level, within manufactured exports, other manufactured goods and machinery and transport constituted major share in most of countries (8 and 6) in 1995; but in 2004, with the increase in share of China, Hong Kong China, Taiwan China and Thailand in exports of machinery and transport, number of countries with major share in machinery and transport exports increased to nine (from 6 in 1995). Japan, Singapore and Korea were the major exporters of machinery and transport (export share above 50 per cent). While China, Hong Kong China and India were major exporters of other manufactured goods (share being 56.9, 54 per cent and 57.6 per cent) in 1995. In 2004, Philippines took a lead in machinery and transport (with share increasing from 22.2 per cent in 1995 to 74.8 per cent in 2004). Cambodia had highest share (96.5 per cent) in other manufactured goods in 2004.

TABLE 5

Trade Structure of Asian Economic Groups (Percent)

Country	Year	All Food Items		Agricultural Raw Materials		Fuels		Ores and Minerals		Manu-factured Goods		Chemical Products		Other Manu-factured Goods		Machinery and Transport		Un-allocated	
		EXP	IMP	EXP	IMP	EXP	IMP	EXP	IMP	EXP	IMP	EXP	IMP	EXP	IMP	EXP	IMP	EXP	IMP
JACIK																			
Japan	1995	0.5	16.0	0.6	6.1	0.6	16.1	1.0	6.0	95.1	53.0	6.7	7.1	18.2	23.3	70.3	22.5	2.1	2.2
	2003	0.5	12.3	0.5	2.9	0.4	21.2	1.3	4.9	92.9	51.0	8.0	7.6	18.0	21.9	66.9	27.5	4.3	1.7
ASEAN																			
Brunei	1990	0.7	—	0.0	—	9.5	—	0.0	—	2.7	—	0.1	—	1.3	—	1.4	—	0.0	—
	2000	0.0	17.6	0.0	0.3	87.7	1.0	0.1	1.0	12.0	79.6	0.1	7.3	6.6	36.9	5.3	35.4	0.2	0.5
Cambodia	2004	1.1	7.8	1.8	2.4	0.0	9.8	0.0	0.3	97.1	78.7	0.1	6.0	96.5	58.8	0.5	13.9	0.1	0.9
Indonesia	1995	11.4	8.8	6.7	6.1	25.3	7.6	6.0	4.6	50.5	72.6	3.3	15.1	38.8	17.3	8.4	40.2	0.1	0.2
	2004	13.6	10.5	5.6	4.9	17.8	19.6	7.1	3.9	55.5	6.0	6.2	17.2	31.5	15.2	17.9	28.5	0.4	0.1
Malaysia	1995	9.5	4.8	6.1	1.2	7.0	2.3	1.3	3.2	74.7	83.6	3.0	7.0	16.6	16.7	55.1	59.8	1.3	4.9
	2004	8.0	5.5	2.4	1.2	11.6	6.4	1.1	3.6	75.4	80.2	5.6	7.9	15.3	14.6	54.6	51.7	1.5	3.1
Philippines	1995	12.8	8.3	1.2	2.2	1.5	9.2	4.3	3.2	40.8	57.8	1.9	9.0	16.8	16.4	22.2	32.4	69.3	19.2
	2004	6.0	7.0	0.6	1.0	1.6	10.1	1.7	2.3	89.8	79.4	1.1	7.9	13.9	13.3	74.8	58.2	0.4	0.2
Singapore	1995	3.9	4.6	1.1	0.9	6.9	8.1	2.0	2.3	83.7	83.0	59	6.4	12.2	18.7	65.6	57.9	2.4	1.2
	2004	1.8	2.9	0.3	0.3	9.7	15.0	1.2	1.3	83.4	79.2	11.6	6.4	10.7	14.2	61.0	58.6	3.6	1.3

Thailand	1995	19.3	3.8	5.3	4.1	0.7	6.8	0.6	3.2	73.1	80.1	3.8	10.2	35.7	22.7	33.6	47.4	1.0	1.9
	2003	14.1	4.9	4.6	2.7	2.7	12.0	1.0	3.3	74.8	75.1	6.5	10.8	24.5	20.8	43.8	43.5	2.8	2.0
Vietnam	2002	25.4	6.2	2.3	3.1	21.2	11.0	0.5	2.8	49.9	76.1	1.5	14.6	40.9	32.5	7.9	28.9	0.7	0.9
China	1995	8.2	7.0	1.8	5.0	3.6	3.9	2.1	4.4	84.0	79.0	6.1	13.0	56.3	26.0	21.1	40.0	0.3	0.9
	2004	3.5	3.8	0.5	3.7	2.4	8.6	1.9	7.3	91.4	76.3	4.4	11.5	41.8	19.7	42.2	45.1	0.2	0.3
India	1995	18.7	4.2	1.3	3.9	1.7	23.7	3.6	6.8	73.2	52.8	8.1	15.3	57.6	17.3	7.5	20.2	1.6	8.5
	2004	11.3	5.3	1.3	3.0	5.9	29.1	4.3	3.9	76.2	49.6	11.6	9.4	54.8	19.3	9.7	20.9	1.1	9.1
Korea	1995	2.3	5.4	1.3	5.3	2.0	14.2	1.0	6.3	91.5	66.5	7.1	9.5	31.9	20.4	52.5	36.6	2.0	2.3
	2004	1.2	4.9	0.8	2.2	4.2	22.5	1.7	6.7	91.0	62.0	9.0	9.0	19.0	19.5	63.0	33.6	1.2	1.8
Pan-Asia (JACIK) + Australia + New Zealand)																			
Australia	1995	52.4	7.4	18.0	1.2	1.6	5.4	4.8	3.5	30.6	82.4	7.6	12.8	14.4	27.5	8.6	42.1	2.6	0.1
	2004	18.4	4.6	4.2	1.4	18.1	9.1	18.2	1.0	20.1	80.3	4.1	11.2	8.9	24.5	9.1	44.6	20.9	4.0
New Zealand	1995	42.4	7.4	18.0	1.2	1.6	5.4	4.8	3.5	30.6	80.4	7.6	12.8	14.4	27.5	8.6	42.1	2.6	0.1
	2004	48.5	7.7	11.2	1.0	1.3	6.4	3.8	2.7	30.7	81.3	5.3	11.7	14.3	25.8	11.1	43.7	4.4	0.9
EAEC																			
Hong Kong	1995	3.0	5.4	1.3	1.6	1.0	1.9	1.7	2.1	92.5	87.0	6.0	7.3	54.0	43.2	32.3	36.5	0.6	2.0
	2004	1.0	3.2	0.7	0.9	0.3	2.4	1.3	1.8	94.2	91.0	4.8	5.9	40.4	34.6	48.9	50.4	2.5	0.8
Taiwan	1995	3.4	5.4	1.5	4.2	0.7	7.0	1.4	6.0	92.8	74.2	6.5	13.0	38.2	21.0	48.0	40.2	0.1	3.2
China	2004	1.3	4.3	1.2	1.9	2.3	12.0	1.3	5.0	93.1	75.1	7.8	12.1	30.3	18.7	55.6	44.3	0.3	1.6

Source: UN: *UNCTAD Handbook of Trade Statistics*, 2005.

The import structure of different Asian nations showed that manufactures constituted major share in imports (share ranging between 52 and 85 per cent in 1995 and between 57 and 91 per cent in 2004). Australia, New Zealand, Hong Kong China and Malaysia were large importers of manufactures in 1995 as well in 2004 (having share above 80%). Within manufactures, in 1995, exports of machinery and transport and in 2004, other manufactured goods along with machinery and transport accounted for major share in imports of Asian countries. Malaysia and Singapore were largest importers of machinery and transport in 1995 as well in 2004 (Philippines in 2004 only); while Hong Kong China was largest importer of other manufactured goods in 1995 as well as in 2004 (Cambodia in 2004 only). Japan, India and Korea were the main importers of fuels in 1995 as well as in 2004. However, countries importing large share of fuels increased to 9 (viz. Indonesia, Philippines, Singapore, Thailand, Vietnam, Taiwan China along with Japan, India and Korea). Import structure of Japan, Brunei and Indonesia consisted of food items also.

Thus diversified export and import structure of Asian nations indicate possibilities of complementarities in trade in case of regional groupings.

2. Revealed Comparative Advantage in Exports

Table 6 shows that of the 67 commodities with highest revealed comparative advantage, China, Hong Kong China, Singapore, Philippines, Myanmar, Malaysia and Brunei have revealed comparative advantage in narrow range of commodities (1 or 2 or 3 out of 10 top exported items). New Zealand had highest revealed comparative advantage in 7 out of 10 commodities, while Lao PDR, India, Australia and Taiwan China have revealed comparative advantage in 5 or 6 commodities. Most of items with highest revealed comparative advantage were under machinery and transport group (16 out of 67), followed by miscellaneous manufactured articles (13), food and live animals (12 items), manufactured goods classified chiefly by materials (9), crude materials in edibles except fuels (6), and chemicals (4). Japan had highest revealed comparative advantage in machinery and transport

TABLE 6

Section-wise Revealed Comparative Advantage

Country	Food and Live Animals	Crude Materials Inedibles except fuels	Mineral Fuels, Lubricants and Related Materials	Animal and Vegetable Oils and Fats	Chemicals	Manu-factured Goods	Machinery and Transport	Misce-llaneous Manu-factured Goods	Commodities and Transactions n.e.s.	Number of commp-dities
1	2	3	4	5	6	7	8	9	10	11
JACIK	6	4	3	1	2	7	14	10	2	49
Japan	—	—	—	—	—	—	4	—	—	4
ASEAN	—	—	—	—	—	—	—	—	—	35
Brunei	—	—	2	—	—	I	—	—	—	3
Cambodia	—	—	—	—	—	—	—	4	—	4
Indonesia	—	—	—	1	—	2	—	1	—	4
Lao PDR	I	1	—	—	—	—	1	3	—	6
Malaysia	—	—	—	—	—	—	2	—	—	2
Myanmar	1	1	—	—	—	—	—	—	—	2
Philippines	—	—	—	—	—	—	3	—	—	3
Singapore	—	—	1	—	I	—	—	I	—	3

(Contd.)

TABLE 6 *(Contd.)*

1	*2*	*3*	*4*	*5*	*6*	*7*	*8*	*9*	*10*	*11*
Thailand	1	1	—	—	—	—	I	—	1	**4**
Vietnam	3	1	—	—	—	—	—	—	—	**4**
China	—	—	—	—	—	—	1	—	—	**1**
India	—	—	—	—	1	3	—	1	—	**5**
Korea	—	—	—	—	—	1	2	—	1	**4**
Pan-Asia	12	7	4	1	3	8	14	10	2	**61**
Australia	1	2	1	—	—	1	—	—	—	**5**
New Zealand	5	1	—	—	1	—	—	—	—	**7**
EAEC	—	—	3	1	3	8	14	5	1	**35**
Hong Kong China	—	—	—	—	—	—	—	1	—	**1**
Taiwan China	—	—	—	—	1	1	2	1	—	**5**
Total	12	7	4	1	4	9	16	12	2	67

Source: UN: *UNCTAD Handbook of Trade Statistics*, 2005.

items (4 out of 16 items), Cambodia in miscellaneous manufactured articles (4 out of 13 items), New Zealand in food and live animal items (5 out of 12 items), India in manufactured goods (3 out of 9 items), Australia in crude materials inedibles except fuels (in 2 out of 6 items), indicating complementarities in export structure. Further, Pan-Asia regional group has more items with highest revealed comparative advantage (61 items) as compared to JACIK (49) and ASEAN (39) indicating scope for widening of Asian Regional grouping. EAEC had only 31 items with highest revealed comparative advantage and EAECI had 35 items. ASEAN and EAECI had almost same number of commodities with highest revealed comparative advantage. India will be gainer as a result of becoming a member of Pan-Asia in the Asian economic grouping.

Commodity-wise analysis regarding highest revealed comparative advantage (RCA) given in Table 7 shows that in food and live animals, New Zealand had highest revealed comparative advantage, in milk and cream (48.65), while Vietnam in Rice (43.5). In crude materials, inedibles except fuels, Myanmar had highest revealed comparative advantage in other wood (104.18), while Lao PDR in wood simply worked and railway sleepers. In mineral fuels section, Australia in coal, lignite and peat (32.53), while Brunei in gas natural and manufactured (28.99). In chemicals, New Zealand in Starches, inulin and wheat gluten albuminoidal substances (24.66). In manufactured goods section, India has highest RCA in pearls, precious and semi precious stones (16.11), and Indonesia in Veeners, plywood, improved (15.13). In machinery and transport, Philippines in thermionic, cold and photo-cathode and Korea in ships, boats and floating structures. In miscellaneous manufactured articles, Cambodia in outer garments and other articles knitted (66.45).

3. Import Share

Tables 8 and 9 show that in the imports of 52 items considered, Brunei, Vietnam and India have sizeable imports in large range of commodities. Machinery and transport account for larger share in imports (15 items), followed by manufactured goods (10 items), indicating larger scope of

TABLE 7

Revealed Comparative Advantage Indices of Asian Regional Economic Groups (2002)

SITC	*Comparative Advantage Category*	*Country with Highest RCAI*	*Other Exporting Countries having RCAI*
1	*2*	*3*	*4*
Section 0—Food and Live Animals		**12**	
011	Meat and edible meat offals, fresh, chilled or frozen	New Zealand (23.29)	Australia (7.96)
022	Milk and cream	New Zealand (48.65)	
023	Butter	New Zealand (84)	
024	Cheese and curd	New Zealand (19.88)	
034	Fish, fresh (live or dead), chilled or frozen	Vietnam (5.69)	
036	Crustaceans and molluscs, fresh, chilled, frozen, salted in brine or dried	Vietnam (36.08)	Myanmar (20.0), India (7.4)
037	Fish, crustaceans and molluscs, prepared or preserved n.e.s.	Thailand (17.8)	
041	Wheat (including spelt) and meslin, unmilled	Australia (12.30)	
042	Rice	Vietnam (43.5)	Myanmar (27.9), Thailand (22.8)
054	Vegetables, fresh, chilled frozen or simply preserved; roots, tubers	Myanmar (27.27)	
057	Fruits and nuts (not including oil nuts), fresh or dried	New Zealand (7.27)	Philippines (2.87), Vietnam (3.91)

Code	Product	Column 2	Column 3
071	Coffee and coffee substitutes	Lao PDR (27.07)	
Section 2—Crude Materials Inedibles Except Fuels		**6**	
232	Natural rubber latex; natural rubber and similar natural gums	Thailand (43.5)	Cambodia (19, 12)
247	Other wood in the rough or roughly squared	Myanmar (104.18)	Lao PDR (44.18)
248	Wood simply worked and railway sleepers of wood	Lao PDR (76.07)	Myanmar (11.71)
268	Wool and other animal hair (excluding wool tops)	New Zealand (54)	
281	Iron ore and concentrates	Australia (28.33)	
287	Base metals, ores, concentrates n.e.s.	Australia (19.3)	
Section 3—Mineral Fuels, Lubricants and Related Materials		**4**	
322	Coal, lignite and peat	Australia (32.53)	
333	Crude petroleum	Brunei (9.11)	Indonesia (1.73), Malaysia (0.69)
334	Petroleum products, refined	Singapore (3.24)	Brunei (0.36), Indonesia (1.00), Malaysia (0.85)
341	Gas natural and manufactured	Brunei (28.99)	Indonesia (7.61), Malaysia (2.71) Myanmar (18.17)
Section 4—Animal and Vegetable Oils & Fats		**1**	
424	Other fixed vegetable oils, soft, crude, refined or purified	Indonesia (30.4)	

(Contd.)

TABLE 7 (*Contd.*)

1	2	3	4
Section 5—Chemicals			
515	Organo-inorganic and heterocyclic compounds	Singapore (3.83)	
541	Medicinal and pharmaceutical products	India (1.22)	
583	Polymerization and copolymerization	Taiwan (1.88)	Korea (1.84)
592	Starches, insulin and wheat gluten, products albuminoidal substances	New Zealand (24.66)	
Section 6—Manufactured Goods Classified Chiefly by Materials		**9**	
634	Veneers, plywood, improved or reconstituted wood	Indonesia (15.13)	
641	Paper and paper board	Indonesia (1.81)	
651	Textile yarn	India (6.43)	
653	Fabrics, woven of manmade fibers	Korea (3.93)	Cambodia (1.06)
658	Made up articles wholly or chiefly of textile materials	India (7.93)	
667	Pearls, precious and semiprecious stones, unworked or worked	India (16.11)	
674	Universals, plates and sheets of iron and steel	Taiwan, China (2.67)	India (2.12), Korea (2.33)
684	Aluminum	Australia (4.64)	
695	Tools for use in hand or in machines	Brunei (1.60)	
Section 7—Machinery and Transport		**16**	
713	Internal combustion piston engine and parts	Japan (2.26)	

728	Machinery and equipment specialized for particular industries	Japan (2.54)	
752	Automatic data processing machines and units thereof	Philippines (4.31)	Malaysia (2.89), Singapore (4.07), Thailand (1.96), China (2.81), Korea (1.96), Hong Kong (1.04) Taiwan (2.66)
759	Parts of and accessories suitable for 751 and 752	Malaysia (4.05)	Japan (1.45), Philippines (3.31), Singapore (3.2), Thailand (2.03), China (1.91), Korea (2.03), Hong Kong (3.04),
761	Television receivers	Malaysia (3.98)	Taiwan(3.53)
763	Gramophones, dictating and sound recorders	China (0.55)	
764	Telecommunications equipment, and parts	Korea (3.29)	Japan (0.89), Indonesia (0.68), Malaysia (1.62), Philippines (0.75), Singapore (1.38), Thailand (1.09), China (1.97), Hong Kong (2.61) and Taiwan (1.46)
772	Electrical apparatus such as switches, relays, fuses and plugs	Taiwan, China (2.33)	Japan (1.73), Malaysia (2.04) Philippines (1.62), Singapore (1.59), Thailand (1.70), Hong Kong (1.77)
773	Equipments for distributing electricity	Philippines (2.44)	
776	Thermionic, cold and photo-cathode valves, tubes and parts	Philippines (10.77)	Japan (1.86), Malayia (5.23), Singapore (6.01), Thailand (1.96),

(Contd.)

TABLE 7 (*Contd.*)

1	2	3	4
			China (0.57), Korea (2.46), Hong Kong (2.09) and Taiwan (3.62)
778	Electrical machinery and apparatus n.e.s.	Taiwan, China (2.42)	Japan (2.22), Singapore (1.31), China (1.58), Hong Kong (1.61)
781	Passenger motor cars for transport and passenger goods	Japan (2.75)	Korea (1.62)
782	Motor vehicles for transport of goods material	Thailand (2.45)	
784	Parts and accessories of 722, 781, 782, 783	Japan (1.73)	Philippines (0.97)
785	Motorcycles, motor scooters and invalid carriages	Lao PDR (17.91)	
793	Ships, boats and floating structures	Korea (8.36)	Brunei (4.31)
Section 8—Miscellaneous Manufactured Articles		**13**	
821	Furniture and parts thereof	Indonesia (2.59)	
842	Outer garments, men's of textile fabrics	Lao PDR (15.85)	Brunei (1.62), Cambodia (1.68), Myanmar (10.33), Vietnam (3.53)
843	Outer garments, women's of textile fabrics	Lao PDR (10.34)	Brunei (1.08), Cambodia (3.34), Myanmar (5.12), Philippines (3.02), China (3.68), India (4.26)
844	Undergarments of textile fabrics	Lao PDR (33.41)	Brunei (3.58)
845	Outer garments and other articles knitted	Cambodia (66.45)	Brunei (2.03), Lao PDR (12.43), Myanmar (13.26),

Code	Commodity		
			Philippines (1.75), Vietnam (4.2), China (4.02), India (2.19), Hong Kong (4.74)
846	Undergarments knitted and crocheted	Cambodia (24.51)	Brunei (2.35), Lao PDR (15.46), Myanmar (6.61), India (5.18)
848	Articles of apparel and clothing accessories	Cambodia (1.83)	
851	Footwear	Vietnam (17 08)	Cambodia (2.46), Lao PDR (2.46), China (4.52), Hong Kong (3.79)
871	Optical instrument and apparatus	Taiwan (11.08)	
892	Printed matter	Cambodia (37.74)	
894	Baby carriages and toys	Hong Kong (6.86)	China (4.7)
897	Jewellery, goldsmiths wares and other articles of precious material	India (7.82)	
898	Musical instruments, parts and accessories	Singapore (3.09)	
Section 9—Commodities and Transactions n.e.s.		**2**	
931	Special transaction and commodities	Thailand (28.29)	Japan (1.82), Singapore (1.6), Australia (3.25), New Zealand (1.66)
971	Gold	Korea (4.96)	Cambodia

Source: UN: *Statistical Yearbook for Asia and Pacific*, 2004.

TABLE 8

Section-wise Import Share (Percent)

Country	*Food and Live Animals*	*Crude Materials Inedibles except fuels*	*Mineral Fuels, Lubricants and Related Materials*	*Animal and Vegetable Oils and Fats*	*Chemicals*	*Manu-factured Goods*	*Machinery and Transport*	*Misce-llaneous Manu-factured Goods*	*Commodities and Transactions n.e.s.*	*Number of commo-dities*
Japan	2	—	1	—	—	—	—	—	—	3
Brunei	1	—	—	—	—	3	4	1	—	9
Indonesia	—	2	—	—	1	—	3	—	—	6
Malaysia	—	—	—	—	—	—	3	—	—	3
Philippines	1	—	—	—	—	—	—	—	—	1
Singapore	—	—	—	—	—	—	2	1	—	3
Thailand	—	—	—	—	—	1	1	—	—	2
Vietnam	—	—	1	—	3	2	1	2	—	9
China	—	—	—	—	1	1	—	—	—	2
India	—	—	2	2	1	2	—	—	2	9
Australia	—	—	—	—	—	—	1	—	—	1
New Zealand	—	—	—	—	—	1	—	1	—	2
Hong Kong China	—	—	—	—	—	—	—	2	—	2
Total	4	2	4	2	6	10	15	7	2	52

Source: UN: *Statistical Year Book for Asia and Pacific*, 2004.

TABLE 9

Commodities with Highest Import Share

Commodity	*Country with Highest Import Share*	*Other Countries Having High Share*
1	*2*	*3*
Section 0—Food & Live Animals Chiefly for Food	**4**	
011 Meat and edible meat offals	Japan (2 01)	
034 Fish, fresh (live or dead), chilled or frozen	Japan (1.8)	
041 Wheat (including spelt) and muslin, unmilled	Philippines (1.15)	
048 Cereals, flour or starch preparation of fruits and vegetables	Brunei (1.95)	
Section 2—Crude Materials Inedible Excepts Fuels	**2**	
251 Pulp and waste paper	Indonesia (3.17)	
263 Cotton	Indonesia (2.17)	
Section 3—Minerals Fuels Lubricants and Related Materials	**4**	
322 Coal, lignite and peat	India (1.75)	
323 Briquettes, coke and semi-coke of coal lignite and peat	India (28.62)	China (7.2), Japan (11.73), Malaysia (1.59), Philippines (9.37), Korea (15.71), Singapore (6.49), Thailand (9.86)

(Contd.)

TABLE 9 (*Contd.*)

1	*2*	*3*
334 Petroleum products refined	Vietnam (10.74)	Indonesia (10.62), Japan (2.3), Malaysia (2.73), Philippines (1.45), Korea (3.11), Singapore (5.57), Thailand (1.86), Australia (1.6), New Zealand (2.99)
341 Gas, natural and manufactured	Japan (4.72)	Philippines (3.33)
Section 4—Animals and Vegetable Oils & Fats	**2**	
423 Fixed vegetable oil, soft, crude, refined or purified	India (0.86)	
424 Other fixed vegetable oils, fluid or solid, crude, refined or purified	India (1.80)	
Section 5—Chemicals	**6**	
511 Hydrocarbons n.e.s	Indonesia (3.32)	
522 Inorganic chemical elements, oxides	India (1.95)	
533 Pigments, paints, varnishes and related materials	Vietnam (3.28)	
541 Medicinal and pharmaceuticals products	Vietnam (4.41)	
562 Fertilizers, Manufactured	Vietnam (3.21)	
583 Polymerisation and copolymerization products	China (4.98)	Hong Kong, China (2.38), Indonesia (1.98), Philippines (1.45), New Zealand (2.12)

Section 6—Manufactured Goods Classified Chiefly by Material		**10**	
641	Paper and paper board	New Zealand (2.08)	
653	Fabrics, woven of manmade fibers	Vietnam (4.21)	
667	Pearls, precious and semiprecious stones	India (9.57)	
672	Ingots and other primary forms of iron and steel	Vietnam (6.7)	Thailand (2.05)
674	Universal, plates and sheets of iron and steel	China (2.84)	
678	Tubes, pipes and fittings of iron steel	Brunei (3.09)	
681	Silver, platinum and other metals of platinum group	India (1.2)	
691	Structure and parts of structures, iron steel and aluminum	Brunei (1.95)	
695	Tools for use in hand or in machine	Brunei (3.09)	
699	Manufactures of metals n.e.s.	Thailand (2.07)	Malaysia (1.99), Korea (1.98)
Section 7—Machinery and Transport		**15**	
713	Internal combustion piston engines and parts	Indonesia (1.72)	
728	Machinery and equipment specialized for particular industries	Malaysia (2.98)	China (2.9), Philippines (2.55), Korea (2.62), Singapore (2.67)
749	Non-electric accessories of machinery	Brunei (1.89)	Indonesia (1.7)
752	Automatic data processing Machines and units thereof	Singapore (4.72)	China (2.19), Hong Kong (2.9), Japan (4.6), Korea (2.37), Australia (4.56), New Zealand (3.33)
759	Parts of and accessories suitable for 751 and 752	Singapore (7.33)	China (2.9), Hong Kong (5.17), Japan (2.17),

(Contd.)

TABLE 9 (*Contd.*)

1	2	3
		Malaysia (4.22), Philippines (6.51), Korea (2.3), Thailand (5.04), Australia (2.1), New Zealand (1.6)
764 Telecommunication, equipment and parts	Indonesia (7.53)	China (5.93), Hong Kong (7.17), Japan (2.33), Malaysia (3.95), Philippines (5.41), Korea (3.18), Singapore (3.59), Thailand (2.6), Brunei (2.3), Australia (5.01), New Zealand (4.6)
772 Electrical apparatus such as switches, relays, fuses and plugs	Thailand (2.96)	China (2.62), Philippines (2.07), Singapore (2.73)
776 Thermionic, cold and photocathode valves, tubes and parts	Malaysia (29.82)	China (10.26), Hong Kong (9.53), Japan (5.22), Philippines (22.49), Korea (12.75), Singapore (22.71), Thailand (13.5), Vietnam (3.35), New Zealand (2)
778 Electrical machinery and apparatus n.e.s	Malaysia (4.44)	China (2.31), Hong Kong (2.28), Philippines (1.39), Korea (1.86), Singapore (2.78), Thailand (12.27), Australia (1.46)
781 Passenger motorcars for transport of passengers and goods	Brunei (4.48)	Japan (1.83)

782	Motor vehicles for transport and goods material	Australia (2.17)	New Zealand (1.92)
784	Parts and accessories of 722, 781, 782, 783	Indonesia (3.34)	Thailand (2.32)
785	Motorcycles, motor scooters and invalid carriages	Vietnam (4.31)	
792	Aircraft and associated equipment and parts	Brunei (4.54)	
793	Ships, boats and floating structures	Brunei (3.28)	Indonesia (2.58)
Section 8—Miscellaneous Manufactured Articles		7	
821	Furniture and parts thereof	Brunei (2.21)	
845	Outer garments and other articles knitted	Hong Kong (2.45)	
847	Clothing accessories of textile fabrics	Vietnam (4.41)	
851	Footwear	Vietnam (3.63)	Hong Kong (2.49)
874	Measuring, checking, analysing, instruments	Singapore (2.00)	Malaysia (1.99), Korea (1.98)
893	Articles of materials of division 58	New Zealand (1.44)	
894	Baby carriage and toys	Hong Kong (3.77)	Malaysia (3.14)
Section 9—Commodities and Transactions n.e.s		**2**	
931	Special transactions & commodities	India (1.80)	
971	Gold	India (8.25)	

Source: UN: *Statistical Yearbook for Asia and Pacific*, 2004.

intra-industry trade among Asian economic group members. Brunei, Indonesia and Malaysia have high import share in most of items of machinery and transport; Vietnam in chemicals; Brunei in manufactured goods (tubes, structures and parts of iron and steel and tools); Japan in fish and meat; Vietnam in textiles and footwear also and India in organic chemicals and in silver and pearls, precious and semi-precious stones.

Thus the study reveals that formation of proposed Asian Economic Regional Groups would facilitate fuller exploitation of the region's resources by increasing intra-regional trade. Intra-regional exports can be increased by expanding exports of India and Asian countries to other members countries through market and trade diversification. For this purpose, deeper and strategic trade liberalisation is needed. The liberalisation process can be expanded in phases. In the first phase, broad product groups like textiles, chemicals, vegetable products and machinery and mechanical appliances can be considered for trade liberalisation. The other important product groups may be chosen in subsequent phases. To enhance competitiveness in these product groups, countries should focus on reduction in tariff and non-tariff barriers, harmonization of product standards, domestic reforms particularly in financial sector and infrastructure. To bring stability in exchange rate and to set-up BOP safety nets, proposal may be considered about setting-up of Asian Monetary Fund, whose working will be free from IMF conditionalities. To develop infrastructure in the community, Asia Development Bank's (ADB) role should be expanded by transferring resources from more developed members to less developed ones.

Notes and References

1. Nanda, P. and Raikhy, P.S., (2004),"Complementarities in Production and Trade among Asian Countries—Prospects of Asian Economic Union", *Indian Journal of Quantitative Economics*, pp. 39-64.
2. United Nations, (2005), "UNCTAD Handbook of Trade Statistics," Geneva.
3. United Nations, (2004), "A Statistical Year Book for Asia and Pacific", Geneva.
4. World Bank, (2005), "World Development Indicators"

Trade Integration in South Asia

Problems and Prospects

Smriti Mukherjee

As trading partners South Asian countries are marked by immense contrasts. They account for 20 per cent of world population but less than 2 per cent of world GDP and trade. Concentrated poverty is manifested in low purchasing power and restricted size of the market. Trade volume with the rest of the world is limited and predictably it is more so with respect to the region itself. Notwithstanding these limitations SAARC is doing a good job in the direction of promoting more meaningful integration. In 1995 a concrete shape to integration approach was given when accord was reached on establishing South Asian Preferential Trading Area (SAPTA). The attempt towards integration got further strengthened by the announcement of SAFTA. A concrete shape to SAFTA was expected to begin in 2006 and then it would be carried over up to 2008. In the process regional integration would surely establish its hold in South Asia.

The uniqueness of SAARC as a regional group flows from the fact that three of its seven members namely India, Pakistan and Bangladesh constituted a single entity up to second week of July, 1947. It was under British rule and even when countries were separated the feeling of different sovereign nations was non existent. The feeling of loss is very much there and this to a large extent explains why these countries do not exactly fit into a frame of mutually respecting nations. Another interesting feature of SAARC is that the group is under the influence of dominant member phenomenon. India is by far the largest partner and is in a position to override the existence of other partners. Integration with a dominant country presence offers some new issues and challenges to the theory of integration itself. And lastly Bhutan, Maldives and Nepal happen to be among the poorest of countries to make SAARC an attractive regional integration area. Heterogeneity in member countries is very high in SAARC.

The present paper seeks to analyse the extent to which SAARC fulfills the condition of a successful regional group and at the same time contributes to faster economic growth.

I. THEORETICAL ISSUES IN QUESTION

Economic issues connected with regional integration dates back to Viner when he talked about trade creation and trade diversion. Several nations trying to form a customs union eliminate tariffs among themselves while maintaining high tariff rate with the rest of the world. Elimination of tariffs within group members leads to promotion of trade at the cost of outside members because after paying tariffs they cannot compete in the market of union members. Union members even if they have higher cost of production may get a preference in relation to more efficient outside producers. Creation of trade is accompanied by trade diversion and ultimate benefit out of customs union is guided by relative strengths of trade creation and trade diversion.

In the later stage of development of customs union theory these effects were characterized as static effects while economies of scale, production cooperation and higher rate of technical progress concomitant upon formation of union came to be known as dynamic effects. In the long run these effects were considered far more important compared to static effects. Another line of research consists in finding out if there is anything like "natural trade partners." Geographical proximity results in lower transport cost and that is one component of being characterized as natural trade partners. Summers (1990) pointed out that if the regional trading partners had experienced disproportionately higher volume of trade prior to the formation of the union possibilities of trade expansion are greater showing that the countries were natural trade partners. Distortions owing to the formation of customs union are much less once the members have an overwhelmingly larger trade share among themselves over a long time. The relationship between regional and multilateral trading arrangements represents another growing area of research. Although multilateralism is always preferred regional agreements can promote better ties and tackle issues that are not properly addressed in a multilateral agreement. Groups so formed may have more intimate knowledge about the needs of individual members and action can be taken more easily outside the frame of multilateral trading arrangements.

Closely related with this issue is the fact that macro-economic changes arising in the context of regional trading arrangements assume a lot of significance and it has already attracted a few researchers to carry out investigations. Transmission of cyclical fluctuations from abroad may become more intense for group members due to greater linkage in trade and investment policy. High incidence of fluctuations may promote or retard the rate of growth in the economies concerned. So what happens to a particular country once it decides to join a regional group offers an area of research with much potential.

Natural Trading Partner Hypothesis

To what extent SAARC members fulfill the necessary condition for a successful regional group offers an interesting area of study. In order to examine that data were collected over a fifteen year period between 1990 and 2004 for individual group members of the SAARC. Direction of Trade Statistics Yearbook published by the IMF served as the basic source of data for the exercise. Time series data on exports and imports were collected for all the partners excepting Bhutan since trade data were not forthcoming for this country. Bhutan figured as a source of trade in other countries' trade data but her own statistics were missing.

The data revealed that dependence of different countries on the group was not uniform. In the first category we had smaller or disadvantaged nations like Maldives and Nepal who depended on the group in a substantial measure. About 95 per cent of Nepal's exports on an average are directed to the group whereas more than 65 per cent of imports are coming from the group. Since the middle of nineties Nepal's closeness with the group has increased in a remarkable manner. For Maldives export shares have diminished compared with the early nineties but still it is more than thirty per cent. Import share however is increasing and though there are fluctuations it sometimes exceeds sixty per cent. In the second category we have Bangladesh and Sri Lanka whose trading relation with the group is quite substantial. Thirty per cent of Bangladesh exports to Asia is directed to the group while import share is slightly less. For Sri Lanka more than sixty per cent of her exports to Asia is accounted for by SAARC whereas imports constitute a little above thirty per cent. In the last category we have India and Pakistan whose export relation with the group is stronger compared to that in the case of imports. Pakistan on an average sends 15 per cent of her aggregate exports to Asia towards SAARC while for India the share stands at 20 per cent. As regards imports the share is less than 5 per cent for India while Pakistan sends 10 per cent of her exports meant for Asian countries in aggregate.

The above findings make it clear that partners of SAARC do not exactly fit into the description of natural trading partners. Excepting the disadvantaged countries no other member depends on the group in an overwhelming manner. For India and Pakistan the dependence is peripheral. There are countries within Asia which are far more important compared to SAARC partners. And what is more the trading relationship is not uniform. As an export market SAARC appears to be more attractive than being a source of import. Such lack of balance in trade cannot promote long-term relationship. Although year to year balancing is difficult to achieve in any trade relationship presence of inherent destabilizing forces prevents the desired expansion in trade. And the reason is not far to seek. India and Pakistan do not find SAARC members to be competent enough to satisfy their import needs. The same type of difficulty arose in the case of India's trade with East Europe. Their imports fell much short of their exports to this country which finally upset the provisions of rupee payment agreement.

One interesting fact about the pattern of regional trade that emerges is that since the mid nineties intra regional trade share is increasing for most of the members. The spate of economic reforms sweeping through the countries might have directly contributed to the phenomenon. Unless upgrading of economic status for Bhutan, Nepal and Maldives takes place it will be difficult for the group to emerge as a dynamic centre of trade.

Trade Intensity Index

One commonly used measure of finding out how closely the regional group members are related refers to the technique of trade intensity index. This measure requires two countries for the purpose of calculation. One we take as the exporting country while the other is its trade partner. First one considers the export side and the second country's share in the country one's export trade is calculated. This is placed in the numerator. In the denominator one deals with another ratio which is concerned with import side. Country two's aggregate imports are expressed as a ratio of world exports net of country one's aggregate imports. If X and M denote exports and imports and i and j stand for country suffixes then country i's exports to country j expressed as a ratio of country i's aggregate exports stand for the numerator. In the numerator one places the country i's imports expressed as a ratio of world imports net of country i's imports. The index as is evident tries to measure whether country j' s imports from the country I is greater or lesser than its from the rest of the world. If the ratio is higher than one it signifies trade intensiveness. A ratio lower than one indicates lack of intensity.

TABLE 1

Exporting Country: Bangladesh, India, Maldives, Nepal, Pakistan, Sri Lanka

	Bangladesh		*India*		*Maldives*	*Nepal*		*Pakistan*		*Sri Lanka*	
	1994	*2004*	*1994*	*2004*	*2004*	*1994*	*2004*	*1994*	*2004*	*1994*	*2004*
Bangladesh	–	–	33.33	17.91	–	–	2.58	22.45	12.23	3.4	2.0
India	0.0010	0.82	–	–	0.35	5.00	45.18	0.95	1.13	1.00	6.46
Maldives	–	–	0.1186	0.50	–	–	–	0.41	1.43	208.3	15.59
Nepal	4.0	3.0	40.35	52.71	–	–	–	4.25	1.11	–	0.28
Pakistan	2.6	2.79	1.33	0.31	–	–	2.84	–	–	5.80	3.58
Sri Lanka	1.2	1.62	17.69	29.25	15.4	3.0	.125	10.95	12.62	–	–

Source: Compiled from Direction of Trade Statistics Yearbook. various issues.

Partner countries are shown along the rows while exporting countries are arranged along columns. Cells coming under partner country exporting to partner country have no entries associated with them. For Maldives trade intensity index could not be calculated for the year 1994 due to lack of data. Results obtained for 2004 only have been given. Cells are mostly credited with entries greater than one signifying presence of trade intensity. But there is no definite trend over time as such; ratios increase or decrease at random. And more important thing is that figures we have derived are not real intensities. To be counted as real intensities they have to be normalized by geographic distance so that one can present a conclusive evidence on natural trade partner hypothesis. If geographic distance has got anything to do with the fact of being close trade partners that variable should be brought into the analysis. Within the group Maldives and Sri Lanka seem to be having a strong trade relation and that is increasing over the years suggesting that they are natural trade partners. Nepal, Bangladesh and Sri Lanka have high trade intensity indices with India which may be more due to India's status of a dominant trade partner. Although we have not calculated trade intensity indices for Asian countries outside the SAARC it is possible that some of SAARC members have more intense trade relationship with outside partners.

Commodity Composition of Intra-regional Trade

Success of a regional group depends to a large extent on the type of market access it provides to the group members. A newly industrializing country will be interested in having a secure market for its manufactured products. Similarly the developing country partners also will be looking for the encouragement the group can provide to export their manufactured commodities. In fact potential for trade expansion is largely determined by the group's ability to absorb finished manufactured goods by the member countries. Coming to members of SAARC one notes that the intra regional market is quite important for three countries namely Bhutan, Nepal and Maldives. For Bhutan the group is important both as sources of imports and exports. For

Maldives the dependence is much more in regard to exports. For Nepal also export dependence is more compared to SAARC's role as a source of imports. Regarding commodity composition of trade it is found that over 90 per cent of Bhutan's exports of simple manufactures are directed to the group. For Maldives manufactures exports are yet to register themselves in the regional market. Nepal shows a very high export dependence (90 per cent) for chemicals while other types of manufactures are mostly diverted to extra regional countries. Side by side with manufactures SAARC provides an important forum for export of food items (over 95%) for Bhutan and Nepal.

The other four group members namely Bangladesh, India, Pakistan and Sri Lanka have different experiences with the group. For Bangladesh among manufactures category only chemicals command a respectable share of about 30 per cent on an average. Other manufactures constitute less than 1 per cent of her global exports. India's exports of manufactures to the group constitute less than five per cent of her world exports For Pakistan share of manufactures is just about 10 per cent of her aggregate value of manufactures exports. Chemicals export from Sri Lanka comprise about 20 per cent of her global export value. Other manufactures account for less than 1 per cent.

Taken as a whole SAARC appears to be a good place for selling chemicals. India, Pakistan and Sri Lanka import negligible quantity of manufactures including chemicals from the group. Nepal, Maldives, Bhutan and to some extent Bangladesh also buy respectable quantity of manufactures from SAARC members which goes to show that intra industry trade is playing a useful role to expand the frontiers of trade in the region. Trade in primary commodities is significant for stronger partners in the sense that India exports more than one third of her tobacco manufactures to this region. Average share•of Bangladesh is also more than 15 per cent of her world level sales. Bangladesh, Pakistan and Sri Lanka sell a sizeable quantity of raw materials to this regional group.

The evidence we have gathered makes it clear that SAARC does not exactly provide any incentive to the stronger partners to sell their manufactures in the home ground. The reasons may be more than one. The most significant explanation seems to be that there is not enough intra regional demand for complex types of manufactures. A country which specializes in producing manufactures has to turn towards markets outside the region. And it may be that size of internal markets is limited so that total intake of SAARC members may not be adequate to guarantee the market clearing sales for bigger partners. In addition to this the need to have diversified trade links with the rest of the world might have prompted the group members to turn towards outside countries in a large measure. Multilateralism has retained its importance in the case of SAARC. Trade displacement experience has been kept to the minimum for the group as a whole.

But this raises important questions for the prospect of the group to emerge as a dynamic centre of trade. Unless reallocation of production takes place according to comparative advantage it is difficult to enjoy economies of scale and process of technological innovation may not take shape. In that event global forces will play the determining role for industrial expansion. Development of a new industry will depend on outside forces and its products also would have to be offered to the rest of the world. The regional group at best will play a supplementing role in absorbing a certain portion of the new industry's output.

Looking at the trade pattern of other Asia-Pacific regional groups one notes that share of intra regional exports in total exports ranged from 37 per cent to 56 per cent while corresponding import shares varied between 39 per cent and 75 per cent. The trade between East and Southeast Asian economies also is expanding at a fast rate, the share on an average being 50 per cent of their global trade. Of course there are fluctuations and Thailand, Vietnam and Philippines are more prone to these fluctuations. But the fact is that the economies involved are more or less similar so that they can take care of each other's needs in a better way. Trade takes place here according to Linder hypothesis where similar economies act complementary to each other. These countries achieved specialization with an eye kept open towards the foreign countries so that mutual flow of trade was of the most beneficial kind. Economies which are too divergent in nature may find it difficult to use the regional group as a source of strength. External world would always be necessary for their proper sustenance.

Reforms and Trade in South Asia

The period of nineties is synonimous with reforms for all the members of SAARC. Withdrawal of quantitative restrictions, slashing down of tariffs, dismantling of licensing system and various trade facilitation measures have marked the era of reform. For the four big partners of the group namely Bangladesh, India, Pakistan and Sri Lanka the reduction in average tariff rate has been commendable during the period. For Bangladesh average tariff rate was more than 80 per cent in 1991. In 2001 it stood at just 20 per cent. For India it was a decline from roughly 80 per cent to 35 per cent. Pakistan showed a decline from 70 per cent to slightly less than 20 per cent. Sri Lankan tariff rate was quite low at a little above 20 per cent in 1991 which came down to 5 per cent in 2001. This decline in average tariff rate signified easing of restriction on trade and higher market access as well. Since lower tariff rate was applied to the entire world in a non-discriminating manner the impact was felt on the aggregate volume of trade. Thus proportion of trade in GDP was 24 per cent in 1985-87 for Bangladesh and it reached 35.5 per cent in 2000-01. During the same period the increase was from 61.5 per cent to 89 per cent in the case of Bhutan, from 14 per cent to 30 per cent in the case of India, from 60 per cent to 169 per cent in the case of Maldives, from 32 per cent to 55 per cent in the case of Nepal, from 34 per cent to 36 per cent in the case of Pakistan and from 62 per cent to 85 per cent in the case of Sri Lanka. The country that benefited least from the reforms seems to be Pakistan while the maximum benefit went to Maldives. Bangladesh and India shared benefit in a modest manner.

The similar movement between trade reform and share of trade in GDP for majority of SAARC members points to a strong correlation between the two. But it is true that trade reforms in conjunction with favorable domestic and international developments can yield the optimum result. For instance both Nepal and Maldives derive benefit from large inflow of tourists. Hence a peaceful international atmosphere will be congenial to development. Growth of terrorist activities is capable of throttling tourist movement thereby lowering economic growth. Similarly East Asian crisis or bird flu epidemic depress trade prospects among nations. Notwithstanding the progress of reforms temporary causes can inflict substantial damage on trade prospects. Sudden loss of crop at home can transform an exporting nation into an importing one Thus reforms can be looked upon as a solid contributory factor to development rather than being the sole cause of trade expansion.

Apart from there being tariff reductions exchange rate changes have been another important area of trade sector changes. Excepting Maldives all other countries in SAARC have introduced floating rate systems to encourage flows of trade. Full current account convertibility has been a feature of several countries in the group. Capital account liberalization may open-up further possibilities of financial flows which have been crucial in the case of East Asian growth. But the thing is growth in trade may promote growth in investment leading to too much interdependence. When a group of neighbouring countries are investing large amounts in each other probabilities of contagion become higher. A shock or disorder experienced by one country quickly reaches another country and the shock engulfs the entire region. Loss of confidence in the capability of a country to honour its commitments leads to panic withdrawal of funds which can only be prevented by the existence of a comfortable amount of foreign exchange reserves. Even in the presence of reserves violent fluctuation in exchange rates becomes a distinct possibility. Therefore those who argue that for a take off in trade SAARC should link-up investment with trade have to think twice. For FDI or portfolio investment it is better to create a common fund which can be utilized in the face of a crisis. Unless global players are there IMF would not send funds to rescue the countries in question. As a first step commodity market integration might be a better alternative than opening of capital account.

The question of higher growth rate in commodity trade is intimately linked with technology development. Thus resource based, low technology, medium technology and high technology industries can always be classified in the sphere of international trade. Low technology manufactures and primary products happen to be important export items from South Asia. About skill based manufactures we can mention IT products where India and to some extent Sri Lanka also seem to have a comparative advantage. Such skill based manufactures have necessarily to depend on extra group sources, as internal market has not yet developed. Preponderance of low technology manufactures is explained by resource endowment position of these countries where low capital availability per worker confines them to textiles, clothing and leather manufactures. In agricultural exports share of processed commodities also is not very much due to variety of reasons. Unless there is a rise in per capita income fruit processing industry turning out products like jams and jellies cannot find a viable market. Marine products and meat preparations have a growing world demand and SAARC partners can look forward to overseas markets for those product lines. Penetrating European Union markets, however, is a distinct challenge as strict quality norms are in existence.

SAARC INFLUENCE ON SOUTH ASIAN TRADE—CONCLUSION

Sometimes formation of regional groups is accompanied by shifts towards manufactured goods because partners provide a strong incentive for that. In this case however no such tendency is insight as exports do not have that much weightage in the economies of South Asian countries. Pull factor operating from the side of other SAARC members is not that strong for any given member of the group so that more industrial diversification will result. Vertical specialization is another possibility after RTAs come into existence. Many countries import certain items from another partner, process them and export to the country of origin, other group members or to the rest of the world. Electronics, auto parts, apparel and raw cashew nuts provide some good examples of exports embodying imports from partner countries. There is evidence from Mexico where growth rate of such industries has far exceeded the growth rate of real GDP over the period 1990-2002. Employment in these industries are however strongly influenced by cyclical factors sweeping through other members of the group. A reversionary trend abroad can throw many people out of employment since no domestic base is there. Intra industry trade can serve as another new direction of trade in the case of countries joining regional trading agreements but in the case of SAARC this possibility is yet to be explored.

References

Karakaovali, B. and Nuno Limao (2005), "The Clash of Liberalizations", *Policy Research Working Paper 3493*, The World Bank, January.

Kose, M. Ayhan and Others (2004), "How Has NAFTA Affected the Mexican Economy?", Review and Evidence, *IMF Working Paper*, WP/04/59, IMF.

Panagariya, A., Preferential Trade Liberalization: The Traditional Theory and New Developments, Vol. xxxviii, No. 2, June 2000, pp. 287-331.

Pitigala, N. (2005), "What Does Regional Trade in South Asia Reveal About Future Trade Integration?" *Policy Research Working Paper 3497*, The World Bank, February.

RIS for the Non-Aligned and other Developing Countries, South Asia Development and Cooperation Report, 2001-02 and 2004.

Yusuf, S. and Others (eds), (2004), Global Change and East Asian Policy Initiatives, The World Bank.

Asian Economic Integration
A Strategic Relevance of Broad Approach

H.H. ULIVEPPA, D.R. ALBAL AND M.N. SIDDALINGAPPANAVAR

INTRODUCTION

Regional economic integration is a new and striking idea for the expansion of foreign trade among the developing countries which seem to have been hypnotized by the success of EU initiated in 1992 achieved by the European Economic Community (EEC) and of NAFTA by the U.S. initiated in 1994 as a means of trade expansion in their area. Particularly, in view of their national markets being rather narrow for the successful operation of modern industrialization and implementation of technological innovations, it is conceived as a regional market to enhance modern industrial development and also to achieve economies of scale in the respective member-nations. Broadly speaking, regional economic integration implies the creation of the most desirable structure of inter-regional economy through the formation of a Customs Union or of a Free Trade Area within the region and deliberately introducing all desirable elements of co-ordination and unification. Generally, such an economic integration would have to pass through three distinct, but inter-dependent stages of co-operation, co-ordination and finally, of full unification. Infact, economic integration may be identified with liberalization of trade as well as factor movements. The harmonization or co-ordination of economic policies as a whole would follow once a Common Market has been set-up. The said integration may take any one or a combination of any of the following forms: (i) Long-term Trade Agreements, (ii) Preferential Trading, (iii) Sectoral/ Partial Integration, (iv) Free Trade Area, (v) Customs Union, and (vi) Economic Union. These different forms of integration visualize different degrees of economic co-operation in the ascending order. It has been highlighted that such a regional economic integration would be able to generate internal impulses for growth besides other favourable effects for the entire region.

There is now a growing recognition of the importance of regional economic integration in Asia for generating growth impulses from within, especially in the wake of the East Asian crisis. Voices emanating from different parts of the region support Pan-Asian co-operation and integration. Against this background, this paper examines the strategic relevance of possible approaches and assess the possibilities/ feasibilities for regional co-operation in Asia.

ASIAN ECONOMIC UNIFICATION PROCESS: AN OVERVIEW

The 21st century is emerged as special era for Asia. Regional economic co-operation in Asia is developing fast and well, with the Association of South-East Asian Nations (ASEAN) as a centre, and with the positive contribution of major Asian nations such as India, China and Japan. The progress in co-operation has shown that Asian economic unification is in motion. It is believed that the economic unification process shall result in an Asian economic community. Integrated co-operation is the best way for Asian nations to promote mutual development; the 'fault lines' suggested in Samuel Huntington's paradigm can be repaired and transcended in the unification process. Guided by this vision, India and others have in recent years, been positively engaging in the globalization process as well as actively participating in efforts towards regional co-operation in Asia.

In Asia, there have been several efforts towards sub-regional, cross-regional, and bilateral regional trading arrangements (Table 1). While bilateral initiatives largely involve ASEAN economies, viz, Singapore and Thailand, some of the notable sub-regional economic co-operation efforts are the Bay of Bengal Initiative among member States for Multi-Sectoral Technical and Economic Co-operation (BIMSTEC) comprising Bangladesh, India, Myanmar, Nepal, Bhutan, Sri Lanka, and Thailand; the Mekong-Ganga Co-operation Group, involving India, Combodia, Laos, Myanmar, Vietnam and Thailand. As may be observed from Table 1, all the major Asian economies, and some of the sub-regional organizations such as Association of South-East Asian Nations (ASEAN) have been pursuing bilateral regional trading agreements (Mukul, G. Asher, Rahul Sen, 2005).

The rapid economic growth rate of around 7 per cent in recent years in the Asian region has laid a solid material foundation for Pan-Asian regional co-operation. China and the ASEAN signed an FTA agreement in November 2002 to establish a free trade zone by 2010. This future free trade zone comprising of 10 ASEAN countries and China (referred to as ASEAN+1) will be the third largest in the world, with 1.7 billion consumers and a trade volume of $ 1.2 trillion annually, next only to the NAFTA and the EU. On October 7, 2003, China, Japan, Korea and the ASEAN also agreed to a plan of setting-up a bigger free trade zone by 2020, embracing the region currently referred to as the ASEAN+3 (Yao Chao Cheng, 2005).

India, the largest economy in south Asia, is also actively taking steps to join east Asia's economic integration movement; and has persistently and purposefully pursued the look East Policy initiated in 1991. It has operationalised bilateral trade agreements with Sri Lanka and Thailand, and has negotiated a comprehensive pact with Singapore and ASEAN (Table 1). India has decided to upgrade all current FTAs to FTA plus, covering non-merchandise trade areas as well. This policy is to be followed in all current and future

TABLE 1

Recently Established or Proposed FTAs in Asia, 1999-2004

Country/ Grouping	*Partners*	*Status of Agreement, 2004*	*Country/ Grouping*	*Partners*	*Status of Agreement, 2004*
1	2	3	4	5	6
ASEAN	China	Framework agreement signed	Malaysia	China	Under negotiation
	India	Framework agreement signed		Japan	Under negotiation
	Japan	Framework agreement signed		USA	Proposed
	Korea	Under study			
	USA (TIFA)	Under negotiation			
	CER	Under study			
	ASEAN+3	Under study			
	EU	Proposed			
China	ASEAN	Agreement signed	Philippines	China	Under negotiation
	Australia	Proposed		Japan	Under negotiation
	India	Under study		USA	Proposed
	Japan	Proposed			
	Hong Kong	Agreement signed			
	Macau	Proposed			
	Malaysia	Under negotiation			
	New Zealand	Proposed			
	Philippines	Under negotiation			
	Singapore	Proposed			

(Contd.)

TABLE 1 (*Contd.*)

1	*2*	*3*	*4*	*5*	*6*
India	ASEAN	Framework agreement signed	Singapore	Australia	Agreement in force
	China	Proposed		Canada	Under negotiation
	Korea	Proposed		China	Proposed
	Japan	Proposed		Egypt	Proposed
	Singapore	Under negotiation		EFTA	Agreement in force
	Sri Lanka	Agreement in force		EU	Proposed rejected by EU
	Thailand	Agreement in force		India	Under negotiation
	BIMSTEC	Framework agreement signed		Japan	Agreement in force
	SACU	Proposed		Jordan	Agreement in force
	COMESA	Proposed		Korea	Negotiations completed
	MERCOSUR	Framework agreement signed		Mexico	Under negotiation
	Mauritius	Under negotiation		New Zealand	Agreement in force
	GCC	Proposed		Sri Lanka	Under negotiation
	Chile	Proposed		Pakistan	Proposed
	SAARC/ SAFTA	Agreement in force		US	Agreement in force
				Panama	Proposed
				Pacific Three (P-3) (New Zealand and Chile)	Under negotiation
Japan	ASEAN	Framework agreement signed	Thailand	Australia	Agreement signed
	Canada	Proposed		Bahrain	Agreement signed
	Chile	Under study		China	Agreement signed
	India	Proposed		India	Agreement in force
	Korea	Under study		Japan	Under negotiation
	Malaysia	Under negotiation		Korea	Under study

	Mexico	Under negotiation	New Zealand	Under study
	Philippines	Under negotiation	Peru	Agreement signed
	Singapore	Agreement in force	South Africa	Under study
	Thailand	Under negotiation	USA	Under negotiation
	Australia	Proposed		
Korea	Australia	Under study		
	China	Under study		
	Chile	Agreement signed		
	India	Proposed		
	Japan	Under study		
	Mexico	Under negotiation		
	Peru	Proposed		
	New Zealand	Under study		
	Singapore	Under negotiation		
	Thailand	Under study		
	USA	Under negotiation		

Source: Rajan and Sen (2004), in EPW: Sept. 3, 2005.

such negotiations. The bilateral agreements with China and Korea have been proposed and joint study groups have been established. An India-Japan study group to examine the feasibility for a similar agreement has also been established. It is hoped that this group will enable the two countries to evolve a strategic partnership. (Mukul, G. Asher, Rahul Sen, 2005). In September 2003, a free trade agreement plan (including 2.5 billion consumers and comprising 75 per cent of the total Asian population) had been reached by the ASEAN, China, Japan, and India, at Jakarta, Indonesia.

It is reported that the agreement shall be gradually implemented between 2012 and 2017. It is quite likely that the set-up will evolve into ASEAN+4 (ASEAN and China, Japan, Korea and India). Also, on December 23-24, 2003, members of the Experts Committee of the SAARC held a meeting in New Delhi to assess and approve the proposed programme of setting-up a South Asia Free Trade Zone. In addition, it is expected that Asia will witness more bilateral 'FTAs' leading up to various other larger regional agreements. The Bangkok Agreement is another notable regional trade arrangement in Asia that includes six countries; three from East Asia (China, Korea and Laos) and three from South Asia (India, Bangladesh and Sri Lanka). The significance of the agreement lies in the fact that it might serve as a platform to link East Asia and South Asia into a broader regional trade agreement (Yao Chao Cheng, 2005).

The statements by the many Asian leaders and experts (for eg; Ramos, 2003, presenting the notion of a Grand Asian Family comprising all Asian nations, Nobel laureate economist Robert Mundel, 2002- stating that Asia would have a single currency in the near future, and Wen Jiabao, 2002- "promote a New Centenial Asian Co-operation with common efforts"—all introducing the concept of constructing a new Asia) show that the Asian nations have already entered the primary stage of economic unification. Chapter VIII of the United Nations also encourages regional, social and economic co-operation. The UN Economic and Social Commission for Asia and the Pacific (ESCAP), promotes economic and social development through regional and sub-regional co-operation and integration in the region. The ASEAN is playing an important role as the main axle of the Asian economic unification process with its well developed political and market mechanisms. The ongoing regional economic unification processes shall make Asia the fulcrum of economic activity in the world and contribute substantially to global security in the 21st century. Even though Asia is too and beset with complicated differences in terms of culture, political systems, economic strengths, as well as religious diversity, the continents' nations can co-operate with each other by developing a consensus on the basis of mutual respect towards existing differences. The main risk of failure does not emanate from the 'fault-lines', but from the ignorance of policy maker who are not working positively on this issue (Yao Chao Cheng, 2005).

The voices emanating from different parts of the region in support of Pan-Asian Co-operation and Integration are ample proof of the growing recognition of the importance of Asian economic integration. At the initiative of Thailand's Prime Minister, the Asian Co-operation Dialogue (ACD) was launched on June 18-19, 2002 at Cha-Am, Thailand. Similarly, the Chinese President Jiang Zemin had launched the BOAO Forum for Asia in 2001 at Boao, in Hainan province of China as a Pan-Asian Economic Forum. The Prime Minister Manmohan Singh has envisioned an Asian Economic Community combining Japan, ASEAN countries, China, India and South Korea (Nagesh Kumar, 2005).

RATIONALE FOR A BROADER ASIAN APPROACH

From the above, it is clear that the ongoing multiple attempts in Asia towards the regional integration at sub-regional and bilateral levels are unlikely to enable the region to exploit the full potential of regional economic integration, but however suggest that there is now a growing recognition of the importance of intensive economic integration at the Pan-Asian level in the region or of the opportunity cost of not doing it. Now it is realized that given the trend of formation of regional trading blocs in the rest of the world, stimulus for future growth has to increasingly come from within the Asian region. The substantial complementarities existing between Asian economies are required to be exploited for their mutual common benefit. In this region, some economies have surplus capital resources, while others have inadequate domestic savings for the rapid development. Similarly, the region is characterised by the complementarities in the demand and supply of other resource such as technology and skilled manpower. The regional co-operation by generating intra-regional demand could supplement the external demand and reduce the vulnerability of the region due to the overdependence on outside regions. And it could also help in exploiting the existing capacities in the region fully. The loss of output due to the under utilization of capacity in Japanese and Korean construction and engineering industries has been reported to be of the order of 10-15 per cent of the GDP of the region or about a trillion dollars a year (Agarwala, 2002). A more intensive and broad co-operation, for matching the underutilized capacity in some countries of the region with unmet demand in others could go a long way in putting the region on a high growth trajectory and help Asian region to reemerge a centre of gravity in the world economy. This Asian region combines some of the fastest growing economies in the world, which together form a huge market growing faster than any other region in the world and could form a vibrant regional grouping that would be roughly of the size of the EU in terms of GDP, will have larger magnitude of trade than NAFTA and international reserves bigger than those of EU and NAFTA put together. The formation of a broader Asian grouping will also help the region to play a more effective role in shaping the emerging world trading and financial system responsive to its needs. The broader regional grouping will also formalize a high level of functional integration that has taken place in Asia especially between ASEAN and its dialogue partners. The intra-regional trade in eastern Asia has increased substantially and now accounts for over a half of their trade and their collective foreign exchange reserves comprise two-thirds of the world (Nagesh Kumar, 2005). Further, this region has its own unique and distinct identity called "Asian identity" shaped by history and cultural exchanges over several countries. There have been not only vibrant flows of goods and services as well as labour and capital amongst Asian countries sustained over several centuries; but also a vibrant exchange of ideas along with the trade. Above all, the ideological influences spread across the nations binding them in ties of religion, Hinduism and with it the art of governance of Chanakya found its sway across to much of Thailand, Malaysia and Indonesia. Similarly, the role of Buddhism is well known, Religion has been a strong unifying factor for with the religious beliefs comes a way of life and as religious influence spread, so did the cultural ties. Pagan, Borobudur and Angkor Wat are only but a small testimony to the vast trading and cultural network that Asia had in ancient times (Shankar, 2004).

Recently, some changed economic imperatives are also working in favour of broader Asian framework. Firstly, the so long existing "flying geese Model" of vertical economic integration, which was Centered on Japan, has been shifted towards that of 'bamboo capitalism' or 'parallel development' based on FDI flows in the region, creating intricate intra-regional production network, based on the exchange of parts, components and other intermediate products, hence, a "horizontal network of trade and capital" with China at its core. There is, therefore, a new division of labour and production across Asia. Secondly, there were fundamentally two models of economic development in East Asia; which tend to be 'converging' today. While one was the Japanese model of large industrial groups which were sponsored and protected to a huge extent by the state and financed by state-led banks, the other was the model built on small and medium-enterprises (or SMEs)—which were based on more private sector-led economic and business development, rather than a state-led approach. These two models appear to be 'converging' today, as the Japanese model' opens-up to Small Private Sector initiatives, just as the state 'scales back', even though it would still be playing an important economic regulatory role. On the other hand, the SME/Private Sector Model appears to have a greater dose of governmental intervention to 'lead' business as in the cases of Taiwan and Hong Kong or Thailand. Thirdly, the social dimension of economic modelling has drastically increased in East Asia, especially in post-SARS Asia today. And finally, the rise of economic nationalism in the Asian region is now more vital than ever. A bigger and more diversified market for Asian economies would stimulate growth through greater Asian trade (especially with China) and foreign investments (from Japan and South Korea as well as by China and ethnic Chinese investments).

STRATEGIC RELEVANCE OF POSSIBLE APPROACHES TO BROADER ASIAN ECONOMIC INTEGRATION

The preceding section has provided a rationale for a Pan-Asian regional economic integration. It is made clear that such a grouping would be able to generate internal impulses for growth besides other fovourable effects for the region. Keeping in mind the experiences of regional economic integration from other regions, a practical approach to regionalization in Asia would be a phased one (Nagesh Kumar, 2005).

As a region and for the creation of a future Asian Community, there are currently three 'regional integration models' which are being highlighted. Asian Economic integration could be achieved by: (i) Weaving a web of existing bilateral free trade agreements (FTAs) together regionwide, thus creating a huge East Asian Free Trade Area, (ii) Finding the means to effectively use the mass of 'unproductive' Japanese savings more efficiently (instead of letting them lie 'fallow' in banks with sub-zero interest rates or as T-bonds in the United States) to urgently develop the weaker economies of Asia through a sort of 'Japanese Marshall for Asia'. The latter economies, however, must also create the conditions for fruitful and sound investment in their weak economies through vigorous and at times, painful reforms; (iii) Creating an integrated East Asian region, centred on China and its enormous potential economic development and growth, through trade (in both goods and services) and investments both ways (China-East Asia as well as east Asia-China), as well as through a new integrated china centred production chain-cum-demand network across the whole region. The current 'ASEAN-CHINA' FTA could be 'expanded' both geographically and intellectually to Japan and Korea, as well as 'deepened' towards an East Asian Comprehensive Partnership or CPA (Eric Teo Chu Cheow, 2005).

The three strategic integrative models for Asia, therefore, would include the following, viz: First, there is a functional and economic trade approach in both north-east and south-east Asia. This functional approach would be to 'weave' a web of FTAs, in a building-block process across the whole region, which could then result in a region wide 'ASEAN+3+1' FTA. ASEAN countries could champion this worthy cause as an Asian end goal. They should hence, like Europe, envision an Asia or 'ASEAN+3+INDIA' free trade area or comprehensive partnership (comprising the free flow of trade in goods, services, investments, human resource/ development and ideas) in the future, as a common and ultimate goal.

Second, there is the model of a Japan-led East Asian growth. There exists some theoretical basis today to reflate and stimulate Japan via East Asia's present 'ASEAN+3' framework. Like the American-led Marshell Plan after second World War, Japan can help to build-up this region, while boosting its own domestic consumption, 'saving' Japanese MNCs and there by stimulating the Japanese economy. The key is for Japan to mobilize its huge domestic savings and private capital in order to 'tap' the vast market of these 14 nations and their three billion population. There is great potential for market integration and competition within this 'ASEAN+3+1' economic space, as Japanese corporations could seek production integration, according to a region wide division of labour. There is also scope for a bigger market share of Japanese services region wide; Japan banks could benefit from fast developing markets in China, India and ASEAN at a time when the Japanese economy seems to have reached a high level of economic maturity. Further more, this region also has total reserves of some US $ 1.5 trillion, including the worlds top five foreign reserves (Japan, China Taiwan, Hong Kong and Singapore), which can be progressively mobilized as fruits of this Japanese-led plan take shape, and as the growing reserves of china, Hong Kong and Singapore supplement Japanese funds progressively.

Lastly, there is potential for a Chian-led (and eventually, an India-co-led) growth model. With the China-ASEAN FTA or partnership (or ASEAN+1), there is more scope for a building block process of networks of partnership across east Asia, subject to market forces; with the central focus being on the vast potential Chinese marketand its 'go West Policy'. Here Japan, South Korea and ASEAN can further tap into vast Chinese market, as they are already doing so, by increasing economic and monetary co-operation, through trade of goods and services and investments, while China modernizes its structures further. Then, this will allow ASEAN, Korea and Japan to dovetail their industries and 'plug' into the vast Chinese market, especially looking for 'niches' in China's industrial and economic development strategy. This is the new regional division of labour in the making, which includes more mobility in terms of human resource deployment, outsourcing in third countries and a flexible supply and logistical chain management between China and its neighbours. The Chinese reckon that the 'ASEAN+3' frame work could be built upon a successful ASEAN-China FTA, as the first building block or initial foundation for regional co-operation. The Chinese envision that the Koreans and Japanese would eventually join in, thus building a greater East Asian cooperation entity, which the 'ASEAN+3' framework is supposed to provide for. Hence, China intends to 'grow' the ASEAN+3 from what they now dub the 'ASEAN+1' today. Similarly, India's impressive economic growth can also centre Asian growth and integration progressively, besides China alone. In this Asian economic integration execise with China, India would need to integrate more pronouncedly with rest of East Asia by encouraging efforts to consolidate trade and investments between India and the 13 East Asian countries.

All these three above models are not necessarily independent of each other. In fact, they are not exclusive models, and a combination of all three could be used effectively to 'integrate' the whole region. However, in all the three cases, the East Asian model for economic and monetary co-operation would be less of an institutional one model (as

FIGURE 1

Emerging (East) Asian Community

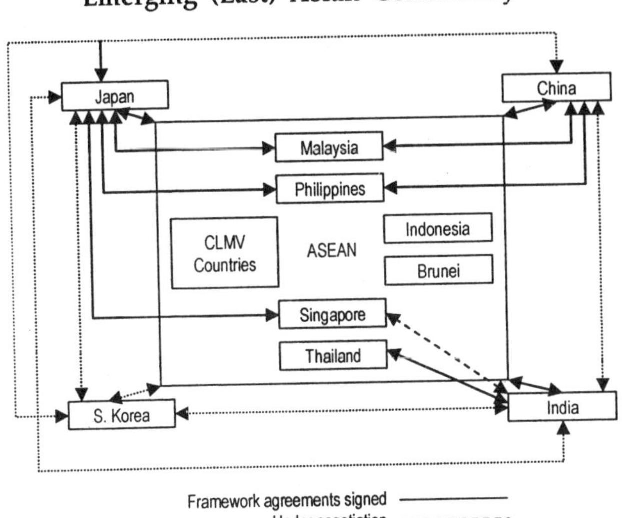

in Europe), than a functional one. Either through an intertwining web of FTA's consolidating an 'ASEAN+3' FTA, or a Japanese investment-led model, or a China/India-inspired East Asian growth and consolidation model, the Asian integrative model should be incremental and functional in nature. The ASEAN+3' and JACIK framework should constitute the primary vehicles to drive this economic and monetary co-operation forward.

The present 'FTAs' between Japan, Korea and China and those between India-China, India-Korea and India-Japan are being examined. As shown in the Figure 1, ASEAN and the four dialogue partners, namely, Japan, ASEAN, China, India, and Korea (JACIK) countries are all engaged in evolving the FTAs between their different pairs. A virtual JACIK FTA is emerging through this complex web of FTAs. However, these FTAs (bilateral or sub-regional) do not allow full exploitation of potential of regional economic integration that exists in view of the substantial complementarities arising from diversity in the factor endowments and levels of development. Hence, a vision for the Asian economic integration is to begin by coalescing these multiple FTAs between the JACIK countries into an overarching regional trading arrangement. This broader overarching framework alone will allow optimal utilization of Asia's resources and synergies for their mutual common benefit. As pointed out by Rowley (2004), "without some form of overall regional framework within which to work, capital, human and natural resources may all be deployed at less than their optimal value."

JACIK approach—as a core of an Asian Economic Community—in supported by a number of Asian leaders including Indian prime minister. Combining 14 of the largest and fastest growing economies of Asia with vast complementarities, the JACIK trade bloc is a potential third pole of the world economy. As shown in Table 2, for instance, they combine between them a population of three billion or a half of the world population and a GNP of over $7.2 trillion comparable to that of EU in 2000. In terms of purchasing power parity, this JACIK grouping will have the gross national income of $ 13 trillion, much larger than either NAFTA or EU. Its exports will add up to $ 1.37 trillion

TABLE 2

Proposed JACIK Community in Relation of European Union and NAFTA in 2000

(Billion US $)

Parameter	*EU*	*NAFTA*	*JACIK (14)*
GDP	7260	11147	7262
Per cent to world total	23.17	35.57	23.17
GNI PPP	8315	11350	13361
Per cent to world total	18.68	25.5	30.02
Exports	2025	1226	1367
Per cent to world total	31.89	19.31	21.53
International reserves (2002)	426	246	2000
Population (millions)	354	411	3012
Per cent to world total	5.85	6.79	49.76

Source: World Development Report, 2002 and WDI, 2001, CD-ROM.

compared to $ 1.2 trillion of NAFTA and its combined official reserves will be much larger ($ 1.3 trillion in 2000) than those of the US and the EU put together. In fact, the latest estimates suggest that foreign exchange holdings of the JACIK countries are nearly US $ 2 trillion. Therefore, the region will have sufficiently large market and financial resources to support and sustain expedited development of the region's economies.

Combining both China and India, the two emerging economies of Asia that are projected to emerge as the two of the three largest economies of the world with their rapid growth in the next three-four decades, JACIK is likely to be the centre of gravity of the world economy. The Table 3, highlights the possible welfare gains from Economic Integration in JACIK countries. It has shown that a trade liberalisation in the framework of an RTA in JACIK could produce efficiency gains worth US $ 147 billions. However, with investment liberalization and mobility of skilled

TABLE 3

Welfare Gains from Economic Integration in JACIK Countries

	Estimated Welfare Gains in US $ Million		
	Scenario I (Trade Liberalisation)	*Scenario II (Trade and Investment Liberalisation)*	*Scenario III (Trade, Investment and Mobility of Skilled Workers)*
Japan	107626	111807	150695
Korea	13043	13317	14076
China-HK	6327	7100	16328
ASEAN (5)	13451	13553	19405
India	6971	7379	9937
JACIK	147418	153156	210441
Rest of the world	-27293	-45306	109916
World	120125	107849	320357

Source: RIS Simulations, see Mohanty *et al.* (2004) for details.

manpower, the gains from integration add up to US $ 210 billion indicating more than 3 per cent of combined GDP of the JACIK economies. What is more, all the JACIK economies benefit from integration. Moreover, the welfare of even the rest of the world also improves by US $ 109 billion in the scenario III, suggesting that Asian economic integration will be Pareto Optimal. Further more, the creation of a regional institutional infrastructure to mobilize even a moderate proportion of the region's considerable savings of about US $ 2 trillion for an investment in creation of regional public goods such as transport infrastructure, gas and oil pipelines, satellites and broad cables, has the potential to generate additional output and welfare effects that could add up hundreds of billions of dollars in view of substantial underutilized capacity in Japan, Korea and other Asian countries in engineering and construction industry. In view of the above, there is a strong case for ASEAN-Japan-China-India and Korea working together to realize the Asian dream of building broad functional Economic Integration.

REGIONAL INTEGRATION—IS IT A FEASIBLE PROPOSITION FOR THE WHOLE ASIAN REGION?

It is held by many that a regional integration is not a feasible proposition for the whole Asian region under the existing circumstances. It has been argued that in view of vast population in the region, its cultural, economic and political diversities, in past and present, it is very difficult to work out a successful integration in Asia. The less-developed countries of the Asian region, have, therefore, been warned against being hypnotized by the success of the EU. The regional co-operation of Western European countries had produced beneficial results, because these countries were industrially advanced, and the economic integration helped them in further division of labour and specialization, standardization and reallocation of resources. But, for the poor and primary producing Asian countries, there does not exist even a remote chance of achieving any gains through an economic integration. It may, therefore, be suggested that these and other 'LDC' countries should instead explore possibilities of effecting co-ordination in economic development programming, projection and execution. Instead of wasting their energies and efforts on tariff and other commercial aspects of foreign trade, these backward countries should concentrate on mutual co-operation for development and up liftment. And, once economic advancement has been attained a full fledged economic union through a common market may follow. But in the present juncture, there is a great risk in this regard.

Further, the welding together of two or more unstable economies makes the task of achieving stability and growth more difficult. A monetary imbalance and inconvertibility in these countries is not very compatible with a regional free trade policy. It requires the creation of some sophisticated monetary device like that of EPU/EU. Further more, most of the countries in Asia swear by the ideals of Socialism/ Religion and resort to severe governmental restrictions and controls, which necessarily implies that their customs union should be accompanied not only by the integration of their national economic programmes but also methods of intervention. Unless this is achieved, no regional co-operation will succeed. And to achieve this is next to impossible under the existing circumstances.

Despite all these difficulties, we may, however, opine that initially some steps are necessary to have regional economic co-operation of some kind to some degrees in Asian continent, since this is the need of the hour as has become evident form the deliberations in the recently held various international/global summits. A sort of regional integration of LDCs would definitely help in solving many of their unsolved problems at international level.

Difficulties may creep in while initiating steps for such a regional co-operation, but where there are difficulties; there should be solutions, too. Even though such steps may result in failures, it is better to make attempts in some form or the other rather than not at all. Because no a priori judgment should be accepted as true without experimentation.

CONCULDING OBSERVATIONS

From the above, we can say that there is a great interest in Asia to build on growing functional economic integration and emerging web of FTAs linking ASEAN and its summit-level dialogue partners, namely, Japan, China, India and South Korea or JACIK into an east Asian community which could eventually grow into broader Asian economic community. There is a strong case for ASEAN-Japan-China-India and Korea working together to realize the Asian dream, although troubled Sino-Japanese relations, as well as the Sino-Taiwanese and Korean non-reconciliation could still cloud the Asian horizon.

Asia and especially East Asia like Europe would symbolically need a D-day type ceremony and reconciliation to erase the painful memories of the last war and bury the awful past altogether. This appears to be the overriding strategic goal of the current increasing economic integration. But who could organize it and where? There is no Asian Chirac or an Asian Normandy for such a setting. Reconciliation indeed sadly remains elusive in Asia, although it is undoubtedly an aspirations for millions of Asians; this despite the accelerating trend of Asian economic integration. But hopes still remain. The most important strategic goal in Asian economic integration, probably with the JACIK as core, would be reconciliation and peace in Asia, at a moment when US strategic goals and influence are on a decline in the region, and when Asians themselves want to be more 'balanced' in their own relations with Washington. Asian regionalism would undoubtedly rise with increased economic integration and regionalism; infact, strategic political, social and cultural enmeshment is now poised to accelerate for China, India, Japan, the Koreas and ASEAN, as they reconcile, co-operate and partner each other to form the Asian economic community one day.

References

Agarwala, Ramgopal (2004), "Reserve Bank of Asia: An Institutional Framework for Regional and Monetary Co-operation in Asia" in

Agarwala, Ramgopal (2004), "Reserve Bank of Asia: An Institutional Framework for Regional and Monetary Co-operation in Asia" in Nagesh Kumar (ed), *Towards an Asian Economic Community: Vision of a New Asia'*, RIS and ISEAS: New Delhi and Singapore, 177-203.

——— (2002), "Towards an Asian Economic Community: Monetary and Financial Co-operation", *RIS Discussion Paper No. 33*, New Delhi.

Alatas, Ali (2001), "ASEAN Plus Three", *Equals Peace Plus Prosperity No. 2*, Institute of South-East Asian Studies, Singapore.

Asher Mukul, G. and Rahul Sen (2005), "India-East Asia Integration: A Win-Win for Asia", *Economic and Political Weekly*, Vol. XL, No. 36.

Bonapare, Tiziana (2005), "Regional Trade and Investment Architecture in Asia-Pacific Emerging Trends and Imperatives", *Economic and Political Weekly*, Vol. XL, No. 36.

Frank Andre Gunder (2004), *Reoriented: Economic Globalisation in Asian Age*, September.

Kumar, Nagesh (2005), "A Broader Asian Community and a Possible Roadmap", *Economic and Political Weekly*, Vol. XL, No. 36.

Miltani, D.M. (1999), *International Economics*, Himalaya Publishing House, Delhi.

Sarma A. and P.K. Mehta (2002), Exploring Indo-ASEAN Economic Partnership in Globalising World, *Bookwell*, New Delhi.

Shankar, Vineeta (2004), "Towards an Asian Economic Community: Exploring the Past" in Nagesh Kumar (ed); *Towards an Asian Economic Community: Vision of a New Asia*, RIS and ISEAS, New Delhi and Singapore, 13-42.

Shinawatra, Thaksin (2001), "Asian Cooperation Dialogue", Speech Delivered in New Delhi on Nov. 28 2001, *Excerpted in RIS Digest*, Dec. 2001.

Teo Eric, Chu Cheow (2005), "Strategic Relevance of Asian Economic Integration", *Economic and Political Weekly*, Vol. XL, No. 36.

Wei, Li (2004), "A Road to Common Prosperity: Relevance of an FTA between India and China, in Nagesh Kumar (ed), *Towards an Asian Economic Community: Vision of a New Asia*, RIS and ISEAS: New Delhi and Singapore, 75-90.

World Trade Organisation (2004), *International Trade Statistics, 2004*; WTO, Geneva.

Yao, Chao Cheng (2005), "China's Role in the Asian Economic Unification Process", *Economic and Political Weekly*, Vol. XL, No. 36.

Agenda for Asian Economic Integration

Problems and Prospects

AMALESH BANERJEE

I. INTRODUCTION

Asian economy is in doldrums. Conflicting forces are at work; some forces are trying for integration while others are harping on division. Inspite of these conflicting aspects there are some common threads that should lend stronger and firmer ground for Asian people unlike Europe, Asia is consisted of countries experiencing diverse level of economic growth. In post-Colonial period Asian countries recorded significant advance and have come now at the frontal battle with European and United States under the banner of W.T.O. Commodity trade, capital flow monetary relation and labour movement and fight against poverty are some central issues which are making strong pull for integration rather than the divisive forces of political game and power demonstration. Regional Associations notwithstanding the economic integration among Asian nations, are thwarted by two reasons: capitalists design and hegemorcy and the political squabble of the some stooges of capitalist power. The greater is the chances of integration and cooperation among Asian nations the larger will be in the interest of the majority of Asian people who are poor and under privileged. India has an important role in Asian unification not only as a regional power but also in the economic and political interest of her own. So instead of being confined in SAARC, India should launch a Pan-Asian hegemonic cooperation for Asian integration. This paper presents briefly in the next section the diversity of Asian nations both in respect of past and present economic and political background. Section III is devoted to the existing regional economic cooperations and their strength and potentiality. Section IV seeks to emphasis on the possible commodity cartel among Asian nations. Section V deals with the central banking and financial relations in the Asian background. Sections VI explains WTOs role and Asian trade relation. Section VII puts the agenda for further integration to combat poverty. Section VIII emphasizes on Indian's role vis-à-vis China. Section IX presents the conclusions.

II. ASIAN DIVERSITY

Asian diverse economic and political map is rewarding to remember. Large part of South and South East Asian countries were under colonial rule which has practically shaped their economics and the life. European colonial powers in the South and South East Asian countries have changed their production base as well as their life and culture. The Gulf countries are exclusively oriented by oil market which has a global ramification.

Global political game largely *veer* around oil production and export. Although they are Asian nations, Gulf oil producing countries are tied up with the USA and UK, i.e. with world capitalist countries. The former socialist countries of Asia are a separate group. With vast natural resources, these former socialist countries are trying to attain high rate of growth. Japan is a class by itself. It has been exerting tremendous pressure on the neighbouring countries of Asia. Japan has gripped the USA market on the one side, and it is extending its network of trade in Asian markets on the other side. Asian socialist bloc comprises China, North Korea,

Vietnam. Economic might is now strongest in the South-East Asian Countries. Two other blocs in Asia are the Association of South East Asian Nations (ASEAN) and the South Asian Association for Regional Cooperation (SAARC).

Economically and Politically these nations are wide apart, while China is experiencing highest rate of growth, Japan has been experiencing low rate of growth in recent years. The consistent high rate of growth of the Chinese economy was comparable to the high rate of growth of Thailand, Singapore and some other South-East Asian countries.

The most phenomenal aspect is the political system of the Asian Nations. While the Gulf countries have a fundamentalist base, their oil economies are controlled by foreign multinationals. Gulf World has therefore restricted freedom, particularly for Women. Central Asian republics have emerged in the democratic system only recently. Socialist blocs have dominant political system which is not like that of Western democracy. South Asian countries including India have strong democrat base.

The implications of these diverse political structure for integration of Asian economy are strong and intractable. Since the political objectives determine the economic inter-action, the diverse political framework hardly leave any scope for deeper economic cooperation. Even then there are scope for common agenda for economic integration among Asian nations. To these, we shall turn in the last section.

III. REGIONAL COOPERATIONS

Inspite of these basic structural limitations, cooperation among the Asian nations began to develop over decades step by step since Non-Aligned conference in *Bundung*. Although it is a political platform, NAM has laid a sound basis for cooperation among Asian-African nations.

Pure economic cooperation among the Asian countries began with the formation of Association of South-East Asian Nation (ASEAN) and the South Asian Association for Regional Cooperation (SAARC). Although limited in scale, SAARC and ASEAN have began to gather momentum over last two decades. SAARC has now stepped in the regime of free trade. The SAARC Free Trade Area has opened the door of closer economic interaction and trade relation among the members of this bloc (Bangladesh, India, Nepal, Sri Lanka, Bhutan, Pakistan and Maldives) and ASEAN members have also developed Asean Free Trade Area.

The interaction between these two blocks have began on a multilateral and bi-lateral basis. SAARC is gradually consolidating. The free trade agreement among the SAARC countries has become operational and the major SAARC nations are negotiating on the list of items of trade and the tariff waiver principles. But the international trade relation of SAARC countries indicate that more than sixty per cent export of these countries go to USA and EU countries and around 35 per cent of their imports are from those countries; only 20 per cent Exports of India, Pakistan and Nepal go to Asian countries and about 25 per cent of their imports are from Asian countries. Intra-SAARC and intra-ASEAN trade is limited; to around, 20 per cent of total world export in case of ASEAN and only 4 per cent in case of SAARC in 2000. SAARC process is slower and weaker than that of ASEAN. SAARC has targeted 2020 for customs Union, which is long way off. Compared to that intra-ASEAN trade is stronger in volume and variety.

China's entry into the WTO has violently affected the regional balance in the South and East Asian Combination. There are two pronged changes: (a) both ASEAN and SAARC countries are trying to woo the Asian as well as world's biggest country, China and bilateral trade relations are developing. (b) new formations of trade and economic relations are developing among nations including China. As for India a slow understanding of economic relation is developing with China, Singapore and Thailand, Bangladesh, and Myanmar. Thailand and Singapore have developed a combine (BIMSTEC), beside the ASEAN had developed a number of ASEAN+relations. There are a number of Preferential Trade Agreements (PTA) such as ASEAN+ China Comprehensive Economic Partnership, ASEAN+India Comprehensive Economic Cooperation, ASEAN+Japan Comprehensive Economic Cooperation, ASEAN+Korea

Comprehensive Cooperation Partnership. Thus by 2005 more then a dozen Preferential Trade Agreements (PTA) have developed involving the Asia-Pacific countries including Australia, New Zealand, Japan, Korea, Singapore, Mexico, Pakistan and Sri Lanka. This over-last five or six years a complex web of interesting bilateral, regional and plurilateral trade agreements have developed in the Asia-Pacific region. What had developed initially as regional economic cooperation has now developed into a completely intra-regional agreements in trade and other fields. Asian economic integration is yielding place to bilateral and opportunistic alliances.

IV. COMMODITY CARTEL

Economic integration may start from (a) production level integration, (b) from financial integration, (c) trade integration, (d) factor market integration, (e) deliberate government agenda against issue like poverty, natural calamities like tsumani, earth quake and (f) defence preparedness. Here we take a few of these channels of integration.

We can remember that fifty years ago European Economic Union started its journey from the agreement on steel. Arcelor-Mittal integration shows that continental integration of production units is a growing phenomeaon is the modern corporate world. If European Steel consortium provided the initial spurt on European Economic union similarly a number of commodity agreement at Asian level may heep the economic integration among many Asian states. Tea, Jute, Oil and Gas, energy are some common items for which production cartel is possible. OPEC has provided a platform for oil producting countries of Gulf World and it has developed a strong bargaining counter with oil buyers.

Recently the effort of the government of India to develop the Iran-Pakistan India pipeline and the Kazakhstan Indian agreement on oil will strengthen the economic integration on specific issues. The recent ASEAN + Comprehensive cooperation and partnership is an important step towards the economic integration in East Asian segments. In fact the ASEAN is a step ahead in the integration process of Asian economy.

Energy sector has wide scope for cooperation, Bangladesh can supply gas to India which has unmet demand for gas, in exchange India can supply hydroper to Bangladesh. There is a strong possibility of integration around production and distribution of energy among the SAARC countries. South Asia has close proximity to Persian Gulf as well central Asia, Both regions being rich in natural gas, Iran possess 15 per cent of the World's gas reserves. Thus, Bangladesh can easily develop in a closenet grid of production and distribution of energy. Similarly there is a strong possibility of cooperation between Nepal, Bhutan, India and Bangladesh as regards hydro electricity. Cooperation may also develop in respect of renewable and non-conventional energy source such as biomass, solar energy. Thus energy cooperation may lead to investment cooperation among nations. This a dormant area. It requires a bold attempt to jointly cultivate natural resources for increased production and employment of the region.

V. FINANCIAL INTEGRATION

Global financial integration has been moving at a rapid pace since the close of World War II. Marshall Plan, IMF structural adjustment programme, World Bank and International Development Assistance, Asian Development Bank and other public financial institutions have been extensively providing financial assistance of reconstruction and economic development of many states-developing and developed. Till sixties global financial network was more or less confined to official assistance. Beginning with oil shocks of sixties, domonitisation of gold global financial market has pushed-up by leaps and bounds and Euro-dollar and petro-dollar emerged in volume. At that stage the multinational Banks leading and debt-trap of the developing nations have become the most sorbid phenomen in late seventies.

Private capital flow in Asian countries at this stage provided strong support for emergence of the Asian Tigers. The flow of new finance capital and the sustained growth of

Tiger countries of Asia have been cited as the new phenomen of Asian integration. This is largely the flow of European and Japanese Capital in Asia and the phase of external capital supported growth of east and South-East Asian countries began. This phases of Asian growth buffeted by export and external capital and multinationals come to a half by East Asian crisis. The irrational upsurge of finance capital and the weakness of domestic production and banking institutions have been the catalytic of East Asian catestrophe. Concentration of finance capital in Asia are in Jakarta, Singapore and Tokeyo. This financial integration of Asia needs to be rationalized in the interest of development of the Asian people.

The Asian regional blocs could not develop any sound financial grid. ASEAN is still under the strong net of finance capital and the monetary coordination among the South-East Asian counties is weak and fragile. Equally SAARC could not yet build-up the financial bull work particularly because smaller SAARC counties like Bangladesh, Nepal are dollarised. A small beginning has been made in SAARC sumit held in Colombo. It was decided to establish a Network of Central Bank and Finance Ministries of the SAARC region. SAARC FINANCE held its second meeting in April 1999. Except staff exchange and seminars noting, substantial about financial flow and monetary policy has yet to be developed even after 25 years of SAARC operation since 1981.

Financial integration of Asian Countries can be strengthened through (a) Central Bank linkage, (b) state level financial assistance, (c) foreign direct investment, (d) exchange rate agreement, (e) the creation of Central Reserve Pool, and (f) creation of common currency. In fact none of these channels are working at present at Asian level. Although there have been banking crisis in South-east Asian countries and in Japan, there was no Asian remedial guideline, the global stand such as Basel-I and Basel-II are stated to be the universal gride lines. Even then the Central Banks of India Japan, China, Singapore, Thailand and South Korea can follow certain guideline so that banks in Asia are not subjected to global web of capital movement. Central banks can follow certain norms for observing the bottom line of money supply, interest rate and inflation. The state level assistance among the Asian at large or regional block level is another channel of monetary flow and monetary integration. Rich states of Asia can assists the poor states in large or regional block level is another channel of monetary flow and monetary integration. Rich states of Asia can assist the poor states in large volume.

FDI Foreign direct assistance in Asian countries is a strong channel of integration of course among the relatively richer states. As it appears in 2002, three recipients (People's Republic of China (PRC), Hong Kong and Singapore) account for 80 per cent FDI. PRC having 57.7 per cent of total FDI to Asian developing counties has only 4-3 ratio of GDP. India's FDI share is .07 per cent and that of Kazakhistan is 10.5 per cent. It appears that FDI is Asia is concentrated only in a few countries whereas small and poor nations are deprived. Liberalization has not made India any more attractive to FDI than the earlier period. However the contribution FDI to the growth of the economy is positive and particularly related to the export sector.

As in China, India is also creating special economic zones in order to attract FDI. In fact FDI inflow in both ASEAN and the SAARC countries is very limited. Recently, ASEAN has instituted ASEAN Investment Area (AIA) in order to attract larger investment in that area. It has taken extra measures for investment cooperation, investment promotion and investment liberalization.

Reserve Pool

Yet another device of monetary unification is the creation of Reserve Pool of foreign exchange of the major countries of Asia. In 2003, the gross external reserve (in US $ million) of China was 4.3, Hog Kong 118, Korean Republic 135, Taipei 207, Singapore 96, Thailand 42, India 107. the reserve pool may be utilized for development of infrastructure or other development activities which may result in further development. This developed pool is a source of investment fund.

Common Currency

Finally one step is the formation of Common Currency for the Asian Countries. At least six or seven leading Asian nation may come to an agreement to form a common currency. This could have been started at a small stage by SAARC. SAARC and the ASEAN countries can thresh out a common currency which will reduce hedge cost of exchange and confusion to the traders. European monetary union and Euro have been evolved in this way step by step. Monetary Integration of Asian nation may proceed step by step and the first step in this reaction is the understanding on the issues like money supply, exchange rate and inflation.

Exchange Rate

Among the monetary tools of cooperation among nations the exchange rate is an important tools, exchanges agreements different phase has strength end the monetary union Europe. In Asian perspective, at least at regional level of SAARC no exchange rate agreement could reached at as yet. This is because the weak currencies of smaller nations are largely aligned with dollar, and the stronger countries have separate denominated dollar currency. Singapore, Hong Kong have their special demoniated dollar. At least the major Asian nations like India, Singapore, Thailand, South-Korea can attempt an exchange rate agreement.

VI. WTO DISINTIGRATION

That W.T.O. multilateral trade machanism is failing to work as an integrating forum. It is now clear that W.T.O. regime is an advance country hegemony. It has neither enhanced investment flow not could apply uniform lowering of tariff for agricultural products. Integration among Asian nations through the W.T.O. trade channel is not possible. Therefore bilateral and preferential trade agreements have multiplied. W.T.O. insistence on Trade Related Investment Measures (TRIMs), and Trade Related Aspects of Intellectual Property (TRIPs) have practically isolated most of Asian, African and Latin American countries. The failure at Doha is a trump for Asia, because it has united the many Asian nations to resist the global trade being controlled by rich nations. G-20 group has been successful in extracting an agreement to eliminate all forms of export subsides within a credible time frame. Thus trade negotiation under W.T.O. was hardly conducive for integration of Asian economy except through indirect resistance to the W.T.O. framework.

VII. ELIMINATION OF HUNGER-AGENDA FOR ASIAN INTEGRATION

Against the cries—cross aspect of Asian integration stated above at least one common agenda can be conceived for united action of Asian nations. It is the robust programme of Human Development the programme of elimination of Hunger. Inspite of the rapid progress that the Asian nations have achieve the continent still remains as the home of hungry people. Asian nations can take this common agenda for actions with all the resource at their disposal. Foreign exchange reserves are polled for commercial expension. But this can be utilized side by side, for reduction of poverty, hunger and diseases. As the UND 2005 observed, the greatest challenge facing the world is the challenge of meeting the millennium development Goals. While the economic growth remains the main objective of the countries, it must have pro-poor growth strategy. Hunger and good security has to be the first step of that growth strategy. Asian nations can seat over a sessions, like another Bundung, to vow for elimination of Hunger. Food stock and distribution has to be the number one goal for which the Asian nations must Wage War. The become the order of development, Asia, which is most affected in this respect, should be united to eliminate this crime committed by society.

VIII. LEADERSHIP—INDIA *VIS-A-VIS* CHINA

Who can give the leadership for integration of Asia? Is it the capitalist and corporate power or the people's power? We have seen the two types of integration process. The so-called Asian miracle tigers and the consolidation of corporate finance is the one process and the other is the alternative agenda for the development of Asian people. The out come of the first course is divergence, differentiation and distortion. To give leadership to the agenda for integration we proposed, the country on the one hand, must have democratic values and hand have attained high standard of human development and equity. While India has the democratic power she lags behind China in respect of human development India must rapidly progress towards human development with high standard of economic power and human development, India can provide leadership in the task of integration of Asia around the agenda of elimination of hunger and poverty.

The market socialism of china is making rapid progress in respect of economic growth and social welfare. But democracy of India is faltering due to low growth rate and low human development. India should have a greater rapport with Asian nations so that her avowed democratic values and pro-poor development strategy can provide leadership for Asian economic integration.

IX. CONCLUSION

Asian countries have diverse experience with colonial past. Different countries of Asia are now in different regional blocs which are not set in any direct destination. Economic growth buffeted by finance capital has not been able to eliminate hunger and poverty from Asia. Integration of finance capital and monetary integration alone can hardly enhance welfare of Asian people. A pro-poor development strategy based on democratic values is the right agenda for Asian development. India is better suited for leadership in Asian integration than China although her market socialism has produced better result both in respect of economic growth and human development. To fulfil this historic task of Asian integration leadership, India must make rapid growth both in respect of physical achievement as well as human welfare.

References

Asian Development Bank (2004), *Outlook 2004,* Oxford University Press.,

Bhagawati, Jagdish, D. Greenaway and A. Panagariya (1998), "Trading Preferentially: Theory and Policy" *Economics Journal*, Vol. 108.

Dasgupta, Biplab (2005), *Globalisation: India's Adjustment Experience*, Sage Publication, New Delhi.

Feridhanusityawam Tubagus (2005), "Preferential Trade Agreements in Asia Pacific Region", *IMF Working Paper*, IMF

Frankel, Jeffrey A. (1997), "Regional Trade Block in The World Economic System", *Institute of International Economics.*

Government of India, (2004), *Economic Survey*, 2004-05, *Ministry of Finances*, Government of India.

Gulati, A. and Kelly, Tin (2001), *Trade Liberalization and Indian Agriculture*, Oxford University Press, New Delhi.

Gupta, K.R. (2003), *A Study of World Trade Organization*, Atlantic Publishers, New Delhi.

Hanna, N. (1994), *Exploiting Information Technology for Development*, World Bank, Washington D.C.

Jumar, N. (2003), "Intellectual Property Rights, Technology and Economic Development: Experiences of Asian Countries", *Economic and Political Weekly*, No. 3, January 18.

Krumm, Kathie and Himi Kharas (ed.) (2004), *East Asia Integrates: A Trade Policy Agenda for Shared Growth.*

Rajan, Ramkrishen (2002), "Liberalization of Financial Services in South-East Asia under the ASEAN Framework Agreement on Services (AFAS)", Centre for International Economic Studies (CIES) *Discussion Paper No. 0226* (University of Adelaide).

Rao, C. Murthy M. and K. Ranganathan (1999), Foreign Direct Invest (FDI) in the Post-liberalization Period: An Overview. *Journal of Indian School of Political Economy*, July-Sept.

Rao, C.H. Hanumantha (2001), "WTO and Viability of Indian Agriculture", *Economic and Political Weekly*, No. 30, September 8-14.

S. Collay, Robert and John Gilbert (2001), *New Rigional Trading Agreement in the Asia Pacific*? Washington: Institute for International Economics.

Schiff, Maurice and L. Alan Winters (2003), *Regional Integration and Development World Bank*, Oxford University Press.

Srinivasan, T.N. (1999), *Global Trading System, the WTO and the Developing Countries*, National Council of Applied Economic Research, New Delhi.

Srinivasan, T.N., Suresh, D. Tendulkar (2000), *Reintegrating India with the World Economy*, Oxford University Press.

United Nations (2005), *Human Development Report 2005*, Oxford University Press.

Wadhava Charan D., (1994), *Economic Reform in India and the Market Economy*, Allied Publishers Ltd., New Delhi.

World Bank (1999), *World Development Report*, 2000-2001.

World Development Report, 2003.

Asian Economic Integration
Issues and Challenges

Krishan K. Kaushik and Kurt K. Klein

INTRODUCTION

"My vision for Asia and the Pacific in the 21st century,—a vision of a region free of poverty—diverse yet united, well integrated within itself and with global economy, and contributing profoundly to the ongoing process of humankind (Haruhiko Kuroda, 2005)."

Economic integration has been the dream of the Asia for many years. Over the recent past, there has been a flurry of regional cooperation activity, including negotiations towards the creation of bilateral, plurilateral, and region-to-region free trade areas. Global economic integration is an unstoppable process that is sweeping aside states, national cultures, and other barriers. It does not simply mean price arbitrage. Market integration encompasses the convergence across regions: production technologies; menus of diverse

* Speech by President (ADB) at the Emerging Market Forum, Oxford, UK, 10th December 2005.

varieties of goods and services; the prices and costs of each variety; and basic contestability conditions for new or cheaper technologies and varieties (Richardson and Parson, 2004).

Asia has once again become the most dynamic growth center in the world economy. Japan is recovering from a decade-long economic stagnation, China is booming and dynamically transforming itself to an open market economy, India is also growing by pursuing liberalization and structural reforms, and other countries in the region are, by and large, demonstrating their strong buoyancy that was severely tested by the Asian crisis of 1997-98. With the overall recovery, economies in Asia are integrating at a fast pace through private sector-led activities such as trade, foreign direct investment and financial flows.

The idea for Asian economic integration is dependent on several aspects. The first is to stabilize intra-Asian bilateral exchange rates by following a unified currency peg to a common basket of trade-related exchange rates. This is pertinent in the case of countries having somewhat diversified export destinations that do not provide obvious single major global currencies (the Dollar, the Euro and the Yen) against which to peg. The second aspect of economic integration is the setting-up of a number of bilateral swap arrangements among regional central banks to further the arrangements made available by the International Monetary Fund. The third aspect of regional financial integration is the strengthening of economic and financial surveillance and exchange of information between agents and events. The fourth aspect of monetary cooperation is the provision of regional public goods and the setting-up of a regional bond market.

The recent push for Asian economic integration is a direct consequence of the Asian economic crisis in 1997. Rising regionalism has become a global phenomenon as nations around the world have used this strategy to respond to global challenges and developments. They integrate their economies because they do not want to lose out in the global competition for export markets and foreign direct investments. A number of proposals for financial and monetary integration have been suggested by government officials, academic researchers and business elites to forestall the disastrous outcomes caused by the Asian crisis. But times are changing. Since the Asian crisis of 1997-1999, East Asian governments have become quite active participants in the global regionalism zeitgeist, with many proposals for preferential trading arrangements (PTA) between countries in the region (e.g., Japan-Korea, Singapore-Japan); between countries and sub regions in Asia (e.g., China –ASEAN); and with countries outside Asia (e.g., ASEAN-CER, Singapore-US).

The Asian governments have embarked on various initiatives for "institutional cooperation" to support market driven integration. First, the region's trade officials have been working relentlessly to forge closer ties through free trade agreements (FTAs). Second, the Chiang Mai Initiative (CMI) has been taken as a framework for regional financial and monetary cooperation by the region's finance officials. Among these, currency union and regional financial schemes such as the Asian Monetary Fund (AMF) have also been established. Third, infrastructural officials have put significant efforts into construction of cross border infrastructure with regulatory coordination. Fourth, leaders of ASEAN countries, China, Japan and South Korea are making efforts to accelerate the process of establishing a common market. In November 2002, the ASEAN leaders decided to study the idea of an "ASEAN Economic Community" (AEC) by 2020.

The idea of an "Economic Community" among the ASEAN countries is evocative and conjures-up the image of the European Economic Community (EEC) experience. EEC was born of small group of very different countries. Market integration happened in some European sectors than in others. The European Coal and Steel Community (ECSC), set-up in 1952, accounted to a sectoral experiment in more institutionally centralized and substantially deeper market integration. The largest continental economies extended the ECSC institutional framework into a general common market in the EEC in 1958. To the social fund was added a promise realized in the 1960s, of a much larger payoff to farmers (under the Common Agricultural Policy). The other major development was the EEC's European Court of Justice. Within this framework the EEC achieved full customs union in the early 1970s. The 1980s and 1990s brought the addition of monetary cooperation and later monetary union. The inauguration of the Euro on January 1, 1999 continued the evolutionary process of almost 50 years that started with the coal and steel company in 1951. The Euro zone will promote regional financial integration, growth, and stability in Europe (Letiche, 2000).

The questions that generally crop-up in debate on Asia's regional economic integration are: (i) how far are Asian countries prepared to go in their endeavors towards regional integration? (ii) How far Asia satisfies the economic feasibility criteria of framing an Asian currency union? (iii) Does Europe's experience provide any guidance to get a common currency in Asia? With this background the present paper is an attempt to seek answers to some of the questions from the theoretical and empirical literature.

ISSUES

How far are Asian Countries Prepared to go in their Endeavors Towards Regional Integration?

The countries in Asia are probably more diverse than any regional grouping across the globe. Asian countries differ historically, economically, socially and culturally. The differences within Asia are not only evident in comparisons across time. They also show-up in comparisons across countries and regions. Initially, all 15 European Union countries were technically developed and had somewhat common backgrounds, especially with the frequent wars throughout the centuries. Asia, on the other hand, features developed "dynamic Asian economies"; middle-income developing countries; and least-developed countries. The coefficient of variation on income levels within ASEAN is three times that of countries in the European Union. Economic integration initiatives are far more complicated and risky in such an environment.

The patterns of integration in Europe and Asia are sensitive and dependent upon contextual factors. Even controlling for differences in the structure of the world economy as have evolved over the past half century, it remains clear that the countries of Europe and of Asia remain contextually specific, that the problems they face are in many ways unique, and that the solutions that would fit within an existing institutional framework are highly idiosyncratic (Jones and Plummer, 2004).

Using integration theory to explain the policy-making process, it is argued that the approach of liberal inter-governmentalism, which looks at member countries as key actors and supra-national institutions as peripheral, is inadequate for many areas. Neo-functionalism is needed for a fuller understanding of context and of the relationships between agents and events. New institutionalism appreciates that institutions themselves can become significant actors, developing their own motivation (Holland, 2002). The main hurdles facing Asian nations are their uneven bargaining power within Asia and the hegemony under *Pax Britanica and Pax Americana.*

The Asian *status quo* today is altogether different from the origins of integration in Europe. First, the contemporary global market place is much more open. The WTO rounds have led to an immense reduction in trade barriers and to huge increases in foreign direct investments (FDIs). This suggests that the price of using regional integration as a form of "fortress", that is, to maximize trade diversion, are consequently much higher than they were in the past, as separating the regional economy from the global production chain has become too pricy.

Economic interdependence among countries has been growing. Looking at East Asia, for example, the intra-regional trade has grown from less than 35 per cent of total trade in 1980 to 54 per cent in 2004. This is higher than the 46 per cent intra-regional trade in the NAFTA region and is in line with intra-regional trade in the EU before the 1992 Maastricht treaty. During 2003 Japan exported more to "greater China" than to the United States. Japanese firms sent cars, computer chips, televisions and other goods worth 13.7 trillion yen west to mainland China, Hong Kong, and Taiwan in 2003, and only 13.6 trillion yen worth of goods east to America (Gresser, 2004). Since intra-regional trade is growing even small intra-regional trade exchange rate misalignments can perturb trade. This indicates the need for intra-regional exchange rate stabilization or a unified currency. Market-driven financial integration has also been underway as a result of the increased deregulation of the financial system, opening of financial services to foreign institutions, and liberalization of the capital account in Asia (Kawai, 2005).

Asia's current advantage is its pairing of China's low labor and land costs with the wealth and technology of its neighbors. The traditional framework for regional monetary unification analysis is provided by the Optimum Currency Area (OCA) theory which is based on the assumption that exchange rate flexibility will absorb negative effects of shocks that effect the demand for exports of a country (Mundell, 1961). Moreover, Frankel and Rose (1996,) showed that trade is an endogenous variable and countries are more likely to satisfy the (OCA) criteria *ex-post* than *ex-ante*. The elimination of exchange rate risks and volatility would decrease transaction costs and uncertainty, which is likely to increase trade among these countries. All of these initiatives are critical to strengthening the financial systems in these countries, building the region's resilience and mitigating the risks of future financial crises. An Asian union has some powerful competitive strength. The challenge is how to manage that integration process to ensure that it will be smooth, equitable and inclusive. The potential of an economically integrated Asia is huge and the one thing that is needed most is to exert leadership to tap this vast reservoir of opportunities.

How far Asia Meets the Economic Feasibility Criteria of Framing an Asian Currency Union?

The evolution of the Euro zone and increasing openness of East Asian economies have drawn greater attention from economic analysts to the potential of an Asian currency union (Bayoumi and Eichengreen,1999) and what could be done with respect to monetary and exchange rate policy at the regional level (McKinnon, 2000; Kwan,1998). In May 2000, the finance ministers of ASEAN and China, Japan and the Republic of Korea (10+3 countries) agreed through Chiang Mai Initiative to plan for closer monetary and financial integration. In order to strengthen the self-help and support mechanisms in East Asia through the ASEAN+3 framework, a need to establish a regional financing arrangement to supplement the existing international facilities has been recognised. As a start, it has been agreed to strengthen the existing cooperative frameworks among the monetary authorities through the "Chiang Mai Initiative." The Initiative involves an expanded ASEAN Swap Arrangement that would include all ASEAN countries, and a network of bilateral swap and repurchase agreement facilities among ASEAN countries, China, Japan and the Republic of Korea. It is important to assess the economic feasibility of framing an Asian currency union that is organized around some well-known theoretical and empirical literature on an Optimum Currency Area (OCA).

Theoretical and empirical literature on monetary integration revolves around the elimination of national currencies and their replacement with a common currency and the likely impact on the economies that give-up their currencies and independent monetary policies. The adoption of a common currency leads to an increase in the number of economic agents using the currency as a medium of exchange. The degree of optimality of currency area is determined by the structural characteristics of member countries and whether the benefits of currency union outweigh costs. While costs are essentially related to the loss of an important macro-economic policy instruments for adjusting to asymmetric shocks, benefits mainly concern potential gains in economic efficiency, the majority of which derive from elimination of exchange rate risks that facilitates trade among the countries. The argument runs as follows: transaction costs, and more importantly currency risks, constitute a barrier to trade and dampens trade that would otherwise take place. Price differences in member countries tend to become more transparent with monetary integration, leading to healthy competition that increases production efficiency.

An optimum currency area is an economic area composed of countries affected systematically by shocks and within which labor and other factors of production flow freely. The literature on optimum currency theory deals at length with the debate on whether or not a common currency zone is plausible (Mundell, 1961; McKinnon, 1963; Tavlas, 1993). The criteria involve factor mobility, trade integration, and similarity of the regional production pattern. First, there should be a commitment to fix the exchange rate with a credible mechanism of adjustment. Second, there should be an establishment of tight monetary arrangements. Third, the national currency should be replaced by the common currency. However, as outlined earlier, bilateral trade agreements among countries are making the process more attractive. Additionally, trade can be encouraged through fixing the exchange rates credibly (Saxena, 2005).

Recent empirical work has lent support to the argument that stable exchange rates encourage trade (Eichengreen and Irwin, 1995; Frankel and Rose, 2002). Asian history is also instructive in this regard. Japan's policy of pegging the yen to the US dollar from the late 1940s until the early 1970s contributed to the country's emergence as a major export power house (McKinnon *et al.*, 1997). The East Asian economic miracle (in part) is due to the commitment of Asian governments to peg their exchange rates at a competitive level. More recently, China's rapid growth is partly a result of China's exchange rate being pegged to the US dollar.

If potential members of a union trade a lot with each other, currency union would reduce transaction costs. More recently, competitive real exchange rates and stable nominal exchange rates have been seen as conducive to growth. Although growth may appear to be faster (even recently) in Asian countries that peg their exchange rates, this pattern may be an artifact of survivor bias (Moreno, 2001). The argument is that the regional economies should be concerned with the stability of exchange rate vis-à-vis one another and not just with respect to the G-3 (Germany, Japan and the U.S.) countries. These concerns were taken notice of when instability in Thailand's baht quickly infected the entire region. Another factor was that trade among the crisis countries was not large.

Trade has been growing over time, which may give this argument more power in the future than in the past (Kwai and Motonishi, 2004). By themselves, countries within ASEAN do not trade much with each other nor do countries within the newly industrialised economies (NIEs). By taking (NIE) countries with China, about 40 per cent of trade was intraregional in 2003, up from 20 per cent in 1980. When Japan is included, more than 50 per cent of trade is intra regional. Taking south Asia, this percentage increases further. This is fairly comparable to the more than 60 per cent intra-regional trade within the European Union.

According to the so-called optimum currency theory, the need for independent monetary policy control, is greater when member countries are exposed to different shocks and lesser when they are exposed to the same or similar shocks. One factor that minimizes the probability of various shocks is high trade integration among member countries. If the countries experience similar shocks, the cost of giving-up monetary policy independence would decrease. Most supporting evidence for the possibility of monetary union comes from observing the correlation of demand and supply shocks for a country willing to join a currency union. It is argued that nations experiencing positive correlated economic shocks are better suited for a currency union because it permits the utilization of union-wide policies to check imbalances (Ng, 2002).

Kwack (2004) assessed the economic feasibility of forming a regional currency block Asia on the basis of theoretical and empirical literature on optimum currency areas. Zhang *et al.* (2004) applied Blanchard-Quah methodology to identify demand and supply shocks from movements in prices and output. The findings suggest of high correlation of demand and supply shocks, though the same was not true in the case of two largest economies (Japan and China). Zhang's analysis suggests that the correlations are more or less similar to those across Europe in the early 1990s (see Bayomi and Eichengreen, 1994). It is also believed that the adoption of a monetary union can lead to more trade integration which, in turn, increases the cross-correlations.

The adjustment to a single monetary policy for a region is easier if the countries in the region have been pursuing relatively similar monetary policies. Another way to look at whether countries in Asia have a similar monetary policy is to look at the correlation of their interest and inflation rates. High (low) correlations across Asian countries means that it may be easy (difficult) to form a currency union that will result in a common interest rate for the whole region.

Saxena's (2004) study using a structural vector auto regression model to estimate the relationship between supply and demand shocks in the south Asian region. Her results confirm that about 50 per cent of the supply shocks (including those in India, Pakistan and Sri Lanka) and 80 per cent of the demand shocks are positive. The speed of adjustment to both kinds of shocks is very fast and most of the adjustment takes place within two years. Hence the loss of policy autonomy would impose a low cost in the South Asian Association for Regional Cooperation (SAARC) region if these countries choose to adopt a common currency. Rose and Engel (2002) found that members of international currency unions tend to experience more trade, less volatile exchange rates, and more synchronized business cycles than do countries that use their own currencies.

Lastly, it is believed that, as in Europe, there is a strong political advantage for the economic integration of Asian countries. The constant disruptive battles between India and Pakistan are a source of instability for the region and combating terrorism has been an unproductive use of resources for India. Once these nations can give-up their political motives and start to think of themselves as a part of the economic integration, it could help bring peace and prosperity.

Does Europe's Experience Provide any Guidance for a Common Currency in Asia?

The European Monetary System (EMS) provides a precedent, and the recently negotiated Chiang Mai Initiative (CMI) provides the requisite mechanism. Though Asia may succeed towards satisfying the optimum currency areas (OPA) criteria, Asian countries will remain very different historically and culturally from each other. This makes it difficult, if not impossible, to follow the European path. Four discrepancies between Asian and European countries stand out.

First, the Asian road to monetary union is long and working towards a common currency is a huge challenge. It implies structural reforms and real convergence among the economies involved. Asian economies differ a lot in terms of income levels, stages of development, and economic structure. However, recent developments offer some cause for optimism. Since 1992, the Greater Mekong Sub-region Economic Cooperation Program has shown the benefits that cooperation can bring in spite of obstacles. The six countries that share the Mekong River—Cambodia, People's Republic of China, Lao People's Democratic Republic, Myanmar, Thailand, and Vietnam—are together reaping the benefits of increased connectivity, competitiveness, and a greater sense of community than would have been possible two decades ago.

Second, in Europe the commitment to collective currency pegs was strong and credible as intra-European trade is so extensive. Intra-Asian trade remains less important by comparison despite the fact that it is growing. Much of the increase in trade within East Asia reflects intra-industry trade in parts, components, semi-finished products and finished goods as multinational companies diversify their operations and create production networks across the region. But the fact of the matter is that 50 per cent of the intra-regional trade is in raw materials and intermediate components that ultimately are exported outside. Asia's situation is, if anything, even more difficult than Europe's (Williamson, 1999).

Third, the two regions differ in terms of interest in political integration. Throughout its existence, the European Monetary System was supported either by capital controls (before 1992) or by a fixed timetable for completing the transition to currency union (after 1992). Above all, the EMS was buttressed by the set of interlocking political, economic, and financial commitments that make what is now known as the European Union. The European project was girded by a commitment to political integration, which was driven by France and Germany. The devaluation of the French franc and revaluation of the Deutsche mark that followed galvanized both France and Germany to agree in principle to economic and monetary union. In contrast to Europe, more than half a century after the end of World War II, Asia does not have regional institutions to devise cooperative economic policies and promote regional stability (Stevenson, 2004). Clearly, the same preconditions are missing in Asia. Little appetite for political integration is apparent because of wide variations among nations in terms of political systems, culture and history.

The fourth discrepancy is that, in contrast to Europe, Asia has little craving for the re-imposition of controls, China and Malaysia to the contrary notwithstanding. Rather governments find that financial liberalization is the best way to solve their financial problems. This lends support to the hypothesis that controls may become more difficult to operate in the future. In Asia, sovereignty concerns have left governments reluctant to delegate significant authority to super-national bodies, at least so far. Having ruled out all other options, the conclusion is that most Asian countries will move towards floating currencies. As Dutta (2003) noted at length, the question of monetary union in Asia has become a popular one since the Asian crisis and especially in light of the successful launch of the Euro.

There exists several studies in the literature which attempt to address the question of whether or not some sort of Asian currency area would be optimal, often using the experience of monetary union in Europe as a yardstick. Perhaps the most comprehensive works on the subject thus far have been undertaken by Bayoumi and Eichengreen (1999), Bayoumi, Eichengreen and Mauro (1999), and Bayoumi and Mauro (2001). A variety of indicators have been used in line with the OCA literature, from analysis of intra-regional trade to association of aggregate supply shocks, to compare the EU prior to Maastricht and Asia/ASEAN today. Thus, the body of work undertaken by Bayoumi and Eichengreen, Bayoumi, Eichengreen and Maura and Bayoumi and Mauro suggests that, in general, Asia comes about as close to meeting OCA criteria as Europe did. However, it is argued that historically the essential preconditions for a durable regional monetary arrangements depend critically on politics rather than economics (Plummer, 2002).

These foregoing discrepancies nevertheless imply that even when the final destination is similar, there are multiple routes to legitimate market integration, routes that depend on the challenges and pressures faced by the integrating units. Overall, despite discrepancies, we think the EU case sketches a fairly robust common profile for the regulatory- institutional frameworks in which successful market integration can be politically sustained.

CHALLENGES

Regional arrangements divide the Asian region into two classes: those that can integrate into regional and global markets and those with currency regimes that have little potential for integration. Conventional wisdom in the west is that emergence of an Asian Union is full of challenges. The economic divergences and asymmetries are too large—the historical divisions too sharp. Diversity and heterogeneity imply that low income countries—where market infrastructure is inadequately developed and institutional capacities are limited—will be slow in trade, investment, financial liberalization, and market opening, and hence, will not be able to integrate quickly with the rest of Asia. This constitutes an obvious impediment to economic integration for the whole of Asia. There is no monetary hegemony like Germany in Europe or the US in the western hemisphere. Japan runs chronic trade surpluses so the yen is not in such wide circulation as the major current international currencies (the United States Dollar and the Euro).

Governments and business elites who have initiated the deepening of Asian economic integration have two major challenges: designing the ancillary thresholds for business regulation that are the needed props to making an Asian single market sustainable, and steering the political-diplomatic mechanisms that help Asia transition from a traditional development regime of national economic polities and priorities to a regime of regionally well managed economic interdependence (Richardson and Parsons, 2004).

The Asian region desires to maintain openness to the rest of the world—particularly North America and Europe, which are important as markets for final products as well as sources of risk capital and innovative ideas. The Asian region must continue to embrace the WTO as a global institution that can reduce cross-bloc impediments to trade and investment flows. It is in the best interest of Asia to regard the WTO principles as the basic infrastructure for international trade rules and achieve trade and investment liberalization by going beyond the commitments under the WTO.

Similarly, the region needs to complement the IMF by ensuring regional financial stability, without which global financial stability cannot be achieved. At the same time, Asia must make efforts to increase its voice in these global institutions for global economic management. Asian countries are also diverse in political systems and in cultural and religious traditions, without shared history of political integration under a hegemonic power. As a result, establishment of a common value, mutual belief or strong political will for economic assimilation is one of Asia's most challenging issues. Monetary union cannot solve all of the economic challenges, in particular those concerning the urgent need to reduce the high level of structural unemployment.

National governments are responsible for carrying out the required structural reforms. In particular, the benefits of carefully prepared integration into the global financial system outweigh the risks. But we should also draw a lesson from the recent crises in emerging markets that in some cases, there was clearly overly-rapid capital account liberalization. Coping safely with volatile international capital flows requires sound domestic financial systems, adequate supervision, prudential regulation, and good risk management capacities in banks and businesses, reinforced by greater transparency and market discipline.

We do not suggest that the European experience is a model that Asia can and should copy. Regional developments in Asia should be driven by its own political dynamics and unique historical background. But trading patterns and geography do make it reasonable to think of the creation of an internal market in Asia as possible, future stage in regional cooperation. And why should this not be a basis for greater monetary integration, if that is what the people of Asia desire?

CONCLUSION

Asia's history and present circumstances—the diversity among its countries, its dependence on extra-regional trade, its political diversity, its lack of strong collective institutions, and its capital mobility—imply that exchange rate stabilization and monetary integration are not easily achievable in the near future. But, there is evidence of growing intra-regional trade and financial cooperation in the region along with the increase in the size of the existing swaps under the Chiang Mai Initiatives with the economic surveillance process by monitoring economic developments in the region. Asian economic integration has been real and deep, comparable to that of Europe, and largely market-driven. But the institutional support to such assimilation has been limited. Certainly, it will not come easily. It has been very rightly said "before any great dream is realized, lots of small obstacles must be dealt with."

In this sense, Asia has great prospects for further economic integration through various types of institutional cooperation. These include: creation of an Asia-wide Free Trade Agreement, development of stronger devices for regional financial stability, increasing stability of intra-regional exchange rates, and provision of various types of regional public goods, all of which would be a basis for a future "East Asian Community." Due to the differences in political and economic systems, the pace of institutional cooperation for Asian economic integration may be sluggish. For this reason, its configuration ought to be flexible and open until a stronger political and economic convergence is achieved.

For the time being, market-driven integration continues to intensify and the region can still gain much by pursuing institutional cooperation to a maximum extent in all key areas, namely, trade and investment, money and finance, and regional public goods. If there are enduring lessons from Europe for Asia, they lie in the area of process and not in the application of specific policies or institutions. Lastly, the idea of creating a single currency in Asia may appear far-fetched and improbable at this point, but it can help to articulate a long-run strategy for regional economic integration.

REFERENCES

Bayoumi, T. and Eichengreen, B. (1994), One Money or Many? "Analyzing the Prospects for Monetary Unification in Various Parts of the World", *Princeton Studies in International Finance*, No. 76.

Bayoumi, T. and Eichengreen, B. (1999), "Is Asia an Optimum Currency Area? Can it Become One?" Regional, Global, and Historical Perspectives on Monetary Relations in S. Collilgnon, J. Pisani-Ferry, and Y.C. Park (eds.), *Exchange Rate Policies in Emerging Asian Countries London*, New York: Routledge, pp. 347-367.

Bayoumi, T. and P. Mauro, (2001), "The Suitability of ASEAN for a Regional Currency Agreement", *World Economy*, Vol. 24. p. 944.

Bayoumi, T., Eichengreen, B. and P. Mauro (1999), On Regional Monetary Arrangements for ASEAN Prepared for the ADB/CEPII/KIEP Conference on Exchange Rate Regimes in Emerging Economies, Tokyo, 17-19 December.

Dutta, M. (2003), "EU and The Euro Revolution: The Theory of Optimum Currency Area Revisited" (John Hopkins University SAIA-Bologna Working Paper.

Eichengreen, B. and Irwin D. (1995), Trade Blocks, Currency Blocks and the Reorientation of Trade in the 1930s. *Journal of International Economics* Vol. 38, pp. 1-24.

Frankel, J. and Rose, A. (1996), "The Endogeneity of the Optimum Currency Area Criteria", *NBER Working Paper*, 7857.

Frankel, J. and Rose, A. (2000), "Is EMU more Justifiable Ex-post than Ex-Ante"? *European Economic Review*, Vol. 41, pp. 753-760.

Frankel, J. and Rose, A. (2001), "Estimating the Effect of Currency Unions on Trade and Output", NBER 7857.

Frankel, J. and Rose, A. (2002), "An Estimate of the Effect of Currency Unions on Trade and Growth", *Quarterly Journal of Economics*, Vol. 20, pp. 437-466.

Gresser, E. (2004), "The Emerging Asian Union: China Trade, Asian Investment, and a New Competitive Challenge", htpp:/ www.chinabusinessreview.com/public/0407/gresser.html

Holland, M. (2002), "The European Union and the Third World", London: Palgrave Macmillan.

Jones, E. and Plummer, G.M. (2004), "EU-Asia: Links and Lessons", *Journal of Asian Economics*, Vol. 14, pp. 829-842.

Kawai, M. and Motonishi, T. (2004), "Is East Asia an Optimum Currency Area?" Paper delivered at the conference on Financial Interdependence and Exchange Rate Regimes in *East Asia sponsored by the Japan Ministry of Finance Policy Research Institute*, December 2-3, 2004. htpp://www.mof.go.jp/english/soken/kiep2005/ kiep2005_04.pdf

Kawai, M. (2005), "East Asian Economic Regionalism: Progress and Challenges", *Journal of Asian Economics*, Vol. 16, pp. 29-55.

Kwack, S.Y. (2004), "An Optimum Currency Area in East Asia: Feasibility, Coordination, and Leadership Role", *Journal of Asian Economics*, Vol. 15, pp. 153-169.

Letiche, J.M. (2000), "Lessons from the Euro Zone for the East Asian Economies", *Journal of Asian Economics*, Vol. 11, pp. 276-300.

McKinnon, R. (1963), "Optimum Currency Areas", *American Economic Review*, Vol. 53, pp. 717-724.

McKinnon, R. Kenichi, O. and Kazuko, S. (1997), "The Syndrome of the Ever-Higher Yen, 1971-95: American Mercantile Pressure on Japanese Monetary Policy", *SIEPR Policy Paper 487*. Stanford University, Stanford, Calif.

Moreno, R. (2001), "Pegging and Macro-economic Performance in East Asia", *ASEAN Economic Bulletin*, Vol. 18, pp. 48-62.

Mundell, R. (1961), "The Theory of Optimum Currency Areas", *American Economic Review*, Vol. 51, pp. 657-665.

Ng, Thiam Hee (2002), "Should the Southeast Asian Countries form a Currency Union?" *The Developing Economics*, Vol. 15, pp. 113-134.

Plummer, M.G. (2002), "The EU and ASEAN: Real Links and Lessons in Financial Integration", *The World Economy*, Vol. 25, pp. 1469-1500.

Richardson, D.J. and Parson, C. (2004), "Lessons for Asia? European Experiences—in American Perspective—in Legitimizing Market Integration", *Journal of Asian Economics*, Vol. 14, pp. 885-907.

Rose, A. and Engel, C. (2002), "Currency Unions and International Integration", *Journal of Money, Credit and Banking*, Vol. 34, pp. 1067-1089.

Saxena, S.C. (2005), "Can South Asia adopt a Common Currency?" *Journal of Asian Economics*, Vol. 16, pp. 635-662.

Stevenson, A.E. (2004), "Regional Financial Cooperation in Asia", *Journal of Asian Economics*, Vol. 15, pp. 837-841.

Tavlas, G.S. (1993), "The 'new' theory of optimum currency areas", *World Economy*, Vol. 16, pp. 663-685.

Williamson, J. (1998), "Crawling Bands or Monitoring Bands: How to Manage Exchange Rates in a World of Capital Mobility", *International Finance*, Vol. 1, pp. 59-80.

Zhang, Z.K.S. and Michael, M. (2004), "Is a Monetary Union Feasible for East Asia?" *Applied Economics* Vol. 36, pp. 1031-1043.

Asian Economic Integration
An Emerging Sub-Paradigm in Regional Groupings

V.N. Attri

INTRODUCTION

Over the last two centuries the nature and scope of Economics has been constantly changing. Though, the fundamental questions to be solved and determined with an economy still remain the same. Yet the economic issues at the turn of the century cannot be analyzed and solved with 'micro' and 'macro' considerations. The development of 'Science and Technology' along with social-political factors has been a key sources of paradigm(s) shift in Economics.

In the present paper, our attempt has been to analyze the major developments in Economics of Regional Grouping at theoretical as well as empirical level in terms of theory of paradigms shift(s) as propounded by Kuhn's theory of paradigm-shift and Lakatosian alternative approach known as Methodology of Scientific Research Programme (MSRP) since the publication of Viner's Theory of Custom Unions (1950). After making in depth study of some of the major developments of classical, Neo-classical; Keynesian; and Post-

Keynesian Economics, we feel that a synthesis of the first two approaches i.e. classical and neoclassical gives us a better insight for analysis of Regional Groupings.

For most of the time in Economic History of the different nations, we find an emphasis on the rules and regulations that were related with the promotion of "free-trade." The classical Economists believed that "Free trade is the best policy" as it leads to the optimum allocation of the world's resources. Despite all this, projectionists' policies were also developed and introduced by different countries and in different periods of time keeping in view economic, political and social conditions.

The basic economic issues have been, till recently, largely analyzed and solved by 'micro' and 'macro' economic considerations within national perspective. International Trade, though being in limelight since the publication of Adam Smith's, "Wealth of Nations" (1776) could not be effective in turning the different national-economies into an International Economy, mainly because of the slow and insufficient progress of "Science and Technology." This becomes evident in the discussion of "Stationary State" among the classical economists. Their advocacy of free trade as the best policy could not be pursued in continuity due to certain political and economic constraints and also because of the upsurge of Neo-Classical Paradigm which shifted the emphasis of economic science to micro analysis as a consequence of marginal revolution in 1871.

However, during 1990's, these issues are being resolved in the light of international perspective which has come into existence due to liberalization and globalization of the world economy. The rise of new paradigms in economics and sub-paradigms in the theory of International Economy is better understood, if we discuss briefly the theory of paradigm-shift in Kuhnian and Lakatosian sense.

PARADIGM AND THEORY OF PARADIGM SHIFTS

According to Thomas Kuhn, a paradigm can be' defined in its generally accepted connotation as a disciplinary matrix, "disciplinary" adopted for the industrialization of the economy. Later on, several empirical and theoretical studies in 1950s, 1960s and 1970s have proved that outward orientation of the economy leads to 'efficient' industrialization. That implies that International Trade, when integrated with the domestic economy provides several 'Direct' and 'Indirect' gains. After World War Second, GATT through "Multi-lateralism" tried to expand and promote International Trade. It (GATT), through article XXIV allowed for the establishment of free trade areas and custom unions, which is the second-best policy. This initiated the beginning of Regional Trading Blocs. A vast literature on the study on Regional Trading Blocs suggests an emergence of new paradigm(s) in theory of International Economy, especially Bhagwati's (1991) concepts of "Building Blocs", and "Stumbling Blocs." If a trading block happens to be a "Building Bloc" then it will be improving the welfare, even maximizing it by moving on the dynamic time-path; and also ensuring world-wide non-discriminatory trade-liberalization.

Regional Trading Blocs are also expected to solve the economic problems of 21st century such as eradicating poverty and discrimination, promoting economic prosperity and ensuring sustainable economic development, by adopting "International Perspective" which gets strengthened through Regional Trading Blocs.

Because it refers to the common possession of the practitioners of a particular discipline, "Matrix", because it is composed of ordered elements of various sorts each requiring further specification[1] though he also identifies a broader, sociological use for the term in which it stands for the entire constellation of beliefs, values, techniques and so on, shared by the members of a given community.[2]

When, a science fails to solve the contemporary problems or queries with the help of existing paradigm, then there is a crisis in a science, and paradigm switch or 'shifts' in the paradigm(s) take place which gets explained with the 'Copernican' and 'Newtonian' paradigms in Physics. But, Kuhn's theory of scientific revolution and his concept of paradigm has been severely criticised as being ill-defined and inapplicable to most of the scientific disciplines—particularly to social sciences like Economics.

Imre Lakatos suggested an alternative approach to Kuhn's concept of paradigm, known as Methodology of Scientific Research Programmes (MSRP) which interprets the history of science in terms of a continuous competition between alternative research programmes rather than as a succession of conjectures and refutations on one hand, or total paradigm-switches on the others.[3]

Later, Kuhn, by rectifying his stand on 'paradigm-switch as being independent and discontinuous, came nearer to Lakatos in accepting continuity and inter-dependence among different paradigm(s) which explain the evolution or development of an idea or theory or group of ideas and theories in science discipline. Therefore, in our analysis, we will apply the 'mix' of the two approaches to explain the evolution of different paradigm(s) in economics in general and International economies in particular with reference to regional-groups (Trading-blocs).

1. Major Paradigm Shifts in Economics

J.A. Schumpeter in his book, "History of Economic Analysis", has divided the developments in Economics in four major paradigms i.e. Classical, Neo-classical, Keynesian, and Post Keynesian/Modern. Even within these major paradigms there can be various 'schools' such as Austrian Schools, Stockholm, Cambridge and Chicago Schools and several others. Similarly the term 'evolution' has been used for certain developments in economics, the "marginal revolution", the imperfect competition revolution, 'Keynesian revolution' etc. These terms were coined well before T.S. Kuhn, therefore, there are no strong reasons to presume that our revolutions are of the Kuhnian class. Not elaborating on the issue, it is essential to point out that the different paradigms in economics cannot be treated independent of each other and that successive paradigm-switch generally took 15-20 years period for preparation for the acceptance of new paradigm. For example, the preparations for marginal revolution and neo-classical economics, went on in 1850s and the 1860s which was a period of relative prosperity for the British economy and also for British economic thought. Ricardian views on value and distribution came under heavy criticism, whereas his analysis of the benefits of International trade and Monetary Policy with bias in favour of free market economy, which he had inherited from Adam Smith, still dominated orthodox economic thinking. The practitioners of Economic Science in Britain and elsewhere in Europe began to provide alternative theories or explanation for the determination of value and distribution. With the publications of the works of Jevons (1871); Menger (1871); and Walras (1874), the so-called marginal revolution which involved a wide-ranging transformation of the characteristic methodology of analytical economics by means of what was essentially a mathematical tool derived from the Calculus, came into existence and this provided new tools of analysis as well as new ideas such as 'utility', 'equilibrium' etc. for solving the problems associated with, value and distribution. Not totally rejecting the classical paradigm, the neo-classical paradigm provided better and comprehensive explanations on value and distribution. Jevons (1876) in the preface of his book, "The Future of Political Economy" stated "The problems of value and distribution which had preoccupied the Ricardians were solved, or more accurately, one might say swept under the carpet, by simple process of definition. The problems of growth were outside the effective range of marginal analysis and further problems of growth consideration of them was consciously postponed."

The above statement indicates that neo-classical paradigm by postponing the problems associated with growth, concentrated on micro economic problems of resource-allocation and optimization and the determination of price-output under different market-forms became the focal point.

The developments during 1914-1919 and thereafter enriched Keynes vision of his excellent work, "The General Theory of Employment, Interest and Money (1936). Again, socio-political and economic compulsions were responsible for the movement towards Keynesian-paradigm. The Great depression of 1930s was strong enough to shake the economists' belief in the fundamental assumption of full-employment. As a consequence of this, pendulum again swung in favour of macro-economics; determining output employment and income in the short-run in a closed economy framework which is essentially static. During 1950s and 1960s, the post World War II developments compelled the economists to think in terms of economic growth which led to a more viable formal synthesis of neo-Walrasian and Keynesian economics-leading to the rise of post-Keynesian or modern paradigm, building macro-superstructures on neo-classical (rather neo Walrasian) micro foundations as well as several neo-classical growth models.

In these neo-classical growth-model; the role of money and technology have been incorporated. Solow (1956) in his model with money, shows that equilibrium growth rates are lower than real economy because savings may not be equal to Investment due to positive balance effect. The marriage between neo-classical and post-Keynesian schools has given birth to several theoretical controversies. Not only this, it has also contributed to the revival of Marxian economics which forms the part of assumptions determining growth and distribution; in addition to Keynes and Ricardian assumption.

In early 1970s the oil-price hikes and 1980s the international debt problem created 'bubbles' in the World Economy which were not soluble within the existing paradigm and specializations like Open-Macro Economics, International Economic Policy Coordination etc. came into existence. Such developments brought the need to focus the solution of economic problems of 1980s and 1990s, which was being faced by the national economies as well as in the world economy with an international perspective rather than in terms of 'micro' and 'macro' outlook.

The three fundamental questions of economics (i.e. what to produce; how to produce; and for whom to produce) can be optimally decided only by focusing on International perspective. This perspective has acquired its place of dominance in economic thinking in 21st Century due to fast and unimaginable developments in science and technology which has reduced the distance; and also increased the mobility of labour and capital. As a consequence of this, the basic assumption(s) of International Trade theories have undergone a sea-change which have led to the emergence of various new paradigms in international Economy.

The above brief account of major paradigm shifts in economics can be explained in terms of socio-political and économic compulsions and developments in Science and Technology in contemporary world. Apart from this, 'situational determinism' also explains a greater part of the evolution of different 'schools' or 'paradigm'. In our opinion in the next 15 years or so the nature and scope or economics may change completely if man succeeds in commercializing the moon-then we might enter into an inter-planetary era; greatly or absolutely changing the present situation.

2. Policy of Free Trade and Emergence of Regionalism

If we analyze the economic history during the classical and neo classical periods; and particularly during the period 1790-1870, we find that free trade legislations have been framed all over the Europe, based on the classical thinking that free trade is the best policy as it increases the welfare of all the trading partners through efficient allocation of resources. During the period 1870-1930, due to rise in marginalism, nationalistic attitude and World War I, protectionist pressures got strengthened and consequently the policy of free trade was abandoned. In the years of First and Second World Wars, there was deterioration in the Volume and value of world trade. After the end of World War II, efforts were made to promote International Trade through GATT. The 1950s and 1960s the golden-periods for International Trade in which it increased many-fold in volume and value through "Multi-lateralism." The GATT, through article XXIV, allowed for the establishment of free trade areas and customs unions which combine free trade with protectionism as they lower the tariffs within the union; and establish a joint outer tariff-wall on the rest of the countries. This is known as the second-best policy. Is there any, conflict between the two? Whether they 'converge' or 'diverge'—these are the issues which need explanation. And for this, first, let LIS discuss the theoretical basis of regional groupings. The subject has been very extensively analyzed in economic literature in recent years; the prominent studies being that of J. Viner (1953),[4] J.E. Meade (1955).[5] Jagdish Bhagwati (1968),[6] (1991[7] and 1993[8]) Summers Lawrence

(1991);[9] T.N. Srinivasan (1993),[10] Gene Grossman and Elhanau Helpman (1995);[11] Arvind Panagariya (1995);[12] and Jagdish Bhagwati and Panagariya (1996).[13]

These studies have analysed almost every aspect related with regionalism beginning from Viner's 'Trade-creation' and 'Trade-Diversion' to Bhagwati's (1991) concepts of "Building Blocks" and "Stumbling Blocks." If trading blocks happen to be "Building Blocks" or having positive trade creation effect (trade creation-trade-diversion) then these blocks will be improving the welfare, even maximizing it by moving on the dynamic time path and also ensuring world-wide non-discriminatory trade-liberalization.

Wilfred J. Ethier (1998)[14] following the non-Vinerian analytical approach to regional integration suggests a relationship between regionalism and multilateralism. He opines that the relationship can be explained by the following these points:

- The new regionalism is, in good part, a direct result of the success of multilateral liberalisation.
- Regionalism is the means by which new countries bring to enter the multilateral system (and in small countries already in it) compete among themselves for the direct investment necessary for their successful participation in that system.
- Regionalism—by internalising an important externality—plays a key role in expanding and presenting the liberal trade order.

Trading Blocs also strengthen free-trade by reducing labour-rigidities through free labour-movements across the member-countries and also ensures less or restricted occurrence of financial-crisis, if these blocs succeed in having single currency. Bhagwati points out that the greatest danger to free trade comes from labour-rigidities but in case of custom unions this danger is reduced, if not fully eliminated, by ensuring free movement of labour.

In addition to this, when each trading bloc will be having a single currency, then instead of having a tripartite monetary agreement among the U.S., Japan and Germany; we would be able to have a multipartite monetary agreement which will be more "effective" in dealing with the problems arising out of monetary-management. This, in our opinion, will strengthen the IMF's ability to maintain and sustain the International Financial System which is at present collapsing under its own burden.

This leads to the conclusion that better supervision and prudent financial policies are needed to provide stability to the international financial system. When financial crisis become frequent (as it is happening in case of East Asian countries and Russia) because of the lack of coordination among the different sectors of the financial system; it leads to fall in the growth rates due to undesirable effects on the real economies—a point emphasized in Solow's model of economic growth (with money). This illustration confirms our opinion that in Economics past paradigams never become irrelevant. It depends on the skill of the economists/policy-makers to arrange a perfect marriage between the two, 'so that, the new emerging 'paradigm' or 'school' may be able to solve the contemporary economic problems in a more convincing way.

The financial stability in future can be attained through better governance, transparency and fighting with corruption. In our opinion, these three points need to incorporated in the 'hard-core' of Economics for developing models for sustainable and environment-friendly growth in this age of globalization. Wherein regionalism, capital-flows, MNCs etc. are becoming increasingly important in the growth process of an economy. As such the new theories/models are being developed by the Economists to meet the requirement of International Economy and this is being done in the light of latest developments in science and technology. This, again makes us believe that in the coming 21st century 'International Perspective' needs to be emphasized for solving the economic issues at national as well as global level.

CHARACTERISTICS OF ECONOMIC PARADIGM OF 21st CENTURY

The present paradigm is different in shape from the

earlier "classical paradigm", some economists have given it the name of "Neo-neo-classical paradigm."

Though it is too early to name it. In our opinion the economic paradigm of 21st century is essentially going to be related to the following main Issues:

(i) To establish an ever-more-open global trading system to eradicate the poverty prevailing in the developing economies.
(ii) To safeguard the lives and livelihoods the health and the safety of families around the world.
(iii) To improve the environment and working conditions of the workers all over the world.
(iv) To minimize the labour-rigidity so that the forces strengthening a promoting free-trade can be restored.
(v) To develop the world economy by tapping the full potential of the Information Age.
(vi) To achieve higher and faster rate of economic growth through the governments that are open, honest, and fair in their practices.
(vii) To evolve mechanism that minimize uncertainties regarding future.

The above-mentioned issues can be settled and solved to a greater extent if we promote free-trade across the world. The growing realization that trade benefits all is leading the negotiators to complete the process of formation of free-trade area(s) in all the continents i.e. Americas, Asia, Africa, and Europe etc. The growth of regionalism (new) is becoming essential as it creates a framework for different region-wide free-trade system, encourages fundamental reforms; promotes labour standards; promotes sound environmental programms and ensures financial liberalization. In a sense, regional-integration is moving the world towards Market Economy through governments' initiative and imagination.

Therefore, it can be concluded that new insight(s) in regional trade integration are helping the economists as well as policy-makers in preserving and strengthening of liberal trade order, democracy, promoting prosperity through economic integration; eradicating poverty and discrimination; and ensuring sustainable development and conservation of environment for the prosperity. Hence in our opinion, adoption of "International Perspective" having the elements of good governance, transparency and corruption-free system is becoming inevitable for the solution of the economic problems of 21st century.

MULTILATERALISM *VS.* REGIONALISM

In the post-World War II period many nations have pursued the objective of trade liberalization. One device used to achieve this was the GATT and its successor, the WTO. Although the GATT began with less than 50 member countries, the WTO claimed 149 members by 2006. Since GATT and WTO agreements commit all member nations to reduce trade barriers simultaneously, it is sometimes referred to as a *multilateral* approach to trade liberalization.

An alternative method used many countries to achieve trade liberalization includes the formation of preferential trade arrangements, free trade areas, customs unions and common markets. Since many of these agreements involve geographically contiguous countries, these methods are sometimes referred to as a *regional* approach to trade liberalization.

The key question of interest concerning the formation of preferential trade arrangements is whether these arrangements are a good thing. If so, under what conditions. If not, why not.

One reason supporters of free trade may support regional trade arrangements is because they are seen to represent movements towards free trade. Indeed, Section 24 of the original GATT allows signatory countries to form free trade agreements and customs unions despite the fact that preferential agreements violate the principle of non-discrimination. When a free trade area or customs union is formed between two or more WTO member countries, they agree to lower their tariffs to zero between each other but will maintain their tariffs against other WTO countries. Thus, the free trade area represents discriminatory policies.

Presumably the reason these agreements are tolerated within the WTO is because they represent significant commitments to free trade, which is another fundamental goal of the WTO.

However, there is also some concern among economists that regional trade agreements may make it more difficult, rather than easier, to achieve the ultimate objective of global free trade.

The fear is that although regional trade agreements will liberalize trade among its member countries, the arrangements may also increase incentives to raise protectionist trade barriers against countries outside the area. The logic here is that the larger the regional trade area, relative to the size of the world market, the larger will be that region's market power in trade. The more market power, the higher would be the region's optimal tariffs and export taxes. Thus, the regional approach to trade liberalization could lead to the formation of large "trade blocs" which trade freely among members but choke off trade with the rest of the world. For this reason some economists have argued that the multilateral approach to trade liberalization, represented by the trade liberalization agreements in successive WTO rounds, is more likely to achieve global free trade than the regional or preferential approach.

Here we present the economic argument regarding trade diversion and trade creation. These concepts are used to distinguish between the effects of free trade area or customs union formation that may be beneficial from those that are detrimental. As mentioned above, preferential trade arrangements are often supported because they represent a movement in the direction of free trade. If free trade is economically the most efficient policy, it would seem to follow that any movement towards free trade should be beneficial in terms of economic efficiency. It turns out that this conclusion is wrong. Even if free trade is most efficient, it is not true that a step in that direction necessarily raises economic efficiency. Whether a preferential trade arrangement raises a country's welfare and raises economic efficiency depends on the extent to which the arrangement causes trade diversion versus trade creation.

EVOLUTION OF ASSOCIATION OF SOUTH-EAST ASIAN NATIONS (ASEAN)

When the East Asian Financial Crisis broke out in July 1997, many people thought the South-East Asian countries would retreat into isolationism and protectionism-ending ASEAN's vision of regional economic integration. The opposite happened.

Even at the height of the crisis, in December 1997, ASEAN leaders had spelled out their vision of an integrated ASEAN economy in the first two decades of the new century. As their ASEAN Vision 2020 put it, the leaders committed themselves to "closer cohesion and economic integration." The Declaration reads: "We will create a stable, prosperous and highly competitive ASEAN Economic Region in which there is a free flow of goods, services and investments, a free flow of capital, equitable economic development, reduced poverty and socio-economic disparities."

And ASEAN did not restrict itself to long-term plans. At their Summit Meeting in Ha Noi in December 1998, the ASEAN heads of state and of government issued a "Statement of Bold Measures"—bold in that these measures met head-on the crisis that was still raging. Without waiting for the financial storm to clear, they decided to accelerate ASEAN's programmes to liberalise trade and investment and to integrate the region's economies. The measures also moved forward the programmes to make South-East Asia a free-trade area from the then 2003 target date to 2002—so that, even now, most of the goods traded in the region enjoy tariffs of no more than 5 per cent. ASEAN also reaffirmed its goal of extending the free-trade concept to include services, and scheduled a round of negotiations on this. It called for the continued implementation of the ASEAN Industrial Cooperation scheme, under which the products produced by and traded between at least two ASEAN companies would be given a preferential tariff of 5 per cent or less. It even waived the 30 per cent national equity requirement for firms participating in the scheme if they apply by the end of 2000. (This deadline has been subsequently extended to the end of 2001.)

The ASEAN leaders also called for accelerating the realisation of an ASEAN Investment Area, in which investments are to flow freely in most sectors. They gave political impetus to ASEAN's programme for developing infrastructure linkages among its members, including the Trans-ASEAN Gas Pipeline Network and the ASEAN Power Grid.

Meanwhile, the ASEAN finance ministers set-up a "collective surveillance process" that would conduct periodic "peer reviews" of the economies of member countries, to ensure the transparency of monetary and fiscal conditions throughout the region. Periodic analyses of macro-economic trends in the region would raise early-warning signals of any recurrence of the sudden, massive and simultaneous pullout of foreign portfolio capital that caused the Asian crisis.

Evolution ASEAN's path to economic integration has evolved over the years. The very first sentence of the "Bangkok Declaration", which set-up the organisation in 1967, spoke of "mutual interests and common problems among countries in Southeast Asia" and called for a "firm foundation for common action to promote regional cooperation." Economic cooperation at the time dealt with programmes for joint ventures and complementation schemes among ASEAN governments or companies, such as the 1976 ASEAN Industrial Projects plan, the 1981 ASEAN Industrial Complementation scheme, and the 1983 ASEAN Industrial Joint Venture Programme.

In the 1980s and 1990s, though, countries all over the world began to dismantle the economic barriers they had set-up from the 1950s to the 1970s. The protectionist economic-development model—of a country shielding its enterprises from foreign competition—had, in most cases, resulted only in inefficiency and underdevelopment. As the phenomenal growth of several Asian nations showed, a country's calculated opening to competition and international markets is the best path to development in our time. What is more, the acceleration of technological developments facilitated—and made inevitable—the flow of people, capital, goods, and services around the world-making isolationism anachronistic and even impossible.

Because of their geographic proximity and their roughly similar level of development, the ASEAN countries realised that the best way for them to cooperate for their development would be to open-up their economies to one another, and eventually to integrate them. Indeed, all over the world, the forces of globalisation and the increasingly rapid advances in technology have been impelling nations to coalesce in various combinations. They have to coalesce to be competitive in today's world-to enlarge their markets, attract investments, cut costs, increase efficiency, improve productivity and thus generate jobs and raise people's incomes.

The most important move towards this new model was made at the Fourth ASEAN Summit in 1992, at which member countries agreed to create the ASEAN Free Trade Area. A market of close to half a billion people would allow corporations in ASEAN to take advantage of economies of scale. They would also have access to the best prices for the raw materials they require, even as competition among them would stimulate their productivity and efficiency. An integrated ASEAN economy would be a potent attraction for investors outside the region—who generally prefer large, integrated and efficient markets to small, fragmented and inefficient ones.

Rather than derailing ASEAN's programme for an integrated region, the Asian crisis may have been a blessing in disguise. ASEAN's growing closeness in the past decade meant that one country's problems affected the others with increasing and accelerated impact. That message was driven home by the Asian financial crisis, which some called the "Asian contagion" for the way it moved swiftly from one country to another to engulf the whole region. But the closeness of the ASEAN countries' economies cannot be reversed; nor can isolationism be an option in an era of irreversible globalisation. The Asian crisis, therefore, has made ASEAN move closer together still—towards the ultimate goal of economic integration.

Through the years ASEAN has taken a number of important decisions to achieve economic integration. These have included establishing the region as a free trade area and an open investment area, and encouraging industrial cooperation.

The ASEAN Free Trade Area

The 1992 agreement to set-up the ASEAN Free Trade Area (AFTA) was the organisation's first breakthrough towards creating an integrated ASEAN economic region. The main implementing mechanism for AFTA is the Common Effective Preferential Tariff (CEPT) scheme, also adopted in 1992.

Under the CEPT, tariffs on a wide range of products traded within the region are progressively either lifted totally or limited to a maximum of 5 per cent. Quantitative barriers-limits on the volume of certain products a country imports—and other non-tariff barriers—such as outright prohibition and unnecessary technical requirements are being eliminated.

AFTA's final goal is to eliminate altogether import duties on all products, to create a truly free-trade, or tariff-less, region. The Third ASEAN Informal Summit in Manila in 1999 advanced the timetable for this goal to 2010, ahead of the original schedule of 2015, for the six original signatories to the CEPT scheme—Brunei Darussalam, Indonesia, Malaysia, the Philippines, Singapore and Thailand. The newer ASEAN members—Cambodia, Laos, Myanmar and Vietnam—have committed themselves to eliminating all import duties by 2015, with some sensitive products to follow these members' original target of 2018.

This year—in compliance with the Bold Measures—85 per cent of the Inclusion List of the six original signatories is already in the zero-to-5-per cent zone.

ASEAN is also working to enhance the linkages among service suppliers in the region by consulting with the Coordinating Committee on Services. It is encouraging meetings among associations of service suppliers to develop a better understanding of the unique characteristics and requirements of each sector and the issues that need to be dealt with in liberalising intra-ASEAN services trade in each sector.

Data show that the AFTA programme has already made an impact on intra-ASEAN trade, which expanded from US $ 43.26 billion in 1993 to US $ 85.4 billion in 1997. Although the East Asian financial crisis contracted intra-ASEAN trade to US $ 68.8 billion in 1998, that trade went-up to US $ 74.4 billion in 1999. Before the crisis, intra-ASEAN exports had been increasing at a much higher rate than the growth rate of all ASEAN exports.

EMERGENCE AND PROSPECTS FOR ASIAN ECONOMIC INTEGRATION

The detailed description of ASEAN games the purpose of highlighting the vitality of ASEAN for the successful emergence of Asian Economic Integration, the Japanese initiative of getting a US $ 100 millions Fund and 10+3+3 model seems to be a bold step in right direction. In addition to 10 original members of a Asian, China, South Korea should be included first and the next three members i.e. India, Australia and New Zealand should be further included. Once this is formed, then the integration should further be extended to cover all the countries in Asia.

India, since 1991 is pursuing the policy of looking towards bank on a consequence of which the trade-share of these East Asian nations in India's foreign trade has increased significantly. Beside this several FTAs have been concluded in the recent years which are as follows:

(i) **India and Singapore** signed an agreement in 2005, known as Comprehensive Economic Cooperation Agreement (CECA) as a consequence of this bilateral trade between the two countries will increase from US $ 7 billion to US $ 15 billion and 30 billion dollars with the whole of ASEAN countries.

(ii) **India and China: Regional Trade Agreement (in Progress):** Both the countries agreed to explore the possibilities of inking a regional trade agreement along with investment protection pact. The bilateral trade between two countries will reach to US $ 50 billion by 2010 as compared to 20 billion dollars in 2006.

(iii) India is also moving in the direction of signing a comprehensive economic pact with Gulf Cooperation Council (GCC). This pact will be achieved by the early 2007. This pact will more than FTA.

(iv) **India and Australia**: Trade and Economic Cooperation Agreement (March, 2006).
This pact aims at enhancing cooperation in fields of energy mining, infrastructure, food and beverage, textiles, clothing, footwear, agriculture and bio-technology.
In service sector, Education, Tourism, Information Technology, Communication and Management of Sports events etc. are covered.

(v) India-South Korea are likely to sign a bilateral comprehensive Economic Partnership Agreement (CEPA) by the End of 2007.

(vi) **Japan-India Trade Pact (2006)**: Work on India-Japan Comprehensive Economic Partnership Agreement (CEPA) is on the fast-track.

The description of the above pacts is a pointer in the right direction that India has chosen since 1991. These developments, though not covering all the initiatives of present and future do suggest that Asian Economic Integration is becoming a reality and there will be no Reversal despite so many hurdles in the way—ASEAN, SAARC are the likely, key building blocks for the integration of the entire Asia Pacific Regions.

FACTORS DRIVING GLOBAL ECONOMIC INTEGRATION

Global economic integration is not a new phenomenon. Some communication and trade took place between distant civilizations even in ancient times. Since the travels of Marco Polo seven centuries ago, global economic integration—through trade, factor movements, and communication of economically useful knowledge and technology—has been on a generally rising trend. This process of globalization in the economic domain has not always proceeded smoothly. Nor has it always benefited all whom it has affected. But, despite occasional interruptions, such as following the collapse of the Roman Empire or during the interwar period in this century, the degree of economic integration among different societies around the world has generally been rising. Indeed, during the past half century, the pace of economic globalization (including the reversal of the interwar decline) has been particularly rapid. And, with the exception of human migration, global economic integration today is greater than it ever has been and is likely to deepen going forward.

Three fundamental factors have affected the process of economic globalization and are likely to continue driving it in the future. These factors are as follow:

1. Improvements in the technology of transportation and communication have reduced the costs of transporting goods, services, and factors of production and of communicating economically useful knowledge and technology.
2. The tastes of individuals and societies have generally, but not universally, favoured taking advantage of the opportunities provided by declining costs of transportation and communication through increasing economic integration.
3. The public policies have significantly influenced the character and pace of economic integration, although not always in the direction of increasing economic integration.

These three fundamental factors have influenced the pattern and pace of economic integration in all of its important dimensions. There are three important dimensions of economic integration:

(i) Through human migration.
(ii) Through trade in goods and services.
(iii) Through movements of capital and integration of financial markets.

1. Interactions Among the Fundamental Factors Driving Economic Integration

Although technology, tastes, and public policy each have important independent influences on the pattern and pace of economic integration in its various dimensions, they clearly interact in important ways. Improvements in the technology of transportation and communication do not occur spontaneously in an economic vacuum. The desire of people to take advantage of what they see as the benefits of closer economic integration—that is, the taste for the benefits of integration—is a key reason why it is profitable to make the innovations and investments that bring improvements in the technology of transportation and communication. And, public policy has often played a significant role in fostering innovation and investment in transportation and communication both to pursue the benefits of closer economic integration (within as well as across political boundaries) and for other reasons, such as national defense.

The tastes that people have and develop for the potential benefits of closer economic integration are themselves partly dependent on experience that is made possible by cheaper means of transportation and communication. For example, centuries ago, wealthy people in Europe first learned about the tea and spices of the East as the consequence of limited and very expensive trade. The broadening desire for these products resulting from limited experience hastened the search for easier and cheaper means of securing them. As a by-product of these efforts, America was discovered, and new frontiers of integration were opened-up in the economic and other domains. More recently, if less dramatically, it is clear that tastes for products and services produced in far away locations (including tastes exercised through travel and tourism), as well as for investment in foreign assets, depend to an important degree on experience. As this experience grows, partly because it becomes cheaper, the tastes for the benefits of economic integration typically tend to rise. For example, it appears that as global investors have gained more experience with equities issued by firms in emerging market countries, they have become more interested in diversifying their portfolios to include some of these assets.

Public policy toward economic integration is also, to an important extent, responsive to the tastes that people have regarding various aspects of such integration, as well as to the technologies that make integration possible. On the latter score, it is relevant to note the current issues concerning public policy with respect to commerce conducted over the internet. Before recent advances in computing and communications technology, there was no internet over which commerce could be conducted; and, accordingly, these issues of public policy simply did not arise. Regarding the influence of tastes on public policy, the situation is complicated. Reflecting the general desire to secure the perceived benefits of integration, public policies usually, if not invariably, tend to support closer economic integration within political jurisdictions. The disposition of public policy toward economic integration between different jurisdictions is typically more ambivalent. Better harbours built with public support (and better internal means of transportation as well) tend to facilitate international trade—both imports and exports. Import tariffs and quotas, however, are clearly intended to discourage people from exercising their individual tastes for imported products and encourage production of domestic substitutes. Sadly, the mercantilist fallacy that seems to provide common-sense support for these policies often finds political resonance. Even very smart politicians, such as Abraham Lincoln (who favoured a protective tariff, as well as public support for investments to enhance domestic economic integration) often fail to understand the fundamental truth of Lerner's (1936) symmetry theorem—a tax on imports is fundamentally the same thing as a tax on exports.

It should be emphasized that the interactions between public policy and both tastes and technology in their effects on economic integration can be quite complex and sometimes surprising. Two examples help to illustrate this point. First, for several centuries, there has been active trade between Britain and the Bordeaux region of France, with Britain importing large quantities of Bordeaux wine. This trade, however, was seriously interrupted (if not completely suppressed) during various periods of hostility between the two countries when one side or the other wished to suppress trade with the enemy. Partly as a result of being cut off from Bordeaux wines, and partly as a means of strengthening its alliance with Portugal, Britain sought to develop imports of Portuguese wines. The existing Portuguese wines, however, did not meet British requirements. A solution was found in creating a new product—Portuguese red wine from the Duoro region, fortified with grape brandy that gave the wine an extra alcoholic kick, retained some of the fruit sugar that would otherwise have been absorbed in fermentation, and helped protect the wine during shipment in hot weather. The result of this technological innovation was a new product—modern Port—that developed and retained a considerable market, especially in Britain, even after barriers to the acquisition of French wines were reduced.

The second example concerns U.S. public policy toward international trade in sugar which, in a bizarre way, is partly the consequence of policies pursued by Napoleon Bonaparte and Admiral Lord Nelson. For many years, the United States has maintained tight import quotas on sugar to keep the domestic price typically at roughly three times the world market level. The domestic political interests that support this policy include some sugar refiners, some producers of cane sugar in the deep south and Hawaii, and a few thousand sugar beet farmers primarily in the upper midwest. Production of sugar from beets is a "new" technology, dating back to the Napoleonic period. Before that time, sugar was produced from cane grown primarily in the West Indies. Admiral Lord Nelson's establishment of naval supremacy over the French enabled Britain to cut off Napoleon's empire from imports of West Indian sugar. In response, Napoleon established a prize for finding a substitute for cane-based sugar which could be produced within his empire. The sugar beet was discovered, and has been with us ever since. Not going into historical details of the process of economic integration, let us conclude by saying that Human Migration, trade in goods and services, reduction in transport cost and international capital movements and trade in financial services etc. Contributed and will keep on contributing in future also to the growth of global economic integration.

MUSSA and Gold Stein (1993) in their article discussed all these issues in greater details. Post Mussa—Gold Stein development can be summed-up in the following points:

1. During the past thirteen years, financial markets, especially wholesale markets for high grade instruments, have tended to become more tightly linked internationally, especially among the industrial countries and also including many important emerging market economies. Most notably and as a clear example of the influence of public policy on economic integration, the advent of EMU (and the anticipation of this event) has eliminated exchange rate fluctuations among the eleven participating countries and has led to a dramatic reduction in interest rate spreads and in the volatility of these spreads. A unified market for bank liquidity emerged very rapidly once EMU started, with the larger banks in each country bidding aggressive for liquidity auctioned by the European Central Bank (ECB) and acting as wholesalers of liquidity to second-tier institutions; these developments are discussed in the IMF's reports on *International Capital Markets* for 1999 and 2000. For the industrial countries, the only significant suggestion of any weakening in international capital markets linkages relates to Japan. When concerns about the financial condition of many large Japanese banks arose during 1997–98, the "Japan premium" paid by large Japanese banks to borrow on international banking markets spiked-up; Government measures to help re-capitalize and restructure Japanese banks was subsequently instrumental in reducing the Japan premium. Nevertheless, many Japanese banks have substantially scaled back their involvement in international financial markets. Also (as described in the IMF's report on *International Capital Markets* for 2000) there are some indications of a degree of detachment of some Japanese financial markets, such as the market for yen-based OTC derivatives, from global financial conditions.

2. For emerging market economies, dramatic evidence of their linkage to global financial markets was provided during the tequila crisis of 1995 and especially during the Asian/Russian/LTCM/Brazilian crises of 1997–99. It is noteworthy that the Asian crisis, which effectively began with

the attack on the Hong Kong dollar and stock market in mid-October 1997, was preceded by a massive surge in gross private capital flows to emerging market countries and a deep compression of spreads for emerging market borrowers. These developments signal a shift in tastes of global investors either toward lower assessments of the risks of investing in emerging markets or toward greater acceptance of such risks. With the onset of the Asian crisis, there was an apparent sudden shift of tastes of global investors away from emerging market risks, especially for Asian emerging market economies and, as gross private capital flows dropped precipitously (especially for Asian emerging markets), spreads for emerging market borrowers spiked upwards. In this episode and in later episodes of the series of crises during 1997–99, many emerging market countries lost effective access to global financial markets. In many cases, the loss of access proved relatively brief—in contrast to the experience of many Latin American countries during the debt crisis of the 1980s—but in a few cases access has not yet been restored. Consistent with Mussa and Goldstein, while some progress has been made, the linkage of developing countries to global financial markets remains weaker and more tenuous than for industrial countries.

3. Although not original to Mussa and Goldstein, the observation that for a country highly open to private international capital flows, the policy requirements for successful operation of a pegged exchange rate regime are quite demanding has certainly proved prophetic. For Mexico in the tequila crisis, for Thailand, Malaysia, Indonesia, and Korea in the Asian crisis, for Russia in 1998, and for Brazil in 1999, the combination of a pegged exchange rate regime with a relatively high degree of openness to private international capital flows proved unsustainable and contributed to substantial financial crises. Countries that supported their pegged exchange rate policies with firm commitments to consistent monetary policies and maintained well-capitalized and well-regulated banking systems—notably Argentina and Hong Kong—were able to weather recent crises without collapses in their policy regimes. However, emerging market countries that maintained more flexible exchange rate

regimes—such as Singapore, Taiwan Province of China, South Africa, and Mexico (after 1995)—were generally better sheltered from the effect of recent financial crises.

The general lesson here (and also earlier from the ERM crises of 1992–93) appears to be that the public policies that support the highest degree of international capital market integration—rigidly pegged exchange rates and free capital mobility—are feasible, but only if other key macro-economic policies, most importantly national monetary policies, are subordinated to this goal of financial integration. Where the requisite degree of subordination is not feasible or not desirable, a choice of public policy orientations must be made. For some countries—notably those that have comparatively weak financial systems and have in place systems of controls on private capital flows—maintenance of some restrictions on private capital flows (at least for some period of time) may be a desirable option that allows greater stability of the exchange rate. For the major currency countries and regions (the United States, the euro area, and Japan) where unrestricted capital mobility is the established norm, and where pursuit of a common monetary policy appears unlikely to be consistent with key goals of macro-economic stability, floating exchange rates will, and should, continue to prevail.

4. In light of the experience of the past seven years, the favourable assessment of the growing role of and prospect for direct investment flows to emerging market economies appears justified; but the relatively sanguine assessment of changes in the composition of portfolio flows and of the "enhanced resiliency of the international financial system in dealing with any future problems" seems somewhat premature. While it is true that flows of foreign direct investment to developing countries have expanded considerably during the 1990s and have come to dominate net flows of private capital to these countries and flows of FDI have also proved to be quite stable during recent financial crises. Nevertheless, the international financial system was certainly not free of important problems during the past years.

5. The emphasis in Mussa and Goldstein on efforts to improve market discipline through better provision of information, heightened transparency, harmonization of accounting standards, etc., and through avoiding generous bailouts of errant borrowers (and their creditors) appears to have successfully forecast much of the agenda for the recent debate on improving the international financial architecture. Already at this stage important progress has been made in these reform efforts; but much remains to be done on the implementation of reforms. It is still to be seen how much these reforms will improve the performance of the international financial system.

In our view, the main omission from the discussion of global capital market integration in Mussa and Goldstein is the relative lack of emphasis on the globalization of the activities of providing financial services—a phenomenon which is part of the broader revolution in this sector brought on primarily by rapid advances in information and communication technology. The rapid reductions in the costs of storing, accessing, analyzing, and communicating information are both dramatically reducing the costs of producing virtually all existing forms of financial services and creating new products and services (such as many OTC derivatives) which would have been prohibitively expensive with older technologies. At the national level, the structure of the financial services sector is changing as the distinctions that used to exist between commercial banks, investment banks, securities dealers, insurance companies, and other financial service providers become increasingly blurred. At the international level, the same basic forces are driving where financial services are increasingly being provided across national boundaries, and public policies are tending to accommodate and/or facilitate this mechanism of global economic integration.

A REVERSAL IN THE TREND OF INCREASING GLOBAL ECONOMIC INTEGRATION?

During the interwar period between World Wars I and II, there was a sharp reversal in the generally rising trend of global economic integration. The volume of world trade contracted sharply. This contraction of world trade was particularly pronounced during the early 1930s, and was partly attributable to, the general decline of economic activity in the great depression. The decline in world trade, however, was much greater than the decline in economic activity (or in goods production). The rise of protectionism, particularly the Smoot-Hawley tariff imposed by the United States in 1930 and the retaliatory responses to it, clearly contributed importantly to the collapse of world trade. At around the same time, capital market linkages among countries weakened substantially, as the international gold standard collapsed and as several countries, led by Germany, began to impose highly restrictive controls on capital movements.

A complex of factors undoubtedly contributed to the general sharp reversal of global economic integration in the interwar period, including especially the economic effects of the great depression. Several studies have suggested economic and political economy explanations for this reversal, especially as relates to developments in the United States. However, I believe that it is not possible to explain an important part of this world-wide phenomenon without recognizing that there was an important change in the politics of several key countries away from sympathy to involvement in an economically integrated global economy and toward nationalism and isolationism. In Europe, the tragedy of the Great War and its aftermath explains much of the change. Russia after the devastation of the war and Bolshevik revolution was invaded by some of its former allies. Mutual suspicion and hostility between communist Russia and most of the rest of the world was reflected in Russia's economic isolation. In Germany, a bitter defeat and a bitter peace fed a new spirit of nationalism. In the United States, the symptoms of the shift toward isolationism took many forms. The Senate refused to ratify the League of Nations Treaty in 1920. The government took repressive action toward imported political ideologies in the red-square. The Ku Klux Klan was reborn and gained prominence outside of the south, expressing antipathy not only to blacks but also to most things foreign. Prohibition was passed, partly based on campaigns that attributed alcoholism to foreign influences. The National Origins Act sharply restricted foreign immigration. All of this transpired during the roaring twenties, before the great depression; the Smoot-Hawley tariff was also passed before the depression took hold. From all of these developments, it seems clear that after World War I and partly in reaction to it, many Americans decided that they wanted substantially less involvement with most things foreign.

What are the chances that something similar might happen again? The protesters in Seattle demonstrated that globalization has its detractors, and we have hardly seen or heard the last of them. However, while we need to remain cognizant of the risk that such protests may gain political momentum, I do not believe that the conditions are ripe for a return to isolationism. The plain fact is that the U.S. economy, and the world economy more generally, have prospered enormously under, and partly because of, favorable policies toward international economic integration—policies that have been championed by the United States in the post World War II era. Despite occasional difficulties such as the recent emerging market financial crises, nations around the world are not seeking to withdraw from the increasingly integrated global economic system. Rather, those that are not yet full participants are generally seeking to become so.

The study of all these historical trend logically leads to the conclusion that emerging awakening and efforts about the Asian Economic Integration is going to be successful and Indian destined to play a vital role in its formation which will certainly in hence employment and production opportunity in the country. Thus, the paper has been successful improving that "The mix of Classical and Neo-classical paradigms in economics through the economics of integration leads to creation of more employment and production opportunities not only the western world but also in Asia and else where in the world economy. The process of Global Economic Integration seems to be a panacea for the contemporary economic problems being faced by the developed as well as developing countries. Thus, the theory of paradigms given by Kuhn and the Lakatosian approach known as Methodology Scientific Research Programme

(MSRP), explains emergence of sub-paradigm in regional groupings, known as Asian Economic Integration.

Notes and References

1. Kuhn, T.S. (1969), "The Structure of Scientific Revolutions", p. 182.
2. ——(1969), Both references are to the postscript added to the second edition, p. 175.
3. Lakatos, See Imre and Musgrave, Alan, (1970) (eds), "Criticism and Growth of Knowledge", p. 177.
4. Levons, W.S. (1876), "The Future of Political Economy", *Fortnightly Review*, p. 620.
5. Brahmananda, P.R., "New Drifts in International Trade Theory", *The Indian Economic Journal*, Vol. 45, Jan.-March 1997-98, No. 3.
6. Viner, J. (1950), "The Customs Union Issue", New York: Carnegie Endowment for International Peace.
7. Meade, James (1955), "The Theory of Customs Unions", Amsterdam: North Holland.
8. Bhagwati, Jagdish (1968), "Trade Liberalization among LDSCS, Trade Theory and GATT Rules", in (Il.N. Wolf, ed.) *Value, Capital and Growth*, Oxford: Oxford University Press.
9. ——(1991), "Regionalism and the World Trading System at Risk", Princeton: Princeton University Press.
10. ——(1993), "Regionalism and Multilateralism: An Overview", in (Melo and Panagariya eds.).
11. ——Summers, Lawrence (1991), "Regionalism and the World Trading System", Federal Reserve Bank of Kanas City, Policy Implications of Trade and Currency Zones.
12. ——Srinivasan, T.N. (1993), "Discussion", in de Melo and Panagariya.
13. ——Grossman, Gene and Helpman, Elhanan, (1995), "The Politics of Free Trade Agreements" *American Economic Review* (September) pp. 667-90.
14. ——Panagariya, Arvind (1995), "Rethinking the New Regionalism." Paper presented at the Trade Expansion Programme Conference of the U.N. Development Programme and World Bank, January.

References

Bhagwati, Jagdish, Bhagwati and Panagariya, (1996), "The Theory of Preferential Trade Agreements: Historical Evolution and Current Trends", *American Economic Review*, Vol. 86, pp. 82-7.

——, Jagdish (1968), Wilfred, J. Ethier (1998), "The New Regionalism", *The Economic Journal*, Vol. 108, No. 449, July, 1998.

Bhagwati, Jagdish, Baldwin, Richard E. and Phillipe Martin, "Two Waves of Globalization: Superficial Similarities, Fundamental Differences," *NBER Working Paper*, No. 6904, January 1999.

——Barraclough, Geoffrey, ed., *The Times Atlas of World History*, London: Times Books, Ltd., 1978.

——Bordo, Michael, Barry Eichengreen and Douglas Irwin, "Is Globalization Today Really Different than Globalization a Hundred Years Ago?" *NBER Working Paper*, No. 7195, June 1999.

——Claessens, Stijn, Thomas Glaessner and Daniela Klingebiel, "Electronic Finance: Reshaping the Financial Landscape Around the World," *Financial Sector Discussion Paper No. 4*, Washington, DC: The World Bank, September 2000.

——Crafts, Nicholas, "Globalization and Growth in the Twentieth Century," *IMF Working Paper*, WP/00/44. Washington, D.C.: International Monetary Fund, March 2000.

——Eichengreen, Barry, "The Political Economy of the Smoot-Hawley Tariff," *Research in Economic History*, 12, pp. 1-43.

——Irwin, Douglas and Randall Kroszner, "Log-Rolling and Economic Interests in the Passage of the Smoot-Hawley Tariff," *NBER Working Paper* No. 5510, March 1996.

——Eichengreen, Barry and Michael Mussa, "Capital Account Liberalization: Theoretical and Practical Aspects," *IMF Occasional Paper*, No. 172. Washington: International Monetary Fund, 1998.

——Edwards, S., "Openness, Productivity, and Growth, What Do We Really Know?", *Economic Journal*, 108, pp. 383-398.

——Fogel, Robert, *Railroads and American Economic Growth*. Baltimore, Maryland: The Johns Hopkins Press, 1964.

——Goldstein, Morris and Mohsin Khan, "Income and Price Effects in Foreign Trade," in Peter Kenen and Ronald Jones, eds., *Handbook of International Economics*, Vol. II. Amsterdam: Elsevier Science Publishers, 1984.

——International Monetary Fund, *International Capital Markets*, November 1999 and October 2000 (forthcoming).

——Johnson, Hugh, *Vintage: The Story of Wine*. New York: Simon and Schuster, 1989.

——Krugman, Paul, "Scale Economies, Product Differentiation, and the Pattern of Trade, "*American Economic Review*, 70:5, December 1980, pp. 950-959.

——Leamer, Edward, "International Trade Theory: The Evidence", in Gene Grossman and Kenneth Rogoff, eds., *Handbook of International Economics*, Vol. 3. Amsterdam: North Holland, 1995, pp. 139-159.

——Lincoln, Abraham, "Lecture on Discoveries and Inventions," in *Selected Writings and Speeches*. New York: Vantage Book, 1992, pp. 200-208.

——(1968), Lerner, Abba, "The Symmetry between Import and Export Taxes," *Economica*, New Series, III, pp. 308-313.

——Mundell, Robert, "International Trade and Factor Mobility," *American Economic Review*, 47:3, June 1957, pp. 321-335.

Bhagwati, Jagdish, Mussa, Michael and Morris Goldstein, "The Integration of World Capital Markets," in *Changing Capital Markets: Implications for Monetary Policy*. Kansas City, Missouri: Federal Reserve Bank of Kansas City, 1993.

——Rodrik, Dani, "How Far Will International Economic Integration Go?" *Journal of Economic Perspectives*, 14:1, pp. 177-186.

——Ohlin, Bertil, *International and Interregional Trade*. Cambridge, Massachusetts: Harvard University Press, 1935.

——Salvatore, Dominick, *International Economics*, Sixth Edition. Upper Saddle River, New Jersey: Prentice Hall, 1998.

——Thucydides, *History of the Peloponnesian War*, as translated and presented in *The Landmark Thucydides*, edited by Robert Strassler. New York: Simon and Schuster, 1996.

Asian Regional Financial Integration
An Analysis of a Possible Road Map

SHRAWAN KUMAR SINGH

THE CONCEPT OF ASIAN REGION

The concept of an Asian economic area must at the outset address itself to three key questions (Rehman Shobhan, 1995): (i) The territorial ambit for Asia; (ii) Why the grouping of countries defined as part of Asia should think of themselves as a group; and (iii) What are the operational and institutional implications of this Asian identity definition and how does the concept of an Asian identity relate to the sub-regional and ex-Asian linkages of various Asian countries which have already developed or may be emerging.

Asia is essentially a *geographical expression*. It covers the *Arabic-speaking* countries in West Asia, Israel, Turkey and Iran. *South Asia* includes Afghanistan, while Burma, occupies a sort of no-man's land between South and South-East Asia. *South-East Asia* includes the ASEAN countries plus the countries which once constituted Indo-China. *East Asia* groups China, the Korean Peninsula and Japan. These countries constitute a variety of ethnic groups, languages and faiths.

Historically, *there has been no evolution of an Asian entity nor has there so far been any contemporary attempt to forge one.*

Any exercise which seeks to define an Asian community will thus have to first agree on what constitutes Asia. This will help to define the geopolitical contours as well as the economic logic of such an Asian community. "The definition of an Asian community cannot satisfy academic purists. It will have to be driven by institutional concerns over why an Asian identity is necessary and what is expected to follow from this definition. The concept itself has to take root in the minds of the thinking people of the region. It is only when a respectable conceptual and empirically validated infrastructure of knowledge has emerged that the idea can be placed before the political leadership of the region. It is upto the respective countries to then decide whether their respective national compulsions can be productively integrated into the concept of a wider regional community. The policy-makers and the economic entities belonging to the integration region should first of all have a sense of awareness about the interacted region as a compact region for their operations. It is here that the concept of the Economic Area becomes relevant. The will to co-operate or the political will for that matter, would be determined by the perceptions of the decision-makers about their belonging to a particular area. Thus, the concept of Economic Area is presented here as a necessary pre-condition for the process of economic integration. It serves as the most common starting point for *attitudinal changes in the decision-making process of the economic agents* in propounding the Asian region as an Asian Economic Area."

"Asian Economic Area is a notion. But acceptance of its existence by the economic agents in the region, including the governments and the intellectuals, would bring about a paradigm of development and international economic relations, which would foster optimal use of the regional resources. The new conceptual frame could do away with the variety of the "*isms*", which have coloured the evaluation of successes and failures. The confusion of the present times can be fully eliminated only through a genuinely new thinking" [*V.R. Panchmukhi*, 1995].

Historically, the Asian countries have not had a strong sense of an *"Asian Identity"*, unlike their European counterparts. But economic developments over the past decade, especially in the wake of the 1997-1998 Asian financial crisis, have altered peoples' attitudes significantly, and a new regionalism is now emerging.

FACTORS CONTRIBUTING TO ASIAN INTEGRATION

ASEAN is experimenting with various other combinations like ASEAN+1 or ASEAN+2 or ASEAN+3, but the real combination has yet to come. So the need is for the big powers of Asia, all 6, or any 2, 3, 4 or 5 to make a beginning. Other things will fall in place automatically. In fact the very talk of an Asian Union will lead to a dialogue between civilizations, so to say.

In recent years, four key developments have forced the Asian countries to review their existing foreign trade policies and reconsider the merits of expanding trade: (i) *The 1997-1998 Asian financial crisis,* (ii) *The rapid development of FTAs in other parts of the world,* (iii) *Rapid trade expansion within Asia* and (iv) *Uncertainty about the future of a multilateral framework.*

As East Asian nations work in earnest for regional trade arrangements, financial co-operation in the area has begun moving quietly onto the agenda of experts, financial technocrats and regional politicians. On their minds is the building of a framework that might help the region avoid the repetition of the disruptive 1997 financial crisis, and enhance the efficiency of financial resource allocation and facilitate economic integration.

And specific steps have been taken to start that kind of financial cooperation. The first initiative to find an institutional alternative was launched at the Thai city of Chiang Mai in 1997. Though nothing came to the *Chiang Mai Initiative* and the subsequent relatively-strong recovery of these economies put such initiatives on the back-burner. The idea that South Asian countries can build an economic union on the lines of the European Union needs to be assiduously worked upon over a period of time. People are getting more educated and are slowly realizing the marvel of "economic prosperity." Thus, the establishment of Asian union would definitely give a boost to the intra member trade and make substantial contribution in the growth and development of these countries. Barring a few exceptions, majority of the countries are very similar *culturally, geographically, socially, economically, in terms of resource endowment, this would facilitate the trade among them. It would also help in the trade between Asia and the rest of the world. However, the countries have to realise the importance of peace and should amicably settle their disputes.* One can go a long way only if one stands together and support each other and work towards the growth and development of Asia as a cohesive unit.

Given the interventionist inclinations of politicians and international agencies, the construction of a single Asian currency is likely to be a complicated and evolutionary process. The twenty-first century can be truly Asia's if the current trend of rapid growth rates in China and India can be sustained. However, what can be achieved in a relatively short period is a freer trade and investment regime promoted by the larger Asian community. Asian economies can discuss a common financial architecture which will help deal with financial crises of the kind that visited East Asia in 1997. While all these are nascent thoughts, it appears there are many big ideas in the larger Asian region whose time may have come [*M.K. Venu, 2005*].

INCREASING FOREX RESERVE OF THE ASIAN REGION

Martin Wolf (2004) is of the view that Asian governments are exporting astonishing quantities of capital, overwhelmingly to the US. "This is not just absurd. It is also economically destablishing. In 2002 and 2003, the principal economies of the Asian region ran a combined current account surplus of $ 540 billion, of which $ 249 billion was Japan's. This aggregate surplus covered more than half of the cumulative US current account deficit of $ 1,023 billion. It would be natural to assume that these huge current account surpluses were the means through which the region exported its excess private savings. But most Asian economies have not been net exporters of private capital."

According to ADB's economist *Ifzal Ali,* Asia's foreign exchange reserves have soared beyond optimal levels and governments must tackle global imbalances by ploughing some money back into the region. Asian economies control more than two-thirds of global foreign exchange reserves and the region's central banks have more than $ 2.5 trillion in their vaults. Most of the money is held in dollar-denominated assets and speculation in the past that Asian central banks could diversify their holdings have undermined the dollar. They have grown far beyond what is the optimal level. It's basically a reflection of a lack of imagination, a lack of innovativeness and to some extent a lack of self-confidence. The mountain of reserves has grown rapidly in recent years as Asian central banks intervened in markets to curb the export-damaging rise of their currencies against the falling dollar. This is mercantilism at its worst. The reserves must be ploughed back into Asia and not sit in North America. Developing Asia must have resilience to unexpected shocks arising from global uncertainties. But they must be seen as active players in addressing and unwinding the global imbalances that we are seeing today. Asia must not rely solely on weaker currencies to boost exports, but take measures to boost domestic consumption and investment and liberalise trade. It must also allow currencies to appreciate to shield economies from high oil prices. Obviously, adjustment and flexibility is being sought mainly in Asia where growth and productivity is expected to explode in the next 10-20 years or so. There must be a joint strategy worked out by the big Asian economies in regard to the nature of this adjustment.

It makes no sense for a region with huge current account surpluses and foreign currency reserves to be so desperate to avoid international financial crises. The US should feel vulnerable instead. A step towards reducing the region's perceived vulnerability would be to create a large *Asian Monetary Fund*. Armed with this insurance, Asian countries could allow their exchange rates to appreciate, generate greater internal demand and then run current account deficits. This would generate global balance of payments adjustment. Moreover, if Asians do wish to lend money generously, why not benefit their own people rather than Americans? [*Martin Wolf*, 2004].

Agnes Belsaisch and Alessandro Zanello (2006) have opined that "The hope of better risk sharing, more efficient allocation of capital, more productive investment, and, ultimately, higher standards of living for all is propelling the drive for stronger connections between financial systems across the world. Asian economies, particularly emerging markets, are taking an active part in this quest, at both the regional and global levels. At the global level, Asia's integration with the international financial system is well advanced. At the regional level, however, integration is more limited."

STEPS TOWARDS FINANCIAL INTEGRATION

The financial integration has been defined as a gradual process through which cross-border capital flows increase, financial markets' co-movements become stronger, and product prices and market infrastructures converge to common standards. In the years since the 1997–98 financial crisis, Asian governments have affirmed their intention to promote financial integration at the regional level with a view to both reducing vulnerabilities and improving the allocation of savings. A series of initiatives have been launched to boost regional self-sufficiency, ranging from information sharing to financing arrangements in foreign exchange. Governments are also taking steps to *deepen regional bond markets to reduce reliance on bank financing and to shelter the regional economy from the possible repercussions of future volatile capital flows originating elsewhere in the world.* "Yet, despite all these efforts, Asia's capital markets remain fragmented. Emerging Asian companies frequently raise capital in industrial country markets rather than at home, and relatively few bond issues are in Asian currencies. In other words, emerging Asian countries are not really investing in each other. Making a dent in the large unfinished agenda for financial integration poses many challenges. The encouraging news is that Asia is well positioned to forge ahead" [Belaisch and Zanello, 2006]. There are various measures of financial integration. They are:

1. *Geographical reach*—that is, regional *versus* extra-regional or global linkages. Asia's integration with *global* financial markets is already well advanced by most standards.
   Limited data complicate an evaluation of *regional* financial integration. Information on bilateral cross-border capital flows within Asia is scant, making it difficult to assess how much cross-border investment in Asian financial markets originates in the region.
2. A second measure of integration is within *asset classes*—the cross-border connections among domestic banking systems, equity markets, and bond markets. This measure also shows financial integration as uneven.
3. On Asian *stock markets,* there are few foreign listings and even fewer regional listings. In some Asian countries, stock markets have a large international presence, but few foreign players come from neighboring countries. The share of foreign listings on Asian stock markets is also decreasing, as borrowers prefer to issue depositary receipts in New York or London. Foreign shareholding and trading.
4. In *bond markets,* regional integration is also limited. Much of the growing foreign currency–denominated bond issuance of Asian sovereign and corporate borrowers is in U.S. dollars and is marketed outside of Asia—about 80 per cent is in the United States and Europe. There is little evidence of Asians investing in the bonds of other neighboring economies to date, notwithstanding initiatives under way to promote cross-border holdings.

While already reaping the benefits of diversification through its participation in the global financial market, emerging Asia could make additional gains from more extensive intraregional ties, including the following [*Belaisch and Zanello,* 2006]: (i) More stable access to capital; (ii) Lower funding costs and greater investment; (iii) Greater market discipline of macro-economic policies. Deeper and better-connected financial markets would thus benefit Asia. Its financial systems are mostly bank based, with equity and private bond markets generally smaller than those in developed economies. The depth of local bond markets has generally increased across Asia, however, because governments have become major issuers to finance bank restructuring and rising fiscal deficits since the financial crisis. In the future, trends in regional trade and abundant liquidity are likely to serve as catalysts for stronger financial linkages throughout the region.

On the liquidity front, there is a local overhang because of a combination of high domestic savings and low domestic investment in much of the region, on top of recent surges in capital inflows and associated (unsterilized) intervention. As a result, Asia has become a net exporter of capital, contributing to large global imbalances in current accounts. Deeper intraregional financial integration could help allocate this liquidity intra-regionally, reviving domestic investment and an orderly decline in external surpluses.

STRENGTHENING THE PROCESS OF INTEGRATION

Asian policy-makers have launched several initiatives (*Belaisch and Zanello*, 2006): (i) In many countries, capital account restrictions no longer stand in the way of cross-border flows; (ii) developing capital markets requires reforms to strengthen issuers, broaden the investor base, and build market infrastructures (including clearing and settlement systems and credit-rating agencies); (iii) Banking supervisory and regulatory norms need to be on par with international best practices, and a framework for consolidated supervision needs to accompany cross-border consolidation. As in the euro area, this can be done through cooperation between national banking supervisors or through the creation of a supranational supervisory unit—perhaps limited to regionally significant financial players; (iv) Under the aegis of ASEAN+3 (the grouping of 10 Southeast Asian Nations, joined by China, Korea and Japan) and other forums, the focus so far has largely been on strengthening bond markets in the context of the Asian Bond Market Initiative; and (v) Ways to strengthen the role of local credit rating agencies are being explored.

"Greater financial linkages bring benefits but also require sound policies and institutions, as well as mechanisms to contain new risks that could arise from more open financial systems. Asian governments have established significant financial support mechanisms in the context of the *Chiang Mai Initiative* to cope with disruptive capital flows and maintain exchange rate stability." For many Asia watchers, advances in financial integration and intraregional trade are seen as heralding eventual adoption of a regional common currency and the establishment of an Asian monetary union—following the euro model. Europe's experience shows that a monetary union imposes such stringent demands on policy coordination and institution building that Asia may well need a clear political will, sustained over generations. It is safe to say that a monetary union for Asia remains, at best, a distant goal. That said, the policy requirements for a strong regional economy also support convergence of economic conditions among its members. For now, Asian economies are best served by exchange rate systems with adequate flexibility to cushion country-specific shocks [*Belaisch and Zanello,* 2006].

RIGHT TIME FOR DEEPER INTEGRATION

Asia has come a long way in opening its financial system and clearly understands how it can benefit from deeper financial integration. Emerging Asia is a global player in international trade and a significant recipient of net private capital flows to emerging markets. The development of regional capital markets offers significant payoffs, particularly as it supports better integration with the global financial system. Nonetheless, many challenges remain and the policy agenda is extensive. The combination of favorable economic conditions and a clear commitment to integration can provide a fitting environment in which the policy debate can flourish—and Asia's financial integration can continue to advance.

J.P. Morgan, the US investment bank, has suggested

that China and its Asian neighbours to tie their currencies together and create an Asian currency unit that could gradually be allowed to float freely against external currencies. The bank claims this would reduce global imbalances, allow Asian countries to strengthen their currencies without losing competitiveness and promote regional stability. J.P. Morgan is calling for a bolder approach to a regional bloc that would free Asian currencies to strengthen on the world stage without any country losing intra-regional competitiveness. This *concept would replicate Europe's exchange rate mechanism, the forerunner of the euro, with Asian currencies trading within a band against each other*. The bank does not predict an eventual single currency, however. But advocates the currencies of *China, Hong Kong, India, Indonesia, South Korea, Malaysia, Philippines, Singapore, Taiwan and Thailand as being suitable for the system*. But China and Taiwan's political differences and economic disparities between some states present hurdles [*Business Standard,* February 1, 2005].

To facilitate a collective response on the nature of future adjustments in the financial systems, we must create an *Asian Monetary Fund* (AMF) whose initial corpus could be 10 per cent of the reserves of all Asian central banks. That will mean a corpus of over $ 200 billion. Who knows it could grow to $ 1 trillion by 2008, given the way capital is flowing to Asia on a sustained basis. A collective response from Asia could facilitate a smoother adjustment in the international financial system. Clearly, Asia must begin to think big now. China, India and Japan could be the main pillars of this initiative [*M.K. Venu,* 2004].

In this context, a small initiative has already been taken in the from of setting-up an *Asia Bond Fund* (ABF), created by Asean nations to help member countries deal with financial crises a la 1997-98. *India has sent a strong message in favour of an alternative financial architecture for the Asian region*. The idea is to eventually minimize dependence on the IMF as a lender of the last resort. At present the corpus of ABF is too small, and at best the fund symbolizes an aspiration which can be realized sometime in the future. However, the prospects of creating a much bigger fund are quite bright given the way the Asian economies are expected to attract capital flows based on future projections of productivity growth in this region. Besides Japan, China has also express strong support for an alternative financial architecture for Asia. Both these countries were part of the famous *Ching Mai Initiative in Thailand* where this idea was born after the 1998 Asian financial crises.

But there is no doubt that the seed of an *Asian Monetary Fund* has been planted. The advantages of establishing a much bigger Asian Fund are obvious: (i) the concerns of most Asian economies would be similar in terms of the impact a widespread readjustment of the international financial system will have on their economies; (ii) such a fund will help check undue volatility in times of a crisis in the financial markets; (iii) it can also negotiate with institutions like the IMF on how to adjust currencies in times of a financial crisis; (iv) The bargaining power will come from AMF's own financial muscle; it will obviate the need for Asian economies to depend heavily on the IMF for bail-outs. These bail-outs come with conditionalities that take away independent policy making ability; (v) an exclusively Asian Fund will help these economies calibrate policies as per their requirements; (vi) would have the advantage of being closer to the countries in the region and thereby would have had a better understanding of their economic and social conditions; and (vii) could be a useful associate of the Asian Development Bank (ADB), that has been responsible for aiding much of the development of industry and infrastructure in Asian countries. Ultimately, the Asian Monetary Fund will succeed or fail based on its governance, its economists, its protocol of supervision and surveillance [*S. Venkitaramanan*, 2005].

According to S. Venkitaramanan, Mr. Kuroda is more keen on creating an *Asian Monetary Fund* rather than merely creating an Asian Currency Unit (ACU). The Asian Monetary Fund can be a critical new ingredient of the coming Asian century. Visualise the AMF starting out as a clearing house for ideas on currency adjustments and helping in times of crisis. The AMF can be a monetary fund with a difference. It can be a monetary physician with a human face.

In the area of monetary cooperation, the creation of a regional unit of account or an *Asian Currency Unit* (ACU), is an important initiative of ADB President Kuroda. However, *Nagesh Kumar* (2006) is of the view that while ADB's initiative needs to be lauded, the present conception of the ACU seems inadequate and would not allow it to exploit its potential. ADB proposes to include in the basket of currencies for determining the value of ACU the currencies of Asean+3 countries, namely, Japan, China and South Korea. It is not clear why ADB is thinking of leaving out the Indian rupee, considering India's growing role in Asia as an engine of economic growth and its growing economic integration with East Asian countries, reflected in her participation in the East Asia Summit. India is the third-largest shareholder of ADB in the region after Japan and China. Further, unlike the currencies of many East Asian countries, the Indian rupee has a market-determined exchange rate. The Indian rupee is convertible on the current account and is moving towards full capital account convertibility. Indian financial and capital markets have considerable depth and are prudently regulated. India's foreign exchange reserves of over $ 165 billion are among the largest in the region. From India's point of view, exclusion from the ACU basket could be costly, as it may increase transaction costs of trading vis-à-vis other players. In view of the emergence of the East Asian countries as our largest trade partners, it may not be prudent to remain outside the ACU basket.

CONCLUSION

The two Asian giants, India and China are about to become powerful superpowers. The momentum in this direction seems irresistible. Demography, once a liability, is turning out to be an asset. The largest proportion of working age young people in the world is giving Asia an advantage over their OECD rivals. Geography, once considered irrelevant, is allowing Asia to forge a thicket of links that will sustain an unprecedented development momentum. Their economies, once considered irremediably stagnant, are likely to remain among the world's fastest growing. The proportion of world trade controlled by Asia is likely to exceed anything the world has seen since the 17th century. Yet there is some uncertainty over the political trajectory of Asia. What will China's political arrangements look like a decade from now? Will India's political institutions be up to the task of managing the complexities of a globalised world? But even in politics, Asian countries come to the new century with a remarkable asset: relatively stable state structures. Strong and stable states are the cornerstone of any great power. The momentum is on Asia's side. While this should energise countries like India, it ought not to breed complacency.

Our future is not constrained by our resources. The only thing that can constrain us is our will. There is no path to true greatness without coming to terms with whom we are and what we want to be. Will we be able to radically restructure the world and its values in new ways? The most uncertain question of all is this: what will the new Asian Century stand for? [*Indian Express*, January 17, 2005]. Asia is, therefore, a force to reckon with, after North America and the Euro currency area. Regional integration can be achieved, step-by-step, through strengthening various cooperation channels under a long-term vision of "*Integrated Asia.*" The best way is to grasp the existing momentum and implement.

References

Belaisch, Agnes and Alessandro Zanello (2006), "Deepening Financial Ties", *Finance and Development,* June.

Kumar, Nagesh (2004 'a'), "Realising the Asian Dream", *The Financial Express,* April 21.

——(ed.) (2004 'b'): *Towards an Asian Economic Community: Vision of a New Asia,* RIS and ISEAS, New Delhi and Singapore, 123-55.

——(2006): Asian Currency Unit Minus Indian Rupee? *The Financial Express,* April 25.

M.K. Venu (2005): An Asian Economic Community?, *The Economic Times,* September 20.

——(2004): Time to Set-up Asian Monetary Fund, *The Economic Times,* February 24.

Panagariya, A. (2004): *"India in the 1980s and 1990s: A Triumph of Reforms", IMF Working Paper* No. WP/04/43.

Panchamukhi, V.R. (1995): Asian Economic Area: What it Means? included in a book *'Towards An Asian Economic Area',* edited by V.R. Panchamukhi and Rehman Sobhan, South-South Centre, Geneva.

Shankar, Vineeta (2004): 'Towards an Asian Economic Community: Exploring the Past' in Nagesh Kumar (ed.) *Towards an Asian Economic Community: Vision of a New Asia,* RIS and ISEAS, New Delhi and Singapore, 13-42.

Sobhan, Rehman (1995): Towards an Asian Economic Area: Some Conceptual Issues, included in a book *'Towards An Asian Economic Area',* edited by V.R. Panchamukhi and Rehman Sobhan, South-South Centre, Geneva.

Venkitaramanan, S. (2005): A Monetary Physician with a Human Face, *The Hindu Business Line,* May 16.

Wolf, Martin (2004): Asia Needs its Own Monetary Fund, *Business Standard,* May 22.

Can South Asia Create a Common Currency?

PRIYANKA GAUR

INTRODUCTION

The empirical result suggests that the SAARC region is not suitable for the Currency Union. However, greater economic integration will reduce the cost of monetary cooperation. A single SAARC currency would symbolize a major step towards the realization of the dream of peaceful, stable and integrated South Asia.

Almost six decades after independence from British rule and two decades after the formation of South Asian Association for Regional Cooperation (SAARC), closer economic cooperation and integration in South Asia (SA) has finally become a real possibility with the improvement in political relation between India and Pakistan. In this context the issue of closer monetary cooperation, including that of single currency has been placed on the regional policy agenda and there is a real possibility that SA may emulate the European Union (EU) and move towards a single currency. This seems an opportune time to examine if the seven SA countries satisfy the criteria to create a single currency for the region.

Formation of SAARC

On Dec. 8, 1985 Bangladesh, Bhutan, India, Maldives, Nepal, Pakistan and Sri Lanka formed a South Asian Association for Regional Cooperation (SAARC). The primary goals of the organisation were to promote greater regional coordination of economic, social, cultural and scientific issues and present a unified voice to the rest of the world. SAARC's process can be separated into two stages. During stage I, output expansion was promoted though trade, investment and technology collaboration under the Integrated Programme of Action (IPA), the seven countries implemented a development strategy that included poverty alleviation, action for the environment, welfare gains for women and children, and social and cultural exchange. During stage II, SAARC members choose to promote a common market and macro-economic coordination that would lead to the SAARC Economic Union. The goal to move towards more economic integration and ultimately towards a common currency in SA was emphasized by the Prime Minister of India, Mr. A.B. Vajpayee, in January 2004. The commitment towards economic integration though free trade agreement has also been evident in the 12th SAARC summit held in Islamabad on Jan. 4-5, 2004.[1]

One of the first significant collaboration agreement of the member States was SAPTA agreement. SAPTA was implemented in Dec. 1995 and since then there have been four rounds of SAPTA negotiations. The successful SAPTA negotiations prompted SAARC leaders to set-up a 'committee of experts' to draft a treaty of SAFTA at the tenth SAARC summit in 1998. With the 'committee of experts' having resolved all the contentious issues during their meeting in Kathmandu from Nov. 29 to Dec. 1, the Agreement SAFTA among the seven member countries of SAARC, came into effect from Jan. 1, 2006. Moreover that expansion of SAARC with Afghanistan's admission as eighth members, China and Japan being accorded observer status was expected to deflect attention and create road block in the path for creating a proper road map for greater monetary cooperation.

At the eleventh SAARC summit, held in Kathmandu in Jan. 2002,[2] the member states have expressed a desire for higher level of economic cooperation, a South Asian Economic Union (SAEU). The SAARC GEP report[3] has in turn provided a roadmap towards economic integration: a free trade area by the year 2010, a Custom Union by 2015 and an Economic Union by 2020. In addition to SAEU, SAARC GEP report, has also mentioned the goal of achieving a "single monetary system, including a common currency."

Therefore, the objective of the paper, is to present some information relevant to this analysis, on the pattern of economic shocks affecting the member states in the region. Countries that face similar shocks are likely to encounter lower cost in giving-up these tool of adjustments as compare to other set of countries facing such shock.

Before I proceed with the paper, certain questions beg some discussions: Should the countries proceed with this Currency Union (CU) in the EU style? It was felt that the SA should proceed in the EU style by encouraging factor mobility and trade integration. Then the following path can be taken to the CU (Mundel 1997): First, there should be a commitment to fix the exchange rate with a credible mechanism of adjustment. Second, there should be an establishment of right monetary arrangements. Third, the national currency should be replaced by the common currency. Of course, to pursue the EU style economic integration, SA has some way to go. However, bilateral trade agreement among countries are encouraging. Additionally trade can be encouraged through fixing the exchange rate credibility. But if the currencies fluctuate persistently, it could lead to competitive depreciation and exchange dumping which could hinder the operation of a Single Market. Evidently, as regional trade initiatives grow, there will be an "increasing need to butters economic integration with monetary integration in other parts of the world as there has been in Europe."[4] Rose (2001) forcibly argues that the benefit of monetary union and common currency are understated. He finds that the pair of countries in a monetary union and CU seems to have substantially higher bilateral trade, holding a host of other factors constant. Even in a survey on the effect of common currency on international trade, Rose and Stanley (2004) documents that most studies find that CU raise trade a lot. Hence no matter what the move towards single currency assumes even more significant when countries want more economic integration though trade.

Again a questions arises, that when the same level of integration could also achieved though policy coordination like Canada and United States or Switzerland and Germany then, why do we need a common currency? 'The movement to a common currency legitimate recognition of political commitment to ensuring regional integration, hence it might be desirable in the SAARC region, where political incentives have outweigthed economic incentives to establish peace and stability which is crucial for growth in that region, even for Europe, the political economy wisdom dedicated that to avoid exchange rate fluctuations and sustain political support for internal market, the move toward common currency was inevitable.[5] The same would be true for SA the goal for the union is not necessarily to become an international currency and be competitive against the dollar and the Euro. The common currency can lead to a large increase in real income by boosting trade.[6] However, the major benefit of this union, will occur in term of peace, which will enhance growth in the region. This sentiment was echoed by Pakistan's President Mr. Musharraf, on his visit to India on April 17, 2005, "We want people in my country, Pakistan, and your country, India to prosper. This can only be done through peace."

ECONOMIC STRUCTURE OF SAARC COUNTRIES

This Section describes some stylized facts about the SA region including the exchange rate arrangements of member states and their growth and inflation performances. Table 1 provides some basic data about the seven member states of SAARC. Table 1 confirms that these countries are diverse in terms of land area, GDP and population, while having similar human and economic development. For example in term of size India occupies a pre-eminent position. It is over 10,000 times larger in geographical area, 3000 times more populous and has GDP over 8000 times greater then the smallest country in SAARC, the Maldives. Politically to, India's size affects the dynamics of interaction among members: India has

TABLE 1

Economic Structure of SAARC Countries, 2004

	Bangladesh	*Bhutan*	*India*	*Maldives*	*Nepal*	*Pakistan*	*Sri Lanka*
Population (mn)	140.5	8.96	1,079.7	0.3	25.2	152.2	19.4
GDP ($bm)	56.8	0.6	691.8	0.7	6.7	95.11	20.05
PCI ($)	44.0	3.60	620	2510	2.60	600	1010
HDI	0.520	0.536	0.602	0.745	0.526	0.527	.755
Area (km)^2	56,977	18,150	1,222,243	115	53,827	307,374	25,332

Source: World Development Report, 2006, World Bank: Human Development Report, 2005, UNDP.

73 per cent, 79 per cent and 77 per cent of the land area, GDP and population respectively of SAARC as a whole. However, despite large differences South Asian Economies are quite similar in several respects: low PCI, relatively poor HDI (with the possible exception of Sri Lanka), and economic structure.[7]

Table 2 shows the trend of regional economic indicators (output growth and inflation) for the period 1980-2004. Table 2 presents that, however, despite the absence of some systematic relationships during this period, there are some indications of a tendency for convergence in recent years,

TABLE 2

Macro Economic Indicator of SAARC Countries, 1980-2004

(In % change of GDP)

	Bangladesh	*Bhutan*	*India*	*Maldives*	*Nepal*	*Pakistan*	*Sri Lanka*
Output growth	4.2	4.6	6.2	7.8	3.4	4.6	4.7
*Inflation	5.0	7.7	7.9	5.0	7.4	8.1	9.7

* Data are available for the period 1980-2003.

Source: World Development Report, 2006, World Bank: Human Development Report, 2005, UNDP.

with Maldives as an exception. Output growth was within a band of 3 per cent to 5 per cent (with the exception of Maldives with a higher rate of 7.8 per cent), while average inflation came down and was limited to a band of 7-9 per cent (again exception for the Maldives and Bangladesh, which had a slightly lower figure of 5 per cent).

Unfortunately, the level of trade and investment linkage and cross border labour mobility in SAARC is quite low. Table 3 shows that intra SAARC trade is less than 5 per cent of regional income in 2001, mainly involving primary products RIS (2003), while regional trade openness was limited to 25 per cent of regional income. This trade pattern compares poorly ASEAN and Euro areas while being similar to that for Mercosur and NAFTA.[8] Similarly investment flows within the region remain low.[9] Labour mobility across countries borders is also quite low, though again there are significant informal movement of labour, particularly, into India from neighbouring countries.

TABLE 3

Regional Trade Pattern

Organisation	*Intra*	*Openness*
SAARC (2001)	4.7%	25%
ASEAN (1998)	23.5%	101.2%
Euro (1998)	24.8%	50.8%
NAFTA (1998)	4.4%	18%
Mercosur (1998)	10.7%	23%

Source: Direction to Trade Statistics Year Book (2002), IMF, International Financial Statistics (2002).

Just as there is huge diversity among the member states, there is considerable diversity at present in exchange rate regime in SA with each country having exchange rate policy independence. India and Pakistan have managed floats, Sri Lanka has free float and Bangladesh, Bhutan, Maldives and Nepal have pegged exchange rate.[10] The peg of Bhutan and Nepal to the Indian Rupee has been freely chosen by those countries though it has been fairly rigid, with one to one convertibility for the Bhutanese ngultrum over the last 20 years and only three adjustments in the exchange rate with the Nepalese rupee over the same period, whose last adjustment occurred almost a decade ago. Maldives has a defected pegged arrangement, maintaining fairly exchange rate relatively to the USD in recent years.

The choice of optimal exchange rate regime for a country remains an area of controversy and debate because each regime has its benefit and drawbacks and the specific economic, institutional and political contexts must be all taken into account in assessing the desirability of a particular region.[11] There is no simple correlation that can be empirically established between economic performance and exchange rate regime. However, where there are perceived gains from closer economic linkage, the issue of a common currency arises, because it had both direct economic as well as symbolic significance. The direct economic benefit of a common currency within a region the ultimate form of monetary cooperation arise from the basic fact that elimination of the multiple currencies and associated exchange rate fluctuations, reduce transaction cost and facilitate the enhancement of trade and investment.

STATISTICAL ANALYSIS AND RESULTS

The paper uses one particular aspect of the criteria for determining OCA—Nature of disturbance affecting SAARC—to determine if they are candidates for a CU.[12] The pattern of shocks indicates the cost of losing the tools of monetary and exchange rates for adjustments. Countries that face similar shocks would likely encounter lower costs in giving-up there tools of monetary and exchange rates for adjustments, then would other set of countries facing economic shocks. Unfortunately, preliminary estimates suggest that the data for a member states would not allow using the VAR technique pioneered by Bayoumi and Eichengreen (1994), is the most widely used in these type of analysis to decompose shocks from responses and allow analyzing the size of the disturbance and the speed of adjustment. For this reason, and to allow comparison across the region, we adopted an approach used by Bayoumi and Ostry (1991), based on a simplex time series model, where growth of real output was regressed on its own lags. Tables 6 and 7 presents a correlation matrix of disturbances for a single and double lags and they confirm observations made earlier of correlation coefficients in Tables 4 and 5. Again there is no clear-cut pattern of disturbances with a large number of both positive and negative correlation coefficients. The statistically

TABLE 4

Correlation of Output Growth, 1980-2004

	Bangladesh	*Bhutan*	*India*	*Maldives*	*Nepal*	*Pakistan*	*Sri Lanka*
Bangladesh	1.00						
Bhutan	0.35	1.00					
India	0.05	-0.07	1.00				
Maldives	0.14	-0.02	0.22	1.00			
Nepal	0.01	-0.35	-0.14	-0.40	1.00		
Pakistan	-0.32	-0.07	0.17	-0.07	0.07	1.00	
Sri Lanka	0.45	-0.14	-0.17	-0.11	0.01	-0.44	1.00

Note: Figures in bold are statistically significant at the 5% level.
Source: IMF, Boyoumi and Mouro (2001).

TABLE 5

Correlation of Inflation, 1980-2003

	Bangladesh	*Bhutan*	*India*	*Maldives*	*Nepal*	*Pakistan*	*Sri Lanka*
Bangladesh	1.00						
Bhutan	-0.35	1.00					
India	0.20	-0.37	1.00				
Maldives	0.01	-0.14	**0.47**	1.00			
Nepal	0.32	-0.22	0.28	0.35	1.00		
Pakistan	-0.17	0.32	**0.45**	0.24	-0.25	1.00	
Sri Lanka	**0.50**	-0.25	0.47	0.38	0.05	0.32	1.00

Note: Figures in bold are statistically significant at the 5% level.

TABLE 6

Correlation of Disturbance, (Single Lag)

	Bangladesh	*Bhutan*	*India*	*Maldives*	*Nepal*	*Pakistan*	*Sri Lanka*
Bangladesh	1.00						
Bhutan	1.08	1.00					
India	**-0.44**	0.25	1.00				
Maldives	**-0.87**	0.04	-0.32	1.00			
Nepal	-0.28	0.40	-0.17	-0.12	1.00		
Pakistan	-0.35	0.42	**-0.55**	**0.57**	-0.01	1.00	
Sri Lanka	**-0.49**	0.38	-0.19	**-0.68**	0.38	**-0.54**	1.00

Note: Figures in bold are statistically significant at the 5% level.

TABLE 7

Correlation of Disturbances, (Double Lag)

	Bangladesh	*Bhutan*	*India*	*Maldives*	*Nepal*	*Pakistan*	*Sri Lanka*
Bangladesh	1.00						
Bhutan	0.03	1.00					
India	-0.17	0.05	1.00				
Maldives	0.00	0.05	0.00	1.00			
Nepal	-0.02	-0.25	0.02	-0.38	1.00		
Pakistan	-0.13	-0.07	0.20	0.21	-1.00	1.00	
Sri Lanka	0.57	-0.47	-0.22	0.00	-0.05	-0.55	1.00

Note: Figures in bold are statistically significant at the 5% level.

significant (at 5 per cent level) correlations showed no consistency in either positive or negative direction.[13] This suggests that the member states did not face symmetrical pattern of shocks during that time period. This is similar to a finding for Africa (Bayoumi and Ostry (1997). The SD of the above residuals are taken as indicators of real shocks volatility faced by SAARC member countries.[14] The descriptive statistics of the SD of the errors are given in Table 8. Most of the SD of errors (for both lags) are in the 2

TABLE 8

Magnitude of Correlations (Std. Dev)

	Bangladesh	*Bhutan*	*India*	*Maldives*	*Nepal*	*Pakistan*	*Sri Lanka*
Single lag	0.006	0.009	0.015	0.015	0.014	0.017	0.010
Double lag	0.009	0.029	0.017	0.032	0.020	0.019	0.013

per cent range with the exception of the Maldives for the double lag and are similar to those calculated for Germany, Japan and U.S. by Bayoumi and Eichengreen (1994). These results suggest that most SAARC member states have faced rather similar levels of volatility in real output.[15]

DISCUSSION AND OBSERVATION

The empirical result shows that the region is not suitable candidate for a CU. The absence of strong positive correlations in shocks suggest that as a group the regions economies do not seem to face syncronised shocks. Further given the low level of intra-regional SAARC trade, factor mobility, there are no market mechanism either that can be ease adjustment.[16] More importantly, the regional and the political commitment to establishing a CU is missing. Thus the absence of both the economic and political justifications argue against the immediate consideration of the highest level of monetary cooperation i.e., a CU. It is natural to ask if the empirical results point to smaller sub-regional currency grouping in SAARC. Here the result indicates some paradoxical conclusions. For example the positive correlation for disturbances in India and Pakistan (Significant in a first lag but not in the second lag) suggest these two countries as candidates for a CU. However the miniscule bilateral trade and virtual absence of factor market interlinkage, not to speak of the on going tension, suggest otherwise. But some what surprisingly, there is no such support for a CU of India with Bhutan and Nepal, which already have a rigid exchange rate with the Indian rupee and stronger trade and factor market linkage.[17] Hence these result do not provide any support for a CU purely on the basis of conventional OCA criteria.

While the data suggest that the member states in SA may not be candidates for a CU during the sample period, the result would certainly change with greater economic integration as envisaged by SAEU. This is simply staining that the cost for joining a CU is endogenous over time (Frankle and Rose, 1998, also Karras and Stockes 2001). Since the SAARC GEP (1997-98) envision SAEU as a long term goal to be achieved at the earliest by 2020, this suggest that the cost of monetary cooperation would decrease with higher level of economic integration. The long time horizon makes sense in view of the present turbulent situation in SA. The implication is that step towards monetary cooperation should continue at a caution pace. In this regard, some important development have taken place recently, with the establishment and formal recognition in the past SAARC summit of SAARC Finance, an organisation of a Governors of Central Banks and Secretaries of Finance of SAARC member states. Presently the activities of this organisation are limited to information sharing, staff visits and organising workshop/ seminars.

It is also important to be aware of the sequencing used to achieve monetary cooperation. Unfortunately, SAARC GEP (1997-98) has not given a time bound road map with clear preconditions for attaining greater monetary cooperation. This is in contrast to economic integration, where the stages are mentioned in relatively greater detail. While the path for monetary cooperation will have to be assessed more comprehensively, movements towards monetary and economic integration may not stay to far from each other. Thus, it would seem reasonable, until a detailed framework is developed. For monetary cooperation to draw on the road map for economic integration as put forth above, to harmonize the respective monetary policies of member states consistent with their level of economic integration.

CONCLUSION

This paper is a modest attempt to answer a policy

question, is SAARC an OAC? We would have to conclude that loss of monetary independence will have non negligible costs for the SAARC economies given the absence of closely synchronized exogenous shocks across the region. The empirical result suggests that the member states were not suitable candidates for the CU during the surveyed period. Thus it suggest that the sequence of monetary cooperation in SA's growth should be structured and harmonized with the level of regional economic integration.[18]

While the above result suggest that the region is not suitable for a CU for this time, greater economic integration will reduce the cost of monetary cooperation. Such integration has the ability to bring, political stability and huge "peace dividend" in its wake. Moreover the nature of shocks will also change over time. Economic development and declining share of agriculture to GDP will make economic performance less sensitive to agricultural shocks. At the same time as the region moves towards SAFTA, the level and diversity of intra regional trade flows increase, terms of trade and financial shocks will became more likely. Thus, the complexity of this issue highlights the needs for comprehensive and integrated plan regarding monetry cooperation in SA including the necessary preconditions.[19] In the interim, the activity of SAARC FINANCE may be considered the start for greater monetary cooperation in the region. SAARC FINANCE may also be able to begin preliminary work for developing a comprehensive and integrated road map toward greater cooperation, which would not be inconsistent with the broad objective organisation.

Though we end on a note of caution we would not want to give the impression that we reject moves towards Single Currency. On the contrary we recognise that a single SAARC currency would symbolise a major step towards the realisation of the dream of a peaceful, stable and integrated South Asia. But the potential political risk of a common currency regime should be underestimated.[20] Particularly because trade and investment and capital market linkages are still at very low level. Thus priority should be given to greater interaction under the SAARC process, to enhance understanding among members and develop a feeling of regional identity. It is our hope that the issue that we have raised as area of potential concern in this preliminary investigation will lead to a region—while cooperative efforts to study the modalities of how best we can progress towards achieving higher level of economic integration, monetary cooperation and ultimately a single currency.

Notes and References

1. See "htp/www.saarc.sec.org/main.php" for details.
2. SAARC (2002), para 1.
3. SAARC (1997-98), pp. 20-21.
4. Eichengreen (1997) pp. 265.
5. Eichengreen (1997) pp. 364.
6. Francle and Rose, (2000).
7. The similarity of SAARC economic and human development is further reflected by the fact that four (Bangladesh, Bhutan, Maldives and Nepal) of the member states are LDCs and the remaining three are developing countries.
8. IMF, IFS (2006).
9. For more details crossment of the political trade-investment nexus in SA See Jayasuriya and Weerakoon (2001).
10. "Bayoumi and Mauro (2001).
11. For an excellent survey of this issue, see corden, (2002).
12. Since Muldell's (1961) and Mckinnon's (1963) Seminal work on OCA, researchers have focused on four interrelationship between the countries that would impinge a benefit of adopting common currency: Extent of trade, nature of disturbances, degree of labour mobility and fiscal transfer.
13. A result is similar to that reported in Maskey, (2001) for an earlier period.
14. Kontonemis and Semei (2000) use the various GDP growth to assess volatility.
15. Our analysis did not indicate any statistically significant differences between pre and post Liberalization period for the group (though admittedly the power of such test is limited by relatively short data series.
16. This point was made by the NRB (2000).
17. Perhaps not surprisingly, Maldives the most distant, the smallest and structurally different economy, has a different economic performance, despite having strong intra SAARC trade links (38% in 2000).
18. The present activities of SAARC FINANCE, as mentioned above are consistent with this.

19. Off course, the end product of greater monetary corporation and a single SA monetary system should be debated. Should it be a common currency member state or some other variation.
20. Recent Disturbance in Nepal and Bangladesh have also created obstacles in the way of smooth implementation of greater monetary cooperation.

References

Athukorala, and S. Jayasuriyas (1994), "Macro-economic Policies, Crises and Growth in Sri Lanka", 1969-90, World Bank, Washington, DC.

Banerjee, Paula (*et al.*) (1999), "Indo-Bangladesh Cross Border Migration and Trade," *Economic and Political Weekly*, September 1999.

Bayoumi, Tamim, and Eichengreen Barry (1994), "One Money or Many? Analyzing the Prospects for Monetary Unification in Various Parts of the World," *Princeton Studies in International Finance*, No. 76.

Bayoumi, Tamim, Eichengreen Barry and Paolo Mauro (2000), "On Regional Monetary Arrangements for ASEAN," *Journal of the Japanese and International Economics*, 14, pp. 121–148.

Bayoumi, Tamim and Mauro Paolo (2001), "The Suitability of ASEAN for a Regional Currency Arrangement," *World Economy*, 24, pp. 933–45.

Bayoumi, Tamim and Jonathan D. Ostry (1997), "Macro-economic Shocks and Trade Flows within Sub-Saharan Africa: Implications for Optimum Currency Arrangements," *Journal of African Economies (UK)*. 6, pp. 412–44.

Blankchard, Oliver Jean and Quah Damy (1989): "The Dynamic Effects of Aggregate Demand and Supply Disturbances", *American Economic Review*, 70(4), pp. 655-73.

Corden (2002): "Too Sensational: On the Choice of Exchange Rate Regimes", MIT Press.

Dasgupta, Amit, and Maskay Nephil Matangi (2003), "Financial Policy Coordination in SAARC; A First Step Toward Monetary Integration in South Asia." Forthcoming in 4(1) of *South Asia Economic Journal.*

Eichengreen, Barry (1997), "*European Monetary Unification: Theory, Practice and Analysis*", MIT Press, Cambridge Massachusetts.

Frankel, Jeffrey A. and Rose Andrew K. (1998), "The Endogeneity of the Optimum Currency Area Criteria," *The Economic Journal*, 108, pp. 1009–25.

Frankel J. and Rose A. (2002): "*An Estimate of the Effect of Common Currencies on Trade and Income*," *Quarterly Journal of Economics*, 117 (4), pp. 437-66

Jayasuriya, S. and Weerakoon, D. (2001): Foreign Direct Investment and Economic Integration in the SAARC Region in T.N. Srinivasan (ed.), Trade, Finance and Investment in South Asia, Social Sciences Press, New Delhi.

Jayasuriya, S., Maskay Nephil Matangi and Vweerakoon Dushni in Collaboration with Yuba Raj Khatiwada and Shalini Kurukulasuriya (2004): "Monetary Cooperation in South Asia", mimeo, prepared for South Asia Network of Economic Institutes (SANEI).

Karras, Georgios, and Stokes Houston H., 2001, "Time-varying Criteria for Monetary Integration; Evidence from the EMU," *International Review of Economics and Finance,* 10, pp. 171–85.

Krueger, A.O. (2002): "Economic Policy Reforms and the Indian Economy", Oxford University Press, India.

———(2002): "South Asian Monetary Integration in Light of the Optimum Currency Area Criteria Patterns of Shocks: A Reply", *South Asia Economic Journal,* 3(2), pp. 281-84.

———(1998): "A Note on a Single Currency for SAARC", *Indian Economic Journal,* 46(I), pp. 118-210.

McKinnon, Ronald (1963), "Optimum Currency Areas," *American Economic Review,* 53 (September), 717-24.

Maskay, Nephil Matangi, 1998, "A Comment on Empirical Estimation of Patterns of Shocks Utilizing the VAR Methodology on Developing Countries," *Journal of Economic Integration,* 13(3), pp. 544–8.

———(2000), "A Cautionary Note in Using Patterns of Shocks to Determine Optimal Exchange Rate Policy; An Exploration of Nepalese and Indian Exchange Rate Relations of 1964–1994," *Applied Economics,* Vol. 32, No. 4, pp. 491–8.

———(2001), "South Asian Monetary Integration in Light of the Optimum Currency Area Criteria Patterns of Shocks," *South Asia Economic Journal,* 2:2, pp. 203-19.

Masson, Paul R., and Taylor Mark P. (eds.), (1993), "Policy Issues in the Operation of Currency Unions," (Cambridge: Cambridge University Press).

Minz, N. (1970), "Monetary Union and Economic Intergeneration" (New York: University Press).

Mundell, Robert (1961), "A Theory of Optimum Currency Area," *American Economic Review,* Vol. 51, pp. 657-65.

Nepal Rastra Bank (2000), "Feasibility of Using National Currencies in SAARC Trade."

———(2001), SAARC FINANCE seminar conference volume, *Issues in Exchange Rate Management,* (Nepal: Nepal Rastra Bank).

Rose, Andrew, (2000), "Currency Unions: Their Dramatic Effect on International Trade," *Economic Policy,* pp. 8-45.

SAARC (1985), *Charter.*

———(1997/98), "SAARC Vision Beyond the Year 2000: Report of the SAARC Group of Eminent Persons."

———(2002), "Declaration of the 11th Summit in Kathmandu, Nepal," January 6.

———Website, available on the Internet at: http://www.saarc-sec.org

———(2004), Declaration of Twelth SAARC Summit in Islamabad, Pakistan," Jan. 4, 5.

Data Sources

International Monetary Fund, *International Financial Statistic* (Washington, DC),: various issues.

International Monetary Fund (2002), *Direction of Trade Statistics* (Washington, DC).

World Bank (2006), *World Development Indicators (2006)*, (Washington, DC).

———(1997), *World Development Indicators (1997)*, (Washington, DC).

United Nations Development Programme (2005), *Human Development Report (2005)* (New York).

CHAPTER

12

Exchange Rate Regimes and Monetary Policy for Asian Countries

PUSPA TARAFDAR

This paper focuses on issues arising from rapid increase in the foreign exchange reserves in Asia consequent on heavy capital inflows. The stock of foreign exchange reserves exceeded $ 1,800 billion including Japan at the end of 2003 which constitute half of total global reserves. Against this background this paper seeks to examine the issues relating to exchange rate regimes in Asia namely exchange rate policies, monetary policies and policies regarding financial flows. The outline of the paper is as follows.

Section I examines the need for broader Asian Integration. Section II examines the characteristics of capital flows. Section III examines the exchange rate policies and monetary policies in Asian emerging economies. The final Section IV draws policy implication on the issue.

There is now a growing recognition of the importance of regional economic integration in Asia in generating growth impulses from within. The East Asian crisis of 1997 also highlighted the importance of regional economic cooperation. The ASEAN is emerging as an important regional economic grouping with the implementation of AFTA and further deepening of the economic integration. The crisis also led to the launch of several regional initiatives such as Chiang Mai Initiative which involves ASEAN+3 (Japan, China and South Korea).

However, it can be argued that the sub-regional or bilateral attempts at regional co-operation that have been initiated under the framework of ASEAN or SAARC are unlikely to exploit the full potential of the regional economic integration in Asia. This is because the extent of complementarities are limited at the sub-regional levels because of similar factor endowments and economic structures within the neighbourhood. At the broader Asian level, on the other hand, the diversities in the levels of economic development and capabilities are quite wide thus providing for more extensive and mutually beneficial linkages.

There is the realisation that stimulus for future economic growth has to increasingly come from within the region given the trend of formation of regional trading blocs in the rest of the world. The substantial complementarities exist between Asian countries that remain to be exploited for their mutual common benefit. The regional co-operation could also help for exploiting the existing capabilities in the region fully. The lost output because of the under utilization of capacity in the Japanese and Korean construction and engineering industries could be of the order of 10-15 per cent of the GDP or about one trillion dollars a year (Agarwalla 2002). A more extensive co-operation for matching the underutilized capacity in some countries of the region with unmet demand in others could go a long way in putting the region on a high growth trajectory and help Asia to reemerge as a centre of gravity in the world economy.

The Asian region combines some of the fastest growing economies of the world. Together they form a huge market that is growing faster than any other region in the world and could form a vibrant regional grouping that would be roughly of the size of the EU in terms of GDP, will have larger magnitude of trade than North American Free Trade Agreement (NAFTA) and international reserves bigger than those of EU and NAFTA put together. The formation of a broader Asian grouping will also help the region to play a more effective role in shaping the emerging world trading and financial system.

Combined foreign exchange reserves of the JACIK (Japan, ASEAN, China, India and Korea) economies now add-up to nearly US $ 2 trillion and comprise the bulk of such reserves in the world. These funds have been invested in low-yielding U.S. treasury bonds and are able to contribute to the Asian development more meaningfully. There is a growing consensus that Asia needs a regional institution for mobilizing these resources for its own development, besides achieving stability for real effective exchange rates and for orderly response to external shocks. Several studies have shown that there is a growing macro-economic interdependence between Japan, Korea and ASEAN. Such interdependence is likely to include China and India besides Australia and New Zealand with ongoing reforms, liberalization and market opening. The formation of a broader Asian grouping will also help the region to play a more effective role in shaping the emerging world trading and financial system.

SECTION II

The behaviour of capital flows during 1990s in the emerging market economies reveals that these flows can increase rapidly but can be highly volatile. Surges in capital flows and the associated volatility have implications for the conduct of monetary, exchange rate and the foreign exchange reserve policies. Emerging market economies, thus, need to be equipped to deal with such volatility in order to ensure monetary and financial stability. A striking feature of the last 3-4 years is two way movement of capital between Emerging Market Economics (EMEs) and mature economies. Notwithstanding the recovery in capital flows, emerging market economies, as a group, have become net exporters of capital to the matured economies since 2000. Three key factors explain the recent movement in capital flows (IMF 2004). First, EMEs have recorded current account surpluses. As against deficit of US $ 65 billion per annum during the 1990s, the emerging market economies recorded a surplus of US $ 149 billion during 2000-03. The emergence of surpluses reflected the adjustment process in response to the financial crisis in Asia and elsewhere. Countries that experienced crisis had to reduce domestic absorption and increase exports to generate a trade surplus. This process is quite high in East Asian Countries which have seen a sharp turnround in their current accounts (Table 1).

TABLE 1

Current Account Behaviour in Select Economies

(Percentage of GDP)

Country	*1991-96*	*1998-2003*
China	0.9	2.4
India	-1.1	-0.1
Indonesia	-1.3	0.5
Korea	-2.3	3.1
Malaysia	-6.4	11.4
Philippines	-3.8	4.6
Thailand	-6.4	8.1
Mexico	-4.2	-2.8

Source: International Economic Trends, Federal Reserve Bank of St. Louis, July 2004, as represented in Report on currency and Finance, 2003-2004).

Countries affected by crisis were also forced external deleveraging, i.e., a reduction in their external liabilities which also explain the pattern of capital out flows since 2001. This process which started in 1997 is still ongoing in some countries. Although non-crisis countries also exhibited some adjustments, burden was mainly borne out by the crisis countries. The crisis countries witnessed an overage outflow of US $ 48.5 billion per annum during 2000-03 as compared with an average outflow of US $ 45.8 billion by non-crisis counties. The order of correction is better gauged when outflows are scaled by GDP, the outflows in the former group of countries at 2.8 per cent of their GDP were more than three times of that recorded by non-crisis countries 0.9 per cent of GDP (during 2000-03) (Table 2).

TABLE 2

Net Capital Flows to Emerging Markets

(US $ Billion)

Items	*1996*	*1997*	*1998*	*1999*	*2000*	*2001*	*2002*	*2003*
All EMEs	74.4	47.3	104.2	5.2	-99.1	-49.9	-90.5	-137.7
Net Inflows	(1.3)	(0.8)	(1.7)	(0.1)	(-1.6)	(- 0.8)	(-1.4)	(-1.9)
Crisis Counties	53.6	64.8	18.7	-21.6	-33.9	-30.4	-57.6	-72.0
Net Inflows	(2.4)	(2.9)	(1.0)	(-1.3)	(-1.9)	(-1.8)	(-3.7)	(-3.9)
Non-Crisis Countries	20.9	-17.5	85.5	26.8	-65.2	-19.5	-32.8	-65.8
Net inflows	(0.6)	(-0.4)	(2.1)	(0.6)	(-1.4)	(-0.4)	(-0.7)	(-1.2)

Notes: 1. Crisis countries include Argentina, Brazil, Indonesia, Malaysia, Philippines.

2. Figures in brackets are per cent to GDP.

Source: Global, Financial Stability Report IMF, September 2004.

Second, global imbalances and a large US current account deficit also explain the reverse capital movements from EMEs. Third, the movements in capital flows reflect the accumulation of reserves to maintain a competitive exchange rate. Reflecting all these factors foreign exchange reserves of the developing countries increased by US $ 1256 billion between 1996 and 2004 (Table 3).

The need for reserves as self insurance emanates from the volatile nature of the capital flows. It also reflects weakness in the existing financial architecture. (Ready, 2003). Capital flows have been observed to reverse quickly, leaving the country exposed to liquidity crisis.

As IMF (2003) finds, the level of reserve accumulation in some of the Asian economies has become much higher

TABLE 3

Total Reserves Accumulation

Area/Country	*Dec. 1996*	*Dec. 2003*	*June 2004*	*Variance@*
All Countries	1647	3156	3463	1816
Industrial Countries	789	1219	1349	560
Japan	217	663	808	591
Developing Countries	858	1938	2114	1256
Asia	495	1248	1385	890
China P.R. Mainland	107	408	475	368
Taiwan Prov of China	88	207	230	142
Korea	34	155	167	133
China P.R. Hong Kong	64	118	121	57
India	20	99	115	95
Singapore	77	96	102	25
Malaysia	27	45	54	27

Note: Variation between June 2004 and Dec. 1996.
Source: International Financial Statistics, IMF.

than warranted by conventional determinants, such as economic size, level of imports, export volatility; and exchange rate flexibility. Decomposing the change in reserves—reveals that 13 sample economies are being grouped into roughly three sub-groups that are experiencing (i) current account surplus and net capital inflows, (ii) current account surplus and net capital outflows, and (iii) relatively small balance of payments activity. All sample economies with the exception of Pakistan and Vietnam reported current account surplus at the end of 2003. One notable observation, however, is a difference in the trade balance. In countries where service sector is strong (i.e. Hong Kong, China; India; Pakistan; Philippines), the current account surplus is supported by the service trade surplus, or more precisely, remittances from residents abroad, e.g. Philippines. (Table 4).

After a period of post crisis drying-up of capital inflows, capital flows turned around to an upward trend during the past few years driven by both "Push"—the recovery of the world economy and low rate of returns outside, and "pull" rapid economic growth of some countries.

TABLE 4

Grouping by Current Account and Capital Account Positions (As of end –2003)

Group A (5 Economies) Current Account-surplus and Capital Inflows	*Group B (5 Economies) Current Account-surplus and Capital Outflows*	*Group C (3 Economies) All Accounts Less than $5 billion*
PRC	Hong Kong, China	Pakistan
India	Indonesia	Philippines
Japan	Malaysia	Vietnam
Korea	Singapore	
Taipei, China	Thailand	

Inflows during the past few years, however, were concentrated in limited countries: PRC; India; Japan; Korea; and Taipei, China (Group A) which attracted more capital than they export. The PRC is the leading capital importer (except for Japan), receiving $ 61 billion in 2003, largely as a pipeline commitments for new foreign investment, followed by $ 17 billion to Korea and $ 11 billion to India.

China was again the largest recipient of FDI, not only in the region but also among all developing countries worldwide. Strong economic growth, an improved policy environment and further opening-up to FDI in certain industries—such as banking and other financial services—contributed to the increase. Investments by private equity and venture capital funds, specially from the United States, have become important sources of foreign investment in China.

Two major components of capital (or more precisely financial) flows are equity investment and commercial bank flows. The PRC has become by far the most attractive destination of equity investment, receiving about $190 billion during the past 4 years or about 4 per cent of GDP on an average. On the other hand, portfolio investments to countries like Korea have recently significantly decreased from about $59 billion in the early 1990s to $ 14 billion accounting for a share of only 5 per cent of the total flow to the sample countries. There was sharp rise in net portfolio capital inflows specially into PRC, India, and Japan as well as Taipei China. In India, portfolio flows (1.7 per cent of GDP) have become more prominent exceeding the direct investment (0.8 per cent of GDP) in 2003. For the PRC direct investment (3.5 per cent of GDP) is still the major part of equity investment (Table 5).

TABLE 5

Net FDI and Porfolio Investment

(Millions of US $)

	Cumulative Flows (1993-1996)	*Share of Total Flows (%)*	*Cumulative Flows (2000-03)*	*Share of Total Flows (%)*
•PRC	132.753	47	187.600	71
India	19.707	7	30.779	12
Korea	58.745	21	13.546	5
Indonesia	14.636	5	10.715	4
Thailand	10.186	4	1.473	4
Malaysia	29.243	10	4.358	2
Philippines	8.204	3	3.757	1
Vietnam	3.226	1	2.260	1
Pakistan	4.473	2	2.042	1
Total	281.173	100	265.530	100

Source: Institute of International Finance.

The trend of commercial bank flows is distinct from that of equity investment. The dramatic change in found around the time of the Asian Financial crisis in 1997. The contagious withdrawal of capital from the region—sudden stop of capital inflows—forces the crisis hit countries to suffer from liquidity crunches. Three crisis hit countries, Indonesia, Philippines and Thailand, still experienced met outflows in 2003. There are only three countries that attracted sizeable bank inflows: PRC, India and Korea. They attracted about $ 4 billion (India), $ 5 billion (PRC), and $ 10 billion (Korea) in 2003 while Malaysia and Vietnam received less than a billion.

Volatility of the capital account may vary due to the different types of flows they are experiencing. Past studies show that FDI tends to be least volatile, while portfolio and bank flows tend to be more volatile. Countries like India, where portfolio and bank flows are more significant than FDI, appear most fragile to capital account development, while it is less so in the PRC. Nevertheless, the volatility and actual magnitude of outflows, are significantly affected by the extent of capital controls that each country adopts.

South East Asia witnessed rise in capital inflows from $ 17 billion in 2003 to $ 26 billion in 2004. Higher capital inflows to Singapore, Malaysia, Indonesia, Myanmar, Vietnam, the Philippines, and Cambodia contributed to the region's increased FDI receipts.

The rapid rise of FDI inflows to the region and the narrowing gap between flows to ASEAN members and China assuaged those concerned that China is crowding out FDI from its neighboring countries. A recent study suggests that FDI in China did not crowed out FDI inflows in South Asian Countries during 1992-2001. (Zhou and Lall 2005). This is based on the fact that export oriented FDI in China may have been so far complementary to that in South East Asian Countries.

In view of improved economic situation in the region, a better policy environment, and significant regional integration efforts, the prospects for FDI flows to Asia and Oceania are highly positive. The recent increase in cross-border M & As in countries such as China, India and the Republic of Korea supports this optimistic assessment of FDI prospects in the region. However, flows are likely to remain concentrated in a few economics.

SECTION III

Monetary authorities in Asia appear committed to strict management of the exchange rate in both variability and level. In Asia, many countries have gradually narrowed their exchange rate fluctuations by actively managing foreign exchange after the crisis of 1997-98. Many East Asian countries are accumulating dollar assets as a by product of a strategy of export-led growth. The stock of foreign exchange assets exceeded $ 1,800 billion ($ 1,200 billion excluding Japan) at end of 2003, equal to half the global total reserves. Asian Central banks used the reserves to finance well over half of the current account deficit and budget deficit of the United States.

McKinnon (2003) argues that American overspending has trapped East Asia into running current account surpluses: the region is forced to acquire dollar assets in order to avoid exchange rate appreciation and deflation.

However, the amount of reserves appears to be more than what would be warranted by economic fundamental (IMF 2003). The accumulation has been particularly significant in people's republic of China (PRC) India, Japan, Republic of Korea, Pakistan, and Taipei, China where growth rate of reserves has exceeded 20 per cent during the last 2 years. In this respect worth mention are the PRC and India, which recorded average growth rates of about 30 per cent in 2001-2003.

The experience of living with capital flows since the 1970s has fundamentally altered the context of monetary policy. In particular, there is a dramatic shift in the still unsettled debate on the determinants of exchange rate and the choice of the appropriate exchange rate regime, although the weight of opinion is clearly in favour of a flexible regime. According to conventional wisdom, it was trade flows which were the key determinants of exchange rate movements. In more recent times, the importance of capital flows on determining the exchange rate movements has increased considerably. On a day today basis, it is capital flows which influence exchange rate and interest rate arithmetic of the financial markets.

The key question is whether there exists a viable and appropriate exchange rate regime for developing economies when major reserve currencies are subject to frequent gyrations and misalignments, and when international capital movements are extremely unstable.

Volatile exchange rate has been proven to have negative impacts on trade and FDI flows. Therefore a shift in the trade relationship would affect the currency regime–

greater stability is preferred vis-à-vis the major trading partners. If U.S. becomes less important as an export destination, the benefit of having stability against the U.S. dollar will be smaller. As the shares of interregional trade have been steadily increasing, particularly in East and South East Asia, the average trade weighted exchange rate has been fluctuating less than that against the U.S. dollar during the past years. Average trade weighted exchange rate has been managed more against trading partner currencies. Also the exchange rate level developments reveal a striking depreciation of trade weighted rates by 8 per cent during the last 4 years. See Tables 6 and 7 "Moving out" of the U.S.

TABLE 6

Average Nominal Exchange Rate Variability

(Trade-weighted vs. US $)

	2001	*2002*	*2003*	*2004*	2005
Trade-weighted	1.98	2.22	1.29	1.22	1.15
Against $	2.63	2.80	1.40	1.31	0.21

Note: Countries include India, Indonesia, Japan, Korea, Pakistan, Philippines, Singapore and Thailand

Source: International Financial Statistics (IMF various years) and Data Stream. As represented in *Asian Development Review*, p. 28.

TABLE 7

Average Nominal Exchange Rate

(Trade-weighted vs. *US $)*

	2001	*2002*	*2003*	*2004*	*2005*
Against $	100.0	108.6	107.0	104.3	102.4
Trade-weighted	100.1	103.6	102.8	105.9	108.4

Note: Countries include India, Indonesia, Japan, Korea, Pakistan, Philippines, Singapore and Thailand.

Source: International Financial Statistics (IMF various years) and Data Stream. As represented in *Asian Development Review*, p. 28.

dollar does not seem a wise option yet, however, there is a motive to rely less on the dollar to pursue export led growth.

As long as the US remains the largest economy, it is unlikely that the U.S. dollar will lose its status as the anchor currency in trade transactions. As Asian economies grow, their currencies would surely become relatively important. So possibilities are there that Asian economies will opt for more flexible exchange rate regimes and grow out of the U.S. dollar in the long-run, but this does not appear feasible in the short-run.

The question arises about the extent to which the exchange rate may be left to be determined in the market. PRC, Hon Kong, China and Malaysia have either currency board arrangement (CBA) or official fixed peg arrangements. While other countries such as Korea and Philippines declare floating regimes, it appears that all central banks of these countries intervene in foreign exchange markets to a certain degree. Although exchange rate regimes, except for India, are found to have moved to more flexibility until 2001, recent data suggest a reversal of this trend. Therefore these countries are apparently shifting towards more managed regimes.

SECTION IV
CONCLUDING REMARKS

Currencies in Asia have increasingly reduced their variability, and appear more managed suggesting monetary authorities' intervention in foreign exchange markets. However, the developments of exchange rate levels suggest that the intervention did not prevent nominal and real appreciation in several economies over the period of review. As inflows persist and reserves accumulates the sterilization policy can not be a lasting solution, and can be costly. Sterilization can be used in liquidity management in the short-run, however, the exchange rate policies and practices may need reconsideration in countries such as PRC and India, in the medium term. The transition would entail partial liberalization of the capital account and greater transparency and stringency in monetary policy.

Nevertheless, moving to capital account convertibility and exiting from intermediate exchange rate regime remains to be a long-run solution for these countries. As these countries are burdened with various problems, the general consensus is that reform effort should go far enough before moving to capital account liberalization.

References

Agarwala, Ramgopal (2003-04), "Towards A Multipolar World of International Finance", *Indian Economic Journal,* July-Sept., Vol. 5, No. 2.

Akiko, Terada-Hagiwara (2005), "Foreign Exchange Reserves, Exchange Rate Regimes and Monetary Policy: Issues in Asia", *Asian Development Review,* Vol. 22, No. 2, pp. 2, 6-8, 26-28.

International Monetary Fund (2003), *World Economic Outlook,* Washington, D.C.

Kumar Nagesh (2005), "A Broader Asian Community and a Possible Roadmap", *Economic and Political Weekly,* Vol. XL, No. 36, Sept. 3, pp. 3926-28

Puspa Tarafdar (2000), "Exchange Rate Behaviour in Developing Countries", in Context of India in Alak Ghosh and Rakesh Raman, (eds), *Exchange Rate Behaviour in Developing Countries,* Deep & Deep Publications Pvt. Ltd., pp. 143-48.

Reserve Bank of India, "Report on Currency and Finance, 2002-03 and 2003-04", pp. 83-85.

United Nation Conference on Trade and Development, UNCTD, 2005.

World Investment Report, 2002, 2005, pp. 52-53.

Integration of the North Eastern Region with the Neighbouring Countries in Trade and Commerce

Look East Policy Implicates

READINGSTAR JOHN NONGBRI

INTRODUCTION

In the present era of globalization, the world has been gradually integrated to a single economic region. Different countries have been unable to resist the powerful forces of globalization. Hence, they (different economies) have to adjust themselves according to the new economic order like internationalization of trade and liberalization of financial transaction.[1] This new economic order is influenced by Trans/ Multi National Corporation (TNC/MNC). As a result of the globalizing force, the political national boundaries seem to have lost their importance and the geographical obstacles are also reduced. The role of TNCs or MNCs in bringing a complex chain of global interdependencies is quite imminent. The growing influence of the forces of globalization, the collapse of USSR and other factors have made India to look within Asia for gaining its own ground as an Asian power[2] and to strengthen its economic ties with the Asian countries especially the emerging fastest growing economies of the South East Asia.

The aim of this paper is to briefly analyse the prospect of trade and economic integration between the Northeast and the Neighbouring Countries. The paper included 6 Sections. Section 1, is an Introduction. Section 2 deals with the regional economic cooperation between India and the South Asian Countries. Section 3 looks into the status of trade between India and the five neighbouring countries of the North-East. Section 4 deals on the trade of the North-East and the Neighbouring Countries. Section 5 look into trade and integration of economy of the North-East and the Neighbouring Countries (NC) in the context of the Look-East policy and Section 6 is the concluding observation.

REGIONAL ECONOMIC COOPERATION BETWEEN INDIA AND THE SOUTH EAST ASIAN COUNTRIES

The Economic cooperation of various forms has impacted on the process of economic development of different economies. Expecting a good implication from economic cooperation, planners of different countries have agreed upon forming economic cooperation on a regional/ sub-regional basis. The Economic Community of West African States (ECOWAS), the European Union (EU), the North America Free Trade Agreement (NAFTA), the Central American Common Market, the East African Community, the Arab Common Market, the Association of South East Asian Nation (ASEAN) Free Trade Area are some economic groupings formed on the basis of economic cooperation among different countries of the world. It is understood that these common economic associations were formed with an objective of mutual help among the member countries.

Guru and Wadhva elaborately discussed the implications and benefits of having economic cooperation among the Asian Countries. Guru[3] examined the implication of various forms of economic cooperation in fostering trade of the developing countries. By citing the example of the regional economic cooperation among Latin American Countries which set-up the Latin America Free Trade Area (LAFTA) and its good result, he urged for regional/economic cooperation among the South East Asian Countries. He contended that such cooperation would not only increase intra-trade among member countries but would also enable the individual member to get a better market for better utilization of resources and to enjoy the benefits of the economic of scale. While Wadhva[4] shows three alternatives for economic cooperation among countries which he terms the *first best*, the *second best* and the *third best*. The *first best* relates to global welfare, the *second best* to regional welfare and the *third best* is the sub-set of the *second best*. He felt that the economic condition of Asia would be more effective with the third best alternative of sub-regional grouping. Goswami and Gogoi also felt that formation of sub-regional zone will benefit the economy. They felt that the three neighbouring countries viz. China, India and Myanmar can form a sub-regional zone.[5]

The expectation of growth from regional, sub-regional grouping/cooperation was felt by planner of Asian Countries. Subsequently, several agreements for trade and economic cooperation were made/formed in the recent past. The Bangladesh-India-Myanmar-Sri Lanka-Thailand Economic Cooperation (BIMST EC), the Mekong-Ganga Cooperation (MGC), the South Asian Association for Regional Cooperation (SAARC), are few examples of agreements for economic cooperation in the Asian region. The SAARC countries in their Islamabad Summit (2004) also move ahead and signed the historic agreement to establish free trade among the member countries, called the South Asian Free Trade Agreement (SAFTA). This agreement which super cedes the South Asian Preferential Trade Agreement (SAPTA) was supposed to have come into force by 1st January, 2006.[6] These agreements on trade and economic cooperation have no doubt impacted positively on trade and development of the member countries. Apart from the formation of regional economic cooperation, the collapse of USSR the near financial default in the early 1990s[7] and the China factor [8] made India to look to the Asian countries for economic ties and other cooperation. Due to this trade between India and the Neighbouring Countries (NC) including the South East Asian countries are improving in recent years (Table 1).

TABLE 1

India's Trade with the Selected Neighbouring Countries including the South East Asian Countries

(Rs. Lakhs)

Year	*Export*	*Import*	*Total*	*Trade Balance*
1992-93	606168	426401	1032569	179767
	(11.29)	(6.72)	(8.82)	
1993-94	880867	461497	1342364	419370
	(12.62)	(6.30)	(9.39)	
1994-95	1030906	883698	1914604	147208
	(12.46)	(9.82)	(11.08)	
1995-96	1536776	1238309	2775085	298467
	(14.44)	(10.09)	(12.11)	
1996-97	1779895	1377930	3157825	401965
	(14.98)	(9.91)	(12.25)	
1997-98	1704478	1750225	3454703	-45747
	(13.10)	(11.35)	(12.15)	
1998-99	1499216	2344999	3844215	-845783
	(10.58)	(13.31)	(12.10)	

Notes: 1. The figures in the brackets indicate the percentage to world trade (export/import).

2. The selected neighbouring countries includes: Bangladesh, Singapore, Sri Lanka, China, Thailand, Malaysia, Indonesia, Nepal, Philippi and Pakistan.

Source: CMIE, Foreign Trade and Balance of Payment, Centre for Monitoring Indian Economy, pp. 110-11, July 1999.

STATUS OF INDIA'S TRADE WITH FIVE COUNTRIES SURROUNDING: THE NORTH-EASTERN REGION

India had trade relation with all the five Neighbouring Countries surrounding the North East. That is, Bangladesh, Bhutan, China, Myanmar and Nepal. Trade between India's North-East and its NC may be classified into official and unofficial (illegal) trade.[9] Most official trade between India and the NC are carried out in the framework of different trade agreements that India signed with them. India had signed trade agreements with Bangladesh (1980), Nepal (1991), Myanmar (1994) and Bhutan (1995).[10] Besides the existence of trade agreement and the decision of SAARC to convert SAPTA into SAFTA, the share of India's trade with

TABLE 2

India's Export and Import with the Neighbouring Countries of the North Eastern Region

(US $ Million)

	April-October					
	2003-04		*2004-05*		*2005-06 (p)*	
	Export	*Import*	*Export*	*Import*	*Export*	*Import*
China	1156.6	2085.8	2012.1	3550.2	2993.4	5218.5
	(3.50)	(5.00)	(4.75)	(6.22)	(5.72)	(6.80)
			{70.0}	{70.0}	{48.8}	{47.0}
Bangladesh	902.2	43.1	803.8	23.9	843.7	40.4
	(2.73)	(0.10)	(1.89)	(0.04)	(1.61)	(0.05)
			{-10.7}	{-44.5}	{5.0}	{68.8}
Bhutan	54.0	29.1	51.7	35.8	45.2	39.2
	(0.16)	(0.06)	(0.12)	(0.06)	(0.08)	(0.05)
			{-4.2}	{23.2}	{-12.6}	{9.4}
Nepal	340.0	136.2	445.1	177.4	426.3	216.3
	(1.03)	(0.32)	(1.05)	(0.31)	(0.88)	(0.28)
			{30.9}	{30.3}	{3.9}	{22.0}
Myanmar	.NA	NA	NA	NA	NA	NA
Total	2452.8	2294.2	3312.7	3787.3	4344.6	5514.4
	(7.43)	(5.50)	(7.82)	(6.63)	(8.30)	(7.19)
			{35.05}	{65.08}	{31.14}	{45.60}
World	33007.9	41681.5	42334.3	57069.1	52284.1	76647.9

Notes: 1. (p)→Provisional.
2. NA→ Not available.
3. Figure in ( ) Implies percentage to the world export or import.
4. Figure in { } Implies the variation percentage with the preceding year.

Source: RBI Bulletin, January 2006, pp. 57, 59.

the Neighbouring Countries is quite small. India's export to Bordering Countries of the North Eastern Region for the period 2003-04, 2004-05, and 2005-06 accounted for 7.43 per cent, 7.82 per cent and 8.30 per cent respectively of India's total export. That is, export to NC increased by 35.05 per cent between 2003-04 and 2004-05 and 31.14 per cent during 2004-05 and 2005-06. For the same period import from these countries accounted for 5.50 per cent, 6.63 per cent and 7.19 per cent indicating a percentage variation of 65.08 per cent and 45.60 per cent between 2003-4, 2004-05 and 2005-06. These figures indicate that India's trade with NC bordering the North East are Increasing both in term of volume and as percentage to India's World Trade (Table 2).

COUNTRY-WISE ANALYSIS OF TRADE RELATIONSHIP

India had trade relation with all trading blocks of the World and all its NC. However, this section deals only with the five countries which have common border with the North Eastern Region.

Indo-Bangladesh Trade

The Bangladesh border is the longest land border that India shares with any of its neighbours. It covers a length of 4,095 kilometers covering the States of West Bengal (2216.70 kms), Assam (263 kms), Meghalaya (443 kms), Mizoram (318 kms) and Tripura (856 kms).[11] Like India, Bangladesh also initiated trade liberalization in the country in the 1990s. Trade liberalization in the form of tariff reduction, non-tariff barrier, simplification of import procedure, export incentives, etc. lead to sharp increase in external trade of the country. The increase in external trade is signified by the increase of export earning which grew by 23 per cent in the first two months of the fiscal year 2000-01.[12] Being a close neighbour, Bangladesh is an important country for external trades with India especially the North Eastern Region. During 1997-98, Bangladesh ranked 11th position with 2.25 per cent of India's export to that country.[13] This position improved during 1998-99. In 1998-99, Bangladesh ranked 9th position with 2.94 per cent of India's total export. In the case of India's import,

Bangladesh ranked 41st position with only 0.15 per cent for 1998-99. It may be mentioned that during 1998-99, besides USA (21.78), UK (5.67), Germany (5.60), Hong Kong (5.60), UAE (5.51), Japan (4.90), Belgium (3.85), and Italy (3.16), Bangladesh was one of the important destination of Indian goods. Though Bangladesh is a least-developed country it occupies a place of importance in India's export trade. The share of Bangladesh for Indian export was 1.92 per cent, 1.93 per cent, 2.45 per cent, 3.30 per cent, 2.60 per cent, 2.25 per cent and 2.94 per cent for the year 1992-93; 1993-94; 1994-95; 1995-96; 1996-97; 1997-98 and 1998-99 respectively. For the same period, the share of Bangladesh to India's import is quite small as it was merely 0.06 per cent, 0.08 per cent, 0.03 per cent, 0.23 per cent, 0.16 per cent, 0.12 per cent and 0.15 per cent respectively (Table 3).

TABLE 3

Indo-Bangladesh Trade 1992-93—1998-99

(Rs. Lakh)

Year	*Export*	*Import*	*Trade Balance*
1992-93	102902 (1.92)	3523 (0.06)	94379
1993-94	134929 (1.93)	2607 (0.08)	132322
1994-95	202413 (2.45)	1985 (0.03)	190428
1995-96	350909 (3.30)	28722 (0.23)	322187
1996-97	308480 (2.60)	22091 (0.16)	286389
1997-98	292287 (2.25)	18885 (0.12)	273402
1998-99	416803 (2.94)	26765 (0.15)	390038

Note: The figures in bracket indicate the percentage to total export/import.

Source: CMIE, Foreign Trade and Balance of Payment, Centre for Monitoring, Indian Economy, July 1999, pp. 110-11 and 282-83.

Indo-Bangladesh trade is highly imbalanced in favour of India. That is, the volume of India's export to Bangladesh is greater than the volume of Bangladesh's export to India. From 1992-93 to 1998-99, India's export to Bangladesh increased by more than four times (from Rs. 102902 lakh to Rs. 416803 lakh) while import increased by more than 7 times (from Rs. 3523 lakh to Rs. 26765 lakh) (Table 3). Though the rate of increase in import from Bangladesh is greater than that of export to Bangladesh, yet, it fails to catch-up with the volume of export during the period in consideration. The increase in the volume of trade can be mainly because of trade liberalization of Bangladesh.[14] This trade imbalance in favour of India also continues in recent years. During 2003-04, 2004-05 and 2005-06 Bangladesh trade deficit with India was US $ 859.1 million 779.9 million and 803.3 million respectively. (Table 4)

TABLE 4

Indo-Bangladesh Trade 2002-04

(US $ million)

Year	*Export*	*Import*	*Trade Balance*
2003-04	902.2 (2.73)	43.1 (0.10)	859.1
2004-05	803.8 (1.89)	23.9 (0.04)	779.9
2005-06 (p)	843.7 (1.61)	40.4 (0.05)	803.3

Notes: 1. P → Provisional.
2. The figure in bracket indicate the percentage to world trade (export/import).

Source: RBI Bulletin, January 2006, pp. 57, 59.

Indo-China Trade

India and China shared a common border of 3440 kms. Of this Arunachal Pradesh has 1125 kms, Jammu and Kashmir 1570 Kms, Himachal Pradesh 200 kms Uttar Pradesh 345 kms, and Sikkim 200 kms.[15] China is one of the biggest markets in the world and is also a growing trade partner of India. During 1998-99 it was the 18th important destination of Indian goods and it absorbed 1.22 per cent of India's export.[16]

The share of China to India's export was 0.76 per cent in 1992-93; 1.25 per cent in 1993-94; 0.97 per cent in 1994-95; 1.05 per cent in 1995-96; 1.84 per cent in 1996-97; and 2.05 per cent in 1997-98 (Table 5). This indicated that Indian goods have not made an impact on the Chinese market in the 1990s. However, the trend improved during the period 2002-04 to 2005-06., as the share on India's export to China increased to 3.50 per cent in 2003-04; 4.75 in 2004-05 and 5.72 in 2005-06 (Table 2).

TABLE 5

Indo-China Trade 1992-93—1998-99

(Rs. Lakh)

Year	*Export*	*Import*	*Trade Balance*
1992-93	40918 (0.76)	36490 (0.58)	4428
1993-94	87533 (1.25)	94697 (1.29)	-7164
1994-95	79824 (0.97)	238890 (2.66)	-159066
1995-96	111288 (1.05)	271606 (2.21)	-160318
1996-97	218254 (1.84)	268703 (1.93)	-50449
1997-98	266871 (2.05)	416006 (2.70)	-149135
1998-99	172438 (1.22)	445852 (2.53)	-273414

Note: The figure in bracket indicate percentage to world trade (export/import).

Source: CMIE, Foreign Trade and Balance of Payment, Centre for Monitoring Indian Economy, July 1999, pp. 110-11 and 282-83.

With regard to India's import China ranked 17th position in the year 1998-99 with 2.53 per cent of India's total import.[17] In the preceding period India's import from China was 0.58 per cent in 1992-93; 1.29 per cent in 1993-94; 2.66 per cent in 1994-95; 2.21 per cent in 1995-96; 1.93 per cent in 1996-97; and 2.70 per cent in 1997-98 (Table 5). The increasing in the case of import from China is also witnessed in the 2000s. In the year 2003-04; 2004-05 and 2005-06 India's import from China was 5.00 per cent; 6.22 per cent and 6.80 per cent of the total import (Table 2).

The Indo-China trade is highly imbalance. Except for the year 1992-93 which India's balance of trade is favourable, in all period it is unfavourable. The trade balance of India with regard to trade with China was Rs. -7164 lakh in 1993-94 and rose to Rs. -73414 in 1998-99 (Table 5). This unfavourable balance of trade with China continues also in the years 2003-04, 2004-05 and 2005-06 (Table 2).

Indo-Bhutan Trade

Bhutan is a land-locked country. It is bounded by India on the west, the south and the east while it is bounded by China on the north. The Indian states which have a common border with Bhutan are Sikkim (33 kms), West Bengal (175 kms), Assam (265 kms) and Arunachal Pradesh (170 kms).[18] Traditionally, most foreign trade of Bhutan was with Tibet. However, by 1960, owing to the closure of the Bhutan-China border and the development of closer ties with India, formal trade with India replaced that with Tibet.[19] Since then most trade of Bhutan was with India. During 2003-04, 2004-05 and 2005-06 India's export to Bhutan was US $ 34.0 million, 51.7 million and 45.2 million which was 0.16 per cent, 1.93 per cent and 0.08 per cent of India's total export. For the same period India's import from Bhutan was US $ 29.1 million, 36.8 million and 39.2 million which was 0.06 per cent, 0.06 per cent and 0.05 per cent of India's total import (Table 6). This clearly shows that there is an imbalance in the trade balance in favour of India. However, the difference between import and export is decreasing during the period in consideration.

Indo-Nepal Trade

Nepal is bounded by India on the West, the South and the East. The states having common border with Nepal are Uttaranchal (180 kms), Uttar Pradesh (665 kms), Bihar (725 kms), West Bengal (92 kms) and Sikkim (85 kms).[20] The North of Nepal is bounded by the People Republic of China. However, most of the Nepal-China border is of little accessibility as more than 90 per cent run through high altitudes with rocks and snow, glacier and ice field which are not inhabited.[21] The ruggedness of Nepal-China border and

TABLE 6

Indo-Bhutan Trade 2003-04—2005-06

(US $)

Year	*Export*	*Import*	*Trade Balance*
2003-04	34.0 (0.16)	29.1 (0.06)	24.9
2004-05	51.7 (1.93)	36.8 (0.06)	15.9
2005-06(p)	45.2 (0.08)	39.2 (0.05)	6.0

Notes: 1. (p)→Provisional.
2. The figure in bracket indicate the percentage to world trade (export/import).

Source: RBI Bulletin, January, 2006, pp. 57, 59.

the proximity to India are the main reasons for India to become the major trading partner of Nepal. Before Nepal opened its international business in the 60s except for the northern part which had trade relation with Tibet, India dominated its external trade and this trend continues up to 1980.[22] Nepal ranks 37th position as an important destination of Indian goods. While in import it (Nepal) ranks 36th position. The share of Nepal in India's export was 0.39 per cent in 1992-93, it rose to 0.50 per cent in 1995-96 and 1996-97 but it came down 0.44 per cent in 1998-99. With regard to India's import the share of Nepal was 0.11 per cent in 1992-93 but it increased to 0.24 per cent in 1998-99. During the period 1992-93 to 1998-99, the Indo-Nepal trade is increasing both in terms of volume and also as a percentage of India total trade (Table 7). From Table 7 it may be seen that Indo-Nepal is highly imbalanced in-favour of India. From 1992-93 to 1995-96 the imbalance increases. However from 1995-96 to 1998-99 it decreased. These trends (trade imbalance in favour of India) continue also in the period 2003 to 2006 (Table 8).

Indo-Myanmar Trade

For quite a long time Myanmar had established trade relation with India. Until the 1960s Myanmar was the major sources of rice for the growing population of India. After the implication of green revolution the demand for rice from

TABLE 7

Indo-Nepal Trade 1992-93—1998-99

(Rs. Lakh)

Year	*Export*	*Import*	*Trade Balance*
1992-93	20974 (0.39)	7169 (0.11)	13805
1993-94	30784 (0.44)	9068 (0.12)	21716
1994-95	37701 (0.46)	11489 (0.13)	26212
1995-96	53536 (0.50)	16440 (0.13)	37096
1996-97	58830 (0.50)	22745 (0.16)	36085
1997-98	63199 (0.49)	35364 (0.23)	27835
1998-99	62832 (0.44)	59724 (0.24)	3108

Note: The figures in bracket indicate the percentage to total export-import.

Source: CMIE Foreign Trade and Balance of Payment, Centre for Monitoring Indian Economy, July 1999, pp. 110-11 and 282-83.

TABLE 8

Indo-Nepal Trade 1992-93–1998-99

(US $ Million)

Year	*Export*	*Import*	*Trade Balance*
2003-04	340.0 (1.03)	136.2 (0.32)	203.8
2004-05	445.1 (1.05)	177.4 (0.31)	267.7
2005-6(p)	462.3 (0.88)	216.3 (0.28)	246.0

Notes: 1. (p)→Provisional.

2. Figure in ( ) indicate percentage to world trade (export/import).

Source: RBI Bulletin, June 2006, pp. 57-59.

Myanmar has decreased tremendously.[23] India's import from Myanmar is dominated by agricultural and forest based products of which pulses, wood and wood products, fruits and nuts constitute the bulk. India's export to Myanmar consists of both primary and manufacturing products. The main items of export to Myanmar in 1996-97 includes primary and semi-finished iron and steel (38.8 per cent), iron and steel bar and rods (18.3 per cent), drugs pharmaceuticals and fine chemicals (6.7 per cent), manufactured metals (3.6 per cent) glass, ceramics, refractory and cement (2.9 per cent).[24] During the period 1991-92 to 1999-00 the percentage of increase of export is more than that of import. However import decreased in 1997-97 and export decreased in 1999-00. Regarding the export-import position between India and Myanmar the trade balance is in favour of Myanmar (Table 9).

TABLE 9

Indo-Myanmar Trade 1991-92—1999-2000

(Rs. Crores)

Year	*Export*	*Import*	*Trade Balance*
1991-92	9.4	125.6	-116.2
1992-93	20.4 (117.02)	335.2 (166.87)	-314.8
1993-94	67.6 (231.37)	379.5 (13.21)	-312.0
1994-95	71.1 (5.17)	398.0 (4.87)	-326.9
1995-96	100.9 (41.91)	543.1 (36.45)	-442.2
1996-97	160.5 (59.06)	629.0 (15.81)	-468.5
1997-98	172.8 (7.66)	611.7 (-2.75)	-438.9
1999-00	144.09 (-16.61)	735.00 (20.15)	-590.91

Note: The figures in bracket indicate the percentage of increase or decrease of export and import.

Source: IIE, Prospect of Border Trade with Myanmar and Bangladesh: Pre-Investment Feasibility Report, p. 56.

Trade of the NER with the Neighbouring Countries

It is well understood that in the past, the North Eastern Region had trade intercourse will the entire NC namely Nepal, Bhutan, China, Bangladesh and Myanmar. However, owing to lack of relevant data we confined our study only to trade with Myanmar and Bangladesh.

The landlocked North Eastern Region is linked to the rest of the country only through a narrow corridor of Siligury or chicken neck. Because of this isolation the region is deprived of the industrial linkage and the benefit of industrialization of the country. The deprivation is in the form of the Region elimination from trade and commerce which the Region had with the Neighbouring Countries in the past.[25] Trade between the north-east and the neighbouring countries take place through both official and un-official channels.[26] Official trade with the Neighbouring Countries (NC) is facilitated by the Custom Department through Land Custom Stations (LCS) set-up at different border points and trade routes connecting the NER and the NC. Among the neighbouring countries, trade with Bangladesh seems to be more important and followed by that with Myanmar. The total volume of trade (official) including both export and import to Bangladesh and Myanmar during 1996-2001 was Rs. 850.96 crores. Of this Rs. 733.11 crores (86.15 per cent) is export and Rs. 117.85 crores (13.85 per cent) is import (Table 10). The main items to Bangladesh includes coal, limestone, stone boulder, fresh ginger etc. while import includes ready made garment, fruit juice, hilsha fish etc. (Box 1). The export basket to Myanmar includes wheat flour, dry chilli, bleaching powder, bicycles, water filter, etc. and the import basket includes pulse and bean, resin, reed broom, rice, etc. (Box 2). From Box 1 and 2 it may be seen that the composition export is more diversified than the composition of import.

Informal and Transit Trade

Besides formal trade which flows through the Land Custom Station and through the official procedure, there was also a large volume of informal or illegal trade which flows through undisclosed channel. However, the volume of informal trade which takes place between the NER and the NC cannot be ascertained due to the unavailability of relevant data. According to different studies, the different commodities are informally traded between the NER and the neighbouring countries. Another noted characteristic of the informal trade between the NER and the NC is that, it is a transit trade. The IIE Report on Prospect of Border Trade with Myanmar and Bangladesh revealed that there were many goods which the NER trade with Myanmar which originated in the third countries or regions. The goods export

TABLE 10

Volume of Trade Throúgh North East with Bangladesh and Myanmar 1996-97—2000-01

(Rs. Crore)

A. (Export)

Year	*Assam*	*Tripura*	*Meghalaya*	*Manipur*	*Total*
1996-97	21.33	4.19	77.00	30.85	133.37
1997-98	110.82	2.31	100.5	23.84	237.03
1998-99	51.91	2.29	93.24	5.02	152.46
1999-00	37.41	4.38	59.56	3.31	105.71
2000-01	23.17	2.45	73.62	5.30	104.54
Total					733.11

B. (Import)

Year	*Assam*	*Tripura*	*Meghalaya*	*Manipur*	*Total*
1996-97	4.80	6.27	–	16.10	27.15
1997-98	4.65	11.17	0.39	35.72	52.53
1998-99	5.52	10.47	–	5.41	21.4
1999-00	0.42	3.38	–	6.583	10.36
2000-01	1.63	2.45	–	2.23	6.41
Total					117.85

Source: IIE, Prospect of Border Trade with Myanmar and Bangladesh: Pre-Investment Feasibility Report, pp. 247 and 248.

through NER to Myanmar which are produced in other part of India includes Automobile Parts, Drugs and Pharmaceuticals, Cement, Cycles and cycles parts, Chemicals Cotton yarn, Handloom, Stainless Steel Utensils, Wheat Flower, Food and Beverages, etc. The goods which imported from Myanmar which are produces in the third country like China, Singapore, Korea, etc. includes Electronic Goods, Synthetic, Man made fabrics, Car batteries, Inverter, emergency lamp, Locks and padlocks, Precious and semi precious stone, Walking shoes, Soap and toiletries, Silk Yarn and cloves, etc.[27] Regarding unofficial export to Bangladesh, commodities like kerosene, sugar, salt foreign liquor,[28] bicycle

Box 1

Commodity Export and Import Through NER to and from Bangladesh

Commodities officially exported to Bangladesh	*Commodities officially imported from Bangladesh*
Coal, lime stone, sanitary items, stone boulder, non-basmati rice, fresh ginger, onion, dry chilly, grapes, apple, Methe, poultry feed, citrus fruits, oranges, garlic, dry fish, cement, tomato, plywood, motor parts, umbrella, batle leaves, marble state, fabric (bed sheet), paper, pears, soya beens, rohu fish, turmeric, jack-fruits, tube-light, pine-a-ple, safety glass, automotive parts, electronic goods, lentil fruits wooden materials, bagles machines, and some other.	Miscellaneous ready made garment, fruit juice, hilsha fish, small fish, fresh fish, dry fish, green chilly, cotton and cotton yarn and waste, garment, foot wear, plastic tables, kitchen ware, potato frozen, mineral water, condensed milk, corn, toilet soap, and some other.

Source: Selected from IIE, Prospect of Border Trade with Myanmar and Bangladesh: Pre-Investment Feasibility Report, pp. 215-39.

Box 2

Commodity Export and Import Through NER to and from Myanmar

Commodities officially exported to Myanmar	*Commodities officially imported from Myanmar*
Wheat flour, p.v.c., dry chilli anise seeds summon rose, cumin seeds, garlic, carrinder seeds, bush essence, rock salt, bleaching powder, agarbatti, soya bari, bicycle, night lamp, mish steel balls etc., hosiery vest and underwear, ammonium chloride, onion, stainless steel rope of pure jute, ball pen, water filter, fenugreek seed, kajur, pitsaw, table cover chewing tobacco, ajwain, maltova, saw blade, flavouring agen, fenugreek, dall, gold fingers, and some other.	Turmeric, red kidney bean, pulse and bean, betel nut, mustard seeds, kuth, resin, reed broom moong bean, cumin seed, chana, serpentine roots, chick pea, rice bean, ginger, urd, mimosa, pudica, dry cager, achar, katha (kathechu), cardamom cane, cumin black, kooth root.

Source: Selected from IIE, Prospect of Border Trade with Myanmar and Bangladesh: Pre-Investment Feasibility Report, pp. 240-46.

and bicycle part, cosmetics, coal, wood/timbers etc.,[29] most of these goods are produced in other Indian states. Similarly imports form like electronic and electrical goods, jackets and other dress materials, utensils, etc. are brought from countries like China, Japan, and the South East Asian Countries.[30] It may also be noted that the goods which are transited through Myanmar to NER, found their way other part of India and those transited through NER to Myanmar found their destination even to China.

Trade Routes with Bangladesh and Myanmar

The NER trade (both formal and informal) with Myanmar and Bangladesh flows through the 15 LCSs and 52 trade routes. Of the 15 LCSs, 14 LCS are on the NER-Bangladesh border while only 1(one) is on the NER-Myanmar border. We may also note that there are also 19 non-functioning LCSs on the NER-Bangladesh-Myanmar border. Of the functioning LCSs, 7 are in Meghalaya, 5 are in Tripura 2 are in Assam and 1 at Manipur. Of the 52 possible trade routes 39 routes link with Bangladesh and 13 routes linked with Myanmar. Again of the 39 NER-Bangladesh routes 27 routes linked with Meghalaya, 3 routes link with Assam, 2 with Mizoram and 7 with Tripupa and of the 13 NER-Myanmar routes, 6 routes linked with Nagaland, 1 route linked with Mizoram, 1 route linked with Manipur, and 5 routes linked with Arunachal Pradesh.[31]

INTEGRATION OF THE NER WITH THE NEIGHBOURING COUNTRIES: THE LOOK EAST POLICY OF INDIA

For quite some time there have been lots of talks at different levels to convert the isolated NER into a commercial hub between India, the SAARC countries and the dynamic South East Asian Countries.[32] Many planners are much exited, optimistic and anticipate that the look-east policy of the government of India will benefit the NER manifolds. The S.P. Shukla Commission Report asserted that there are great potential of external economic relation between North-east and the Neighbouring Countries especially when Nepal,

Bhutan, Bangladesh and India have agreed of the formation of sub-regional cooperation within the ambit of SAARC. The Commission recommended for activating the external (trade and transit) sector in the Region.[33] The UN-SCAP, Study on India's Border Trade with Selected Neighbouring Countries talked about the integration of the Indian economy with its neighbours through regional grouping.[34] In this grouping the NER will also be affected. Suter analyzed the benefit which Bangladesh as well as NER can deliver from transport linkage and transshipments through Bangladesh.[35] Besides, in the past, the NER is linked to the NC through different trade routes.[36]

The Government of India's Look East Policy' has raised mixed feeling among the North Eastern economists. There are feelings of doubts mixed with feelings of optimism about the prospect of the Region economically integrating with the prosperous South East Asia. While talking about the economic integration with the economics of East and South East Asian Countries, it has to be noticed that the economics of different states within the North Eastern Region are far from integrated. It is felt that the Region has much to gain by integrating into one strong economy at the first instance. It is highly necessary that the constituent states should place more emphasis on strengthening the structure of their local economy lest it gets drained out by the more powerful and much more prosperous economies of the South East Asian Countries. These feeling were also aired to the Members of the Planning Commission when they visited Shillong on 8th and 9th July, 2006, for consultation on the Draft Approach Paper to the 11th five year plan.

Besides the doubt raised local economists, about the look-east policy, the region may face difficulty in its integration with the Neighbouring Countries. To mention a few, there are disputes over the sharing of water of the Ganga between India and Bangladesh. This has been a source of much discontentment and bitterness in the Indo-Bangladesh relation.[37] So far Myanmar opened only one border point with India but it had open 3 and 2 border points with China and Bangladesh respectively.[38] This may implies Myanmar preference to China and Bangladesh rather than to India in its trade. The Government of India may not be willing to fully open the NER border with Bangladesh and Myanmar because of security reasons and drugs trafficking etc.

CONCLUDING OBSERVATION

Through different studies done by different scholars and the present study, it seems that linking the NER with the NC and more especially with the vibrant South East Asian countries will open a new chapter for the Economy of the NER. In order to enable the NER to harness the South and South East Asian Market the following steps may be considered by the planners of India (especially that of the NER):

- Development of road infrastructure is highly recommendable in all states of the region. This is because (a) so far, the states in the NER are not properly integrated among themselves (or even there was no proper integration within the states themselves), (b) Most border areas are yet to have access to market due to poor or absence of connectivity. Immediate steps for road connectivity is badly needed to harness the rich resources.
- The services of most Land Custom Station are far from satisfactory because of infrastructure deficiency. Land custom station required urgent infrastructural facilities like development storage facilities (warehousing), parking lot, banking services and many others amenities.
- The government of India needs to pursue with the Myanmar government to open Land Custom Station in the Myanmar-Arunachal Pradesh-Nagaland-Mizoram border and some more LCS on Manipur border besides the existing ones at Tamu.
- The existing un-official trades need to transform into official trade as they have already penetrated even to the most interior part of the region.
- Most export from the NER to NC is carried without any value addition; the region will

acquired more benefit if the exportable goods are sold in manufactured forms.

- Creation of Special Economic Zones is urgently needed to attract more investment in potential sector/industries.

It may now be concluded that NER's economy requires lots of self-integration before its integration with the NC including Bangladesh, Myanmar, China, Bhutan, Nepal and the South East Asian Countries take place. Partial or sectoral integration will be better given preference than complete integration for the moment as intelligent trade relation is very likely to be better than fully open trade. Indian policy-makers (more importantly the local political leadership of north eastern region) should carefully consider creation of a strong foundation for an internationally competitive sector to sustain trade and development.

Notes and References

1. Steger, M.B. (2003), *Globalization: A Very Short Introduction*, Oxford University Press.
2. Choudhury, S. (2006), 'North-East India and the Look East Policy: A Contextual Analysis', in B.B. Kumar (ed.), *Dialogue* (*Quarterly*), Delhi, Astha Bharati, Vol. 7, No. 3, January-March, p. 134.
3. Guru, D.D. (1972), 'Asian Economic Co-operation: An Analysis of the Possible Form', in IEA, *Asian Economic Co-operation*, Bombay, Popular Prakshan Pvt. Ltd.
4. Wadhva, C. (1972), 'Asian Economic Co-operation through Sub-Regional Grouping', *ibid*, pp. 24-31.
5. Goswami, H. and J.K. Gogoi (2002), "Economic Prospect of the Stillwell Road—An Analysis", in J.K. Gogoi (ed.), *Assam Economic Journar*, Vol. XV, Department of Economics, Dibrugarh Uninersity, pp. 1-10.
6. Sharma, G.K. (2004), "Regional Economic Cooperation Signing of SAFTA", in *Yojana* (*A Development Montly*). Vol. 48, Feb. 2004, No. 2, p. 11, New Delhi, Ministry of Information and Broadcasting.
7. Choudhury, S. *op cit*.
8. Batabyl, A. (2006), "Balancing China in Asia: A Realist Assessment of India's Look East Strategy", in *China Report (A Journal of East Asian Studies*), Delhi, Sage Publication, Vol. 42, No. 2, April-June, p. 181.
9. Das, G. (2000), 'Trade Between the North-Eastern Region and

Neighbouring Countries: Structures and Implication for Developmen'. In G. Das and R.K. Purkayastha (ed). *Border Trade (North-East India nad Neighbouring Countries),* New Delhi, Akansha Publishing House, p. 23.

10. Rao, V.L., S. Baruah, R.U. Das (1997), *India's Border Trade with Select Neighbouring Countries.* New Delhi. Research and Information System.
11. Sachdeva, G. (2000), *Economy of the North East: Policy, Present Condition and Future Possibilities,* New Delhi, Konark Publishers Pvt. Ltd.
12. Indian Institute of Entrepreneurship (IIE), (2001), *A Report of the Study on the Prospect of Border Trade With Myanmar and Bangladesh Pre-Investment Feasibility Report.*
13. Das, G. *op cit.,* p. 25.
14. IIE, *op cit.,* p. 85.
15. Sachdeva, G., *op. cit.*
16. CMIE Foreign Trade and Balance of Payment, p. 111.
17. *Ibid.,* p. 283.
18. *Ibid.*
19. Bhutan-India address httptt://rds. Yahoo. Com/_ylt=A0geutWf3s VEiJ8ApMtXNyoA;
20. Sachdeva, G., *op. cit.*
21. Sing Kansakar, V.B. (2001), 'Nepal India Open Border: Prospect, problems and Challenges', An updated version of the papers presented in a series of Seminars organized by the institute of Foreign Affairs and FES in Nepalguni, Birguni, Biratnagar and Katmandu, email. http://rds.yaboo.com
22. Arya, R.C. (2000), "Indo-Nepal Trade: Some Reflection", in G. Das and R.K. Purkayastha (ed.), p. 23. *op cit.*
23. Das, G., *op. cit.*
24. IIE, *op. cit.*
25. Gassah, L.S. (1984), "Effect of Partition on the Border Marketing of Jaintia Hills", in J.B. Ganguly (ed.), *Marketing in North-east India,* New Delhi, Omson Publication.
26. Das, G., *op. cit.*
27. IIE Table, 11.11.2 and Table 11.11.2.
28. Nongbri, R.J. (2005), "Cross Border Trade between Meghalaya and Bangladesh: A Case Study of Informal Trade along the Shella, Mawdon and Balat Border", A Paper presented in the International Seminar on Indo-Bangladesh Border Status and Prospects, on 12th and 13th July, 2005, NEHU, Shillong.
29. Das, G., p. 39, *op. cit.*
30. Nongbri, R.J., *op. cit.*
31. IIE, *op. cit.*
32. Sachdeva, G. (2000), p. 145, *op. cit.*
33. Shukla, S.P. (1997), *Transforming the Northeast: Takling Backlog in the*

Basic Minimum Services and Infrastructures Needs, New Delhi, Planning Commission.

34. Rao, V.L, S. Baruah, R.U. Das (1997), *op. cit.*
35. Sutar, S. (2005), 'Cooperation through Communication: An Approach to NER-Bangladesh Transport Link', Paper presented at the International Seminar on Indo-Bangladesh Border Trade, NEHU, Shillong, India, 12-13 July, 2005.
36. Kumar, B.B. (2000), 'The Border Trade in North-East India; The Historical Perspective', in G. Das and R.K. Purkayastha ed., *op. cit.*, pp 4-11.
37. Sobhan, F. (2006), 'Estranged neighbours', in Seminar, No. 557 (*A Journal of the Confederation of India industries*), January.
38. Choudhury, S., *op. cit.*, p. 151.

References

Arya, R.C. (2000), 'Indo-Nepal Trade: Some Reflection' in G. Das and R. K. Purkayastha ed., p 23, *op. cit.*

Batabyl. A. (2006), 'Balancing China in Asia: A Realist Assessment of India's Look East Strategy' in *China Report (A Journal of East Asian Studies)*. Delhi, Sage Publication, Vol. 42, No. 2, April-June, p. 181.

Choudhury, S. (2006), 'North-East India and the Look East Policy: A Contextual Analysis'. In B. B Kumar (ed). *Dialogue* (*Quarterly*), Delhi, Astha Bharati, Vol. 7, No. 3, January-March, p. 134.

Choudhury, S., *op. cit.*

Choudhury, S., *op. cit.*, p 151.

Das, G. (2000), 'Trade Between the North-Eastern Region and Neighbouring Countries: Structures and Implication for Developmen', In G. Das and R.K. Purkayastha (ed.), *Border Trade (North-East India nad Neighbouring Countries)*, New Delhi, Akansha Publishing House, p. 23.

Das, G., *op. cit.*, p. 25.

Gassah, L.S. (1984), 'Effect of Partition on the Border Marketing of Jaintia Hills' in J.B. Ganguly, (ed.) *Marketing in Notth-east India*, New Delhi, Omson Publication.

Goswami, H. and J.K. Gogoi (2002), 'Economic Prospect of the Stillwell Road—An analysis' in J.K Gogoi (ed.), *Assam Economic Journal*, Vol. XV, Department of Economics, Dibrugarh Uninersity, pp. 1-10.

Guru, D.D. (1972), 'Asian Economic Co-operation: An Analysis of the possible form' in IEA, *Asian Economic Co-operation*, Bombay. Popular Prakshan Pvt. Ltd.

IIE, Table 11.11.2 and Table 11.11.2.

Indian Institute of Entrepreneurship (IIE) (2001), *A Report of the Study on the Prospect of Border Trade with Myanmar and Bangladesh Pre-Investment Feasibility Report.*

Kumar, B.B (2000) 'The Border Trade in North-East India; The Historical Perspective', in G. Das and R.K. Purkayastha ed., *op. cit.*, pp. 4-11.

Nongbri, R.J (2005), 'Cross Border Trade between Meghalaya and Bangladesh: A Case Study of Informal Trade along the Shella, Mawdon and Balat Border', A Paper presented in the International Seminar on Indo-Bangladesh Border Status and Prospects on 12th and 13th July, 2005, NEHU, Shillong.

Nongbri, R.J., *op cit.*

Rao, V.L., S. Baruah, R.U. Das (1997), *India's Border Trade with Select Neighbouring Countries*, New Delhi, Research and Information System.

Rao, V.L, S. Baruah, R.U. Das (1997), *op. cit.*

Sachdeva, G. (2000), *Economy of the North East: Policy, Present Condition and Future possibilities*, New Delhi. Konark Publishers Pvt. Ltd.

Sachdeva, G., *op. cit.*

Sachdeva, G. (2000), p. 145, *op. cit.*

Sharma, G.K. (2004), 'Regional Economic Cooperation Signing of SAFTA', in *Yojana* (*A Development Montly*), Vol. 48, Feb. 2004, No. 2, p. 11, New Delhi, Ministry of Information and Broadcasting.

Shukla, S.P. (1997), *Transforming the Northeast: Takling Backlog in the Basic Minimum Services and Infrastructures Needs*, New Delhi, Planning Commission.

Sing Kansakar, V.B. (2001), 'Nepal India Open Border: Prospect, Problems and Challenges', An updated version of the papers presented in a series of Seminars organized by the institute of Foreign Affairs and FES in Nepalguni, Birguni, Biratnagar and Katmandu, email. http://rds.yaboo.com

Sobhan, F. (2006), 'Estranged neighbours', in Seminar, No. 557 (*A Journal of the Confederation of Indian Industries*), January.

Steger, M.B. (2003), *Globalization: A Very Short Introduction*, Oxford University Press.

Sutar, S. (2005), 'Cooperation through Communication: An Approach to NER-Bangladesh Transport Link', Paper presented at the International Seminar on Indo-Bangladesh Border Trade/NEHU, Shillong, India, 12-13 July, 2005.

Wadhva, C. (1972), 'Asian Economic Co-operation through Sub-Regional Grouping', *ibid*, pp. 24-31.

India's Regional Trading with the SAARC Countries

Some Issues

M.S. Sidhu, Lavleen Kaur and Pashupati Ray

INTRODUCTION

The emergence of regionalism and regionalisation in Europe paved the way for regional cooperation in other parts of the world. According to Ben Rosamond, "regionalism" emplies *de jure,* formal state led projects and "regionalisation" refers to *de facto* transitional regional economies that emerge in the context of networks of production and exchange among private market actors. From this point of view, South Asia drastically failed in regionalism which prohibited the process of regionalisation (Gill, 2005). South Asia is one of the most integrated regions (geo-economical) in the world but having unnatural fractured border (geo-strategically). Unlike in Europe, the people here are not the opinion maker (*Ibid.*).

As a region, South Asia is the poorest and the most over populated. About 40 per cent of its populations live below poverty line. India alone represent 72 per cent of the region's population and 79 per cent of its Gross Domestic

Product (GDP) of the region. More than one sixth of the world's labour force live in South Asia. Despite huge differences in physical and demographic factors, all the South Asia countries have low income, high population densities and poor health.

With the framework of South Asian Association of Regional Cooperation (SAARC), the South Asia Free Trade Area (SAFTA) was first proposed in 1998 at the SAARC Summit in Colombo. The SAFTA agreement which drastically reduce trade barriers among South Asia countries. However, the SAARC has a long way to go before it can even think of emulating ASEAN. Although South Asia is home to 1.5 billion people, intra-regional trade accounts for less than five per cent whereas trade within the ASEAN region is about 63 per cent (Basu, 2004; and Cherian, 2004). Trade among the SAARC countries will be beneficial to each country. Fear of Indian domination are unfounded because trade is a two way street. It may be stated here that freight is an element that already goes against countries like Pakistan and Bangladesh. It roughly costs Rs. 1000 for one ton from Pakistan to Bangladesh via land route through India as compared to something like Rs. 3600 for ton for shipping from Pakistan to Bangladesh (Kumar, 2005). Keeping in view all this, the present study has been undertaken to examine the India's regional trading with the SAARC countries in the recent years.

RESULT AND DISCUSSION

Some indicators of socio-economic development in the SAARC countries. About one-fourth of the world's population live in the South-Asian countries. Out of these 150 crore people, about 40 per cent earn less than US $ one per capita per day. After Sub-Saharan African countries, the South Asian countries are the poorest in the world. In Sub-Saharan Africa, about 46 per cent of the population earn less than US $ one per capita per day during the year 1998. For the world as a whole, this figure was about 24 per cent. There are seven countries in the SAARC. India, Pakistan, and Sri Lanka are the developing countries, whereas Bangladesh, Bhutan Maldives and Nepal are the least developed countries

(Vasudeva, 2004). It may be mentioned here that seven persons commit suicides in Pakistan every day because of poverty and the number of those living below poverty line has risen to 31 (possibly 34) per cent of the population (Haqqani, 2003). Even in India, about 26 per cent of the population live below poverty line. The trade among any group of countries always depends on the level of its socio-economic development. In case the various indicators of socio-economic development are dismal, the volume of trade and other business will also be low and vice-versa. The data given in Table 1 show that in the SAARC countries, the Human Development Index (HDI) was the highest in Maldives (0.752) followed by Sri Lanka (0.740), India (0.595), Bhutan (0.536), Bangladesh (0.509), Nepal (0.504) and Pakistan (0.497). India and Pakistan are two big countries of this region. India's per capita income was US $ 487 during the year 2002. The per capita income of Maldives, Sri Lanka and Bhutan was high. This was mainly on account of small size of these countries. Moreover, the inflow of tourists was more in these countries due to location factor. Nepal and Bangladesh had low per capita income as compared to other SAARC countries. Therefore, an inference can be drawn that trade within the SAARC countries can not be at par with the European Union (EU), which is a region trade and business association of the developed countries.

INDIA'S EXPORT TO THE SAARC COUNTRIES

The information about India's export to the SAARC countries is given in Table 2. India's total export to all countries of the world had increased from US $ 33.50 billion in 1996-97 to US $ 63.62 billion in 2003-04. Similarly, the export to the SAARC countries had increased from $ 1.70 billion to $ 4.04 billion in the corresponding period. In percentage terms, the exports, had increased from 5.08 per cent in 1996-97 to 6.34 per cent in 2003-04. This increase in trade may be attributed to improvement in bilateral political and diplomatic relation between India and Pakistan as well as India and Bangladesh. In the recent year, the Indian exports related with Information Technology (IT) have increased very

TABLE 1

Some Indicators of Socio-economic Development in the SAARC Countries, 2002

Particulars	*India*	*Pakistan*	*Sri Lanka*	*Nepal*	*Bangladesh*	*Bhutan*	*Maldives*
Life Expectancy at Birth	63.7	60.8	72.5	59.6	61.1	63.0	67.2
Adult Literacy Rate (%age) 15 years above	61.3	41.5	92.1	44.0	41.1	47.0	97.2
Combined Primary, Secondary and Gross Enrolment ratio (%)	55	37	65	61	54	33*	78
Human Development Index (HDI) Value	0.595	0.497	0.740	0.504	0.509	0.536	0.752
GDP per capita (US $)	487	408	873	230	351	695	2182

Note: *Related to the year 1998.

Source: UNDP (2004).

TABLE 2

Share of India's Export to the SAARC Countries in the Total Export, 1996-97 to 2003-04

(US $ million)

Year	*India's total exports*	*Export to SAARC countries*	*%age share of SAARC countries in total export*
1996-97	33498	1703.08	5.08
1997-98	35049	1612.91	4.60
1998-99	33211	1678.79	5.05
1999-00	36760	1396.06	3.79
2000-01	44147	1858.13	4.21
2001-02	43976	2032.91	4.62
2002-03	52856	2731.20	5.17
2003-04	63623	4036.15	6.34

Sources: (i) CMIE (2003); (ii) CMIE (2004).

fast to the developed and developing countries. In India, the IT sector is creating wealth worth Rs. 60000 crore every year (Shourie, 2004). But the SAARC countries except India has limited scope to absorb the IT due to low level of industrial and infrastructural development and other service sector.

INDIA'S IMPORTS FROM OTHER SAARC COUNTRIES

The information regarding India's imports from other SAARC countries has been given in Table 3. India's total imports from all our the world had increased from US $ 39.17 billion in 1996-97 to US $ 77.24 billion in 2003-04. During the corresponding period, the imports from the SAARC countries had increased from $ 0.24 billion to $ 0.64 billion. In this way, India's exports to the SAARC countries exceeded her imports by about $ 3.4 billion during the year 2003-04. In percentage terms, India's imports from the

TABLE 3

Share of India's Import from SAARC Countries to the Total Import, 1996-97 to 2003-04

(US $ million)

Year	*India's total imports*	*Import from SAARC*	*%age share of SAARC countries in total import*
1996-97	39165	241.78	0.62
1997-98	41535	234.58	0.56
1998-99	42379	465.45	1.09
1999-2000	49799	398.11	0.80
2000-01	50056	435.09	0.87
2001-02	51588	573.46	1.11
2002-03	61572	513.30	0.83
2003-04	77237	640.87	0.83

Sources: (i) CMIE (2003); (ii) CMIE (2004).

SAARC countries remained less than one per cent in most of the year. It was only marginally higher than one per cent in 1998-99 and 2001-02.

COMPOSITION OF INDIA'S EXPORT TO THE SAARC COUNTRIES

The data regarding India's exports to the SAARC countries from 1996-97 to 2003-04 are given in Table 4. The major items of export were cotton yarn fabric made-up, etc. transport equipment, non-basmati rice, drugs, pharmaceuticals and fine chemicals, machinery and equipment, etc. It may be mentioned here that India's and Pakistan are the only exporter of basmati rice in the global market and therefore they can protect their economic interest by hard bargaining with other countries (Sidhu and Bhullar, 2005). The geographical indicators in case of basmati rice can also be

TABLE 4

Composition of India's Export to SAARC Countries, 1996-97 to 2003-04

(US $ million)

Sl. No.	Commodities/year	1996-97	% Share	1997-98	% Share	1998-99	% share	1999-2000	% Share
1	2	3	4	5	6	7	8	9	10
1.	Cotton yarn fab made-ups etc.	401.88	23.59	345.26	21.40	197.44	11.70	236.19	16.92
2.	Transport equipment	148.04	8.69	119.06	7.38	116.14	6.92	134.68	9.64
3.	Wheat	119.04	6.99	0.07	0.004	0.31	0.02	-	-
4.	Prim and semi fin. Iron and Steel	79.03	4.64	83.55	5.18	38.33	2.28	57.79	4.14
5.	Non-basmati rice	67.60	3.96	134.42	0.08	540.05	3.22	103.40	7.41
6.	Machinery and equipment	110.10	5.89	106.62	6.61	91.70	5.46	77.41	5.54
7.	Manufacturers of metals	106.35	6.24	52.53	3.25	46.23	2.75	46.87	3.36
8.	Drug, pharm and fine chemicals	11.00	0.64	83.87	5.10	97.96	5.84	97.63	6.99
9.	Oil meals	20.51	1.20	34.22	2.12	35.22	2.09	36.48	2.61
10.	Glass/glassware/ceramics/cements	38.07	2.24	57.05	3.54	35.22	2.09	40.65	2.91
11.	Dyes, intermediates etc.	47.00	2.76	26.20	1.62	25.05	1.49	22.87	1.64
12.	Sugar	31.30	1.84	39.39	2.44	0.75	0.04	0.47	0.03
13.	Plastic and linoleum products	54.42	3.19	31.06	0.02	24.90	1.48	31.27	2.24
14.	Fresh vegetables	29.56	1.74	22.26	1.38	15.73	0.94	29.80	2.13
15.	Manmade yarn fab made-up	22.87	1.34	33.13	2.05	31.14	1.85	38.65	2.77

16. In-org/org/agro chemicals	23.29	1.37	23.43	1.45	21.13	1.26	23.58	1.69
17. Paper/wood products	31.88	1.87	36.18	2.24	29.05	1.73	38.83	2.78
18. Electronic goods	23.24	1.36	23.96	1.48	15.44	0.92	21.97	1.57
19. Cotton raw incl. waste	24.99	1.47	16.57	1.02	2.40	0.14	0.34	0.02
20. Rubber manufactured products	28.68	1.68	37.22	2.31	29.64	1.76	25.74	1.84
21. Coal	10.02	0.59	23.80	1.47	32.72	1.95	27.28	1.95
22. Spices	29.08	1.70	19.46	1.21	25.41	1.51	37.34	2.67
23. Other cereals	8.50	0.49	0.44	0.03	0.49	0.03	0.29	0.02
24. Pulses	4.76	0.28	27.85	1.73	23.33	1.39	49.61	3.55
25. Misc. processed items	5.07	0.29	13.19	0.82	10.24	0.61	12.50	0.89
26. Iron and steel bar/rods	6.39	0.38	8.61	0.53	7.31	0.44	7.87	0.56
27. Fresh fruits	27.02	1.59	12.78	0.79	8.73	0.52	12.78	0.91
28. RMG of cotton incl. accessories	12.65	0.74	6.63	0.41	6.36	0.38	16.00	1.15
29. Other ores and minerals	15.71	0.92	10.65	0.66	8.26	0.49	14.73	1.06
Total	1703.08	100.00	1612.91	100.00	1678.79	100.00	1396.06	100.00

(Contd.)

TABLE 4 *(Contd.)*

Sl. No.	Commodities/year	2000-01	% Share	2001-02	% Share	2002-03	% share	2003-04	% Share
1	2	11	12	13	14	15	16	17	18
1.	Cotton yarn fab made-ups etc.	258.24	12.02	244.32	12.02	228.81	8.38	298.19	7.39
2.	Transport equipment	156.21	8.74	177.62	8.74	214.76	7.86	290.48	7.19
3.	Wheat	25.35	4.51	91.78	4.51	116.16	4.25	235.88	5.84
4.	Prim and semi fin. Iron and steel	69.37	3.08	62.64	3.08	142.68	5.22	228.00	5.65
5.	Non-basmati rice	72.11	1.45	29.54	1.45	131.15	4.80	211.74	5.25
6.	Machinery and equipment	114.03	6.89	139.99	6.89	128.44	4.70	194.70	4.82
7.	Manufacturers of metals	76.52	3.43	69.74	3.43	72.61	2.66	170.35	4.22
8.	Drug, pharm and fine chemicals	117.73	5.46	111.10	5.46	140.99	5.16	156.50	3.88
9.	Oil meals	50.53	2.40	48.76	2.40	59.17	2.17	126.80	3.14
10.	Glass/glassware/ceramics/cements	80.59	3.25	66.04	3.25	64.61	2.36	105.41	2.61
11.	Dyes, intermediates etc.	23.74	1.17	23.78	1.17	37.20	1.36	95.06	2.36
12.	Sugar	76.48	7.33	48.94	7.33	153.07	5.60	93.11	2.31
13.	Plastic and linoleum products	51.15	3.36	68.32	3.36	89.01	3.26	91.39	2.26
14.	Fresh vegetables	31.62	1.63	33.05	1.63	32.25	1.18	88.88	2.20
15.	Manmade yarn fab made-up	53.82	2.14	43.48	2.14	65.04	2.38	85.90	2.13
16.	In-org/org/agro chemicals	60.83	2.15	43.64	2.15	58.35	2.14	80.70	1.99
17.	Paper/wood products	57.53	3.45	70.26	3.45	69.91	2.56	80.21	1.99
18.	Electronic goods	21.05	1.92	38.95	1.92	44.00	1.61	70.89	1.76
19.	Cotton raw incl. waste	4.02	0.03	0.66	0.03	0.72	0.03	66.71	1.65

20. Rubber manufactured products	27.96	1.57	31.84	1.57	40.36	1.48	63.04	1.56
21. Coal	35.86	2.61	52.96	2.61	53.01	1.94	57.59	1.43
22. Spices	40.86	1.64	33.30	1.64	39.92	1.46	49.87	1.24
23. Other cereals	4.10	0.62	12.52	0.62	8.48	0.31	41.22	1.02
24. Pulses	45.34	1.78	36.12	1.78	31.44	1.15	37.63	0.93
25. Misc. processed items	23.74	1.39	28.20	1.39	16.64	0.61	36.45	0.90
26. Iron and steel bar/rods	11.38	0.59	12.11	0.59	23.06	0.84	32.43	0.80
27. Fresh fruits	16.35	1.26	25.57	1.26	15.74	0.58	31.22	0.77
28. RMG of cotton incl. accessories	20.83	0.72	14.57	0.72	22.64	0.83	30.09	0.77
29. Other ores and minerals	14.52	1.19	24.16	1.19	18.12	0.66	28.52	0.71
Total	1858.13	100.00	2032.91	100.00	2731.20	100.00	4036.15	100.00

Note: The export of individual commodities are not equal to the total exports because all items of exports are not included. Similarly, the total of percentages are not equal to 100.

Sources: (i) CMIE (2003); (ii) CMIE (2004).

protected unitedly. It may be stated that SAFTA became operative from July 1, 2006. Pakistan has decided not to accord Most Favoured Nation (MFN) states to India as well as tariff concessions due under the SAFTA. Pakistan has been stating in the recent months that it will not open-up its trade front to India without the resolution of the Kashmir issue (Varma, 2006).

SAARC countries had already announced their "negative lists" which are also called "sensitive lists" which contained the products that were not open for tariff concessions.

As per negative lists announced earlier, Bangladesh will have 1254 items, Bhutan 157, India 884, Maldives 671, Nepal 1310, Pakistan 1183 and Sri Lanka 1065. The biggest obstacle to normal direct trade between our two countries is Pakistan's positive list approach to imports from India when India gives Pakistan MFN access to the Indian market. India accorded the MFN status to Pakistan in 1996. A feasible solution to strengthen trade can be found in a viable give and take between the two countries. Pakistan can offer trade concession to India under SAFTA, while India can reciprocate by playing an effective role in removing non-tariff barriers. The resulting broader trade relations could in fact help improve the political climate (Taneja, 2004).

COMPOSITION OF INDIA'S IMPORTS FROM THE SAARC COUNTRIES

The data regarding India's imports from the SAARC countries from 1996-97 to 2003-04 are given in Table 5. The major items of imports were non-ferrous metals, in organic chemicals, iron and steel, non made filament/spun yarn waste, spices, textile, yarn, fabric made etc. articles, pulses, fruits and nuts, etc. It may be mentioned here that India's imports from the SAARC countries were to the extent of just US $ 0.64 billion during the year 2003-04. The overall size of Indian economy is big as compared to the other SAARC countries. India's GDP during the year 2004 was US $ 675 billion as compared to just US $ 91 billion of Pakistan, US $ 61 billion of Bangladesh and US $ 20 billion of Sri Lanka

TABLE 5

Composition of India's Import from SAARC Countries, 1996-97 to 2003-04

(US $ million)

Sl. No.	Commodities/year	1996-97	% Share	1997-98	% Share	1998-99	% share	1999-2000	% Share
1	2	3	4	5	6	7	8	9	10
1.	Non-ferrous metals	0.56	0.23	1.23	0.52	1.34	0.28	4.41	1.11
2.	In-organic chemicals	20.97	8.67	17.89	7.63	11.35	2.44	28.74	7.21
3.	Iron and steel	8.04	3.33	1.52	1.13	3.01	0.65	8.10	2.03
4.	Man-made filament/spun yarn waste	-	-	-	-	-	-	25.89	6.50
5.	Spices	9.58	3.96	11.32	4.83	18.75	4.03	19.06	0.05
6.	Other text, yarn, fab, made-ups articles	-	-	-	-	-	-	7.19	1.81
7.	Pulses	9.02	3.73	1.02	0.43	7.07	1.52	8.93	2.24
8.	Fruits and nuts	28.38	11.74	22.54	9.61	24.17	5.19	22.94	5.76
9.	Readymade garments woven and knit	-	-	-	0.26	-	-	3.06	0.77
10.	Electronic goods	0.37	0.15	0.60	0.11	0.96	0.21	0.85	0.21
11.	Electrical machinery	0.25	0.10	0.26	5.15	0.61	0.13	2.54	0.64
12.	Essential oil and cosmetic preparation	4.09	1.69	12.08	1.13	3.45	2.89	30.47	7.65
13.	Primary steel pig iron based items	8.11	3.35	2.65	0.52	0.43	0.09	6.28	1.58
14.	Vegetable oils (edible)	1.75	0.72	1.21	0.29	1.54	0.33	1.35	0.34

(Contd.)

TABLE 5 *(Contd.)*

1	2	3	4	5	6	7	8	9	10
16.	Metal ferrow ore and metal scrap	10.34	4.28	9.41	5.80	6.46	1.39	8.50	2.14
17.	Jute raw	21.36	8.83	13.61	5.80	20.52	4.41	32.19	8.08
18.	Paper board and manufacturers	0.19	0.08	0.38	0.16	1.63	0.35	2.36	0.59
19.	Non-metal mineral manufacturers	-	-	0.11	0.05	0.31	0.06	0.40	0.10
20.	Wood and wood products	14.06	5.82	5.06	2.16	6.07	1.30	4.74	1.19
21.	Cotton yarn and fabrics	-	-	-	-	-	-	0.68	0.17
22.	Pulp and waste paper	1.29	0.53	2.98	1.27	2.65	0.57	3.41	0.86
23.	Made-up textile articles	-	-	-	-	-	-	12.27	3.08
24.	Manufacturers of metals	1.25	0.52	0.60	0.26	0.97	0.21	3.03	0.76
25.	Non-electrical machinery	1.23	0.51	0.94	0.40	0.80	0.17	1.48	0.37
26.	Cereal preparations	1.65	0.68	2.12	0.90	2.59	0.56	2.41	0.61
27.	Tea	-	-	-	-	-	-	3.05	0.77
28.	Chemical material and products	-	-	0.92	0.39	0.74	0.15	0.29	0.07
29.	Organic chemical	-	-	2.58	1.09	2.56	0.55	3.26	0.82
Total		241.78	100.00	234.58	100.00	465.45	100.00	398.11	100.00

(Contd.)

Sl. No.	Commodities/year	2000-01	% Share	2001-02	% Share	2002-03	% share	2003-04	% Share
1	2	11	12	13	14	15	16	17	18
1.	Non-ferrous metals	21.62	4.97	54.22	9.45	27.04	5.27	101.23	15.79
2.	In-organic chemicals	31.43	7.22	28.52	4.97	34.32	6.68	47.93	7.48
3.	Iron and steel	9.78	2.25	12.81	2.23	37.33	7.27	44.51	6.94
4.	Man-made filament/spun yarn waste	25.14	5.78	33.76	5.58	23.15	4.51	32.86	5.12
5.	Spices	22.79	5.24	41.77	7.28	43.54	8.48	32.06	5.00
6.	Other text, yarn, fab, made-ups articles	4.82	1.11	11.14	1.94	15.65	3.05	27.59	4.31
7.	Pulses	10.60	2.44	14.88	2.59	20.59	4.01	26.09	4.07
8.	Fruits and nuts	26.73	6.14	27.75	4.83	11.76	2.29	16.10	2.51
9.	Readymade garments woven and knit	4.64	1.07	7.68	1.33	4.99	0.97	13.77	2.15
10.	Electronic goods	1.46	0.34	1.35	0.24	5.65	1.10	13.69	2.14
11.	Electrical machinery	2.46	0.57	3.53	0.62	3.11	0.61	13.06	2.04
12.	Essential oil and cosmetic preparation	34.19	7.86	44.94	7.84	45.56	8.87	12.84	2.00
13.	Primary steel pig iron based items	7.37	1.69	8.52	1.48	12.51	2.44	12.56	1.96
14.	Vegetable oils (edible)	1.00	0.22	2.17	0.38	2.02	0.39	12.11	1.89
15.	Artificial resins, plastic matrix etc.	1.94	0.45	2.25	0.39	9.36	1.82	12.05	1.88
16.	Metal ferrow ore and metal scrap	7.63	1.75	5.17	0.90	8.58	1.67	11.69	1.82
17.	Jute raw	17.39	3.99	20.13	3.51	27.87	5.43	10.83	1.69
18.	Paper board and manufacturers	5.36	1.23	5.09	0.88	6.82	1.33	8.90	1.39
19.	Non-metal mineral manufacturers	0.67	0.15	2.01	0.35	1.40	0.27	8.81	1.37

(Contd.)

TABLE 5 (*Contd.*)

1	2	11	12	13	14	15	16	17	18
20.	Wood and wood products	7.23	1.66	6.64	1.16	6.15	1.19	8.26	1.29
21.	Cotton yarn and fabrics	2.20	0.51	3.29	0.57	2.52	0.49	7.51	1.17
22.	Pulp and waste paper	2.39	0.55	3.08	0.54	1.85	0.36	7.38	1.15
23.	Made-up textile articles	24.60	5.65	12.28	2.14	2.14	0.42	7.22	1.13
24.	Manufacturers of metals	2.59	0.59	2.42	0.42	3.13	0.61	6.45	1.01
25.	Non-electrical machinery	2.68	0.62	1.67	0.29	1.39	0.27	5.89	0.92
26.	Cereal preparations	2.01	0.46	3.99	0.69	5.05	0.98	5.64	0.88
27.	Tea	3.45	0.79	2.95	0.51	3.98	0.78	3.33	0.52
28.	Chemical material and products	0.57	0.13	1.44	0.25	2.75	0.54	2.97	0.46
29.	Organic chemical	2.47	0.57	3.75	0.65	1.49	0.34	2.95	0.46
Total		435.09	100.00	573.30	100.00	513.30	100.00	640.87	100.00

Note: The import of individual commodities are not equal to the total imports because all items of imports are not included. Similarly, the total of percentages are not equal to 100.

Source: (i) CMIE (2004); (ii) CMIE (2005).

TABLE 6

Composition of India's export to Bangladesh, 1996-97 to 2003-04

(US $ million)

Sl. No.	*Commodities/year*	*1996-97*	*% Share*	*1997-98*	*% Share*	*1998-99*	*% share*	*1999-2000*	*% Share*
1	*2*	*3*	*4*	*5*	*6*	*7*	*8*	*9*	*10*
1.	Non-Basmati rice	40.96	4.71	96.96	12.31	533.74	53.62	83.53	13.11
2.	Wheat	9.67	1.11	-	-	-	-	-	-
3.	Cotton yarn fab made-ups etc.	337.19	38.77	273.60	34.75	123.40	12.40	157.20	24.68
4.	Manufacturers of metals	12.15	1.40	13.17	1.67	12.70	1.28	14.24	2.44
5.	Machinery and equipments	55.89	6.43	47.29	6.01	36.03	3.62	24.88	3.91
6.	Transport equipment	66.68	7.69	34.67	4.40	25.00	2.51	40.49	6.36
7.	Oil meals	0.28	0.03	1.44	0.18	1.79	1.18	7.08	1.11
8.	Prim and semi-finished iron and steel	39.08	4.49	34.49	4.33	16.50	1.66	32.78	5.15
9.	Fresh vegetables	10.34	1.19	7.07	0.90	3.88	0.39	14.25	2.34
10.	Coal	14.88	1.71	18.94	2.40	27.24	2.74	22.05	3.46
11.	Drugs, pharm and fine chemicals	16.15	1.86	21.52	2.73	23.86	2.40	21.58	3.38
12.	Electronic goods	16.80	1.93	17.70	2.25	8.17	0.82	10.73	1.68
13.	Plastic and linoleum products	5.37	0.62	9.43	1.20	7.87	0.79	9.83	1.54
14.	Other cereals	0.71	0.08	0.08	0.01	0.31	0.031	-	-

(Contd.)

TABLE 6 (*Contd.*)

1	2	3	4	5	6	7	8	9	10
15.	Rubber manufactured products	24.15	0.79	18.77	2.38	15.88	1.60	12.70	1.99
16.	Sugar	4.69	0.54	0.03	0.004	0.02	0.002	0.08	0.013
17.	Inorganic/organic/agrochemicals	6.83	0.79	6.44	0.82	5.62	0.57	7.30	1.45
18.	Manmade yarn fab made-ups	14.85	1.71	15.59	1.98	13.66	1.37	14.02	2.20
19.	Pulses	0.18	0.02	1.12	0.14	0.10	0.01	19.18	3.01
20.	Cotton raw inclusive waste	-	-	13.93	1.77	2.09	0.21	0.04	0.006
21.	Fresh fruits	11.45	-	11.08	1.41	7.81	0.79	12.24	1.92
22.	Glass/glassware/ceramics/cement	33.53	3.86	41.35	5.25	24.21	2.44	23.00	3.62
23.	Dyes intermediates etc.	16.52	1.90	14.49	1.84	12.06	1.22	11.89	1.87
24.	Aluminum other than products	10.22	1.18	3.57	0.45	4.48	0.46	4.41	0.69
25.	Paper wood products	21.62	2.49	10.94	1.39	7.98	0.81	10.29	1.62
26.	Other ores and minerals	24.23	0.03	9.07	1.16	6.35	0.65	11.11	1.74
27.	Spices	2.20	0.25	2.65	0.35	4.31	0.43	10.91	1.71
28.	Machine tools	-	-	3.16	0.40	1.79	0.18	1.26	0.20
29.	Residual chemical and allied product	2.86	0.34	2.48	0.31	2.09	0.22	2.21	0.35
	Total	869.69	100.00	787.41	100.00	995.37	100.00	636.92	100.00

(*Contd.*)

Sl. No.	Commodities/year	2000-01	% Share	2001-02	% Share	2002-03	% share	2003-04	% Share
1	2	11	12	13	14	15	16	17	18
1.	Non-Basmati rice	65.01	7.43	16.89	1.68	114.95	9.75	192.13	11.64
2.	Wheat	25.26	2.89	86.27	8.58	96.83	8.21	189.26	11.47
3.	Cotton yarn fab made-ups etc.	175.99	20.13	166.41	16.55	138.68	11.76	173.01	10.48
4.	Manufacturers of metals	31.32	3.70	34.22	3.42	22.79	1.93	101.45	6.15
5.	Machinery and equipments	57.46	6.57	73.33	7.29	41.47	3.52	91.43	5.54
6.	Transport equipment	60.81	6.95	78.39	7.30	57.40	4.87	96.38	4.63
7.	Oil meals	21.78	2.49	31.68	3.15	38.14	3.23	68.39	4.14
8.	Prim and semi-finished iron and steel	26.03	2.98	27.73	2.76	62.01	5.26	67.49	4.09
9.	Fresh vegetables	9.75	1.12	16.67	1.66	11.23	0.95	59.68	3.62
10.	Coal	29.95	3.43	42.56	4.23	44.39	3.75	48.63	2.95
11.	Drugs, pharm and fine chemicals	29.85	3.41	26.79	2.66	35.28	2.99	41.82	2.53
12.	Electronic goods	8.74	0.99	27.00	2.68	27.53	2.33	37.88	2.30
13.	Plastic and linsleum products	9.22	1.05	18.57	1.85	29.98	2.54	34.46	2.09
14.	Other cereals	3.08	0.35	12.02	1.19	7.78	0.66	34.18	2.07
15.	Rubber manufactured products	13.21	1.51	16.32	1.62	17.71	1.50	33.40	2.02
16.	Sugar	10.94	1.25	37.87	3.77	67.84	5.75	31.61	1.92
17.	Inorganic/organic/agrochemicals	22.04	2.52	19.06	1.90	17.15	1.45	29.86	1.81
18.	Manmade yarn fab made-ups	23.28	2.66	15.99	1.59	26.69	2.26	29.20	1.77
19.	Pulses	18.01	2.06	21.61	2.15	27.55	2.34	27.36	1.66

(Contd.)

TABLE 6 (*Contd.*)

1	2	*11*	*12*	*13*	*14*	*15*	*16*	*17*	*18*
20.	Cotton raw inclusive waste	2.13	0.24	0.42	0.041	0.17	0.014	24.42	1.48
21.	Fresh fruits	15.41	1.76	24.43	2.43	13.07	1.11	24.20	1.47
22.	Glass/glassware/ceramics/cement	38.32	4.38	20.71	2.06	13.02	1.10	22.71	1.38
23.	Dyes intermediates etc.	13.95	1.59	14.10	1.40	15.39	1.31	21.31	1.29
24.	Aluminum other than products	7.50	0.86	11.82	1.18	7.88	0.67	19.42	1.17
25.	Paper wood products	20.94	2.39	30.94	3.08	23.32	1.98	19.41	1.18
26.	Other ores and minerals	11.18	1.28	19.07	1.89	11.39	0.97	18.85	1.14
27.	Spices	15.53	1.78	10.57	1.05	10.34	0.88	13.64	0.83
28.	Machine tools	5.79	0.66	7.43	0.74	2.67	0.23	8.71	0.53
29.	Residual chemical and allied product	3.41	0.39	6.27	0.62	5.53	0.47	7.79	0.47
Total		874.41	100.00	10059.59	100.00	1179.05	100.00	1650.43	100.00

Note: The export of individual commodities are not equal to the total exports because all items of exports are not included. Similarly, the total of percentages are not equal to 100.

Sources: (i) CMIE (2003); (ii) CMIE (2004).

(Tata Services Ltd., 2006). This shows that India's base of agricultural and industrial sectors is strong as compared to other SAARC countries. Therefore our dependency on South Asia is less as far as imports are concerned. It may be mentioned here that India's economy is 78 per cent of the region and it contains 76 per cent of South

Asia's 1.5 billion people (Zaidi, 2003). In the decade of 1990's, Indian economy grew at a rate of more than six per cent compared to Pakistan's 3.7 per cent (*Ibid.*). In this period, India's GDP per capita in purchasing power parity terms rose by 104 per cent; Pakistan's rose by mare 36 per cent (*Ibid.*). The sophisticated capital intensive technology, which India needs for its industrial sector is not available in the SAARC countries. Therefore we have to import such items from the developed countries. Moreover, the political environment has not been very conducive in South-Asia in the recent year, which was a major bottleneck for the free flow of goods and services in this region. The SAARC countries should concentrate on fighting poverty and hunger instead of fighting among themselves.

COMPOSITION OF INDIA'S EXPORT TO BANGLADESH

The information about composition of India's export to Bangladesh from 1996-97 to 2003-04 is given in Table 6. India's exports to Bangladesh were to the extent of US $ 870 million during the year 1996-97 which increased to US $ 1650 million in 2003-04. Our main items of exports to Bangladesh were non-basmati rice, wheat, cotton yarn fabric made-ups, manufacturers of metals, machinery and equipment, transport-equipment, oil meals, primary and semi finished iron and steel, fresh vegetables, coal etc. India has positive trade balance in case of Bangladesh but this trade surplus is lower subject to fluctuations (Thakur and Padamadeo, 2004).

COMPOSITION OF INDIA'S EXPORT TO PAKISTAN

The data about composition of India's export to Pakistan from 1996-97 to 2003-04 are given in Table 7. India's

TABLE 7

Composition of India's Exports to Pakistan, 1996-97 to 2003-04

(US $ million)

Sl. No.	Commodities/year	1996-97	% Share	1997-98	% Share	1998-99	% share	1999-2000	% Share
1	2	3	4	5	6	7	8	9	10
1.	Dyes intermediates etc.	10.58	6.72	9.90	6.91	11.06	10.43	9.31	10.00
2.	Cotton raw inclusive waste	-	11.04	-	-	0.02	-	-	-
3.	Oil meals	18.39	11.69	18.65	13.22	24.48	0.019	19.81	21.29
4.	Drugs, pharm and fine chemicals	2.86	1.82	7.68	5.36	14.34	13.52	16.69	17.93
5.	In-org/organic/agro-chemicals	3.08	1.96	3.12	2.18	2.24	2.11	2.42	2.60
6.	Rubber manufactured products, etc.	0.21	0.13	9.04	6.31	6.50	6.13	6.83	7.44
7.	Cotton yarn fab made-up etc.	0.14	-	0.30	0.21	0.51	0.48	0.71	0.76
8.	Iron ore	3.60	2.29	8.94	6.24	6.16	5.81	1.64	1.76
9.	Plastic and linoleum products	0.17	0.11	2.52	1.76	0.56	0.53	2.51	2.70
10.	Tea	0.18	0.11	6.49	4.53	0.90	0.85	0.44	0.47
11.	Manufactured of metals	1.43	0.91	9.67	6.75	1.62	1.53	1.37	1.47
12.	Prim and semi-finished iron and steel	0.62	0.39	1.38	0.96	0.79	0.74	1.66	1.78
13.	Sugar	86.69	55.22	35.75	24.94	0.09	0.08	-	-
14.	Paper/wood products	1.22	0.76	1.18	0.82	1.04	0.98	0.90	0.97
15.	Machinery and instruments	1.94	1.23	1.99	1.39	2.15	2.03	1.45	1.56

16. Residual chemical and allied products	0.52	0.33	2.51	1.75	1.09	1.03	1.10	1.18
17. Spices	11.89	7.56	9.54	6.67	12.88	12.14	11.18	12.01
18. Paints/enamels/varnishes	3.03	1.93	2.23	1.56	2.96	2.79	2.97	3.19
19. Ferro alloys	-	-	0.18	0.13	0.18	0.17	0.22	0.24
20. Other ores and minerals	-	-	0.58	0.40	0.64	0.60	2.28	2.45
21. Basmati rice	-	-	-	-	-	-	-	-
22. Glass/glassware/ceramics and cement	0.53	0.34	0.09	0.06	0.24	0.23	0.42	0.45
23. Fruits/vegetables seeds	1.09	0.69	1.25	0.87	2.27	2.14	1.44	1.55
24. Guar-gum meal	-	-	0.82	0.57	0.56	0.53	0.11	0.12
25. Shellac	0.04	0.03	0.28	0.20	0.08	0.08	0.57	0.61
26. Cosmetics/toiletries	0.40	0.25	0.34	0.23	0.34	0.32	0.26	0.28
27. RMG of cotton inclusive accessories	0.01	0.006	0.03	0.02	0.06	0.06	0.05	0.05
28. Processed vegetables	-	-	0.01	0.006	-	-	0.01	0.01
29. Iron and steel bar/rods	-	-	0.43	0.30	1.66	1.56	0.27	0.29
Total	157.35	100.00	143.32	100.00	106.08	100.00	93.06	100.00

(Contd.)

TABLE 7 (*Contd.*)

Sl. No.	*Commodities/year*	*2000-01*	*% Share*	*2001-02*	*% Share*	*2002-03*	*% share*	*2003-04*	*% Share*
1	*2*	*11*	*12*	*13*	*14*	*15*	*16*	*17*	*18*
1.	Dyes intermediates etc.	8.32	4.46	7.40	5.12	18.73	9.06	69.55	24.21
2.	Cotton raw inclusive waste	-	-	-	-	-	-	40.50	14.10
3.	Oil meals	18.29	9.80	4.42	3.06	7.44	3.60	26.26	9.14
4.	Drugs, pharm and fine chemicals	18.39	9.85	18.46	12.75	21.95	10.62	25.28	8.79
5.	In-org/organic/agro-chemicals	20.58	11.03	6.78	4.69	16.33	7.90	18.12	6.31
6.	Rubber manufactured products, etc.	8.03	4.30	8.18	5.66	13.61	6.58	14.34	5.00
7.	Cotton yarn fab made-up etc.	0.11	0.06	0.85	0.59	1.18	0.57	9.75	3.39
8.	Iron ore	3.73	1.99	4.74	3.28	16.38	7.92	8.42	2.93
9.	Plastic and linoleum products	14.03	7.52	22.19	15.36	27.56	13.33	6.78	2.36
10.	Tea	6.81	3.65	3.03	2.09	4.19	2.03	6.54	2.28
11.	Manufactured of metals	2.05	1.09	1.76	1.22	2.85	1.38	5.89	2.05
12.	Prim and semi finished iron and steel	1.42	0.77	0.28	0.19	6.80	3.29	4.96	1.73
13.	Sugar	56.69	30.38	42.89	29.68	6.40	3.10	3.75	1.31
14.	Paper/wood products	0.89	0.48	0.45	0.31	1.24	0.60	3.05	1.06
15.	Machinery and instruments	1.78	0.95	2.92	2.02	3.68	1.78	2.83	0.98
16.	Residual chemical and allied products	2.83	1.51	2.78	1.92	3.58	1.73	2.69	0.94
17.	Spices	7.72	4.14	3.24	2.24	3.54	1.71	2.36	0.82
18.	Paints/enamels/varnishes	2.48	1.33	1.70	1.18	1.84	0.89	2.00	0.70
19.	Ferro alloys	0.50	0.27	0.65	0.45	0.31	0.15	1.89	0.66

20. Other ores and minerals	0.02	0.01	1.05	0.73	1.44	0.70	1.37	0.48
21. Basmati rice	-	-	-	-	0.01	0.005	1.23	0.43
22. Glass/glassware/ceramics and cement	0.38	0.20	0.44	0.31	0.50	0.24	1.15	0.40
23. Fruits/vegetables seeds	0.82	0.44	0.75	0.52	1.94	0.94	1.13	0.39
24. Guar-gum meal	0.51	0.27	0.06	0.04	0.09	0.04	0.74	0.26
25. Shellac	0.73	0.39	0.38	0.26	0.58	0.28	0.66	0.23
26. Cosmetics/toiletries	0.21	0.11	0.38	0.26	0.72	0.35	0.63	0.22
27. RMG of cotton inclusive accessories	0.12	0.06	0.37	0.25	2.29	1.11	0.54	0.19
28. Processed vegetables	-	-	0.48	0.33	0.01	0.005	0.47	0.16
29. Iron and steel bar/rods	0.15	0.08	0.15	0.10	0.26	0.13	0.42	0.15
Total	186.62	100.00	144.50	100.00	206.70	100.00	287.31	100.00

Note: The export of individual commodities are not equal to the total exports because all items of exports are not included. Similarly, the total of percentages are not equal to 100.

Sources: (i) CMIE (2003); (ii) CMIE (2004).

TABLE 8

Composition of India's Exports to Sri Lanka, 1996-97 to 2003-04

(US $ million)

Sl. No.	Commodities/year	1996-97	% Share	1997-98	% Share	1998-99	% Share	1999-2000	% Share
1	2	3	4	5	6	7	8	9	10
1.	Transport equipment	54.36	11.38	57.16	11.67	72.36	16.56	64.50	12.90
2.	Cotton yarn fab, made-ups, etc.	57.41	12.02	65.46	13.36	67.73	15.50	73.69	14.74
3.	Prim and semi finished iron and steel	22.33	4.67	25.88	5.28	16.01	3.66	20.00	4.00
4.	Sugar	25.24	5.28	2.89	0.29	0.04	0.009	0.04	0.008
5.	Manmade yarn fab made-ups	8.74	1.83	9.82	2.02	15.14	3.46	23.30	4.66
6.	Machinery and instruments	32.06	6.71	36.68	7.45	34.64	7.93	37.47	7.50
7.	Drugs, pharm and fine chemicals	24.79	5.91	27.83	5.68	34.42	7.88	31.13	6.23
8.	Wheat	-	-	-	-	-	-	-	-
9.	Glass/glassware/ceramics/cement	10.97	2.30	9.44	1.93	6.47	1.48	10.20	2.04
10.	Manufactured of metals	18.87	3.95	23.41	4.78	27.01	6.18	25.69	5.14
11.	Paper/wood products	17.74	3.71	17.80	3.63	14.87	3.40	22.18	4.44
12.	Plastic and linoleum products	12.68	2.65	16.76	3.42	14.11	3.23	15.61	3.12
13.	Oil meals	10.41	2.18	13.56	2.77	8.81	2.02	9.48	1.90
14.	RMG of cotton inclusive accessories	3.00	0.63	5.16	1.05	4.85	1.11	14.23	2.85
15.	In-org/organic agro-chemicals	9.33	1.93	9.97	2.04	10.85	2.48	10.58	2.12
16.	Non-ferrous metals	54.19	0.15	0.40	0.08	0.39	0.089	0.75	0.15

17. Spices	7.49	1.57	3.68	0.75	5.51	1.26	11.32	2.26
18. Fresh vegetables	17.80	3.73	13.16	2.69	8.85	2.03	14.25	2.85
19. Electronic goods	5.06	1.06	4.16	0.85	5.23	1.20	6.80	1.36
20. Misc. processed items	3.72	0.78	6.48	1.32	4.55	1.04	3.87	0.77
21. Iron and steel bar/rods	4.54	0.93	5.23	1.07	3.36	0.77	5.53	1.11
22. Rubber manufactured goods	6.58	1.38	8.57	1.75	5.85	1.34	4.25	0.85
23. Cosmetics/toiletries	2.68	0.56	4.04	0.84	5.31	1.22	4.08	0.82
24. RMG of wool	-	-	-	-	0.15	0.03	0.10	0.02
25. Residual chemicals and allied products	1.91	0.40	2.64	0.54	3.08	0.70	3.16	0.63
26. Other cereals	-	-	0.35	0.07	0.17	0.04	0.28	0.06
27. Paints/enamels/varnishes	1.04	0.22	1.97	0.40	2.45	0.56	2.48	0.50
28. Gems and jewellery	-	-	0.55	0.11	1.36	0.31	3.11	0.62
29. Tea	-	-	3.01	0.61	2.13	0.49	1.81	0.36
Total	477.81	100.00	437.03	100.00	437.03	100.00	499.78	100.00

(Contd.)

TABLE 8 (*Contd.*)

Sl. No.	*Commodities/year*	*2000-01*	*% Share*	*2001-02*	*% Share*	*2002-03*	*% share*	*2003-04*	*% Share*
1	*2*	*11*	*12*	*13*	*14*	*15*	*16*	*17*	*18*
1.	Transport equipment	79.40	12.59	49.71	7.85	105.25	11.40	148.27	11.20
2.	Cotton yarn fab, made-ups, etc.	77.42	12.28	70.36	11.11	79.24	8.58	84.28	6.37
3.	Prim and semi finished iron and steel	38.57	6.12	28.06	4.43	35.60	3.86	75.80	5.73
4.	Sugar	7.44	1.18	62.94	9.94	74.87	8.11	53.96	4.08
5.	Manmade yarn fab made-ups	26.30	4.17	24.49	3.87	34.05	3.69	51.33	3.89
6.	Machinery and instruments	41.48	6.57	41.48	6.55	53.61	5.81	51.20	3.87
7.	Drugs, pharm and fine chemicals	38.02	6.03	32.12	5.07	46.88	5.08	50.43	3.81
8.	Wheat	-	-	5.35	0.85	17.43	1.89	44.28	3.34
9.	Glass/glassware/ceramics/cement	38.59	6.12	37.24	5.88	36.61	3.97	40.34	3.05
10.	Manufactured of metals	36.76	5.83	24.88	3.93	33.77	3.66	39.83	3.00
11.	Paper/wood products	31.71	5.03	29.13	4.60	35.09	3.80	39.37	2.97
12.	Plastic and linoleum products	23.90	3.79	20.72	3.27	22.74	2.46	34.46	2.60
13.	Oil meals	10.08	1.60	12.44	2.02	13.13	1.42	27.24	2.06
14.	RMG of cotton inclusive accessories	16.97	2.69	11.82	1.87	13.84	1.50	23.97	1.81
15.	In-org/organic agro-chemicals	14.79	2.35	13.02	2.06	18.68	2.02	22.32	1.69
16.	Non-ferrous metals	0.81	0.13	1.54	0.24	8.36	0.91	20.04	1.51
17.	Spices	13.02	2.07	14.25	2.25	17.28	1.87	19.54	1.48
18.	Fresh vegetables	19.86	3.15	13.95	2.20	16.50	1.79	18.92	1.43
19.	Electronic goods	9.19	1.46	7.10	1.12	10.97	1.19	17.61	1.33

20. Misc. processed items	4.49	0.71	5.74	0.91	6.79	0.74	17.05	1.29
21. Iron and steel bar/rods	7.56	1.20	3.66	0.58	7.74	0.84	16.58	1.25
22. Rubber manufactured goods	5.79	0.92	4.78	0.76	5.50	0.60	9.99	0.75
23. Cosmetics/toiletries	6.35	1.01	8.65	1.37	7.08	0.77	8.96	0.68
24. RMG of wool	2.79	0.44	2.05	0.32	5.07	0.55	8.28	0.62
25. Residual chemicals and allied products	3.57	0.57	4.37	0.69	4.48	0.49	5.44	0.41
26. Other cereals	1.02	0.16	0.36	0.06	0.46	0.05	5.29	0.40
27. Paints/enamels/varnishes	3.26	0.52	3.61	0.57	4.39	0.48	5.20	0.39
28. Gems and jewellery	2.29	0.36	1.29	0.20	1.40	0.15	4.14	0.31
29. Tea	1.91	0.30	2.51	0.40	2.75	0.30	3.68	0.28
Total	630.48	100.00	633.04	100.00	923.37	100.00	1323.88	100.00

Note: The export of individual commodities are not equal to the total exports because all items of exports are not included. Similarly, the total of percentages are not equal to 100.

Sources: (i) CMIE (2003); (ii) CMIE (2004)

exports to Pakistan were $ 157.35 million in 1996-97 which increased to $ 287.31 million in 2003-04. The strained political relations between India and Pakistan have haunted the two countries since 1947. On the surface, it may, therefore, appear as though trade between them has been completely jeopardised. Statistical evidence, however, suggests that despite political tensions, trade has been taking place. Since 1947, trade has been negligible only for nine years between 1965-74 following the Indo-Pakistan was in 1965. Bilateral trade did resume in 1975-76 following the 1974 protocol for the restoration of commercial relations on a government to government basis, signed by the two countries after the 1971 war but it remained at an insignificant level till very recently (Taneja, 2004). Since 1996, trade between the two countries has been at much higher levels than before. Interestingly, no direct correlation (inverse) can be drawn between political tensions between the two countries and the level of bilateral trade (*Ibid.*). Estimates of informal trade is placed at US $ 2 billion, which is traded through third countries such as Dubai, CIS countries and Afghanistan.

The principal item exported to Pakistan though official trade, route were dyes intermediate, etc. cotton raw inclusive waste, oil meals, drug, pharmaceuticals and fine chemicals, in organic and organic chemicals, rubber manufactured products, etc.

COMPOSITION OF INDIA'S EXPORTS TO SRI LANKA

The information about composition of India's export to Sri Lanka is shown in Table 8. India's exports to Sri Lanka were worth US $ 478 million in 1996-97 which increased to US $ 1324 million in 2003-04. The principal items of exports were transport equipment, cotton yarn fabric made-up, primary and semi-finished iron and steel, sugar, man-made yarn fabric made-up, machinery and equipment, drugs, pharmaceutical and fine chemicals, wheat, glass/glass were, manufactured metals, paper/wood products, etc.

It may be stated here that during the last two decades, India's exports to Sri Lanka were several time higher than the values of India's imports from Sri Lanka making a huge trade balance. Sri Lanka was in 17th position in India's exports basket by exporting 1.4 per cent of total exports of India in 1996 (Abeywickrama, 2003). The position has been upgraded to 15th place by exporting 1.7 per cent of total exports of India in 2001 (*Ibid.*). In 1996, Sri Lanka's position of India's import basket was 69 by importing 0.07 per cent of total imports of India. It has been increased up to 49th place in 2001 by importing 0.26 per cent of the total import of India. India and Sri Lanka have increased their exports at faster rates (23.8 per cent and 16.04 per cent respectively) than that of the world average exports at 12.57 per cent in the triennium of 1999-2001 over the triennium of 1995-97 (*Ibid.*). If both countries revise the commodities included in different lists to be compatible with potential trade flows on a scientific basis, both would benefit with increased trade flows. Vertical and horizontal integration of production and trade of competitive spices and tea market of the two countries will increase the bargaining ability in the world market rather than acting as rivals.

CONCLUSION

Liberalization of trade policies has been a prime concept of economic policy reforms in both the developed as well as developing countries in the recent years. The developing countries pursued an Import Substitution Industrialization (ISI) strategy from 1950's but failed to achieve rapid economic growth and eradicate poverty. The SAARC countries have also realized the importance of free trade in the Islamabad Summit held in January, 2004. The SAFTA agreement will drastically reduce trade barriers between South-Asian countries despite give problems. Pakistan has not accorded MFN status to India so far. However, the SAARC countries have a long way to go before it can even think of emulating ASEAN. Although South Asia is home to 1.5 billion people of the world, intra-regional trade accounts for about five per cent whereas trade within the ASEAN region is around 23 per cent. Indian exporters control over 70 per cent of the intra-regional shipment. The six SAARC countries have a trade deficit of about US $ 3.4 billion with India. Such fears of Indian domination are unfounded because trade is a two-way traffic, not one way.

India's exports to the SAARC countries had increased from US $ 1.70 billion 1996-97 to US $ 4.24 billion in 2003-04. In percentage terms, the share of India's exports to the SAARC countries was about six in her total exports to all over the world. The major items of exports to the SAARC countries were cotton yarn fabric made-up etc., transport equipment, sugar, primary and semi-finished iron and steel, drugs, pharmaceutical and fine chemicals, non-basmati rice, machinery and equipment, wheat, etc. With the opening of Wagah border, the Indian Punjab will have comparative advantage for the export of agricultural commodities to the Pakistan. It will reduce transportation cost. During the year 2003-04, India's imports from the SAARC countries were to the extent of about US $ 0.64 billion. It mainly consists of essential oil and cosmetic, spices, iron and steel, inorganic chemicals, manmade filament/spun yarn/waste, non-ferrous metals, jute raw, pulses, etc. India's base of agricultural and industrial sector is strong as compared to other SAARC countries. Therefore, our dependency on South-Asia is less as far as imports are concerned.

Freight is an element that already goes against SAARC countries like Pakistan and Bangladesh. It roughly costs Rs. 1000 per ton from Pakistan to Bangladesh via land route through India as compared to something like Rs. 3600 per ton for shipping from Pakistan to Bangladesh. Therefore all the SAARC countries may take all this as an economic opportunity for economic upliftment of the people.

References

Abeywickrama, L.M. (2003), *Emerging Trends in Indo-Sri Lanka Farm Trade: Problems and Prospects in the Context of Liberalisation*. Ph.D. Thesis (Unpublished), Deptt. of Economics, PAU, Ludhiana, pp. 1-197 + XIII.

Basu, Tarun (2004), SAARC can Make South Asia Economic Power: PM: *The Financial World*, Chandigarh, Vol. III (243), January 5, pp. 1&4.

Cherian, John (2004), Looking Ahead, *Frontline*, Vol. 21 (2), January 17-30, pp. 12-14.

CMIE (2003), *Foreign Trade and Balance of Payments*, Economic Intelligence Service, Centre for Monitoring Indian Economy, Mumbai, pp. 1-392.

CMIE (2004), *Foreign Trade and Balance of Payments*, Economic Intelligence Service, Centre for Monitoring Indian Economy, Mumbai, pp. 1-392.

Gill, P.K. (2005), South Asia: Greater Scope for Regional Cooperation, *The Sunday Tribune*, Chandigarh, Vol. 125 (273), October 2, p. 12.

Haqqani, Husain (2003), For General's Knowledge, Nation is not Army Parade, *The Indian Express*, Chandigarh, Vol. 26 (262), June 13, p. 9.

Kumar, Manoj (2005), Cloud of Uncertainty Looms Over SAFTA, *The Sunday Tribune*, Chandigarh, Vol. 125 (321), October 20, p. 21.

Shourie, Arun (2004), The Painful Task of Self-Improvement: The Reforms Mandate Part II, *The Indian Express*, Chandigarh, Vol. 27, (157) Feb. 5, p. 11.

Sidhu, R.S. and A.S. Bhullar (2005), Patterns and Determinants of Agricultural Growth in the Two Punjabs, *Economic and Political Weekly*, Vol. XL (53), December 31, pp. 5620-27.

Taneja, Misha (2004), India-Pakistan Trade Relations: Opportunities for Growth, *Economic and Political Weekly*, Vol. 39 (4), January 24, pp. 326-27.

Tata Services Ltd. (2006), *Statistical Outline of India* 2005-06, Deptt. of Economics and Statistics, Bombay House, Mumbai, pp. 1-302.

Thakur, A.K. and K.B. Padamdeo (2004), Regional Trade Liberalization Under SAPTA and India's Trade Linkages with South Asia. *The Indian Economic Association 87th Conference Volume*, pp. 911-16.

UNDP (2004), *Human Development Report, 2004*, Oxford University Press, New Delhi, pp. 1-285.

Varma, K.J.M. (2006), Pakistan Not to Give MFN Status to India, *The Tribune*, Chandigarh, Vol. 126 (180), July 1, p. 11.

Vasudeva, P.K. (2004), SAFTA for Growth of SAARC Countries, *The Financial World*, Chandigarh, Vol. III (252), January 15, p. 6.

Zaidi, S.A. (2003), The Single South-Asian Currency, *Sunday Hindustan Times*, Chandigarh, Vol. II (50), December 21, p. 10.

Free Trade between India and the European Union-15

A General Equilibrium Approach

Chandrima Sikdar

The European Union was formally established on November 1, 1993. It comprised of 15 member countries, namely, Austria, Belgium, Denmark, France, Finland, Germany, Greece, Ireland, Italy, Luxembourg, The Netherlands, Portugal, Spain, Sweden and the United Kingdom till it was joined on May 1, 2004 by ten other European countries. These countries are namely, Cyprus, Czech Republic, Poland, Estonia, Hungary, Latvia, Lithuania, Malta, Slovakia and Slovenia. The EU-15 represented just 6 per cent of the world's population. But it accounted for roughly 20 per cent of global imports and exports (European Commission, 2002). With its enlargement in May 1, 2004 the union at present comprises of as much as 7.7 per cent of world population and more than 20 per cent of the world trade (Europa, 2004).

Thus, the EU emerged as the leading trade power of the world. It exhibits a strong interest in creating conditions in which trade can prosper. It aims at free but fair world trade. This refers to a system where all countries are given opportunities to trade freely with one another on equal terms and without protectionist barriers. To achieve this, the EU's strategy is to open-up its own market while others do like-wise. It seeks to remove obstacles to trade gradually and at a pace, which the EU and others can sustain, to settle disputes peacefully and to build-up a body of internationally agreed rules.

Opening-up of markets means removal of trade barriers between countries. This was a basic goal of the union right from the days of its inception. That is why, in 1992, the EU launched its single market by removing its non-tariff barriers to trade in goods, and also by opening-up trade in services within the union. Such opening-up of trade serves to stimulate the economy as a whole. It boosts the revenues of exporting countries and offers consumers in the importing countries a wider choice of goods and services at lower prices because of increased competition. Ultimately it allows all countries to produce and export the goods and services with which they are best placed to compete.

Thus, EU's trade policy now covers a broader canvas, beyond trade liberalization. It is about updating and improving international rules, and giving them a wider coverage to ensure fair trade and harnessed globalisation (European Commission, 2002).

INDIA-EU EXISTING TRADE RELATIONSHIP

Traditionally, India had a multi-dimensional relationship with the EU, which is our largest trading partner, the biggest source of our foreign direct investment, a major supplier of our developmental aid, an important source of technology and also a home to a large and influential Indian diaspora (India-EU relations, 2002). India attained the status of the EU's largest trading partner as early as 1993 and since then has maintained a steady growth not only in volume of its trade with the EU but also in diversity, with a third of Indian exports reaching the EU destinations. India's strength lies in traditional exports like textiles, agriculture and marine products, gems and jewellery, leather and engineering and electronic products. Sectors like chemicals, carpets, granites and electronics have exhibited the fastest growth in the last five years. Indian exports from Europe, on the other hand, comprise mainly gems and jewellery, engineering goods, chemicals and minerals.

EU has been enjoying a favourable balance of trade with India throughout the last decade. However, from 1999 this gap started reducing and stood at US $ 807.28 million in 2003. Total trade between EU and India rose from US $ 24.0 billion in 2002 to US $ 28.3 billion in 2003, thereby registering a growth of 17.9 per cent. The Indian exports to the EU registered a positive growth rate throughout the mid-nineties. However, the first year of the millennium, when Indian exports to the EU recorded a figure of US $ 9.96 billion, witnessed a negative growth rate of –5.84 per cent in 2001. Thereafter, the exports from India to the EU picked-up and stood at US $ 13.7 billion in the year 2003. This could be attributed to the developing country status of India, due to which India's exports to the EU is subject to lower tariffs under EU's Generalized System of Preferences. EU's exports to India during the same period (2001 to 2003) also increased from US $ 10.5 billion to US $ 14.5 billion. The India- EU trade has shown an impressive growth over the years, from US $ 18.6 billion in 1995 to US $ 28.2 billion in 2003. EU accounts for as much as 21.73 per cent of India's exports and 20.42 per cent of total India's imports according to the latest available data. Trade with the EU represents almost a quarter of Indian's total world trade. However, India accounts for a meagre 1.6 per cent of total imports of the union and 0.8 per cent of its import of services. Moreover, though the EU happens to be India's largest source of foreign direct investment yet India attracts only 0.3 per cent of the investments that flows out of the European Union to the various countries of the world.

Thus, there exists an enormous potential for improving trade and investment flows between EU and India. In its Communication on an "EU-India Strategic Partnership" the European Commission proposes to take a more comprehensive and ambitious approach to enhancing trade and investment between India and the EU. At the EU-India

Business Summit held in Copenhagen in 2002, a target was set to increase the bilateral trade between the two countries to US $ 31.28 billion by 2005 and to US $ 44.68 billion by 2008. Moreover, the EC-India Country Strategy Paper (2002-2006) mentions that the EU will assume a special responsibility of assisting India in its task of tackling its second generation of economic reforms. Accordingly, the EC will bring on stream a special Trade and Investment Development Programme. This programme builds on the industry driven "EU India investment and trade enhancement initiative" and offers to

- assist India with mainstreaming its tariff, tax and regulatory infrastructure with international practice, including standardization, conformity assessment, safety inspection as well as sanitary and phyto-sanitary systems.
- facilitate training for officials and industry on multilateral trade and WTO.
- promote industry driven studies on improving the trade and investment environment in key industrial and service sectors.
- encourage the involvement as much as possible of the main stakeholders through dialogue stimulated by relevant think-tanks, civil society groups and private sector.

The last decade has been momentous for both Europe and India. It has seen the EU getting transformed from a community to a union. The year 2002 witnessed the successful launching of the Euro while May 1st, 2004 witnessed the accession of ten new member states. After this expansion from 15 to 25 States, the union's territory surged to 3.9 million square kilometers from 3.2 million square kilometers, while the population of the union rose by 75 million bringing the total to around 453 million. This in turn further expanded the single market launched by the EU earlier. The EU's GDP also went-up by 5 per cent following this enlargement. On the other hand, India too has transited from a mixed economy to a market economy. Today, India is a strong and powerful nation which has emerged on the world stage. The country has consolidated her national strength in every sense of the term. It has averaged 6 per cent growth over the last decade and has set a target of 8 per cent over the next five years. Inflation has been at a record low during all this time. The country's foreign exchange reserves are over US $ 70 billion. From a country that has been subject to severe shortages of foodgrains, India has emerged as an exporter and donor of food grains today. The nation's software industry has made a progress commendable enough to be the envy of the world. Her space, nuclear science, bio-tech and other high-tech capabilities are also matter of pride. Most of all, it is widely acknowledged that the human resources of India are among the best in the world.

Against this backdrop it is obvious that India's image in the EU is gradually changing as a dynamic trailblazer with a knowledge-based economy. Given the advantage of this image in Europe, India is expecting to enter into a big-bang relationship with the new European Union. Trade is the bedrock of the multidimensional relationship that the subcontinent already enjoys with the European Union. Therefore the immediate and direct effect of the enlargement of the EU for India will be burgeoning trade prospects as the enlargement will augment the EU market place making it the biggest market in the world- bigger than the US–Mexico–Canada combined, accounting for more than one-fifth of global trade and contributing a fourth of the world's Gross Domestic Product (GDP).

Given that the two sides—India and the EU are meeting frequently as members of a high-level trade group formed during an EU-India summit in the Indian capital in September 2005. The present paper attempts to explore the potentials of having free trade between India and the EU and aims at identifying the possible gains that would accrue to each of the economies.

This paper is organized as follows. Section 1 provides a brief review of the selected literature on promotion of free bilateral trade between the countries of the world. The model that describes the pattern of trade flow between India and the

EU-15 in a perfectly competitive world characterized by free bilateral trade is presented in section 2. Section 3 briefly discusses the data used for the empirical implementation of the theoretical model developed in section 3. The results of the model are presented in section 4. Section 5 discusses the gains from free trade accruing to either country. The paper finally concludes with a summary of the theoretical model that it proposes along with the policy implications.

1. SURVEY OF SELECTED LITERATURE

In recent times contemporary researchers have shown considerable interest in promoting free trade among the various countries and regions of the world. This concern has seen the development of a substantial volume of literature on this topic in recent years.

Chan (1999) made a cost and benefit analysis of forming a free trade area among the Forum island countries and came-up with the suggestion that establishment of a free trade area should only be a stepping-stone to further trade liberalization in the Pacific and not protectionist regional block. Faber (1999) makes a similar study in which he addresses the question whether FTAs between the ACP countries and the European Union will produce better results than the existing one and provides an economic analysis of the FTA approach for the future EU-ACP relations. Nori and Patnaik (2003), attempt to study the trade synchronization of the SAARC region as a whole with another regional bloc, namely, the European Union (EU) in the framework of globalization. It is observed that the SAARC countries have been exporting mainly to the EU countries in comparison to other industrialized countries like USA and Japan.

Apart from these empirical works that relate to the promotion of bilateral trade between countries, there is quite a substantial volume of literature which deals with theoretical model building exercise that helps to explain the pattern of bilateral trade flows between countries.

Roy and Chakraborty (2000) locate the comparative advantages of India *vis-à-vis* Bangladesh. In their paper, they have developed three linear programming models, which maximize foreign earnings of India and Bangladesh at given world prices subject to material balance and factor endowments of the economies. In all the three models in their work by Roy and Chakraborty the foreign earnings of India and Bangladesh are maximized at given world prices subject to the material balance and factor endowments of the two economies. On the basis of the results obtained, the comparative advantages of the respective economies are identified and export potentials of either economy are located.

Raa and Mohnen (2001) postulate a model of free trade in a world characterized by perfect competition involving the two economies of Europe and Canada. They also locate the comparative advantages of these two economies but by constructing a competitive benchmark based only on the fundamentals of the two economies: endowments, preferences and technologies. Sikdar, Chakraborty and Raa (2005) apply a similar theoretical framework to explain trade flows between the two South Asian countries of India and Bangladesh.

These are some of the important works which are based on theoretical model building that help to analyze the prospects and possibilities of bilateral trade between various countries of the world. However, very little work has been done regarding the bilateral trade relations between the two economies of India and the EU-15. In this context a mention may be made of a very early work by Raa and Chakraborty (1991). They locate the comparative advantages of the Indian economy vis-à-vis the European economy. They use a linear programme that maximizes the foreign earnings of India and Europe at given world prices subject to the material balances and factor endowments of either economy. With this maximization exercise, they arrive at a solution that shows positive output for some sectors of the economies. These sectors are identified as the ones, which have comparative advantages in production. However, in the context of today's world more important to India is not her relation with Europe alone but with the European Union as a whole. A comprehensive approach towards the analysis of the possibilities of bilateral trade between India and the EU is lacking in the existing literature. The present paper aims at filling this gap by contributing to this area.

2. THE MODEL

The model developed in this paper allows country specific endowments, preferences and technologies which are the fundamentals of an economy according to the neoclassical theory of trade and on the basis of these fundamentals a competitive benchmark is constructed by solving a linear programme and this linear programme then is used for locating the comparative advantages of the economies and assessing their gains from free trade. This model is a general equilibrium version of Raa and Mohnen (2001).

Thus, the model that is set-up in the following section is a neoclassical model of international trade. It begins with the assumption that each economy has fixed domestic endowments, with tradable and non-tradable commodities, which are used for intermediate as well as final consumption. Leontief functions are used to represent technologies and preferences i.e., there are fixed input coefficients and fixed proportions of final consumption and investment in each economy. The efficient allocation of resources is obtained by maximizing the level of domestic final demand (including consumption and investment) in one economy, subject to a given proportion of final consumption in the other. The novelty of this model lays in the fact that it proposes a new way to locate the comparative advantages of the two economies of India and the EU-15 linked by international trade. It constructs a competitive benchmark based only on the fundamentals of the two economies: endowments, preferences and technologies. No statistics or constructs beyond the fundamentals of the economies are used in the model. In particular, it employs no price statistics. Nor does it admit of any artificial limitations on the direction of trade. This model provides a truly general equilibrium determination of the commodity pattern of trade. In addition, one important point about the model which is worth noting is that though the model is worked out for the two economies of India and Bangladesh, yet, since it is based on fundamentals with all prices endogenous, the incorporation of rest of the world as a third economy would be a straightforward extension of the model.

The model may be formally stated as follows:

Let 'c' denote the level of final consumption in India and 'c*' the same for the EU and let $c^* = gc$ i.e. 'g' is EU-Indian final consumption ratio, g being chosen such that the actual bilateral balance of payments is maintained.

The linear programme is

$$\max_{x,x^*,c} e^T (y+y^*g)c$$

subject to

$(I-A)\,x+(I-A^*)\,x^* \geq (y+y^*g)\,c+z+z^*$ ... for tradable commodities ...(1)

$(I-A)\,x \geq yc,\ (I-A^*)\,x^* \geq y^*g\,c$ ... for non-tradable commodities ...(2)

kx £ K, lx £ L........................ for factor inputs in India ...(3)

k*x* £ K*, l*x* £ L*................. for factor inputs in the EU ...(4)

where,

$$e^T = (1..........1)$$

y, y* = domestic final demand vector (including consumption and investment, excluding trade) in India and the EU respectively.

z, z* = net exports vector (except for bilateral trade) in India and EU respectively.

A, A* = input-output coefficients matrix in India and EU respectively.

K, K* = capital stock in India and EU respectively.

L, L* = labour force in India and EU respectively.

k, k* = capital input coefficients row vector in India and EU respectively.

l, l* = labour input coefficients row vector in India and EU respectively.

For every value of the final consumption ratio, 'g', we denote the optimum (Indian) consumption level by c(g) and the outputs in the two countries by x(g) and x*(g), respectively. For low values of 'g', consumption of EU is not important and the bulk of the net output is exported to India. Similarly, for high values of 'g' the trade balance shows an Indian surplus.

For tradable commodities, Indian net exports to the EU are given by the vector:

$$(I\text{-}A)\ x\ (g)\ \text{-}y\ c\ (g)\ \text{-}z \qquad ...(5)$$

In a general equilibrium framework, the supporting competitive prices are given by the shadow prices of the linear programme. Let us denote those for tradable commodities by p(g). Indian surplus on bilateral trade account is equal to the product of p(g) and (5) and is denoted by s(g).

For 'g' low, s(g) is negative, and for 'g' high, s(g) is positive. For some intermediate value, s(g) matches the observed surplus on the bilateral trade account,

$$S^0 = e\ (x^0 - Ax^o\text{-}y\text{-}z) \qquad ...(6)$$

where x^0 is the observed value of the gross output vector x. We shall find the intermediate value of 'g' by the Newton-Raphson algorithm,

$$g_{n+1} = [\{s(g_n) - s^0\}\ g_{n-1} - \{s(g_{n-1}) - s^0\}g_n\ ]/[s(g_n) - s(g_{n-1})] \qquad ...(7)$$

given initial values $g_0=0$ and $g_1=1$

The limit process (7) solves s (g) = s^0 and this gives the general equilibrium value of the India-EU final consumption expansion ratio, g =**c*/c**

For this value, the linear programme determines the levels, c(g) and c*(g), the allocations, x(g) and x*(g) and the bilateral trade vector, (5). The comparative advantages of the two economies are located on the basis of the sign pattern of the bilateral trade. This is done solely on the basis of the parameters or fundamentals of the two economies—taste (y, y*), technology (A, A*; k, k*; l, l*) and endowments (K, K* and L, L*), and the rest of the world (z, z*) which is fixed.

Thus, the model determines the comparative advantages of the two economies on the basis of their fundamentals only without recourse to any exogenous prices. In fact, all prices in the model–prices of tradables (shadow prices corresponding to constraint 1), prices of non-tradables (shadow prices corresponding to constraint 2), and factor prices (shadow prices corresponding to constraints 3 and 4) are endogenous.

A comparison of the expansion of final demand of the two economies under autarky and free trade scenarios enables one to find out the gains accruing from free trade to either economy. By making technology and taste represent input proportions and consumption respectively we make a short cut. In a strict sense, technology is a blue book of techniques and the relative prices chosen decide the choice of technique. The observed input-output coefficients reflect the techniques prevailing in each economy under observed prices. Thus, if prices change to the general equilibrium values then the choice of technique as also the input-output coefficients may be different. Thus, any induced change of techniques within the technology blue book is likely to prompt further reallocations of endowments and gains to specialization. A similar analysis holds for consumption also. Taste is a blue book of consumption coefficients and these consumption coefficients may adjust. However, the model proposed in this section restricts the blue book of technology as also that of consumption to a single page for each economy and thereby ignores the further reallocations. Hence the results of this model are likely to be conservative to some extent. However, this may not be treated as a serious limitation of this model. This is because the purpose of this paper is to primarily demonstrate how endogenous patterns of productive activity can create significant gains to free trade. Hence ignoring such reallocations may well be allowed in the context of the Leontief framework that underlines the proposed model.

3. DATA

The application of the model developed in section 3 requires data on the following:

- Input-output coefficient matrices for India and the EU-15 (A, A*);
- Sectoral capital and labour coefficients for India and the EU-15 (k, l, k*, l*);
- Sectoral consumption coefficients for India and the EU-15 (y, y*);
- Stocks of capital and labour for the two economies of India and the EU-15 (K, L, K*, L*).

The basis of the data of this study are the two Input-Output Tables of the Indian Economy for the year 1991-92 (Planning Commission, Government of India, 1995) and of the EU for the year 1995 (Eurostat, Brussels, 2003). The input-output table for the Indian economy consists of 60 sectors while the same for the EU consists of 25 sectors. These two input-output tables have been aggregated into 14 sectors only in a way such that all the sectors are common to the input-output tables of the two economies.

From this aggregated input-output table of each of the country, the input-output coefficient matrices (A for India and A* for the EU-15) and the sectoral consumption coefficients (y for India and y* for the EU-15) have been computed. The sectoral labour coefficients (l for India and l* for EU-15) for each economy have also been computed from the sectoral employment and sectoral output data of the respective economies. Given the employment data, wage rate and the value added for each sector the sectoral capital coefficients (k for India) are calculated. The same for the EU (k*) is calculated from the capital stock and the sectoral output data for the economy. Finally, we have obtained data on the total labour force (L for India and L* for EU-15) and capital stock (K for India and K* for EU-15) of each economy.

The detailed description of this data underlying the model and their necessary adjustments are given in the Appendix.

4. RESULTS AND DISCUSSIONS

In this section we present the results of the above model. The results are shown in Tables 1 and 2. The gross output figures, (Table 1) show the commodities which each of the economy would produce under perfect competition and free bilateral trade. Though the actual trade or observed trade figures show that both countries have positive outputs of all the fourteen commodities mentioned in Table 1, but in a perfectly competitive world with free bilateral trade as postulated by the model presented in section 2, India produces only eight out of fourteen goods. These are Agriculture, Fishing and Forestry, Food, Beverages and Tobacco, Textile, Non-metallic Minerals, Metal Products, Transport and Communication Equipment, Construction and Other Services. On the other hand, the EU specializes in the production of seven goods; namely, Fuel and Power Products, Chemicals, Paper and paper products, Machinery, Mining and Miscellaneous manufacturing, Trade and transport services and Other Services and obtains the remaining six commodities from India. Thus, taken together the two nations produce fifteen goods. Out of the goods mentioned in the Tables 1 and 2 India and the EU both produce Other Services. As noted from the observed trade data Other Services is actually a good which is non-tradable between the two economies. Thus, the result of the model showing positive output of this good for both the economies seems quite justified. Besides this, all the other goods that India produces constitute a complementary set to the set of goods that the union produces. Thus, a perfect condition for mutually benefiting bilateral trade is created. However, the actual extent of gain accruing to either nation is to be identified. This issue would be addressed in section 5.

The respective comparative advantages of the two economies are located on the basis of the sign pattern of bilateral trade. The effect of perfect competition and free bilateral trade on the pattern of trade between India and the EU-15 would be as given in Table 2.

The figures in Table 2 reveal that in a competitive set-up with free bilateral trade as postulated by the model in section 2 India enjoys comparative advantage in all the eight commodities it produces under perfectly competitive conditions. The six commodities that she imports from the European Union are Fuel and Power Products, Chemicals,

TABLE 1

Actual and Free Trade Gross Output Figures for India and the EU-15

(Million US Dollars)

Sl. No.	*Sectors*	*India*		*European Union*	
		Observed trade	*Free trade*	*Observed trade*	*Free trade*
1.	Agriculture, Fishing and forestry	67397.91	147880.94	374370.37	0
2.	Food, beverages and tobacco	16320.91	52257.92	813268.78	0
3.	Fuel and Power Products	17019.25	0	709728.49	24970.63
4.	Chemicals	12608.97	0	498127.90	140155.64
5.	Textile	24019.40	77061.95	309012.53	0
6.	Paper and paper products	2721.15	0	377866.72	36187.66
7.	Non-metallic minerals	3823.68	25167.33	221559.75	0
8.	Metal products	11688.40	81787.14	330549.00	0
9.	Machinery	13042.95	0	910374.13	237711.70
10.	Mining and Misc. manufacturing	15810.04	0	701803.83	74213.06
11.	Transport and communication equipment	10728.86	151717.76	546808.77	0
12.	Construction	22484.39	53618.39	970916.45	0
13.	Trade and transport services	50374.06	0	876544.80	188567.79
14.	Other Services	49512.09	99770.29	7872486.88	364207.90

TABLE 2

Free Bilateral Trade from India to the EU-15 Contrasted with Actual Trade Figures

(Million US Dollars)

Sl. No.	*Sectors*	*Actual Exports of India to the EU*	*Free Net Exports of India the EU*
1.	Agriculture, Fishing and forestry	1153.25	3803.26
2.	Food, beverages and tobacco	1868.92	20070.99
3.	Fuel and Power Products	-469.08	-15444.35
4.	Chemicals	-749.20	-27817.56
5.	Textile	2003.22	28593.12
6.	Paper and paper products	-263.61	-3957.33
7.	Non-metallic minerals	-2189.84	11561.17
8.	Metal products	-827.41	30536.18
9.	Machinery	-4646.11	-23829.46
10.	Mining and Misc. manufacturing	10581.64	-14933.91
11.	Transport and communication equipment	-9170.67	61763.38
12.	Construction	34.34	12758.60
13.	Trade and transport services	2.97	-95779.14
14.	Other Services	0	10013.91
	Total	-2671.58	2661.14

Paper and Paper Products, Machinery, Mining and Miscellaneous Manufacturing and Trade and Transport Services mentioned. However, India's observed trade figures suggest that she imports as many as seven commodities from the EU. These are Fuel and Power Products, Chemicals, Paper and Paper Products and Machinery as is obtained in our free trade model also. However, it also imports Non-metallic minerals, Metal Products and Transport and Communication Equipment which she is found to export under conditions of perfect competition. Mining and Miscellaneous manufacturing are exported by the country to the EU-15. However, free trade conditions lead the country to import these products rather than export them. The EU-15 exports six commodities to India, namely, Fuel and Power Products, Chemicals, Paper and Paper Products, Machinery, Mining and Miscellaneous Manufacturing and Trade and Transport Services under conditions of free trade. Though the union specializes in the production of other Services, yet it imports this good from India.

Thus, it is seen that the comparative advantages of the economies as obtained by solving the linear programme are close to the observed pattern for most of the goods mentioned in Table 2. However, there also arise few contrasts of the free trade figures with the actual trade figures of the countries. Thus, the pattern of comparative advantage resulting from the model often departs from the observed trade pattern. This contrast arises due to numerous distortions existing in the real world, which cause the private cost of production of a good to diverge from its social cost in which case the free trade pattern do not confirm the observed pattern of trade. Examples of such distortions are monopoly power, externalities, tariffs and other impediments. The model assumes away all such market imperfections and departures from a simple perfectly competitive model.

However, there are some departures from the competitive benchmark that cannot be separated from the fundamentals, but are embedded in the physical structure of the economies. Particularly, worth mentioning are the phenomena of product differentiation and scale economies. The model in this paper assumes away the possibility of two-way trade, which is the consequence of product differentiation existing in the real world. For instance, in Mining and Miscellaneous manufacturing the dominant item of India is manufacturing (like leather or gems or jewellery) which is a major export item for the country. Thus, given free trade India is likely to export these goods to the EU. But this in turn is likely to be countered by the EU exports of some minerals to our country. This may end-up in export of Mining and Miscellaneous manufacturing from EU to India. Moreover, the quality of some goods for instance a leather handbag (included in Miscellaneous manufacturing) of EU is often different from the same product of Indian origin. Such differences in product quality are ignored in this model and any product considered here is taken to be the same in quality irrespective of its place of origin. However, since the purpose of this model is the determination of comparative advantages on the basis of the fundamentals of the economies I selected the most disaggregated classification of products that I could reconcile given the available input-output tables of the two economies. As such the possibility of product differentiation and hence two way trade is not considered in this model. However, even at this level of disaggregation trade must be two way. This is no doubt true but following Raa and Mohnen (2001). I would like to opine that the only correct way of modeling this is to go in for further disaggregation of the data. This view deviates from the view dominant in literature, where product differentiation is imposed by taking into account the origin of commodities (the so-called Armington assumption, Harris, 1984 and Srinivasan and Whalley, 1986). Consideration of such two-way trade may be practical for obtaining a good approximation but it is not necessary for the location of comparative advantages, particularly when they are not assumed to be revealed by international trade statistics.

As far as scale economies are concerned, such scale induced changes in technical coefficients could be very much relevant for detecting comparative advantages of the economies, particularly, given the fact that monopoly power is a priori excluded from this model. But the effect of such scale economies is ignored by the model. Its inclusion would reinforce the gains to free trade. But one would find it interesting to note that significant gains to free trade can be explained (section 5) with the help of this model even without the use of scale economies. However, the inclusion of scale economies might alter the locational pattern of comparative advantages, but they may not be very high.

Thus, the model developed in section 2 provides with a new method of locating the comparative advantages of the economies of EU-15 and India linked by international trade in a perfectly competitive world of free bilateral trade. Moreover, the model also enables one to probe into the related issue of gains from such free trade. This is discussed in the following section.

5. GAINS FROM FREE TRADE

The solution to the linear programming model developed in section 2 yields g = c*/c and c. The consequent expansion factors for final consumption in India and the EU are

$$c = 1.781 \text{ and } c^* = 0.033 \qquad ...(8)$$

Thus, free bilateral trade in a perfectly competitive world would fetch for the Indian economy a total gain of 78.1 per cent while for the economy of the EU-15 the extent of gains would be only 3.3 per cent. Thus, both the economies gain from free bilateral trade but the magnitude of gain is significantly high for India as compared to that of the EU. This shows that free bilateral trade between India and the EU-15 as proposed by the theoretical model in section 2 is likely to fetch substantial gains for our country.

It is now possible to isolate the gains from free trade only. For this we have to solve yet another linear programme, which will enable us to determine the domestic efficiency gains (gains by eliminating the domestic waste of resources due to misallocation and less than full utilization of resources) that the economies can achieve without having departed from the bilateral trade pattern, which was obtained by solving the previous linear programme.

The linear programme, which we now have to solve to find India's domestic expansion factor is

$$\text{Max } e \text{ y d} \qquad ...(9)$$

subject to

$$(I - A)x^3 \text{ yd} + z \qquad ...(10)$$

$$kx \text{ £ } K, \ lx \text{ £ } L \quad (11)$$

where,

d is the level of final consumption in India and z the full net exports vector of India.

TABLE 3

Gains from Free Trade Accruing to India and the EU-15

Sl. No.	*Countries*	*India*	*EU -15*
1.	Total Gains from trade	78.1%	3.3%
2.	Gains by eliminating domestic waste of resources	70.3%	1.9%
3.	Gains from free trade only	7.8%	1.4%

The solution to this linear programme yields

$$d = 1.703 \qquad ...(12)$$

We likewise solve a linear programme to obtain the domestic expansion factor for the EU. The linear programme is,

$$\text{Max } e\ y^*\ d^* \qquad ...(9)$$

subject to

$$(I - A^*)x^* = y^*d^* + z^* \qquad ...(10)$$

$$k^*x^* = K^*,\ l^*x^* = L^* \qquad ...(11)$$

where d^* is the level of final consumption in the EU and z^* the full net exports vector of the EU.

From the solution we obtain

$$d^* = 0.019 \qquad ...(12)$$

Given the results in (12) and (12′) we obtain that the efficiency gains of India due to the elimination of domestic waste of resources is 70.3 per cent while that of the EU-15 is 1.9 per cent ($d = 1.703$ and $d^* = 0.019$).

Thus, given (8), (12) and (12′) it follows that the total efficiency gains of India from bilateral free trade with the EU is 78.1 per cent while similar gains for the EU is only 3.3 per cent. However, out of this 78.1 per cent of efficiency gains of India as much as 70.3 per cent is due to specialization in production. Such gains from specialization in production obtained by eliminating domestic waste and misallocation of resources for the EU are only 1.9 per cent. Hence, while for India only 7.8 per cent of total gains can be ascribed to its free trade with EU-15, for the EU similar gains from exchange are only 1.4 per cent. Thus, the extent of India's gains from free bilateral trade with the European Union turns out to be substantial.

Free bilateral trade as postulated by the model not only multiplies the volume of trade between the two economies of India and the EU-15, but also enables the relatively smaller economy, India to reap significant gains. Moreover, such a free bilateral trading arrangement allows India to specialize only in eight sectors (Table 1). While all the rest of the commodities considered in this model can be imported from its trading partner the European Union while reaping significant gains from such trade. Thus, absolute free trade between the two economies seems to be a very gainful proposition for India.

Therefore, to sum-up we may say that by solving a linear programme we have obtained the pattern of bilateral trade between India and the EU-15 in a world of free and perfectly competitive trade. The comparative advantages of the two economies are obtained from the sign pattern of the bilateral trade and this is done solely on the basis of the parameters of the two economies—taste (y and y*), technology (A,A*, k,k*, l,l*) and endowments (K,K*, L,L*), the rest of the world trade being fixed and represented by vector 'z'. Thus comparative advantages of the two economies are located absolutely on the basis of their fundamentals without recourse to exogenous prices. The resulting bilateral trade between the economies increases the volume of trade between them and allows both the countries to gain. In particular India's gains turn out to be substantial.

CONCLUSION

EU and India are two important regional and global

players of today's world and as such any sort of partnership between these two largest democratic entities is an important constituent towards stabilization of global peace, stability and progress. India's image in the EU is gradually changing as a dynamic trailblazer with a knowledge-based economy. India's move in this direction is really note worthy but to make quantum leaps the subcontinent has to forge strategies and develop new paradigms for enhancing trade and investment in the economy.

Bilateral trade has been the bedrock of the India-EU relationship right from the days of the latter's inception. This trade has shown an impressive growth over the years and at present India shares a healthy trade relationship with the EU. Therefore the immediate and direct effect of the enlargement of the EU for our country will be burgeoning trade prospects. With new members acceding to the EU, the tariffs on some products are likely to be raised to the common external level. Under such circumstances, it is imperative that India formulates its trade policy in such a way that it is able to effectively combat the problem of non-tariff barriers. Against this backdrop the present paper attempts to study bilateral free trade between India and the EU-15 by constructing a competitive benchmark, based only on the fundamentals of the two economies: endowments, preferences and technologies. A linear programme along with an input-output framework helps to determine endogenously the direction of trade taking place between the countries in a perfectly competitive world characterized by free trade.

The empirical implementation of the model developed in this paper considers trade in fourteen sectors consistent with input-output tables of the two economies. The result shows that India exports eight goods, namely, Agriculture, Fishing and Forestry, Food, Textile, Non-metallic minerals, Metal products, Transport and communication equipment, Construction and Other Services—all of which it produces. EU, on other hand, exports Chemicals, Fuel and power products, Paper and paper products, Machinery, Miscellaneous manufacturing and Trade and transport services. The study also isolates the gains from free trade accruing to the two economies. For this two more linear programmes are solved. The extent of gain in this trading arrangement is as high as 78.1 per cent for India while for its stronger trading partner EU it is only 3.3 per cent.

Over the years, the EU has emerged as India's largest trading partner with nearly a quarter of our exports going to the EU. Thus, it is imperative that India takes special care to strengthen its trade relations with the EU. In particular, India can explore the possibility of a free trade arrangement with the EU so as to gain, at least to some extent, preferential and duty-free access to the European market. Such a free trade arrangement is likely to go a long way towards deeper integration of India with the biggest trade power of the world. In particular, it will fetch substantial gains for India by improving her over-all competitiveness through access to the marketing network, skill and technology of the EU. Moreover, such a free trade agreement between India and the EU will add new dimensions to the much talked about strategic partnership between the two nations and will serve to deepen the economic and political ties between the two sides: one which is the second most populous country with a 260 million middle class population and the other with a 25 country (with 10 more countries joining the EU-15) with 455 million people who are making all possible efforts to emerge as a global powerhouse. Similar suggestion has not only come-up from various policy making levels in the two countries, but has also been put forward by various contemporary researchers in their writings. However, any work, which is based on theoretical model building that helps to analyze the viability of free trade between these two economies, has not been attempted to the best of the knowledge of the present researcher. The present study thus makes a modest contribution to this area.

References

Census of India (1991), *Economic Tables*, Government of India, Various Volumes.

Chan, Y.Y.Y. (1999), "The Costs and Benefits of a Free Trade Srea Smong the Forum Island Countries", *Pacific Economic Bulletin*, Vol. 14, pp. 81-86.

EC Country Strategy Paper (2002), *India (2002-2006)* http://www.europa.eu.int/comm/external relations/india/csp/0206en.pdf.

EU-LDC Network (2003), *EU-LDC Themes-Regional Focus Policy—The EU and the SAARC*, <http://europa.eu.int/comm/external-relations/saarc/intro/index.htm.

Europa (2004), *Activities of the European Union, External Trade*, <http://www. EUROPA—Activities of the European Union-Transport.htm> Europa-Trade Issues [2004] *Bilateral Trade Relations, Trade issues*, <http://www.Europa-Trade—Trade issues1.htm>.

European Commission (2002), "The EU Continues to Open its Textiles and Clothing Market, Evolution of Trade in 1995-2000", *European Commission, Directorate-General for Trade.*

Eurostat (2003), *Statistical Office of the European Community*, Data Shop Brussels.

Eurostat (2003), *Statistical Office of the European Community*, Data Shop Copenhagen.

External Relations (2002), *Overview, The EU's Relations with Bangladesh*, http://www.europa.eu.int/comm./external-relations/Bangladesh.

Faber, G. (1999), "Free Trade Areas as a Model for Future EU-ACP Relations", *ECSA Sixth Biennial International Conference*, held at Pittsburg Pennsylvania, Economic Institute, Utrecht University, the Netherlands, June 2-5 1999.

Harris, R. (1984), "Applied General Equilibrium Analysis of Small Open Economies with Scale Economies and Imperfect Competition", *American Economic Review*, 74, pp. 1016-1032.

Indiachemicalexporters.com (2003), Indiachemicalexporters.com <http://www.indiachemicalexporters.com>

India-EU Annual Report (1999), *EU-India Trade, 1999, Mission of India to the European Union, Brussel.* <http://www. India_EU Annual Report 99.htm>

India-EU Relations (2002), *Discover India*, http://www.meadev.nic.in/foreign/intro.htm

Nori, U. and Patnaik, U. (2003), "Globalization and Trade between Trading Blocs—A Study of SAARC and EU with special reference to India", *University of Hyderabad, India*, <http://blake.montclair.edu/~cibconf/conference/DATA/Theme1/India1.pdf>

Planning Commission, Government of India (1995), *A Technical Note to the Eighth Plan of India (1992-97).*

Raa, T.T. and Chakraborty, D. (1991), "Indian Comparative Advantage *vis-a-vis* Europe as Revealed by Linear Programming of the Two Economies", *Economic Systems Research*, 3, pp. 111-150.

Raa, T.T. and Mohnen, P. (2001), "The Location of Comparative Advantages on the Basis of Fundamentals Only", *Economic Systems Research*, 13, pp. 93-108.

Roy, C. and Chakraborty, D. (2000), "Location of Comparative Advantages in India and Bangladesh", *Journal of Applied Input-Output Analysis*, 6, pp. 17-35.

Sikdar, Chakraborty and Raa (2005), "A New Way to Locate The Comparative Advantages of India and Bangladesh on the Basis of Fundamentals only", in Rajat Acharya (ed.), *Essays on International Trade Allied Publishers, Kolkata,* 2005.

Srinivasan, T.N. and Whalley, J. (1986), *General Equilibrium Trade Policy Modeling,* Cambridge, MIT Press.

World Bank (Various Issues) *World Development Report,* New York, Oxford University Press.

APPENDIX

Data

The application of the model developed in section 2 requires data on the following:

1. Input-output coefficient matrices for India and the EU (A, A*);
2. Sectoral capital and labour coefficients of India and the EU (k.l.k*.l*)
3. Sectoral consumption coefficients of India and the EU (y y*)
4. Stocks of capital and labour for the two economies (K, L, K*, L*).

The data on these have been obtained from various sources—official, semi-official, and studies of other researchers. Since the data are not always available in these forms, we now describe the manipulation of data for each of the above mentioned four categories.

A.1. Input-Output Coefficient Matrices

The basis of the data of this study are the three Input-Output Tables of the Indian Economy for the year 1991-92 (Government of India, Planning Commission, 1995) and of the EU for the year 1995 (Eurostat Data, Brussels, 2004).

As mentioned earlier a detailed sector by sector study of the input-output tables of the economies undoubtedly comes-up with a more comprehensive analysis but requires more resources. Therefore given the constraint of resource we are compelled to go for aggregation of the sectors of the input-output tables. The Input-Output Table for the Indian economy consists of 60 sectors while that for the EU consists of 25 sectors. These two input-output tables have been aggregated into 14 sectors only in a way such that all the sectors are there in the available input-output tables of the two economies. The sectors are: (1) Agriculture, fishing and forestry, (2) Food, beverages and tobacco, (3) Fuel and power products, (4) Chemicals, (5) Textile, (6) Paper and paper products, (7) Non-metal minerals, (8) Metal products,

(9) Machinery, (10) Transport and communication equipment, (11) Mining and miscellaneous manufacturing, (12) Construction, (13) Trade and transport services and (15) Other services.

From the aggregated input-output table of each of the country, the input-output coefficient matrices have been computed (A for India and A^* for the EU) using the standard input-output rule:

$$A = z\ x^{-1} \qquad \text{...(1)}$$

and

$$A^* = z^*\ x^{*-1} \qquad \text{...(2)}$$

Where z is the inter-industry transaction matrix of India (14×14) and x is the diagonal matrix representing its sectoral outputs while z* is the inter-industry transaction matrix of the EU (14×14) and x is the diagonal matrix representing the economies sectoral outputs. Tables A.1 and A.2 represents the two input-output coefficient matrices for India and the EU respectively.

A.2. Labour Coefficients

In this study, sectoral labour coefficients for each sector have been computed from the sectoral employment and sectoral output data of the respective economies. In other words,

$$l = L\ x^{-1} \qquad \text{...(3)}$$

for India and

$$l^* = L^*\ x^{*-1} \qquad \text{...(4)}$$

for the EU,

where l is the row vector of labour coefficients of India, L is the row vector of labour employed in each sector in the Indian economy, l* is the row vector of labour coefficients of the EU-15, L* is the row vector of labour employed in each sector in the EU economy.

The employment figures for majority of the sectors of the economy of India are available for the year 1991-92 from the economic tables (Census, different years). For some agricultural sectors like Rice, Wheat, Jute, Sugarcane, Cotton the employment figures are obtained from website indiaagristat.com. Employment figure for Tea is available from the website www.teauction.com. The employment figures for all the sectors of the economy of the EU for the year 1995 are available from the economy's input-output table (Eurostat, Brussels, 2004).

A.3 Capital Coefficients

An indirect method has been used to derive the sectoral capital coefficients from the available information for the economy of India. The following formula is used:

$$k = (v - wL)\, x^{-1} \qquad ...(5)$$

for India, where k, is the row vector of capital coefficients of India, v, denotes the row vector of value added at factor cost by sectors of India, w denotes the wage rates in the economy and L is the row vector of labour employed in the sectors of the economy.

However, for the EU as a whole capital employed in each sector is available from the input-output table (Eurostat data, Brussels, 1995). These capital stock figures along with the output figures for each of the sectors are used to obtain the sectotal capital coefficients for the EU according to the following formula:

$$k^* = K^*\, x^{*\,-1} \qquad ...(6)$$

where k* is the row vector of capital coefficients of the EU and K* is the row vectors of capital employed in the different sectors of the EU.

The sectoral capital coefficients, thus computed for all the two economies are presented in Table A.3.

A.4. Capital and Labour Stocks

In order to estimate the total capital stock of an economy, we require data on the degree of capacity utilization of that economy. For India, we obtained the rate to be roughly around 60 per cent from Raa and Chakraborty (1991). The declining trends in capacity utilization in major industries over the years, the low efficiency of the private sector companies in terms of capacity utilization and extensive system of industrial licensing and price controls which resulted in bureaucratic controls over foreign trade are some of the factors which explain the reasons for this low degree of capacity utilization in India. Given this rough estimate of capacity utilization, the total capital stock for the Indian economy is obtained by using the formula

$$K= kx/s,$$

where s is the degree of capacity utilization in India.

The data on total capital stock for the EU is directly available from the Eurostat data, Copenhagen (2003).

The figures for the total labour force for the economies are the total economically active population, which includes persons employed, as well as those who are willing to supply labour. For India this figure is available from Government of India, Planning Commission (1995) and for the EU this is available from the Eurostat data, Copenhagen (2003). The figures for the capital and labour stocks for the two economies are shown in Table A.4.

TABLE A.1

Input-Output Coefficient Matrix for India (A)

Sl. No.	Sectors	1	2	3	4	5	6	7
1.	Agriculture, fishing and forestry	0.167	0.377	0.0004944	0.0178619	0.073	0.023	0.004
2.	Food, Beverages and Tobacco	0.009	0.121	3.742E-05	0.013	0.001	0.002	0.0001
3.	Fuel and Power Products	0.022	0.023	0.182	0.097	0.051	0.057	0.079
4.	Chemicals	0.049	0.020	0.0108	0.227	0.073	0.0496	0.0098
5.	Textile	0.004	0.0096	0.0005	0.0198	0.255	0.0098	0.0298
6.	Paper and Paper products	0.0001	0.007	0.0008	0.015	0.004	0.266	0.002
7.	Non-metallic minerals	0	0.006	0.0009	0.006	0.0001	0.0009	0.056
8.	Metal products	0	0.0015	0.002	0.007	0.0016	0.017	0.0196
9.	Machinery	0.00	0.005	0.021	0.004	0.006	0.007	0.005
10.	Transport and comm. equipment	0.0017	0	0.281	0	0.022	0.042	0.163
11	Mining and misc. manufacturing	0.0011	0.032	0.0002	0.065	0	0	0
12.	Construction	0.0145	0.004	0.006	0.0020	0.002	0.002	0.004
13.	Trade and transport services	0.054	0.149	0.085	0.1016	0.113	0.095	0.124
14.	Other Services	0.010	0.047	0.014	0.043	0.052	0.066	0.034

(Contd.)

Sl. No.	Sectors	8	9	10	11	12	13	14
1.	Agriculture, fishing and forestry	0.00125	0.001	0.00097	0.079	0.025	0.0004272	0.0227935
2.	Food, Beverages and Tobacco	0	0	0	0.0001	0	0.0007	0.007
3.	Fuel and Power Products	0.104	0.023	0.013	0.051	0.026	0.062	0.007
4.	Chemicals	0.011	0.017	0.007	0.084	0.017	0.0002	0.029
5.	Textile	0.0008	0.001	0.0006	0.014	0.0015	0.002	0.0008
6.	Paper and Paper products	0.0001	0.003	0.0018	0.005	0.001	0.006	0.009
7.	Non-metallic minerals	0.004	0.002	0.001	0.0096	0.102	0.0003	0.0005
8.	Metal products	0.299	0.213	0.076	0.113	0.128	0.001	0
9.	Machinery	0.005	0.149	0.040	0.032	0.035	0.004	0.0011
10.	Transport and comm. equipment	0	0.006	0.029	0.085	0.0008	0.054	0.0018
11	Mining and misc. manufacturing	0.122	0.038	0.088	0.018	0.098	0.020	0.014
12.	Construction	0.006	0.003	0.0019	0.009	0	0.008	0.0189
13.	Trade and transport services	0.117	0.067	0.032	0.097	0.121	0.116	0.032
14.	Other Services	0.040	0.065	0.027	0.057	0.023	0.074	0.028

TABLE A.2

Input-Output Coefficient Matrix for The EU (A^*)

Sl. No.	Sectors	1	2	3	4	5	6	7
1.	Agriculture, fishing and forestry	0.131	0.244	0.0003	0.0018	0.021	0.014	0.0006
2.	Food, Beverages and Tobacco	0.120	0.149	0.0008	0.0159	0.016	0.003	0.0005
3.	Fuel and Power Products	0.043	0.020	0.269	0.072	0.026	0.031	0.072
4.	Chemicals	0.055	0.009	0.009	0.274	0.0599	0.037	0.029
5.	Textile	0.002	0.0006	0.0002	0.002	0.257	0.004	0.002
6.	Paper and Paper products	0.004	0.026	0.003	0.023	0.012	0.254	0.019
7.	Non-metallic minerals	0.003	0.007	0.004	0.013	0.0005	0.0026	0.159
8.	Metal products	0.005	0.017	0.005	0.015	0.013	0.005	0.009
9.	Machinery	0.014	0.005	0.021	0.011	0.007	0.011	0.017
10.	Transport and comm. equipment	0.003	0.001	0.002	0.001	0.0008	0.002	0.004
11.	Mining and misc. manufacturing	0.008	0.017	0.013	0.027	0.024	0.014	0.028
12.	Construction	0.008	0.002	0.015	0.003	0.003	0.004	0.006
13.	Trade and transport services	0.019	0.028	0.026	0.035	0.026	0.042	0.058
14.	Other Services	0.112	0.151	0.092	0.166	0.169	0.147	0.167

(Contd.)

Sl. No.	*Sectors*	*8*	*9*	*10*	*11*	*12*	*13*	*14*
1.	Agriculture, fishing and forestry	0	0.0001	0.013	0.0001	0.0004	0.0004	0.003
2.	Food, Beverages and Tobacco	0.0004	0.0006	0.0009	0.0005	0.0004	0.0025	0.014
3.	Fuel and Power Products	0.023	0.015	0.059	0.016	0.0139	0.055	0.016
4.	Chemicals	0.0195	0.014	0.076	0.014	0.013	0.002	0.007
5.	Textile	0.002	0.0015	0.010	0.007	0.003	0.002	0.002
6.	Paper and Paper products	0.0099	0.013	0.011	0.005	0.003	0.011	0.018
7.	Non-metallic minerals	0.015	0.0105	0.015	0.012	0.103	0.0009	0.001
8.	Metal products	0.098	0.056	0.029	0.067	0.041	0.003	0.003
9.	Machinery	0.030	0.170	0.020	0.083	0.038	0.009	0.009
10.	Transport and comm. equipment	0.002	0.080	0.003	0.178	0.001	0.019	0.006
11	Mining and misc. manufacturing	0.162	0.005	0.1997	0.105	0.066	0.013	0.005
12.	Construction	0.004	0.004	0.005	0.003	0.062	0.013	0.017
13.	Trade and transport services	0.030	0.028	0.048	0.024	0.027	0.114	0.028
14.	Other Services	0.1298	0.201	0.182	0.192	0.169	0.158	0.276

TABLE A.3

Sectoral Labor, and Capital Coefficients of India and the EU

Sl. No.	Sectors	India		European Union	
		Labour Coeff. (L)	Capital Coeff. (K)	Labour Coeff. (L*)	Capital Coeff. (k*)
1.	Agriculture, fishing and forestry	32.50	0.42	27.76	3.55
2.	Food, Beverages and Tobacco	10.40	0.05	5.49	0.84
3.	Fuel and Power Products	1.11	0.25	2.75	2.96
4.	Chemicals	1.15	0.27	4.82	1.13
5.	Textile	7.41	0.21	14.69	1.08
6.	Paper and Paper products	8.29	0.22	8.56	1.19
7.	Non-metallic minerals	17.91	0.29	8.87	1.44
8.	Metal products	1.64	0.21	12.3	1.08
9.	Machinery	3.35	0.26	9.2	0.87
10.	Transport and communication equipment	1.30	0.48	8.46	1.66
11	Mining and miscellaneous manufacturing	26.65	0.09	6.61	1.01
12.	Construction	7.97	0.29	12.7	0.61
13.	Trade and transport services	18.44	0.46	11.31	2.95
14.	Other Services	18.62	0.52	14.52	3.12

CHAPTER

16

An Economic Overview of Asian Integration with Special Reference to Indo-Korean Economic Alliance

Sita Ram Singh and Mohan Prasad Shrivastava

INTRODUCTION

Asian economic integration specially among the economic giants like India, China, Korea and Japan is the need of hour to meet the global challenges; maintain sustainable development; create massive job opportunities and to become economic super power by competing European and American Mission. In this paper, we aim at to make an economic overview of Asian Economic Integration under various economic challenges and opportunities particularly with reference to Indo-Korean Economic Relation. We both Asian nations India and Korea have emerged as the global leader. Various experts and studies conducted across the global envisage India, China and Korea to rule the world in the 21st century. For over a century the United States has been the largest economy in the world but major development have taken place in the world economy since then, leading to the shift of focus on the US and the rich countries of Europe to the Asian giants, India, China and Korea. The rich countries of Europe have seen the greatest decline in global GDP share by 4.9 percentage points, followed by the US and Japan with a decline of about 1 percentage point each. Within Asia, the rising share of Korea, Japan and India has more than made-up the declining global share of Japan since 1990.

Many experts are of the view that the share of the US in the world GDP is expected to fall (from 28% to 18%) and that of India to rise (from 7% to 10% is 2025) and hence the latter emerge as the Third pole in the economy after the US and China.

By 2025 the Indian economy is projected to be about 60 per cent the size of the US economy. The transformation into a tri-polar economy will be completed by 2035, with the Indian economy only a little smaller than the US economy but larger than that of western Europe. By 2025, India is likely to be a larger growth driver than the six largest countries in the EU, though its impact will be a little over half that of US. India, which is now fourth largest economy in terms of purchasing power parity, will overtake Japan and become third major economic power within 10 years.

In India more than 70 per cent of country's population depends on agriculture, a sector producing only 20 per cent of GDP. Today, India is the largest producer of tea, Jute, and Jute like fiber and is also largest consumer of tea also in the world, which accounts for around 14 per cent of the world Tea. Indian tea is exported in various forms such as; bulk tea, packet tea, tea bags, instant tea, etc; to more than 80 countries of the world. Similarly, Indian milk production is the highest in the world. India has also the privilege of having the 1st rank in total irrigation land in area terms in the world. However, the full potential of Indian agriculture as a profitable activity has not been realized yet.

CHALLENGES OF GLOBAL ECONOMIC INTEGRATION

The concept of globalisation can be traced to the phenomenon of nation states. In the distant past, there were just human communities. For much of human history, most people remained confined to their communities, villages or local areas. With developments in communication and economic activity, it has progressively become easier to move from the local to the regional and then from the regional to the national level, and finally across nations.

In managing the process of economic integration that is driven by several forces, developing countries face challenges from a world order that is particularly burdensome on them. Yet, it is necessary for the public policy to manage the process with a view to maximizing the benefits to its citizens while minimizing the risks; but the path of optimal integration is highly country-specific and contextual. On balance, there appears to be a greater advantage in achieving a well-managed and appropriate integration into the global process, which would imply more effective—but not necessarily intrusive or extensive—interventions by governments.

INDO-KOREAN OUTFIT

Agriculture in South Korea

South Korea's agriculture had many inherent problems. South Korea is a mountainous country with only 22 per cent arable land and less rainfall than most other neighboring rice-growing countries. A major land reform in the late 1940s and early 1950s spread ownership of land to the rural peasantry. Individual holdings, however, were too small (averaging one hectare, which made cultivation inefficient and discouraged mechanization) or too spread out to provide families with much chance to produce a significant quantity of food. The enormous growth of urban areas led to a rapid decrease of available farmland, while at the same time population increases and bigger incomes meant that the demand for food greatly outstripped supply.

Rice was the most important crop and yields were impressive. As noted by Donald S. Macdonald, however, rising wage levels and land values have made it expensive to produce. Rice represented about 90 per cent of total grain production and over 40 per cent of farm income; the 1988 rice crop was 6.5 million tons. Rice was imported in the 1980s, but the amount depended on the success of domestic harvests.

Barley was the second most important crop. Its production declined from about 1.5 million tons in 1970 to about 561,500 tons in 1988. Other crops included such grains as millet, corn, sorghum, buckwheat, soybeans, and potatoes. Fruits and vegetables included pears, grapes, mandarin oranges, apples, peaches, Welsh onions, Chinese cabbage, red peppers, persimmons, cabbage, peaches, and radishes. Other important cash crops included cotton, hemp, sesame, tobacco, and ginseng. In 1988, livestock heads included native Korean cattle (2 million), hogs (4.9 million), and poultry (almost 59 million).

Poor prospects on the farm depleted farm villages as the young left and the old died. Parents sent their children to the towns and cities for a better education. Young farmers who could not find wives also left for the cities.

The government initiated various programs to improve rural conditions. The most extensive of these was the New Community Movement (Saemaul undong, known as the Saemaul Movement). Its goal was to mobilize villagers in their own service. At first Saemaul projects were aimed at improving household living conditions. Later, projects were directed more to the village as a whole and included the construction of roads, bridges, irrigation ditches, and common compost plots. Next, the program focused on more economic concerns—group farming, common seed beds, livestock production, forestation, and even joint marketing and factories. Better health and sanitation as well as beautification of the environment also became program goals.

South Korean farmers have always used the nation's forests for fuel and household products, but centuries of over utilization and poor resource management had practically denuded the countryside by the end of the Choson Dynasty (1392-1910). World War II interrupted Japanese efforts to replace the ravaged forest stock and the Korean War brought to a peak the destruction of Korea's forests. After the 1950s, Seoul slowly developed the organizational and technical expertise to save the nation's trees. Despite frequent setbacks, reforestation had proceeded fairly successfully by the 1970s; the total volume of timber had grown from a low of 30.8 million cubic meters in 1954 to over 164.4 million cubic meters in 1984. The density of the woodlands expanded from an average of 4.8 to 17.8 cubic meters per hectare of forest during the same period.

INDO-KOREAN CONTRIBUTION TO WORLD GDP

Both India and Korea contribute significantly in the world GDP. Korea is among the few Asian countries that are counted among the developed countries of the world; India too has a growing stature and increasing role in international affairs.

In a bid to boost bilateral ties, India and South Korea on June 1, 2005 decided to step-up efforts to take their economic partnership to higher levels by utilising synergies in trade, investment and hi-tech areas. The two sides held ministerial discussions and hoped that negotiations for the $ 12 billion integrated steel plant to be set-up by Korean company Posco at Paradip in Orissa would be concluded at an early date. Negotiations for the mega project are at an advanced stage and when completed it would be the largest single foreign investment by any country in India.

South Korea is ranked 24th in the world in terms of population with 48.233 million people residing there in mid 2004. According to data obtained from World Bank Indicators, national growth rate in Korea during 1997-2003 was 0.7 per cent, more than world average of 1 per cent.

Korea is densely populated country with 490 persons living per sq. km. in 2004, 80 per cent of which live in urban areas. Life expectancy at birth in Korea is 74 years, somewhat less than other OECD high income countries, according to (1997-2003) World Bank figures.

South Korea under High Income Countries of the World

South Korea is characterized among the high-income countries of the world. Total gross national income in 2003 was US $ 576426 million. Per capita income was US $ 12,020, however, in terms of purchasing power parity, it was slightly higher at US $ 17930 in 2003. The growth rate of GDP was 3.1 per cent in 2003 as against 7 per cent in 2002 and 8.6 during 1983-93. Unemployment rate was 3.4 per cent (2003).

Main agriculture products are rice, root crops, barley, vegetables, fruit; cattle, pigs, chickens, milk, eggs; fish. Main Industries are electronics, telecommunications, automobile production, chemicals, shipbuilding, steel.

A striking feature of South Korea's economic structure is its heavy dependence on international trade

In 2003, the value of merchandise trade was equivalent to 35.7 per cent of GDP, compared with 10 per cent of GDP in the early 1970s, following the export-oriented industrialization drive initiated by the then president, Park Chung-hee.

Korean Imports and Exports

Korean exports mainly consist of electronic products, machinery and transport equipment, Semi-conductors, wireless telecommunications equipment, computers, steel, ships and petrochemicals. The main exports partners of Korean republic are China (18.2%), US (17.8%), Japan (9%), and Hong Kong (7.6%). (figures in the bracket indicate these countries' share in 2003). Imports commodities are machinery, electronics and electronic equipment, oil, steel, transport equipment, organic chemicals, plastics. In 2003, the share of different countries from which Korea imported these products was—Japan 20.3 per cent, US 13.9 per cent, China 12.3 per cent, Saudi Arabia 5.2 per cent.

During late 1950s, South Korea GDP per capita was comparable with levels in the poorer countries of Africa and Asia. Today its GDP per capita is 18 times North Korea's and equal to the lesser economies of the European Union. This success through the late 1980s was achieved by a system of close government/business ties, including directed credit, import restrictions, sponsorship of specific industries, and a strong labour effort. The government promoted the import of raw materials and technology at the expense of consumer goods and encouraged savings and investment over consumption.

State Capitalism and Free Enterprise

The economic system incorporated elements of both state capitalism and free enterprise. The economy was dominated by a group of chaebol (large private conglomerates) and also was supported by a significant number of public corporations in such areas as iron and steel, utilities, communications, fertilizers, chemicals, and other heavy industries.

The government guided private industry through a series of export and production targets utilizing the control of credit, informal means of pressure and persuasion, and traditional monetary and fiscal policies.

Significant economic policies included strengthening key industries, increasing employment, and developing more effective management systems. Because South Korea was dependent on imports of raw materials, such as oil, a major government objective was to significantly increase the level of exports, which meant stressing greater international competitiveness and higher productivity.

The government combined a policy of import substitution with the export-led approach. Policy planners selected a group of strategic industries to back, including electronics, shipbuilding, and automobiles. New industries were nurtured by making the importation of such goods difficult. When the new industry was on its feet, the government worked to create good conditions for its export. Incentives for exports included a reduction of corporate and private income taxes for exporters, tariff exemptions for raw materials imported for export production, business tax exemptions, and accelerated depreciation allowances.

Korean Investments in India

South Korea is one of the top ten leading investing countries in India. In 2003, it invested US $ 24 million in India. South Korean business groups such as LG, Samsung and Hyundai have not only established their presence in the Indian business scene but are also looking at diversifying their businesses into different sectors.

Korea accounts for about 2.64 per cent of total FDI inflows, amounting to US $ 2.601 billion (excluding amount approved for ADRs/GDRs).

The main sectors attracting foreign direct investment from South Korea are transportation industry accounting for over 1/3rd of the share, fuels (power and oil refinery), electrical equipment (computer software and electronics), chemicals (other than fertilizer) and commercial, office and household equipments.

There have also been technical collaborations with South Korea—areas include transportation industry, electrical equipment including computer software and electronics, chemicals other than fertilizers, metallurgical industries and industrial machinery.

In addition to the above sectors, studies have also revealed that the two countries could set-up joint collaborations in the sectors of infrastructure—power, ports, telecommunications, ship building and ship repair, petrochemicals, automobile ancillary, electrical and electronics, office equipment, banking and financial services, software as well as iron and steel.

Out of 44 contracts awarded for National Highway Development Project, 9 have been won by Korean companies in collaboration with Indian companies or independently. Recently, Hyundai Heavy Industries have won two mega projects including one pipeline project worth US $ 600 million.

Indian Investment in Korea

With the growing amount of globalization and liberalization, not only Korean companies are making their presence felt in India, Indian firms too are establishing themselves in Korea.

Last year in February, Tata Motors, Mumbai signed an agreement for acquiring Daewoo Commercial Vehicles, Kunsan (South Korea) at a cost of US $ 102 million.

Further, it is essential to make competitive pressure stronger by overcoming the regime of extensive government intervention in the economy, improving competition policy. Given the role played by international trade and foreign direct investment in Korean success, continuing with the policy of openness will be justifiable.

India at A Glance in Asia

Poverty and Social	*India*	*South Asia*	*Low Income Countries*
1	2	3	4
POPULATION, mid year (millions) 2003-04	1064.4	1425	2310
Average Annual Growth, 1997-03			
Population (%)	1.6%	1.8%	1.9%
Labour force	2.1%	2.3%	2.3%
Poverty (% of population below national poverty line)	29		
Urban Population (% of total population)	28	28	30
Life expectancy at birth (years)	63	63	58
Infant mortality rate (per 1000 births)	65	68	82
Child Malnutrition (% of children under 5)	47	48	44
Acess to an improved water source	84	84	75
Illiteracy	39	41	39
Gross primary enrollment (% of school age pop)	99	95	92
Male	107	103	99
Female	90	88	85
Some More Indicators On People			
Population Growth	1.5 for the year 2003-04		
Fertility Rate (births per woman)	2.9 for the year (2002-03)		

(Contd.)

India at A Glance in Asia *(Contd.)*

1		*2*	*3*	*4*
Child immunization, measales (% of under 12 mos)		67 for the year (2002-03)		
Technology And Infrastructure				
Fixed lines and mobile telelphones (per 1000 people)		51.9 (for the year 2002-03)		
Personal computers (per 1000 people)		7.2 (for the year 2002-03)		
Internet users		16.6 million (for the year 2002-03)		
Key Economic Long Term Trends				
	1983	1993	2002	2003
GDP (US $ billions)	212.3	273.9	510.2	603.3
(average annual growth)	1983-93	1993-03	2002	2003
GDP	5.4	5.9	4.6	8.3
GDP per capita	3.3	4.2	3	6.7
Exports of goods and services	8	13.4	21.8	7
Structure of The Economy (% of GDP)	1983	1993	2002	2003
Agriculture	36.6	31	22.7	22.2
Industry	25.8	26.3	26.6	26.6
Manufacturing	16.3	16.1	15.6	15.8
Services	37.6	42.8	50.7	51.2
Private Consumption	71.8	67.4	65	64.9
General Govt. Consumption	10.6	11.4	12.5	12.8
Imports of Goods And Services	8.1	10	15.6	16
Average Annual Growth				

	1983-93	1993-03	2002	2003
Agriculture	3.1	2.4	-5.2	9.1
Industry	6.4	5.9	6.4	6.7
Services	6.7	8.1	7.1	8.7
Private Consumption	5.2	4.5	-0.8	7.6
General Govt. Consumption	5.6	7.1	3.1	9.9
Gross domestic investment	5.3	7.5	9.5	12
Imports of Goods And Services	6.3	10.6	8.1	11.1
Prices and Government Finance	1983	1993	2002	2003
Consumer Prices	14.4	5	4.1	3.7
Government Finance (% of GDP, includes current grants)	1993	2002	2003	
Overall surplus/Deficit	-8.3	-10.2	-9.3	
Trade				
(US $ millions)	1983	1993	2002	2003
Total Exports (fob)	9861	22,683	52,512	62,952
Total imports (cif)	16,575	26,739	65,422	79,658
Balance of Payments				
(US $ millions)	1983	1993	2002	2003
Current Account Balance	-3595	-1526	3727	8160
Financing items (net)	2777	10160	13253	8820
Changes In Net Reserves	818	-8634	-16980	-16980

A remarkable feature of South Korea is its transformation from a developing country in 1950s to a high-income country of the world with a substantial per capita income. The economic reforms of 1990s in India have been influenced with East-Asian success and South Korea was among the chief countries to have an impact on Indian policy makers' thinking process. Though Consular relations between India and South Korea were set-up in 1962, it was in 1973 with the establishment of formal diplomatic ties that a new chapter was opened in the history of Indo-Korean cooperation.

Traditionally India's exports were limited to a few primary commodities such as cotton, oil cakes, iron ore, iron and steel, organic and inorganic chemicals, and electrical machinery and equipments. During the last few years, however, the commodity composition of our exports, though still dependent on low value-added items has expanded to cover a wider range of industrial products. For the last 2-3 years, India has been exporting wheat to Korea. Indian industry is of the view that our exports to Korea, valued at US $ 650 million, are not commensurate with the vast opportunities for trade that still remain untapped. Iron ore, chemicals and allied products, marine products, processed food; cotton yarn fabrics, gems and jewellery, and leather are some of the sectors that offer tremendous potential.

India imports Korean machinery and equipment and these are set to grow rapidly in face of likely investments by South Korea in transportation, construction and infrastructure sectors in India. Already, several Korean construction companies are engaged in highways, power plants, chemicals, petrochemicals and metro rail projects in India. Other sectors where Korean and Indian companies can mutually benefit are the shipbuilding, telecommunications, aviation and energy sectors.

INDO-CHINA ECONOMIC INTEGRATION: AN OVERVIEW

Economics experts and various studies conducted across the globe envisage India and China to rule the world in the 21st century. For over a century the United States has been the largest economy in the world but major developments have taken place in the world economy since then, leading to the shift of focus from the US and the rich countries of Europe to the two Asian giants—India and China.

The rich countries of Europe have seen the greatest decline in global GDP share by 4.9 percentage points, followed by the US and Japan with a decline of about 1 percentage point each. Within Asia, the rising share of China and India has more than made-up the declining global share of Japan since 1990. During the seventies and the eighties, ASEAN countries and during the eighties South Korea, along with China and India, contributed to the rising share of Asia in world GDP.

According to some experts, the share of the US in world GDP is expected to fall (from 21 per cent to 18 per cent) and that of India to rise (from 6 per cent to 11 per cent in 2025), and hence the latter will emerge as the third pole in the global economy after the US and China.

By 2025 the Indian economy is projected to be about 60 per cent the size of the US economy. The transformation into a tri-polar economy will be complete by 2035, with the Indian economy only a little smaller than the US economy but larger than that of Western Europe. By 2035, India is likely to be a larger growth driver than the six largest countries in the EU, though its impact will be a little over half that of the US.

India, which is now the fourth largest economy in terms of purchasing power parity, will overtake Japan and become third major economic power within 10 years.

Globalisation, is seen to be the world's "mega-trend" over the next 15 years, causing the global economy to grow by about 80 per cent compared with 2000, and raising average income per head worldwide by about 50 per cent over the same period. The benefits will be unevenly distributed but there will be a much richer world.

Economists world over believe, that most of this growth will be in Asia, especially in China and India, driving Asia to displace the west over the next 15 years as the focus of global economic dynamism. The impact of that shift will be economic and political, pulling Washington's attention away from Europe and the Middle East and towards the emerging 21st century superpowers.

Emergence of Indo-China as Asian Giants

More recently, however, a debate in the rest of the world has been in evidence on the challenges likely to be faced by the global economy on account of progressively increasing global integration of the Indian economy. There is a need to have an ongoing appreciation of how the global economy is responding to the challenges of our integration while we move forward with our own agenda of securing an optimal integration.

The Present Day World

Currently, the major issue in the global economy appears to be the significant build-up of current account imbalances. The current account deficit of U.S.A. has been rising and is around 5 per cent of GDP, while current account surpluses are noticed in Asia and to some extent in Latin America and Russia.

Further, the simultaneous emergence of China and India with significant competitive strengths in trade in goods as well as services will have to be accommodated by the global economy. Thus, the issue for the immediate future is that both, correcting current global imbalances and integrating the two Asian giants, may have to take place simultaneously in the global economy.

It is evident that China and India will have to give a high priority to generating employment. Both these emerging economies are poised for substantial increases in productivity. Consequently, the global economy will have to consider the implications of these developments on prices, exchange rates, wages and structures of employment in industrialised countries. Over the medium term, it is felt that outsourcing will grow in geometric progression, particularly to India, and may also cover high-end research and development. One sector where the industrialised economies continue to show considerable strength and dominance is the financial sector, partly attributable to the confidence factor in financial markets that favours the industrialised economies and traditional international financial centres. It is essential for India to carefully monitor the developments in both real and financial sectors, and to modulate her policies in accordance with the global developments so that global integration continues to be a positive sum game for all the countries. Global economic integration is technology induced and policy-managed. While the economic integration of India with the global economy will continue to take place, a successful integration, with due regard to the interests of a vast majority particularly, the poor would be possible only through sound public policies—evolved and redesigned from time to time.

In order to harness the demographic advantages, the quality of labour force, (in terms of relevant skills which need to be sustained, reoriented and upgraded in a globally competitive era) and the physical health of the workforce become crucial. Education and health, therefore, provide the link between supply and demand for labour through increases in productivity.

Since independence Indian economy has thrived hard for improving its pace of development. Notably in the past few years the cities in India have undergone tremendous infrastructure up gradation but the situation in not similar in most part of rural India. Similarly in the realm of health and education and other human development indicators India's performance has been far from satisfactory, showing a wide range of regional inequalities with urban areas getting most of the benefits. In order to attain the status that currently only a few countries in the world enjoy and to provide a more egalitarian society to its mounting population, appropriate measures need to be taken.

Currently Indian economy is facing these challenges:

- Sustaining the growth momentum and achieving an annual average growth of 7-8 per cent in the next five years.
- Simplifying procedures and relaxing entry barriers for business activities.
- Checking the growth of population; India is the second highest populated country in the world

after China. However in terms of density India exceeds China as India's land area is almost half of China's total land. Due to a high population growth, GNI per capita remains very poor. It was only $ 2880 in 2003 (world bank figures).

- Boosting agricultural growth through diversification and development of agro processing.
- Expanding industry fast, by at least 10 per cent per year to integrate not only the surplus labour in agriculture but also the unprecedented number of women and teenagers joining the labour force every year.
- Developing world-class infrastructure for sustaining growth in all the sectors of the economy.
- Allowing foreign investment in more areas.
- Effecting fiscal consolidation and eliminating the revenue deficit through revenue enhancement and expenditure management.
- Empowering the population through universal education and health care. India needs to improve its HDI rank, as at 127 it is way below many other developing countries' performance. The UPA government is committed to furtering economic reforms and developing basic infrastructure to improve lives of the rural poor and boost economic performance. Government had reduced its controls on foreign trade and investment in some areas and has indicated more liberalization in civil aviation, telecom and insurance sector in the future.

THE THREE PILLARS OF INDIAN ECONOMY

Agriculture

More than 58 per cent of country's population depends on agriculture, a sector producing only 22 per cent of GDP. The agriculture and allied sector witnessed a growth of 9.1 per cent in 2003-04, which fell steeply to 1.1 per cent in the current fiscal year. Favourable monsoon facilitated an impressive growth rate of 9.6 per cent in 2003-04 on the back of negative growth in the preceding year. However, deficient rainfall from the southwest monsoon is estimated to have caused a significant decline in kharif crops production in the current year.

While looking at some of the agricultural products, one finds that India is the largest producer of Tea, jute and jute like fibre. India is not only the largest producer but also largest consumer of tea in the world. India accounts for around 14 per cent of the world trade in tea. Indian tea is exported in various forms such as bulk tea, packet tea, tea bags, instant tea etc, to more than 80 countries of the world. Among livestock cattle and buffalo are found maximum in India. Indian total milk production is highest in the world. India has also the privilege of having the 1st rank in total irrigated land in area terms in the world. Among cereals production, India is placed third, having second largest production in wheat and rice and the largest production in pulses. However, the full potential of Indian agriculture as a profitable activity hasn't been realized yet. Agriculture upliftment will not only benefit farmers and a large section of the rural poor, but also will give fillip to overall growth of the economy through the backward and forward linkages of agriculture with the rest of the economy.

Priority to Second Green Revolution

Priority must be given to livestock's and fisheries, horticulture, organic farming, commercial crops and agro-processing, as these are the potential areas of high growth. Further, rationalization of minimum support price regime and introduction of other risk- mitigation measures, improvements in rural infrastructure are essential for sustaining high agricultural growth. It is conceived that reforms in legislations, strengthening R&D and improvements in post harvest management technologies will give a further boost to Indian agriculture. While acceleration in agriculture growth to 4-4.5 per cent is imperative, even with such growth rate; share of agriculture in total GDP is likely to reduce further. Therefore, there is a need to absorb excess agricultural labour in other sectors, notably industry. Rapid growth of agro-processing industry close to the agricultural production centers can bring about this shift without moving people from rural to urban areas. Also, public investment in agriculture needs to be augmented, especially in rural infrastructure, irrigation, and agricultural research and development. Better access to institutional credit for more farmers, is also high on priority list. The New trade policy gives focus to agriculture and all the hurdles in Indian agriculture will be crossed gradually.

Textile Sector

Textile industry is the largest industry in terms of employment economy from the current US $ 37 billion to $ 85 billion by 2010 creation of 12 million new jobs in the textile sector and modernization and consolidation for creating a globally competitive textile industry. With the phasing out of quota regime under MFA, from Jan 1st 2005, developing countries including India with both textile and clothing capacity may be able to prosper.

Automobile, Pharma and I.T. Sector

Automobile sector has demonstrated the inherent strengths of Indian labour and capital. The pharma industry and the IT industry are two sunrise sectors for India. Among the sectors that have experienced the greatest transformation in India, the pharmaceutical is perhaps the most significant.

India's WTO involvement during the last decade has encouraged our pharma companies to adopt a strategy of R and D based innovative growth. Indian pharma exports were 14000 crore Rupees and accounts for more than a third of the industry's turnover. Apart from manufacture of drugs, the pharma industry offers huge for outsourcing of clinical research. A vast pool of scientific and technical personnel and recognized expertise in medical treatment and health care are India's strength, India can take advantages of its strength once patent protection is given to the result of the researches. By participating in the international system of intellectual property protection, India unlocks for herself vast opportunities in both exports as well as her potential to become a global hub in the area of R and D based clinical research outsourcing, particularly in the area of bio-technology.

The three main sub-sectors of industry viz Mining and quarrying, manufacturing, and electricity, gas and water supply recorded growths of 5 per cent, 8.8 per cent and 7.1 per cent respectively.

Apart from infrastructure, particularly adequate and reliable power supply at reasonable cost and transportation facilities, there is need for stepped-up investment in manufacturing. Industry needs to grow rapidly not only to boost the overall growth rate in the economy but also to generate gainful employment for the existing unemployed, as well as the new entrants. In a diverse range of industrial activities, several Indian firms have succeeded in getting integrated into global production chains and realized rapid growth of exports. This experience suggests that with appropriate scale, investment and technology, rapid industrial growth is indeed possible.

While in most parts of the developed world, the services sector's share of employment rose faster than its share of output in India there has been a relatively slow growth of jobs in the service sector. This is primarily because of the rise in labour productivity in services in sectors such as information technology that is dependent on skilled labour. Growth in tourism and tourism-related services such as hotels, holds a large potential for employment generation.

IT enabled services, such as Business Process Outsourcing have been growing rapidly in the recent past and will continue to rise. India's large number of English speaking skilled manpower has made India a major exporter of software services and software workers. However, the emergence of somewhat inexplicable protectionist tendencies in some developed countries is a disturbing trend.

Also India outsourcing companies need to work more closely with their customers. In the complex BPOs, customers would like to have hybrid processes to control value. Indian companies need the right mix of domain expertise and process expertise, further, mere knowledge of English is not sufficient; management skills are also needed. Education for the offshoring industry needs to be given impetus too.

A growth rate of above 8 per cent was achieved by the Indian economy during the year 2003-04 to 2005-06 and in the advanced estimates for 2006-07, Indian economy has been predicted to grow at a level of 6.9 per cent. Growth in the Indian economy has steadily increased since 1979, averaging 5.7 per cent per year in the 23-year growth record. In fact, the Indian economy has posted an excellent average GDP growth of 6.8 per cent since 1994 (the period when India's external crisis was brought under control). However, in comparison to many East Asian economies, having growth rates above 7 per cent, the Indian growth experience lags behind. The tenth five year plan aims at achieving a growth rate of 8 per cent. For the first time after Independence, India has achieved growth rate of 8 per cent continuously for three year as Prime Minister Manmohan Singh has stated on 15th August, 2006.

S. Mahendra Dev, Director CESS, Hyderabad (*Economic Times,* 22 August, 2006) has rightly observed that an 8 per cent plus economic growth can be achieved and sustained agriculture and manufacturing sectors grow at high rates of 4 per cent and 12 per cent per annum respectively. For sustainability of growth, equity matters and it has to be employment intensive.

Many factors are behind this robust performance of the Indian economy in 2006-07. High growth rates in Industry and service sector and a benign world economic environment provided a backdrop conducive to the Indian economy. Another positive feature was that the growth was accompanied by continued maintenance of relative stability of prices. However, agriculture fell sharply from its 2003-04 level of 9 per cent to 1.1 per cent in the current year primarily because of a bad monsoon. Thus, there is a paramount need to move Indian agriculture beyond its centuries old dependency on monsoon. This can be achieved by bringing more area under irrigation and by better water management.

INDIA'S APPROACH IN THE NEW MILLENNIUM FOR ASIAN ECONOMIC INTEGRATION

In the 21st century, there has been a dramatic shift in India's approach to external sector management in tune with the changing circumstances. First, with the emergence of marginal current account surplus, the sustainability of India's current account deficit may not be a problem though the deficit on her trade account persists and has been increasing. Second, the main contributors to the positive outcome in India's current account are workers' remittances and export of software, both being a result of process of global integration. Third, the exchange rate regime as well as external debt management has served India well, especially the avoidance of sovereign debt through commercial borrowings. The new policy regime helped India withstand several global crises while maintaining a respectable growth. Fourth, the management of capital account has acquired the primary focus rather than the current account. Fifth, a judicious integration with the global trade regime has imparted some competitive efficiency and confidence to the domestic industry and perhaps, even to commercial agriculture though to a limited extent. Finally, it has become evident that the management of the external sector is closely linked to the domestic sector and the major thrust of Indian public policy is now on managing the integration.

Indo-Korean Joint Venture

Thus, these two countries India and Korea should decided to set-up joint vehture in sectors of infrastructure, power, ports, telecommunications, shipbuilding and ship repair, petrochemicals, automobile ancillary, electrical and electronics, office equipment, banking and financial services, software as well as iron and steel.

In addition to this, out of 44 contracts awarded for National Highway Development Projects in India I have been own by Korean companies in collaboration with Indian companies or independently. Recently, Hyundai Heavy Industries have won two mega projects including one pipeline project worth US $ 600 millions.

From Indian side, since February, 2004 Tata Motors, Mumbai and other are also investing in Korea at a cost of US $ 102 million.

Indian economy is very much impressed with the programmes, policies, plans, achievements, performance of Korean economy in all the fields particularly for building high-technology, chemical and bio-engineering etc. We Indians should also take lesson from Korean National Agricultural Co-operative Federation (NACF) which was established in 1961 but merged in National Livestock Co-operative Federation (NLCF) in 2000 forestry and fishing money and banking etc.

In brief, India has moved from managing external sector to implementing an optimal integration of domestic and external sectors, and the global economy. Economic growth can be sustained with higher agriculture and manufacturing growth and infrastructure investment, labour-intensive growth, reduction in social and religious disparities. The challenges for achieving more inclusive growth and equitable development are much greater than for stepping-up the GDP growth.

Thus, in this background India's global integration has to be a two way process, encompassing movement of people with some caveats, trade in a free and equitable manner and financial integration on a specially sequenced basis.

The Eleventh Plan Approach Paper envisages a need to restrict central government expenditure to roughly the same level as now as a ratio to GDP while raising plan expenditure significantly. This will require much political consensus to focus more on building of assets. Major derivation from this strategy will imply that fiscal imbalances will lead to lower investment spending threatening the growth objective.

As such, we Indian shall be quite happy if Korean economy comes forward in promoting its heavy investment with Indian collaboration in our country in different fields in meeting the basic challenges of poverty alleviation, eradication of unemployment and correction of imbalances. We must take lesson from the trend of economic supremacy of China, Japan, Korea and Thailand and should make every effort to Asian economic integration in eco-friendly system.

References

Abraham, James and Agrawal, Neeraj (2006), "Race to the IT Pinnacle", *The Economic Times,* Kolkata, 22 August.

Asian Outlook, 2004-05

Cho, David (Paul) Yonggi (1996), *The Fourth Dimension;* Seoul Logus Co., Inc., Korea.

Dev, S. Mahendra (2006), "How do We Sustain 8 per cent Plus Growth Rate?", *The Economic Times,* Kolkata, 22 August, 2006.

Economic Survey, Government of India, Ministry of Finance from 2000-01 to 2005-06.

Economic Times (2006), 22 August, *"Unnecessary Law on FDI: Don't Target China and West Asia."*

Economic Times (2006), 23 August, *"India Still Far From Selling."*

Human Development Report from 2000-01 to 2005-06, Oxford University Press.

Ki, Kim Yong (2005), *The Unique Canaan Farm of Korea;* The Great Light Publishing Company, Korea

World Development Report from 2000-01 to 2005-06, Oxford University Press.

With Special Reference to Indo-Nepal Trade Relation

S.P. Saha and Vinod Kumar Choudhary

INTORDUCTION

Regional cooperation has become an important force in modern business and trade environment. It is a process by which two or more countries work together towards finding solutions to their common problems. It works in the sprit of friendship, trust and understanding. It is based on mutual respect, equity and shared benefits. Discriminations existing along national boarders are progressively removed. We have seen the disappearance of the so-called super power rivalry and era of the cold war. There have created expectations of a peaceful future and fostered an environment conductive to the enhancement of regional cooperation in the social and economic fields. The world is witnessing a general movement of the restructuring of economies away from command and central system to market based ones. The winds of change have affected Asia also. There has been rapid integration of the Asian Economy in recent times with emergence of the Asian Economic Community or Asian Economic Union. The unifying forces of global development in the region should cement mutual relations and create a climate of confidence and faith.

The world economic scenario presents a varied picture, while in certain parts, such as the developed countries, great progress has been made; there are other parts, through not yet as developed, that are witnessing substantial and consistently high rates of growth. This establishes the complementarity's that needs to be exploited for securing overall global welfare. The fast growing economies provide just the opportunities that the economies in recession require, to achieve revival. It is important that the developed countries of EU, USA and Japan and developing countries of should understand this

Asian region alike. The need of our times is for cooperation—not confrontation. The countries of Asian region except Japan need to appreciate the desire of these countries to catch-up with the rest of the world. It would be counter-productive to create problems on narrow short-term considerations. It is in this perspective that the free flow of resources, capital technology and market access has become more relevant than ever to give a strong impetus to global economic growth in general and a regional development in particular.

While East Asia's stunning economic growth has been powered by a rapid rise in exports and its more favorable level of human development, South Asia has started from much a lower level of human development and been slower to liberalize. Even so, while South Asia has chosen a different path from East Asia, they may reach the same destination: high growth, high trade and high human development.

Regional trade cooperation in the sub-region has been slow to develop. The trade liberalization programme of the new South Asian Free Trade Area (SAFTA) offers a very limited reduction in import duties for intra-regional trade, which is not much more than that offered under the World Trade Organization.

Led by India, South Asia has done much better than East Asia on exports of services such as business process outsourcing, short-term labour migration and special-interest tourism; services now comprise 26 per cent of South Asia's exports.

Employment growth has remained fairly constant in South Asia, despite jobless growth occurring in some of the most successful economies of East Asia. This is because the vast majority of South Asian merchandise exports are still natural resource-based or labour-intensive.

Regionalism has gained popularity in Asian sub-continent itself because it is seen as a faster route to reach global free trade than the multilateral negotiations. Moreover, the idea of regional cooperation in South-Asia led to the establishment of South Asian Association for Regional Cooperation (SAARC) in 1985 by India, Pakistan Nepal, Bhutan, Bangladesh, Sri Lanka and Maldives. The people of South Asia constitute more than one fifth of mankind, they are heirs to great civilization and yet face momentous problems of poverty, illiteracy and deprivation. Since its inception, the member countries of SAARC have made sincere efforts to improve the condition of their people these attempts are often thwarted by multifarious religious, ethnic and linguistic problems. The tribulations faced by such a huge mass leads to enormous discontent and frustration, which emboldens subversive forces to exploit national inadequacies. The solution to these problems is widely met by SAARC under an atmosphere of bilateral dialogue, mutual cooperation and friendship. The objections of peace, freedom, social justice and economic prosperity in the underdevelopment region can be achieved only by fostering mutual understanding, good neighborly relations and meaningful cooperation among member states which are bound together by close historical and cultural ties through SAARC.

The summit is the highest authority of SAARC, which consists of the heads of states or government and meets annually. Its fourteen summits have already been held: Dhaka (1985), Bangalore (1986), Kathmandu (1987), Islamabad (1988), Male (1990), Colombo (1991), Dhaka (1993), New Delhi (1995), Male (1997), Colombo (1998), Kathmandu (2002), Islamabad (2004), Dhaka (2005), and New Delhi (2007).

IMPETUS TO REFORMS IN TRADE AND COMMERCE

India has always endeavored to forge strong trade and economic linkages with its neighbors. Formation of South Asian Preferential Trade Agreement (SAPTA) is a major step towards raising the trade within the region. Under SAPTA, the member governments have offered preferential tariff concessions for trade among themselves on selected products. SAPTA is based on the following principles; first, overall reciprocity and mutuality of advantages; second, step-by-step negotiations and extension of preferential trade agreement in stages, third, inclusion of products covering all stages of processing and fourth, special and favorable treatment to the Least Developed Countries (LDCs). In SAARC, the least developed countries are Bangladesh, Bhutan, Nepal and Maldives. These countries will be granted higher level of tariff concessions, more liberal rules of origin as well as technical assistance for accelerated economic and social progress.

The Tenth Summit (Colombo, 1998) decided that in order to accelerate progress in next round of SAPTA negotiations, deeper tariff concessions should be extended to products, which are being activity traded, or are likely to be traded, among members; that discriminatory practices and non-tariff barriers should be simultaneously removed on items in respect of which tariff concessions are granted or have been granted earlier. Measures to remove structural impediments should also be taken in order to move speedily towards the transition of SAFTA towards a Customs Union, Common Market and Economic Union. In 1995, sixteenth session of the council of ministers held in New Delhi agreed on the need to strive for realization of SAFTA and to this end an Inter-government Expert Group (IGEP) was set-up in 1996 to identify the necessary steps towards moving into a free trade area. The Male Summit in 1997, recognized the importance for achieving a Free Trade Area by 2001. SAFTA is now a reap forward in promoting free trade in SAARC region. The arrangement was signed on January 6, 2004.

The SAARC submit held in Kathmandu, Nepal in 2002 visualized establishment of a south Asian Economic union by

2010 to usher in a new era of prosperity for this higher to neglected region of the world. It is well known that regional of the world. It is well known that regional cooperation is meaningless without economic cooperation mainly in business and trade.

Economic agenda, including poverty alleviation has been given a high place on the SAARC agenda since 1991. Trade fairs have been organized. SAPTA, signed on January 2004 has been emerged as a landmark for regional economic and trade cooperation and SAFTA is a move towards South Asian Economic Union (SAEU).

According to the World Development Report, 2002, the share of SAARC in World Trade is 1.03 per cent. It means that there is tremendous scope for intra-regional trade. India stands as the largest and strongest economy of the SAARC region. India's exports to SAARC countries have never been above 56 per cent of its total exports. The trade among SAARC countries continues to remain marginal and confined mainly to primary commodities. On the contrary trade between SAARC region and development countries and even developed blocs like EEC remains significant.

Therefore, a broad trade policy with trade liberalization will be a useful tool in the expansion of trade in the region. Political differences need to be resoled and focus should be on economic developed of the region. In view of India's strong position in the region, it has become incumbent upon India to take the initiative, give-up the policy of reciprocity in economic liberalization within SAARC. Serious doubts have been raised whether India would be a fair partner or a bully in the region. Small countries like Nepal, Bhutan, Maldives and Bangladesh complain that India is a major exporter but a minor importer in intra-SAARC trade. India has accorded MFN status to Pakistan while Pakistan continues to defy WTO guidelines. Such apprehension and stumbling blocks need to be removed before *a de facto* trade regime can take place in South Asia.

METHODOLOGY

The present study uses data from central statistical

organization and other profiles of SAARC relating to marketing and trade among the member countries. The basic aim of the study is to examine.

(i) The market potential of SAARC countries including Nepal.
(ii) The impact of SAPTA and SAFTA on the Asian business environment and possible benefits to India and Nepal.
(iii) The role of SAARC on Indo-Nepal trade relation.

In view of these basic objectives of the present study the use of primary and secondary data have been used. An attempt has been made to find out the degree of business size between India and Nepal and among member countries. The analysis is also based on the null hypothesis (HO); the coefficient of regression is zero or there is no correlation between the various dependent and independent variables.

MARKET SIZE AND MARKET POTENTIAL OF SAARC

A market is any context in witch the sale and purchases of products takes place. People and their purchasing power and the key determinants of market size.

SAARC is a regional grouping of seven South Asian countries-Bangladesh, Bhutan, Indian, Maldives, Nepal, Pakistan, Sri Lanka. The region has 22 per cent of the World's total population, but it covers only 3.3 per cent of the world's land area. It is poorly endowed with mineral resources. But it is rich in the resources of the Himalayas and the seas.

The population-related indictors of the market size of SAARAC are in: Table 1 as:

- Size of population
- Growth of population
- Urban population
- Growth rate population of

In 2003, South Asia had a total population of 1396 million. Of this, India had 76.2 per cent, Pakistan 10.6 per

TABLE 1

Market Size Indicators of SAARC

Country	*Population Million (2003)*	*% of SAARAC*	*Population Growth % (1990-2003)*	*Urban Population % (2002)*	*Urban Population Growth % (1980-95)*
Bangladesh	138.1	9.9	1.7	24.0	5.6
Bhutan	0.9	0.1	2.9	8.2	5.4
India	1064.4	76.2	1.7	28.1	3.1
Maldives	0.3	0.1	2.5	28.4	–
Nepal	24.7	1.8	2.4	14.6	7.8
Pakistan	148.4	10.6	2.4	33.7	4.6
Sri Lanka	19.2	1.3	1.3	21.1	1.6
Total	1396.0	100	1.8		

Source: World Development Report, 2005.

cent, Bangladesh 9.9 per cent, Nepal 1.8 per cent, Sri Lanka 1.3 per cent, and less than 0.1 per cent for Bhutan and Maldives. India's market size is the largest in terms of population.

- In terms of population growth rate, during 1990-2003, Maldives had 2.5 per cent, Pakistan 2.4 per cent, Nepal 2.4 per cent, Bhutan 2.9 per cent, Bangladesh 1.7 per cent, India 1.7 per cent, and Sri Lanka 1.3 per cent. Growth indicates the growing size of the market.
- Urbanization has been growing in South Asia. In 2002, share of urban population was: 28 per cent, Maldives, 34 per cent Pakistan, 8 per cent Bhutan urbanization indicates concentration of market.
- Nepal has the highest rate of urban population growth (7.8%), followed 5.6 per cent for Bangladesh, 5.4 for Bhutan, 4.5 per cent for Pakistan, 3.1 per cent for India and the lowest 1.6 per cent for Sri Lanka.

- The market size of SAARAC in terms of population-related indicators is growing at a high rate.

MARKET POTENTIAL OF SAARC

Market potential is the total sales volume expected during a stated time period in a specific market. It is the maximum market demand.

Market potential of SAARAC is the expected combined maximum market demand during a stated time period of all the seven member countries.

The indicators of market potential are in Table 2 as:

(a) Size of Gross Domestic product (GDP),
(b) Per capita income and its growth rate,
(c) Structure of GDP,
(d) People blow poverty line, and
(e) Foreign trade.

Size of GDP

Size of GDP is an important indictor of market potential. It provides purchasing power. The total GDP of SAARC in 2003 was US $ 745 billion. It represented 2 per cent of world GDP. India accounts for 80 per cent of SAARC GDP, followed by 9 per cent for Pakistan, 7 per cent for Bangladesh, 3 per cent for Sri Lanka, 1 per cent for Nepal and less than 0.1 per cent for Nepal and Maldives.

Per capita income and its Growth Rate

SAARC suffers from low per capita income averaging about US $ 500 in 2003. It ranges from $ 240 for Nepal to $ 2300 for Maldives. The growth rate of per capita income rages from 0.7 per cent for Nepal for 6.4 per cent for India. Low per capita income and its low growth Constrains the market potential of SAARC.

Structure of GDP (Gross Domestic Product)

Structure of GDP indicates the market potential of specific category of products. In SAARC countries, the share of services is dominant and is 52 per cent in GDP. The share of industry is 25 per cent. Agriculture is important for Nepal and Bhutan.

Poverty and Human Development

People below poverty line indicate inequity in distribution of income. 2002, Nepal had 38 per cent of the total population below poverty line. It was 35 per cent in India, 36 per cent for Bangladesh, 7.1 per cent for Sri Lanka and 13 per cent for Pakistan. Market potential of SAARC has been adversely affected by high incidence of poverty. SAARC is a region of medium human development.

Foreign Trade

- Foreign trade is an important indicator of market potential. In 2003, SAARC accountant for 1.2 per cent of total world trade. In 2002, exports accountant for 20 per cent of GDP and imports accountant for 19 per cent of GDP. Exports as per cent of GRD ranged form 14 per cent for Bangladesh to 88 per cent for Maldives.

As a result following key points are to be considered for Asian Business Environment from SAARC.

- SAARC has high market potential. The high population growth adds to this potential. Bet low per capita income constrains this potential.
- Structure of GDP indicates high market potential for services.
- Foreign trade, an important indicator of market potential is growing. The intra-region trade is low its potential has remained untapped, which can be exhibited in the following box:

Economic Dynamics of India and SAARC Increasing

Globalization is growing in India. Liberalization of the economy has facilitated it. Foreign direct investment in the industrial sector is on the increase. The Indian economy is gradually being integrated with the global economy.

Indian multinational companies are operating in many courtiers. Till 2003, India's overseas foreign direct investment was $ 5 billion. It was mainly in IT-related services and pharmaceuticals.

Foreign Trade

India's exports amount to 15 per cent of GDP. They account for two-thirds of total exports of SAARC region.

Indian imports are 16 per cent of GDP. They account for 65 per cent of total imports of SAARC region.

Major export products of India are: pearls, precious stones, jewellery, clothing, machinery, vehicles, metal products, tea, jute, iron ore, cotton products, handicrafts, pharmaceuticals, leather products, software, etc.

Major import products of India are: petroleum products, machinery parts, precious stones, iron and steel, chemical products, edible oils, vehicles, fertilizers, etc.

Nepal's 98 per cent of SAARC region exports are to India. So are 96 per cent of SAARC imports from India.

Agricultural Development

Agriculture plays an important role in Indian economy. It provides employment to more than 60 per cent of labour force. Its share in GDP is about 23 per cent. It contributes a great deal to exports. Agro-oriented industries depend largely on agricultural raw materials. Diversification is increasing in India's agriculture. New technology is getting important.

Impact of India's Economic Dynamism on Nepal's Business Sector.

The trade relations between India and Nepal under SAARC have been strengthened since 1996 after signing on SAPTA and creation of SAFTA. The extent of trade creation is reveled by the value of regression coefficient. Among SAARC countries, Indo-Nepal trade relation occupies an important position as an import destination for India. the Simple Linear Method is used to explain the relationship between the total export and the value of export to Nepal by SAARC countries including India. India's total import from SAARC countries including Nepal has been experienced a variation, ranging between 60–80 per cent in respect of SAARC Trade relations.

India is the Southern neighbor of land-locked Nepal. There are both positive and negative impacts of India's economic dynamism on Nepal's business sector.

Positive Impact

The positive impact is as follows:

(a) Extended Market

Nepal is heavily dependent on India for its exports and imports. The economic dynamism of India provided market accessibility for Nepal's exports. It also ensures steady supply of raw materials and technology for Nepal's industrial sector.

(b) Increased Foreign Direct Investment

Foreign direct investment flow from India to Nepal is facilitated by India's economic dynamism. Indian global companies are gradually extending their operations in Nepal. This provides opportunities for employment and income generation in Nepal.

(c) Increased Foreign Aid

India is an important donor for Nepal. Economic dynamism of India may increase India's aid to Nepal. Trade can also increase between India and Nepal.

Negative Impact

(a) Increased Competition

India's growing economic dynamism provides greater competition to Nepalese products. Global Indian companies adversely affect the competitive capacity of Nepalese industries.

(b) Policies and Prices

Nepal and India share long open-border. The growing economic dynamism of India affects Nepalese economic policies and prices. Smuggling increases from India to Nepal and from Nepal to India to take advantage of price differentials. In practice, Nepalese business sector is subservient of Indian economic policies. The 1700 km long open border has been responsible for this state of affairs.

CONCLUSION

The study concludes that the goals of establishment of SAARC have been met significantly to accelerate the process of economic, social and cultural development through optimum use of available resources. The principles of SAPTA provided for gradual reduction and eventual elimination of tariffs within SAARC and paved the way to raise trade relationship between India and Nepal in a separate manner. Moreover, it is SAFTA, which is considered a major milestone that would enable regional South Asian Trade and Indo-Nepal Trade to double in five years. The present study shows that there are tremendous opportunities for boosting India's export to, as well as, import from, among members of SAARC in general and between India and Nepal in particular. For this purpose, new initiatives would be required in order to enable us to take advantage of the expanding unified Indo-Nepal Trade Market. India will have to be prepared to face new challenges and convert them into opportunities, and act as a "Big brother", not as a 'Big Bully' in the SAARC.

References

Bhattacharya, B., June (2005), SAPTA: A Step Forward, *Yojna*, Vol. 49, No. 6, pp. 17-19.

Dhanjal, Gursharan (1994), SAARC: On the Move; *Mainstream*, Vol. XXX, No. 12, pp. 12-14.

Dubey, Muchkund (1991), SAARC: New Imperatives; *Strategic Digest*, Vol. XXI, No. 7, pp. 39-49.

Kumar, Dhruba (1992), Remaking south Asia: Major Trends and Imperatives; *BIISS Journal* (Dhaka), Vol. 13, No. 3, pp. 16-44.

Mansoor, Ahmad (1996), India-SAARC Trade: A Dwindling Feature, *India Quarterly*, Vol. 46, No. 6.

SAARC at the Crossroad: The Islamabad Summit and Bajon: Spotlight on Regional Affairs (Islamabad), Vol. XXI, No. 3, July 2006.

Asian Economic Integration

Issues, Challenges and Future Prospects thereof

Dev Raj

INTRODUCTION

Economic Integration is the process by which barriers of goods, services and capital are reduced, allowing the freer play of market forces. It refers to reducing barriers among countries to transactions and to movements of goods, capital, and labour, including harmonisation of laws, regulations, and standards. Common forms include FTAs, customs unions, and common markets. Sometimes classified as shallow integration *vs.* deep integration. The process, which can be spontaneous or induced by trade liberalisation agreements among governments, has been described as "shallow" integration. It is distinguished from "deep integration", which is seen to occur when governments alter domestic policies to harmonise policies or converge with the economic performance of their partners. Regional integration can be either market or policy driven.

In the last decade, regionalism has become the most important trend in the global economy. The Asian economic integration (AEI) can by exploiting the synergies, expand the economic opportunities available and strengthen growth prospects in the Asian countries. But the geographical distribution of RTAs is still uneven. RTAs are a major and perhaps irreversible feature of today's Multilateral Trading System (MTS).[1] The number of preferential agreements as well as the world share of preferential trade has been steadily increasing over the last eleven years. As per WTO's estimates, preferential trade now represent over 90 per cent of the total international trade; for other MFN trade relations are limited to a handful of Members.

The drive towards the conclusion of Regional Trade Agreements (RTAs) which gathered pace in the 1990s continues unabated. As of July end, 2006 all 149 WTO Members, currently participate in or are actively negotiating RTAs. Further, the sluggish progress of the Doha Development appears to have accelerated the rush to forge RTAs. It is estimated that more than half of World Trade is now conducted under RTAs. The total number of notified preferential agreements in force had increased to 197 RTAs as of July, 2006 are in force have been notified to the GATT/ WTO. This is an important step towards ensuring that RTAs become building blocks, not stumbling blocks to World Trade. Approximately about 20 more RTAs are due to enter into force upon completion of their respective ratification procedures.

Asian countries need to complete the transition to full-fledged market economies to be able to complete in an increasingly integrated and globalised economic environment. Key areas of reform like improving the investment climate and reducing the cost of doing business, particularly through improvements in legal and regulatory systems and tackling governance problems forcefully can further stimulate the process of AEI to a great extent. The international community has an important role to play in support of the Asian Economic Integration and development. Recent efforts to advance regional financial integration have focused on two areas namely: (i) local currency bond funds are being introduced under the Asian Bond Market Initiatives (ABMIs); and (ii) existing arrangements to swap foreign exchange reserves in case of liquidity crises are being expanded under the Chiang Mai Initiative (CMI). Preferential trade agreements are proliferating around the world, including in the Asia and Pacific region.[2]

OBJECTIVES OF THE PAPER

The objectives of this paper is to examine the following aspects of the AEI:

(i) To strengthen international competitiveness of the Asian countries;
(ii) AEI to work as an "Engine of growth";
(iii) To provide a brief update of recent developments, trends and developments in the direction of Asian integration;
(iv) To make an analysis of the various issues and challenges coming in the ways of forming an AEI; and
(v) The future prospectus of the AEI.

This article will puts together these reflections and will aid to their further dissemination and discussion. These reflections present visionary perspectives and a body of current thinking in the region on many issues of current development concerns in India-Asia a part of the world that will be found useful for policy-makers and research scholars in addressing the issues and challenges in the years to come.

GEOGRAPHICAL BORDERS OF ASIAN REGION

On the basis of cultural similarities, nature and geographical proximity of the Asian Countries, we can put the Asian countries as under:

1. East Asia;
2. South East Asia;
3. South Asia;
4. West Asia; and
5. Central Asia.

Now, we may put the details of the countries in striatum in these groups as under:

1. East Asia (4)

(i) People's Republic of China including Hong Kong,
(ii) Japan,
(iii) North and South Korea, and
(iv) Taiwan (Republic of China).

2. South East Asia (10)

(i) Indonesia,
(ii) Philippines,
(iii) Thailand,
(iv) Malaysia,
(v) Myanmar (previously called Burma),
(vi) Vietnam,
(vii) Cambodia,
(viii) Laos,
(ix) Singapore, and
(x) Brunei.

3. South Asia (4)

(i) India,
(ii) Pakistan,
(iii) Sri Lanka, and
(iv) Bangladesh.

4. West Asia (9)

(i) Iran,
(ii) Iraq,
(iii) Kuwait,
(iv) Saudi Arabia,
(v) UAE,
(vi) Israel,

(vii) Jordan,
(viii) Syria, and
(ix) Turkey.

5. Central Asia (4)

(i) Tajikistan,
(ii) Kyrgyzstan,
(iii) Kazakhstan, and
(iv) Afghanistan.

In other word, the following grouping of the Asian Region can be employed and can be put as under:

- The Emerging Asia refers to China, India, Hong Kong-SAR, Korea, Singapore.
- Taiwan Province of China, Indonesia, Malaysia, the Philippines, and Thailand.
- The Industrial Asia refers to Japan, Australia, and New Zealand.
- Asia refers to emerging Asia plus Industrial Asia.
- Newly Industralised Economies (NIEs) refers to Hong Kong-SAR/Korea, Singapore, and Taiwan Province of China.
- ASEAN-4 refers to Indonesia, Malaysia, the Philippines, and Thailand.
- Low-Income countries in Asia (LIAs) include Bangladesh, Cambodia, Lao P.D.R., Mongolia, Sri Lanka, Nepal and Vietnam

ISSUES IN ASIAN ECONOMIC INTEGRATION

The most fundamental rationale behind the **emergence of regional economic cooperation is the deepening of regional economic interdependence in the Asian countries.** Economic integration can resolve the "collective action" problem and internalise externalities and spill-over effects that arise from interdependence. Further, with the Asian

Economic Integration in the areas like Trade and FDI integration, Financial and macro-economic interdependence, and Institutionalisation will also be taken care off. It has been observed that the Asian region put together accounts for 26.8 per cent of global exports, and 24 per cent of the global imports in the year 2004, and 25 per cent of global International Reserves. During the year 2005, the Asia's share in world exports increased to 27.40 per cent and imports to 24.80 per cent. The Asian region combines some of the fastest growing economies in the World. Together they form a huge market, which is growing faster than any other region in the World and could form a vibrant regional grouping. Moreover, the formation of Asian Economic Community (AEC) will also help the region to play a more effective role in shaping the emerging world trading and financial systems. The Asian region has a distinct identity, shaped by history and cultural exchanges over the several centuries. Asia is now the fastest growing region in the world, contributing close to 50 per cent of world growth.

COVERAGE OF THE ASIAN ECONOMIC INTEGRATION

The following aspects of the Asian Economic Integration will be analysed in this article:

(i) Possibilities and constraints of Asian Economic Integration;
(ii) Capital, labour and technology flows among Asian countries;
(iii) Trade development and capital flows among the Asian economies;
(iv) Monetary, financial and trade integration in Asian countries;
(v) Multilateral trade agreements, the trading agreements in Asian countries, the trading blocs/ SAARC, ASEAN and South Asian Countries;
(vi) To restore and build new infrastructure links between Central and South Asia; and
(vii) To analyse the possibilities of sustainable integration among all the Asian counties.

EMERGENCE OF ASIAN ECONOMIC INTEGRATION

Following are the main reasons for the emergence of AEI:

1. General trend towards regionalism of the world, like the formation of NAFTA, APEC, EU, and MERCOSUR, etc.
2. A strong regionalism has emerged in weak workability of WTO.
3. Currency and financial crises in Asian countries in 1990s.
4. Physical deepening of economic integration in the Asian region through increased, intra-regional trade, capital transactions, and strong human networks.

LATE START OF ECONOMIC INTEGRATION IN THE ASIA

The AEI have initiated efforts toward greater institutionalisation of trade and FDI interdependence essentially owing to the reasons like: (i) Defensive response to proliferation of regional trade arrangements among the Asian Countries; (ii) Dis-satisfaction with the slow progress on trade/investment liberalisation among Asian countries and intra-regional levels; and (iii) Prevailing sense of security among neighbours countries. Asian Economic Integration needs to be implemented and encouraged in a phased manner like the approach adopted by the successful blocs of EU, NAFTA and other blocs. To make a more successful AEI group of all the Asian countries have to adopt the more refined strategic thinking process, effective planning; collaborations which facilitate the evolutionary process to convert the dream into a reality like EU and NAFTA. To make the AEI a reality the following guiding principles are to be adopted by all the Asian countries such as: transparent, comprehensive; open-ended policy, minimal trade and investment diversion, no undermining WTO rights and obligations, and Multi-lateral trading system.

PRESENT DEVELOPMENT AND OUTLOOK OF ASIAN REGION

The real GDP growth in the Industrial Asia, Emerging Asia, NIEs, ASEAN-4 and Asia as a whole can be put as under:

TABLE 1

Real GDP Growth (Year-on–year percentage change)

Economic Groupings/ Year	*2004*	*2005*	*2006*	*2007*
	(Actual)		*(Projected)*	
1	2	3	4	5
A. Industrial Asia	2.5	2.7	2.8	2.2
Of which:				
Japan	2.3	2.7	2.8	2.1
Australia	3.6	2.5	2.9	3.2
New Zealand	4.3	2.0	0.9	2.1
B. Emerging Asia	8.4	8.3	8.0	7.7
Of which:				
China	10.1	9.9	9.5	9.0
India	7.4	8.0	7.3	7.0
C. NIEs	5.9	4.5	5.2	4.5
ASEAN-4	5.8	5.2	5.1	5.7
ASIA	7.1	7.1	6.9	6.6

Source: IMF, APDCORE database, and staff estimates, "World Economic and Financial Surveys: Regional Outlook, Asia and Pacific", May, 2006, p. 5.

ISSUES: IN THE WAY OF ASIAN ECONOMIC INTEGRATION

1. Free Trade Agreements (FTAs)

FTAs help economic development but cannot solve "diversity problems" among the Asian member countries such as **income disparity** in particular. Proactive actions to correct such discrepancies are necessary for faster Asian economic integration. FTAs will not only be an important for proactive action but will also stimulate economic operation, among the Asian countries. In this process the Japanese government proposed economic partner agreements (EPAs) to its neighbours, rather than mere FTAs. Japan should take the initiative by providing the financial support, intellectual contributions, and good rules, as well as social capital in the Asia. Japan's trade and industrial structure are supplemental to those of China and ASEAN countries. A revival of its economic growth is being awaited. If Japan revives, then a virtuous circle would begin with more exports, imports, and FDIs. That will work as a stimulant to East Asian countries' integration. In fact, China is harshly competing with ASEAN countries, in its external trade. ASEAN countries have recognised this phenomenon as inevitable, and are trying to find new opportunities in their trade and tourism with China as a regional partners. Like in trade, China and ASEAN countries are competing in attracting FDI from Japan and rest of the world.

Asian countries cannot set-up an EU-type community in near future. Meanwhile, the sub-regional grouping and good sequencing toward the final target will be a realistic approach. To realise FTAs and EPAs one after another on a bilateral, sub-regional or regional basis will be Ashortcut to the final destination. Moreover, an obligation of the members of East Asia will pay the cost of regional public goods. Further, India on August 18, 2006 sought to review the FTA talks with ASEAN by offering to prune the list of sensitive items to 569 from 852 earlier.

2. Moves for Regional and Bilateral FTAs

Recently, several economies in East-Asia have embarked on RTAs on a large scale. Notably, Japan concluded a bilateral FTA with Singapore and made effective in November, 2002, and came to *de facto* conclusion with Mexico. It has also begun, bilateral negotiations with Korea, Malaysia, Thailand, Philippines and Australia. In particular, Japan and Korea have already completed the negotiations in 2005. The rapid economic growth rate of 7 per cent, in recent years in the Asian region has laid a solid material foundation for Pan Asian Regional Cooperation. The China and the ASEAN signed an FTA agreement in November, 2002 to establish a free trade zone by 2010. This future free trade zone comprising of 10 ASEAN countries and China (i.e. ASEAN+1) will be the third largest in the world with 1.7 billion consumers and a trade volume of US $ 1.42 trillion as of 2005. Which will be next only to the APEC, EMFTA, ACS and the EU. On 7th October, 2003, China, Japan, Korea and the Association of South-East Asian Nations (ASEAN) also agreed on to a plan of setting-up a bigger free trade zone by 2020, embracing the region currently referred to as the ASEAN+3.[3]

India, the largest economy in the South Asia, is also actively taking steps to join East Asia's economic integration movement. In September 2003, a free trade including 2.5 billion consumers and comprising 75 per cent of the total Asian population, agreement plan had been reached by the ASEAN, China, Japan, and India, at Jakarta, in Indonesia. It is further reported that the agreement shall be gradually implemented between 2012-17.[4] Under these circumstances, there are three initiatives for the Asian Economic Integration namely: Multilateral surveillance; financing emerging market economies; and IMF governance. Over the coming years, the author see a particular need for multilateral consultations to deal with the growing global economic imbalances which threaten the world's prosperity. For example, large deficits in current account of the balance of payments of the US, i.e. 6.5 per cent of GDP in 2005, which is expected to be the same during the year 2006.

Bangkok Agreement is another notable regional trade arrangement in Asia that includes six countries; three from the East Asia, i.e. China, Korea and Laos and three from the South Asia, i.e. India, Bangladesh and Sri Lanka. Of the agreement lies in the fact that it might serve as a platform to link East Asia into a broader regional trade agreement.[5] Even in 2003, at the annual meeting of BOAO Forum for Asia, Mr. Ramos, former president of the Philippines had formally put forward the concept of **building-up a Grand Asian Family comprising of all the Asian Countries.** In April 2002,

Dr. Robert A. Mandel (Nobel laureate for economics) said in his speech at the Sun Yat-Sen University, Guangzhou, South China, that Asia would have a single currency in the near future. On June 22, at the opening ceremony of the Third Session of the Foreign Ministers of the Asian Cooperation Dialogue, in Qingdao, China, the Chinese Premier Wen Jiabao made a speech entitled, **"Promote a New Centennial Asian Cooperation with Common Efforts," introduced the concept of constructing a new Asia.**

3. Precautions for the Formulation of Sustainable Integration

The following precautions, the Asian countries have to take to ensure the Asian Economic Integration a success:

(i) To ensure not to repeat the 1990s crises in future;
(ii) To nurture Asian Bond Markets;
(iii) To stabilise the exchange rates of the regional currencies;
(iv) To finalise altogether an East Asian or ASEAN–wide social infrastructure;
(v) To reduce income disparities among the member-countries;
(vi) To protect the business environment in the region;
(vii) To fight against the terrorists and pirates; and
(viii) To further cooperates on energy-saving and conservation efforts.

Here, the questions arises, who should pay the cost ? The answer to this is, none other than member-countries. China, Japan and Korea have to pay a sizable portion of the cost, as these countries are relatively big economic powers and be the main players in the Asia.

4. Financial Integration in Asia

One measure of financial integration is geographical reach—that is, regional *versus* extra-regional or global linkages. As we have seen in the preceding pages that Asia's financial integration with global financial markets is already well advanced by mort standards. For example, Asia has been a major beneficiary of a surge in net private capital flows to emerging markets, home to half of the global supply of such flows in 2003 and 2004. Asia's emerging markets receive a large share of the total net private flows to global emerging markets. Some of the Asian countries like Hong Kong, Singapore, Malaysia, Indonesia, Philippines are much bigger holder of foreign liabilities than others like India and China are at the low level. Information on bilateral cross-border capital flows within Asia is scant, making it difficult to assess how much cross-border investment in Asian financial markets originates in the region. The low cross-border correlation of consumption growth in emerging Asia suggests untapped potential for diversification.

The second measure of financial integration is within asset classes—the cross-border connections among domestic banking systems, equity markets, and bond markets. In this measure of assessment also reflect that the financial integration as of 2005 is uneven. For banking sector data as of 2004 show that the major foreign lender is EU or American. While, the Japanese banks rank third, except in Thailand, where they rank first. However, anecdotal evidence suggests a growing interest in cross-border acquisitions, especially by Singapore banks with a consistent trend with rising outward FDI in the Asia. Further, on Asian stock markets, there are few foreign listings and even fewer regional listings. In some of the Asian countries, stock markets have a large international presence, but few foreign players come from neighbouring countries such as Hong Kong SAR, Japan, Thailand, Korea, India, Taiwan POC and China.

Further, in bond markets, regional integration is also limited. It has been observed that much of the growing foreign currency-denominated bond issuance of Asian sovereign and corporate borrowers is in US $ and is marketed outside of Asia—about 80 per cent is in the US and Europe. Moreover, there are evidences that Asian Investors in these marks absorb large amount of the issues. However, the high degree of integration of foreign currency-denominated bond markets does not carry over to Asia's markets for local currency-denominated bonds. Further, it has been observed that there is little evidence of Asians investing in the bonds of other neighbouring countries, notwithstanding initiatives under way to promote cross-border holdings. Emerging Asia could make an additional gains from more extensive intra-regional ties, including the following such as: more stable access to capital lower funding costs and greater investment, and the greater market discipline of macro-economic policies. Thus, we can say that deeper and better-connected financial markets would benefit Asia. Asia's financial systems are mostly bank-based, with equity and private bond markets generally smaller than those in developed countries. However, Malaysia and Korea are exceptions owing to their corporate bond markets, as a percentage of GDP, are among that largest in the world following the collapse of bank lending in the late 1990s. The depth of local bond markets has generally increased across Asia, owing to the governments being the major issuers to finance bank restructuring and rising fiscal deficits since the financial crises.

While, on the other hand, stock market activity has since declined, in part because of the migration of credit-worthy Asian Corporate to mature markets. However, overall Asia's growing intra-regional trade will catalyze greater financial integration and, in turn, be stimulated by it. On the liquidity front Asia is a local overhang because of a combination of high domestic savings and low domestic investment in much of the Region. Asia has become a net exporter of Capital, contributing to large global imbalances in current accounts. Deeper intra-regional financial integration could help to allocate this liquidity intra-regionally, reviving domestic investment and an orderly decline in external surpluses.

Greater financial linkages bring benefits but also require sound policies and institutions, as well as mechanisms to contain new risks that could arise from more open financial system. Mindful that financial integration could magnify the channels through which shocks are transmitted across borders or across asset markets within a crises. For example, ASEAN+3 countries are strengthening information sharing to better monitor short-term capital flows. Further, surveillance groups have also been established to provide a basis for policy-makers to exchange information and to cooperate in a regulatory capacities. Asian governments have established significant support mechanisms in the context of the Chiang Mai Institute to cope with disruptive capital flows and maintain exchange rate stability.

5. Asian Monetary Integration

With the advances in the financial integration and intra-regional trade in Asia are seen as heralding eventual adoption of a regional common currency and the establishment of an Asian Monetary Union on the line of the euro model. EU's experience shows that a "monetary union" impasse such stringent demands on policy coordination and institution building that Asia may well need a clear political will, sustained over generations. An other obstacle include a lack of common institutions, widely different economic structures, and uneven development patterns. Then, differences in production patterns are particularly problematic because they increase the likelihood of asymmetric shocks that call for different monetary responses at the national level—something that would be impossible within a monetary Union. It is safe to say that a monetary union for Asia remains, at best, a distant goal. The policy requirements for a strong regional economy also support convergence of economic conditions among its members like EU.

Further, Asian economies are best served by Exchange Rate Systems with adequate flexibility to cushion country-specific shocks. Although, some aspects of financial integration for example the transformation of local markets into an all-encompassing regional market may not be possible in the absence of a common currency, flexible exchange rate systems can facilitate ongoing efforts to foster closer regional economic ties. For example, North America's experience with its FTA underscores the benefits of flexible exchange rates and monetary policies targeting low inflation, provided that excess volatility can be contained. Notwithstanding fluctuations in their bilateral exchange rates, North American countries have developed highly articulated supply chains, large intra-regional FDI flows, open capital accounts, and stable financial systems.

Thus, we can say that Asia has come a long way in opening its financial system and clearly understands how it can benefit from deeper financial integration. Emerging Asia is a global player in international trade and a significant recipient of net private capital flows to emerging markets. The development of regional capital markets offers significant pay off, particularly as it supports better integration with the global financial system. In the course of foregoing the path ahead, regional policy-makers will tackle difficult issues, including the appropriate sequencing of reforms; the desirable balance between domestic and regional priorities; possible trade-offs between global and regional financial integration; and the relative roles of governments and markets in shaping the process. The combination of favourable economic conditions and a clear commitment to integration can provide a fitting environment in which the policy debate can flourish—and Asia's financial integration can continue to advance.

6. Asian Economic Integration: Need for Motivation and Outcome

Regional economic integration is undergoing an unprecedented boom all over the world. While, Asian Economic Integration is a late comer in this process. However, since the late 1990s its integration has been accelerating at multiple levels, with ASEAN being the hub, and ASEAN+1 and ASEAN+3 being two main pillars. During this process, the economic relationship between China and India—two countries that have experienced similar after effects of colonialism in their history are opening-up their economies through similar reforms at present, and that share long geographical borders—is attracting greater attention around the world. This process will not only affect the two countries themselves but will have a great impact on the Asian economic integration in connecting East Asia and South Asia and, to a greater or lesser extent, on the emerging future shape of the world.

We know that both China and India are the great ancient countries and civilisations with a long history. These two countries had a centuries-old traditional friendship. Further, it may be mentioned that owing to numerous historical, political and economic reasons, relations between China and India were basically left at a standstill in the past few decades owing to the border disputes between China and India. For the historical reasons, there has been no officially defined border line between China and India, which restricted the development of Sino-Indian relations to a large extent and made these two countries to keep a watchful eye on each other even long after the border war. Owing to this, China and India have had highly limited economic exchanges for a along time in the past.

Sino-Indian economic relations, ignited by the Indian systematic reform and series of cooperation agreements signed by the two governments, have been accelerating since the end of the 1990s, as represented in trade, investment, technological cooperation and other exchanges and communications, etc. Then, from 1999 to 2005, bilateral trade increased from US $ 1.99 billion to US $ 13.6 billion, respectively. Further, Sino-Indian investment is also thriving. Moreover, the two countries have reached a consensus on guidelines for solving the border problem. **The Sixth round of trade negotiations, held in September, 2005 and brought the negotiations to a substantial phase**. However, still there are also a series of impediments like conflicts of interests among domestic interest groups in both the countries, geopolitical consideration and the coexistence of economic cooperation and competition in the two countries.

Mr. Soogil Young, President, National Strategy Forum, South Korea said in "the East Asia Summit a harbinger for Asian integration," that the most serious threat to the continuation of Asian dynamism stemmed from proliferation of FTAs with the "spaghetti bowl effect", failure of the Doha Round of trade negotiations, and continued stalemate over the global payments imbalances. He further said that the East Asian summit should play the role of coordinating the various prevailing schemes in the management of the global development process.[6] Mr. Yao Chao Cheng, of China's Shanxi University of Finance and Economics, remarked in one of the meeting that among all Asian nations, social and civilian exchanges were too little. He further added that the Asians should discover their common cultural identity by repairing the **"cultural fault lines"** by managing the internal disputes and conflicts. As a strategic approach, Governments of the Asian nations should take effective steps to encourage and promote the mass flow of people, scholarism particularly the younger generation, to improve understanding and minimise mis-understanding among the Asian people.[7]

The integrated cooperation is the best way for Asian countries to make common development and to remove the "fault lines" as proposed in Samuel Huntington's paradigm[8] can be repaired and transcended in the unification process. At this stage, the question arises how integration of Capital markets has helped to allocate Savings and Investment more efficiently, which has also increased the risks from volatile capital flows and financial contagion. The defence against crises must be a sound macro-economic framework, including appropriate monetary and fiscal policies as explained in the preceding pages. Further, it has been observed that the globalisation of production creates tremendous opportunities but also potentially serious challenges for the Asian countries. To meet the challenges of global competition in production, there is an urgent need for the flexible policies to promote the Capital Markets (CMs) and labour market. Moreover, measures to improve the business environment, which would encourage new investment and innovation, would also help to face the challenges.

7. Pillars of Regional Economic Integration

This inherent dynamism provides a sustainable basis for long-term integration,. by rooting it in market forces and aligning with the interests of the region's businesses and the real comparative advantages, we find in different areas. There are four key pillars of regional cooperation and economic integration as given in Figure 1.

RECENT DEVELOPMENTS IN ASIAN ECONOMIC INTEGRATION

The hope of better risk sharing, more efficient allocation of capital, productive investment, and, ultimately, higher standards of living for all is propelling the drive for stronger connections between financial systems across the world. At the global level, Asia's integration with the system

FIGURE 1

Pillars of Regional Cooperation and Economic Integration

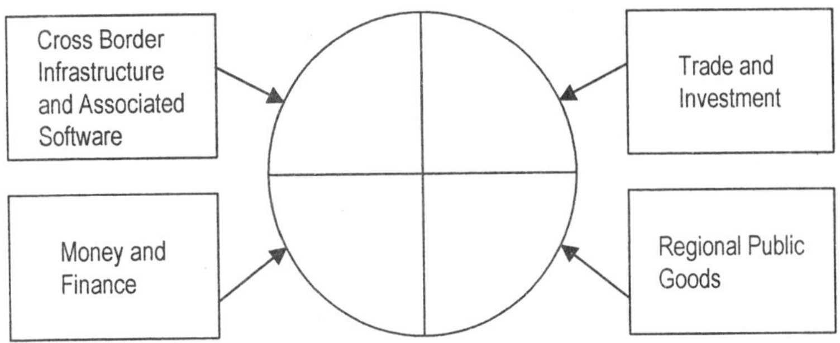

is well advanced. However, at the regional level financial integration is more limited. Emerging Asian countries are not ready in investing in each other country in the region. Moreover, making a dent in the large unfinished agenda for financial integration poses many challenges. However, the encouraging news is that Asia is well position to forge ahead. At present the East Asia's Economic Integration will refer to the 15 economies comprising of ASEAN; People's Republic of China; Hong Kong, China; Japan, Republic of Korea; and Taipei, China, a region that has proven to be a natural hub for the economic integration. What has distinguished the East Asian Economic Group now named as East Asia Economic Caucus (EAEC) formed in 1990 having exports of US $ 1777 billion in 2004 experience from that of EU and North America is that until recently the process has been almost entirely market-driven, rather than relying on more formal arrangements. Intra-regional exports have been growing by more than 12 per cent per year for more than two decades.

As FDI flows to China and India is increasing, it also continues to flow to the ASEAN region from 2003 to 2005. FDI into ASEAN grow by 20.4 per cent, surpassing flows into China of 13.2 per cent and slightly below the amount going to India at 27.9 per cent. China in particular has become an important engine of growth for Asia. India, too, has been emerging as a growth engine, albeit from a much lower base.

Both China and India are still in the early stages of developments, with much more scope for domestic consumption levels to rise. For example, China's middle class is still relatively small at 5 per cent only of the total population of 1.3 billion and could increase by almost 10-fold over the next decade. While, India's middle class could expand from about 57 million now, to about 160 million by the end of the decade. The rise of China and India will redefine regional divisions of labour and trade and help the Southeast Asian economies take off on a new and higher growth trajectory. It is expected that the China and India will bring Asia into the centre of the global economy in the near future. The rise of both countries will be helping Asia not only in growth, but also to become more integrated. Now, the Asian countries are working to create a cohesive Asian community which will allows for both complementary growth and positive competition. The success of an Asian community depends on the following key factors:

- Growth in China, India, Japan and Korea must continue to catalyse economic integration in Asia;
- They must continue to adopt mutually beneficial developmental and foreign policies which respect to the other Asian countries; and
- Other Asian countries must continue to reform and integrate their own economies and present themselves to China, India, Japan and Korea as valuable and viable partners.

RESERVES AND INFRASTRUCTURAL NEEDS IN DEVELOPING ASIA

We may now, examine the other aspects of the Asian economic integration as under:

Beside trade, there is a great potential for integration in financial, cross-border capital flows and financial crisis recovery plans. Asia has the highest saving growth rate in the world with 38 per cent of GDP in 2004. The Asian official foreign reserves increased to US $ 2 trillion in 2004. Asia has an estimated 2.3 million high-net-worth individual compared to 2.7 million in the US and 2.6 million in Europe in the year 2004. Further, their number is expected to grow by 7 per cent a year. Although, Asian investors have traditionally looked to Western markets for their investment and financial needs, but now their savings are increasingly being intermediated within Asia for investing globally. Though, Asia has a high saving growth rate, but its financial needs are equally high, as it have to grow consistently and rapidly on a continuous basis. Across Asia, there is a huge demand for funds to finance infrastructure projects. Developing countries in Asia will need to spend an estimated total of US $ 377 billion per year between 2006-10 or approximately US $ 2 trillion in a five year period in infrastructure sectors such as roads, railways, airways, ports and electricity. For India alone, need for investment in infrastructure of US $ 367 billion during 2006-10 as against the estimated US $ 215 billion during 2001-06.[9] Further, private companies are also eager to raise funds to feed the growth of their business. With the greater integration of Asian financial markets and intermediation of funds within Asia will allow it to partially fund its own growth.

Asian countries have built-up huge reserves as a buffer against future problems. The integration of capital markets has helped to allocate savings and investment more efficiently, but it has also increased the risks from volatile capital flows and financial contagion. The **"savings glut"** view contends that Asia is flooding the world with excess savings, driving down world interest rates to artificially low levels and fostering counterpart external deficits in the US. The "investment slump" view maintains that investment has been depressed since the Asian crises. How to reduce domestic vulnerabilities prevent future crises, and create international and regional safety nets for insurance against large and volatile capital flows remains a key challenge. A number of factors are worth examining, including the effects of financial and corporate sector restructuring, competition from China, and perceptions that the investment environment is riskier. The increase perceived risk seems pervasive, whereas the other factors are more country-specific.

Mutual economic benefits and economic integration have been possible owing to the ASEAN + China, India,

Japan and Korea have chosen to pursue development strategies characterised by peace and partnership. They support the vision of a peaceful, progressive, and inclusive Asian community and have shown a willingness to engage and cooperate with regional neighbours for enhancing regional stability and cohesiveness. India is today an import ASEAN + JACIK dialogue partner and a member of the ASEAN Regional Forum, and, in December, 2005, it became an inaugural member of the East Asia Summit (EAS). As the web of bilateral and multilateral relations grows, the Asia will become more stable and cohesive. This will be the key to successfully managing and integrating the rising Asian region. This way the emerging Asian economic integration must not become an insular rival to other regions but a globally connected and engaged partner. China and India have already taken a lead in connecting the Asian countries to the rest of the world.

RTAs AMONG ASIA-PACIFIC AND OTHER ASIAN COUNTRIES

The RTAs in Asia-Pacific was formed in 1989 as a Asia Pacific Economic Cooperation (APEC) as of 2004. It has a total 21 members countries as of 2004. The debate over RTAs in Asia-Pacific Economic Cooperation has further intensified in 2004. Singapore which is also the member of APEC has signed FTA with Jordan. And for Australia and new Zealand, negotiating for an FTA between them and ASEAN countries were launched in early 2005. In South Asia, India has been the main focus of RTA activities. With its SAARC counterparts comprising of Bangladesh, Bhutan, India, Maldives, Nepal, Pakistan and Sri Lanka, it has signed the South Asian Free Trade Agreement (SAFTA), designed to revamp the SAPTA, and a Framework Agreement under the name BIMSTEC, i.e. Bangladesh, India, Myanmar, Sri Lanka, Thailand—Economic Cooperation. It is also engaged in FTA negotiations with ASEAN and Thailand, having signed Framework Agreements with both, and is negotiating a Comprehensive Economic Cooperation Agreement (CECA) with Singapore. Further, India has signed a partial scope agreement with MERCOSUR, as a preliminary step to an FTA and is considering FTAs with Chile, the GCC and SACU.[10]

In addition to the CIS free trade agreement and a customs union agreement between the Kyrgyz Republic, the Russian Federation, Kazakhstan and Tajikistan, Armenia, Georgia and the Kyrgyz as WTO Members have notified a number of bilateral agreements between them and other regional partners. It would appear that most of the other regional countries have similar networks of bilateral RTA overlapping like SADC, COMESA, ECOWAS, CEEAC, and the Arab Maghreb Union, have been designated as pillars of the AEC. The focussed sectors of the Central Asia are energy, transportation, and communications. Goal behind the Central Asia's integration is to facilitate the development of needed infrastructure to foster regional cooperation and economic development though trade in Central Asia. It has been observed that the East and South (Asia minus the Gulf countries) alone accounts for 20 per cent of global imports, 23 per cent of global exports; and 23 per cent of foreign exchange reserves. It has been further observed that the trade of South Asian countries with the East Asian countries is much larger than the intra-regional trade. The same is the case with ASEAN. At the pan-Asian level, the diversities in the levels of economic development and capabilities are quite wide, thus providing for more extensive and mutually beneficial linkages. The diversity in economic structure provides its own indigenous capacity and markets for dynamic industrial restructuring within the region on the basis of **"flying geese."**[11]

INTRA-REGIONAL EXPORTS AND SHARE IN WORLD EXPORTS

The world total exports increased from US $ 5138 billions in 1995 to US $ 10121 billions in 2005. It has been observed that the expansion, widening and deepening of RTAs has resulted in a situation whereby intra-regional trade accounted for 40 per cent of the world trade (merchandise imports) in 2000 and has increased to 50 per cent in 2005 as per the WTO Trade Report 2006. The large proportion of "global" intra-RTA trade would be accounted for by the existing large RTAs, including APEC-72 per cent, CIS-63.6 per cent, EU-60.7 per cent, NAFTA- 55.9 per cent and the FTAA-60.1 per cent as on 2004. Intra-regional exports of the EU alone accounted for about 39.4 per cent of merchandise exports, while NAFTA intra-exports represented around 14.6 per cent and FTAA 9.8 per cent in the year 2005. Further, the value of total exports increased from 221 in 1996 to 324 in the year 2004. The share of developed countries in world exports which was 69 per cent in 1980 came down slightly to 68.7 per cent in 2004. While, the percentage share of exports of the developing countries which was 26 per cent in 1980 increased to 34.02 per cent in the year 2005 in the total world exports.[12]

INTRA-REGIONAL TRADE SHARE FOR THE YEARS 1990-2004

The data given below in Table 2 summarises changes in the share of intra-regional trade intensity Index for various groupings of countries in the world for the period of 1990-2004 as under:

TABLE 2

Intra-regional Trade Share during the Years 1990-2004

(in percentage)

Regions	*1990*	*1995*	*2000*	*2001*	*2002*	*2003*	*2004*
APEC	68.3	71.8	73.1	72.6	73.4	72.6	72.0
EAEC	39.7	47.9	46.6	46.6	48.2	49.4	49.8
EMFTA	68.5	65.3	64.6	63.3	63.3	63.9	63.6
ASEAN	19.0	24.6	23.0	22.4	22.7	22.2	22.2
NAFTA	41.4	46.2	55.7	55.5	56.6	56.1	55.9
European Union: 25	65.9	62.4	61.6	60.8	60.6	61.1	60.1
ECO	3.2	7.9	5.6	5.5	5.9	6.7	6.3
FTAA	46.6	52.5	60.7	60.6	60.8	60.1	60.1
SAARC	3.2	3.8	4.1	4.3	4.8	5.7	5.6
MERCOSUR	8.9	20.3	20.0	17.1	11.5	11.9	12.6

Source: World Development Indicators, 2006, The World Bank, 2006, pp. 332-34.

The above Table 2 summarises changes in the share of intra-regional trade for various groupings in the world over the period of 1990-2004. From the Table 2, it may be observed that the share of intra-regional trade for APEC has risen from 68.3 per cent in 1990 to 72 per cent in 2004. While in case of EU it decreased from 65.9 per cent in 1990 to 60.1 per cent in 2004. The share of intra- regional trade within ASEAN increased from 19 per cent in 1990 to 22.2 per cent in 2004.Which is lower than that in the EU 60 per cent, and still there is scope to increase the intra-regional trade in the Asian countries.

EUROPEAN *VIS-A-VIS* ASIAN ECONOMIC INTEGRATION PROCESS: A COMPARISION

While making a retrospective analysis of the European Integration it has been observed that how political factors and economic opportunities/constraints have interacted in the progressive design of an unprecedented form of federalism. Political reconciliation of former enemies, i.e. France and Germany, modesty of the first steps of economic integration, i.e. market for steel and coal, then of manufactured goods, prolonged by an extension to agricultural products, creation of an institution in charge of defending the Common Market and the general interest of Europe as such (European Commission), trial and error process in order to preserve the single European Market in the era of financial instability from EMS to euro, progressive building of political institutions in order to get legitimacy an approval by the citizen (European Parliament). Should the same strategy and criteria apply for contemporary economic integration processes, as observed in Latin-American (NAFTA versus MERCOSUR) but also in the Asian Economic Integration. Can an economic integration take place at the only initiative of multinational firms and is it possible to build new supranational coordinating mechanisms in the era of financial globalisation? Paradoxically enough, regional integration is more necessary than ever but it has never been so difficult to achieve.

RTAs: ITS SYNERGISATION WITH RULES OF ORIGIN, BILATERAL AND MULTILATERAL TRADING SYSTEMS

With the increasing trend in block and other preferential the global trading system is becoming complex owing to the following developments like: (i) Rules of Origin, (ii) Bilateral Preferential Relationships, and (iii) Synthesizing RTAs with the Multilateral Trading System. Let us now, we may discuss them in details as under:

(1) Rules of Origin

Rules of Origin (ROOs) are an inherent feature of the FTAs where each country maintains its own tariff structure *vis-à-vis* third parties as a means of determining whether goods are eligible for preferential treatment in the importing country and to prevent "trade diversion", i.e. the transhipment of products from non-parties to an RTA through a low-tariff RTA-party to one which maintains higher tariffs. ROOs are also frequently used in customs unions, particularly a transitional measure. The complexity of these regimes vary: some are based on a general rule applicable across the board for all tariff items; others contain multiple rules depending on the product in question.

Often it has been observed that the rules of origin fall into distinct families or groups, though each has its own idiosyncrasies. A country's membership in different RTAs each with its own set of rules of origin may require exporters to tailor their products in accordance with a daunting array of product-specific criteria in order to qualify for preferential treatment in different markets. Various Studies have shown that exporters may choose to forgo the preferential rates offered under an RTA, if offset the administrative burden of complying.[13] This may have particular resonance in RTAs concluded between developed and developing countries, or between low and high tariff countries. Although, the exporter facing the low MFN tariff may forego preferential treatment, the exporter exporting to the market where higher MFN tariffs exist has a greater incentive to comply with origin rules to secure the higher preference margin.

(ii) Bilateral Preferential Relationships

The current trend towards the conclusion of bilateral FTAs, rather than customs unions, has led to an ever-increasing number of crisis-crossing and overlapping FTAs, each with its own tariff liberalisation schedules and distinct rules of origin. For example, if the parties to an RTA adopt a "big bang" approach and liberalise all tariffs on all products on the date of entry into force of an agreement, there would be no need to negotiate tariff liberalisation schedules. However, this is rarely the case in practice. In general, RTA contain a time table for the progressive reduction of duties on a bilateral basis. Tariff liberalisation schedules may be asymmetric, allowing one country a longer transition period to implement tariff reductions; most countries negotiate longer implementation periods or exclusions for their most sensitive products

(iii) Synthesizing RTAs with the Multilateral System

The economic impact of an RTA depends on its particular architecture, the trading impact of the parties involved, and the degree of liberalisation undertaken, particularly with regard to sensitive sectors. It is notoriously difficult to assess the trade creation and diversion effects for a single RTA; the empirical evidence on the subject remains ambiguous. Given the wide variety of motives that induce countries to pursue the regional path, RTAs are likely to remain popular no matter how well the multilateral system functions. The most important challenge is to seek ways to maximise RTAs' welfare effects and their compatibility with the WTO, while minimising any negative effects.[14]

The adoption of certain principles in RTAs could help to consolidate and build-upon the benefits of preferential trade agreements and promote a more effective multilateral system. *First* would be for countries to engage only in regional commitments which they would be willing, sooner or later, to extend to the multilateral setting. Countries could signal their willingness to do so by concurrently lowering MFN tariffs alongside preferential tariffs, thus reducing the likelihood of trade and investment diversion. *Secondly,* countries could promote the principle of transparency by ensuring that comprehensive information on tariffs, regulations, and rules of origin of their RTAs is publicly and easily available and that all such RTAs are notified to the WTO in a timely fashion. *Third,* by agreeing to a consultative system to map and monitor RTAs and by redefining, where necessary, the rules applicable to RTAs, a more effective link might be forged between regionalism and multilateralism.

REGIONAL ECONOMIC INTEGRATION AND THE WTO

The WTO rules on RTAs date back to GATT 1947. Article XXIV of GATT, complemented by its Understanding negotiated during the Uruguay Round, provide the legal foundation for RTAs in the area of trade in goods. The Enabling Clause adopted in 1979 provides for the mutual reduction of tariffs on trade in goods among developing countries. Rules covering trade in services in RTAs, negotiated during the Uruguay Round, are set out in Article V of the GATS. On this basis, Ministers agreed to launch negotiations aimed at clarifying and improving the relevant disciplines and procedures under existing WTO provisions with a view to resolve the impasse in the CRTA, exercise better control of RTAs dynamics, and minimise the risks related to the proliferation of RTAs. The CRTA was established in 1996, in particular (a) to oversee, under a single framework, all regional trade agreements, and (b) to consider the implications of such agreements and regional initiatives for the multilateral trading system and the relationship between them. However, this body has enjoyed little success so far in assessing the consistency of the RTAs notified to the WTO, due to various political and legal difficulties, most of which were inherited from the GATT years.

The 1990s have witnessed a strong trend of Regional Trading Blocs in the different parts of the world especially the blocs. These attempts include formation of the Single European Market (SEM) in the European Union and North American Free Trade Area (NAFTA). The formation of these trade had been promoted? by the increasing emphasis on competitiveness with the conclusion of Uruguay Round negotiations. An immediate effect of these regional integration agreements (RIAs) has been the rising proportion of the World trade that is conducted within the Trading Blocs. Over half of world trade is now conducted with in RTAs and its proportion is growing fast.

COUNTRIES' MOTIVATIONS FOR THE ASIAN ECONOMIC INTEGRATION

There are the following two motivations behind the RTAs namely the Economic Rationale and Political reasons. In the economic rationale the major points are:

(i) Search for larger markets;
(ii) Deeper integration;
(iii) Defensive necessity;
(iv) Competition;
(v) Lock in investment; and
(vi) More secure access to developed markets than GSP programs.

While, in the political reasons, the main points are namely:

(i) Increased bargaining power;
(ii) Prevent back sliding on political/economic reforms; and
(iii) To ensure or reward political support.

Effects of RTAs on the Multilateral System can be summed-up as under:

(A) Positive Effects

(i) Economies of scale;
(ii) Laboratories for change;
(iii) To provide competition;
(iv) To attract FDI; and
(v) Allow countries to hone negotiating skills.

(B) Negative Effects

In the negative effects the points comes like:

(i) Strains negotiating capacity;
(ii) Dampens enthusiasm for multilateral negotiations;
(iii) Creates vested interests;
(iv) Labyrinthine rules of origin;
(v) Trade and Investment diversion; and
(vi) Weakest countries are left out.

SAARC REGIONAL COOPERATION

We have seen that the present international economic scenario is witnessing on the one hand a movement towards globalisation, deregulation, privatisation, liberalisation, etc. while on the other hand there are on-going efforts towards creating regional blocs among the countries located in a geographical region, to promote intra-regional economic cooperation. It is evident from the development scenario emerging in different parts of the world, and a perceptible shift in the world power, politics from geo-political to geo-economic considerations, that regional cooperation is vital for accelerating economic growth. In fact, regional cooperation constitutes a major policy approach both in developing as well as developed economies. South Asian Association of Regional Cooperation (SAARC) is one such efforts to bring the developing countries of the region together and has laid the foundation for regional cooperation in South Asia, linking India, Pakistan, Bangladesh, Nepal, Sri Lanka, Bhutan and the Maldives. In the year 2004, SAARC block was having a meagre merchandise exports within block to the tune of US $ 5.7 billion.[15]

DIVERSION OF TRADE AND INVESTMENT BY TRADE BLOCKS

One main reason that could explain why RTAs in Asia appear to have been more trade-creating than other RTAs to date, the fact that RTA in Asia followed a long period of unilateral liberalisation during the 1980s and 1990s.

Subsequently, regional integration efforts proceeded in parallel with multilateral liberalisation. In fact, many Asian countries acceded to the WTO in the mid-1990s, and lowered their MFN tariff rates substantially, thereby limiting the risk of possible trade diversion under subsequently agreed RTAs.

FUTURE POTENTIAL OF ASIAN ECONOMIC INTEGRATION

A more intensive cooperation for matching the under utilised capacity in some of the countries of the region with unmet demand in others could go a long way in pulling the region out of the current slump. Further, we observed that Asian Economic Integration is having the potential for mutual beneficial co-operation in the areas namely: Petroleum and Natural gas, Agriculture, Agro-based Technology, Bio-technology, Power and Telecommunications; Information Technology, Railways and Roads, Civil Aviation, and Financial Services. India's compulsions of integrating with ASEAN have assumed a new urgency with the failure of the WTO Ministerial meeting at Cancun and the threat issued by the US by passing WTO for bilateral trading arrangements. Thus, by pushing the idea of closer ties with ASEAN, Japan, China, India and South Korea, India should ensure that a roadmap being charted for a new economic cooperation in the region at the earliest. India has agreed to eliminate tariff by 2011 for Brunei, Cambodia, Laos, Indonesia, Malaysia, Myanmar, Singapore, Thailand and Vietnam and they will reciprocate and eliminate their duties for India in the same year. The new ASEAN member states—Cambodia, Laos, Myanmar and Vietnam—will do so by 2016. The exchange of tariff concessions and elimination of tariff on an agreed common list of 105 items based on common reciprocity between India and ASEAN-6 will take place within four years. It is true that India's to have an FTA with ASEAN by 2010 and the proposed creation of ASEAN + Three East Asian Economic Community member countries.

India's exports to Asian and Oceania countries has steadily gone-up from US $ 29.6 billion in 2003-04 to US $ 37.6 billion in 2004-05. The quantum of Sino-ASEAN trade during the year 2003 was US $ 55 billion and China has targeted a trade level of US $ 100 billion with the region in 2005. As China, Japan and South Korea have offered economic cooperation with ASEAN, India's integration with the Association is also expected to facilitate greater cooperation between India and these countries. India has already put forward the idea that ASEAN should be more closely integrated with India, Japan, China and South Korea to form an Asian Economic Community that would more efficiently exploit synergies. Moreover, JACIK has 14 of the fastest growing economies with vast complementarities. These countries have a population of 3.8 billion or half of the world population as on 2004, and a GDP of over US $ 8.43 trillion, which is comparable to the EU in 2004. Exports of JACIK countries adding-up to US $ 2.035 trillion compared to US $ 1.3 trillion of NAFTA in 2004. The combined official reserves of JACIK economies are at about US $ 2.089 trillion in 2004, would be much larger than those of the US and the EU put together. Thus, the region would have sufficiently large market and financial resources to support and sustain expedited development of the region's economies. The Indian Government signed the Framework for the India-ASEAN Free Trade Area by 2012. China and ASEAN countries also signed a similar framework last year to bring the FTA into operation not later than 2010.

At present, the Asian Economic Integration may be looking as a overlapping and inter-locking agreements. However, once the successful integration emerges, it will be the world's largest trade alliance covering Asia as a whole with a GDP of more than US $ 10 trillion. ASEAN itself, under the "Bali Concord", will become an integrated economic community only by 2020. While at present even the JACIK is having a GDP of US $ 8.43 trillion as of 2004. Now, the ASEAN Free Trade Area (AFTA) has reconciled to remove the barriers on the following sectors latest by 2020. These sectors are: Wood-based products, Rubber, Fisheries, Electronics, Textiles, Automobiles, Healthcare, and Air-travel and Tourism. The emergence of China as one of the world's strongest economies with explosive export growth rates and huge reserves has dramatically transformed the outlook for

Asia's future. While, 43 per cent of China's exports were to Asia, and 58 per cent of China's imports in 2002 came from the rest of Asia. Intra-regional trade in ASEAN totalled US $ 122 billion in 2004, 22.2 per cent of the bloc's total exports and with a global share of 6.1 per cent. The main reason behind the integration of ASEAN countries with the China, is the realisation that it cannot ever depend on US market alone. This has also partly moderated the concern of ASEAN over its declining share of foreign direct investment flows, with China attracting the maximum to the tune of US $ 52 billion in 2002 and US $ 55 billion in 2004. Asia has more than half of the inward stock of FDI US $ 1,400 billion in the developing world and, notwithstanding the slowdown, foreign investments so far in ASEAN countries account for a sizeable ratio of GDP. India was to bring down the higher tariffs by 20 per cent, closer to Asian levels, by 2005. As of 2004, India's weighted tariffs were brought down to 25.3 per cent for all the countries as of 2004.

To kick-start its FTA with ASEAN, China signed a protocol on "early harvest" of benefits, with tariff reductions on agricultural and manufactured goods from January 1, 2004 onwards. Work on lowering tariffs within the framework of FTA was to begin from 2005. The China-ASEAN FTA will be the biggest, with 1.7 billion consumers and GDP of about US $ 2.4 trillion as on 2004. By 2010, it will cover the original ASEAN-6 and by 2015, the other four member-countries. Already, the two-way trade is rapidly growing at annual rate of US $ 70-75 billion, and Chinese officials expect it to touch US $ 100 billion in 2005. India also invited business leaders to take advantage of India's liberal investment regime, its high return and record of profit repatriation. India at present is having the strengths, particularly in IT, financial, pharmaceuticals, health and entertainment sectors. India has set a target of two-way trade at US $ 30 billion by 2007, against the present level of US $ 12.5 billion. This proactive effort on India's part clearly suggests a policy shift. Traditionally a supporter of multilateral trade negotiations, the country has finally woken-up to the importance of being in an influential trade bloc and rightly so, the India-ASEAN FTA, to come into effect in 2011, has the basic objective of enhancing trade relations, but this would entail significant liberalisation by India. Time and again it has been seen that the multilateral option is time-consuming, as a wide range of issues need to be reconciled in it.

India's exports to ASEAN countries' trade grew from US $ 27.2 billion in 2003-04 to US $ 37.9 billion in 2004-05. The trade trend shows that India has been trading mainly with four ASEAN members. There is a need to increase our exports to other countries in the group as well. The major items of imports to the group are gems and jewellery, electronic goods and organic chemicals. The India-ASEAN pact is not merely restricted to trade, it also cover enhancing investments as well. This is because, in the changing international scenario, FDI is a major pre-requisite for growth and development, especially in developing world. From January 1991 to May 2002 the cumulative FDI approvals from the ASEAN to India was Rs. 14,000 crores, nearly 6 per cent of the total FDI into India. But the actual inflow during the period was only 3.5 per cent of the total FDI. Thus, given India's huge population and market size, the scope for increased investment from the ASEAN is immense. For strong Asian Economic Integration the following points are to be taken on a priority basis. These points are: Monetary Cooperation for Exchange Rate Stability; Financial Cooperation for Reviving Demand; Sub-regional Cooperation; To promote trade and investment links; Coordination on Global Issues; Biotechnology and Food Security; Space Remote Sensing and Sustainable Development; Health and Development; Global Technological Order and Innovation among the Asian Developing Countries; Crucial Role of Corporate Governance in the Asian Countries in a Global scenario; and Cultural Identity of Asian Countries in the world trade and development.

CONCLUSION

The Asian Economic Integration is taking shape indeed, but slowly. In the course of process of Integration, there will be occurring many disputes and conflicts with clashing economic interests amongst the Asian countries. But the

Integration may provide a dynamic platform for democratic exchange and peaceful negotiations within the framework of International Laws for the Common good. In this process of integration, the national interests can find a higher gratification and fulfilment in the International Integration and cooperation and can increase synergetic efficiency of all the Asian countries and globe as a whole. However, the Regional Economic Integration process in Asia as part of economic globalisation shall no doubt produce a Pan-Asian economic community. Asians shall have their own unified currency in future, perhaps in more than 50 years time or even longer, as experienced by the European Union.

The case for Regional Integration is both economic and political in the case of India joining the ASEAN. The case for integration is typically not accepted by many groups within a country and other countries of the World, which explains why most attempts to achieve regional economic integration have been contentious and halting. It also encourages FDI to transfer technology, necessity and managerial know-how to host nations. Moreover, the role of knowledge in stimulating economic growth, opening a country to FDI also is likely further to stimulate economic growth. In sum, economic theories and experience suggest that free trade and investment is a positive-sum game, in which all participating countries stand to gain. While the political case for Asian economic integration has also loomed in most attempts to establish free trade areas, Customs Unions, and the like. By linking neighbouring economies and making them increasingly dependent on each other, incentives are created for political cooperation between the neighbouring states. In turn, the potential for violent conflict between the states will be reduced. In addition, by grouping their economies, the country (India) can enhance their political weight in the World. Despite the strong economic and political integration, it has never been easy to achieve and sustain for two main reasons, i.e. (i) Although economic integration benefits the majority, it has its cost. While, a nation as a whole may benefit significantly from a Regional Foreign Trade agreement, certain groups may lose; and (ii) A second impediments to integration arises from concerns over national sovereignty.

The tide has been running strongly in favour of the Regional Foreign Trade Agreements in recent years. Some of the economists have expressed their concern that the benefits of regional integration have been over soled. While the costs have often been ignored. They point out that the benefits of Regional Integration are determined by the extent of Trade Creation as against opposed to a trade diversion. Further, trade creation occurs when high-cost domestic producers are replaced by low-cost procedures within the Free Trade Area. Trade diversion occurs when lower-cost external suppliers are replaced by higher-cost suppliers within the free trade area. A regional free trade agreement will benefits the world only if the amount of trade it creates exceeds the amount it diverts. However, we can conclude that joining the ASEAN trade group, India have to reduce the tariff and non-tariff barriers while, on the other hand India will be gaining the relations which will further boost the India's prestige in the trade scenario and regional economic integration.

The JACIK group of Asian countries can face these challenges much more effectively as a group rather individually. The regional economic integration can, by exploiting the synergies, expand the economic opportunities available and strengthen the growth prospects. The foregoing discussion has shown that Asian Economic Community is an idea whose time seems to have come. It is clear from the voices emanating from different places. Therefore, formation of a broader Asian Economic Community could enable the region to resume its rapid growth despite the uncertain global economic outlook and emerge as the centre of gravity in the Global scenario. Regional trade liberalisation accompanied by freer movements of investment, technology and skills among the Asian countries would generate substantial efficiency gains by enabling the participants to exploit their complementarities to mutual advantage. Furthermore, regional Keynesianism based on cooperation in finance and monetary policy has the potential to help the region to recover hundreds of billions of dollars of potential output lost due to under utilisation of capacity and pull the major economies such as Japan out of prolonged recession. As Asia looks to the future, the most important challenge it faces is how to adapt to globalisation with its wide-ranging impact on trade patterns, production processes, employment opportunities, and financial linkages. However, an ambitious programme such as this has to be implemented in a phased manner as explained earlier. Further, one should not underestimate the political challenges to getting an ambitious programme such as this off the ground. These challenges are no more than those faced by the European countries when they began their plans for economic integration in the beginning. The most significant of these is the trend towards further, globalisation of the world economy accompanied by a progressive liberalisation. There is globalization in trade, in production and in finance, and all of these are all closely connected, yet quite distinct. The globalisation trend in trade, especially intra-industry trade, is connected with the globalisation trend in production, whereby different stages of manufactures production are being split-up and located in different geographical regions. The globalisation of production is connected with—though not synonymous with—the globalisation of firms. Firms have increased the volume of their international transactions, and corporate strategies are increasingly geared towards specific regions of the world in terms of both supply, i.e. organisation of production and demand (i.e. the servicing of markets). Hence, we can say that there are no more exclusively regional or global markets. Related to this is the increased competition among enterprises. Large and small firms have responded to this by regionalising, specialising via product differentiation and often by forging business alliances on the supply, marketing and production fronts. Developing Asian Economic Integration is a home to nearly two thirds of the world's poor people. Asian Economic Integration can be a powerful tool to help all the countries to sustain high levels of economic and employment growth, to spread the benefits of growth more equitably, and to realise the dream of an Asian region free from poverty.

Notes and References

1. WTO's Discussion Paper No. 8: "The Changing Landscape of Regional Trade Agreements" by Jo-Ann Crawford and Roberto V. Fiorentino, 2005.
2. World Economics and Financial Surveys: "Asia and Pacific Regional Economic Outlook, May, 2006, p. 72.
3. Hu Yue Qiang: "The (10+3) Meeting of Leaders of the ASEAN, China, Japan and Korea", p. 2, September 30, 2003.
4. "ASEAN to Form Free Trade Zone with China, Japan and India", Tempointeraktif.com, September 5, 2003.
5. Li Wei, "A Road to Common Prosperity: Examination of An FTA between India and China." RIS Discussion Paper 49, March 2003, pp. 1-2.
6. The Two-day Conference, jointly organised by the RIS with the Institute of South East Asian Studies (ISEAS), Singapore and supported by the Sasakawa Peace Foundation, Japan and UNDP, at New Delhi from 18-19 November, 2005.
7. RIS, Discussion Papers No. RIS-DP# 89/2005, entitled " China's Role in the Asian Economic Unification Process", by Mr. Yao Chao Cheng, Associate Professor, Faculty of International Trade of Shanxi University of Finance and Economic, 696, Wu Cheng Road, Tsiyuan, China.
8. Host Rolly, "Concerning India and China, Huntington see no way of removing the existing fault line between the two nations", p. 354, 1999.
9. Government of India: "Estimated in India Infrastructure Report", 1996.
10. Jo-Ann Crawford and Roberto V. Fiorentino: WTO Discussion Paper No. 8 entitled, "The Changing Landscape of Regional Trade Agreements", WTO, 2005, p.15.
11. Mr. Sobhan Rehman, "Towards An Asian Economic Area: Some Conceptual Issues", RIS and South Centre, New Delhi, Macmillan, 1995.
12. WTO: "World Trade Report: 2006: Exploring the links between subsidies, trade and the WTO, 2006" and WTO: "International Trade Statistics, 2005, WTO: 2005, pp. 9-11 and 89.
13. Estevadeordal Antoni, and Kati Suominen, "Rules of Origin: A World Map", Preliminary Draft, April 2003.
14. The World Bank's Annual Report-Global Economic Prospects 2005: Trade, Regionalism and Development 2005", The World Bank, 2005.
15. Danielle Goldfarb, "The Road to a Canada-US Customs Union", C.D. House Institute, No. 184, June 2003, pp. 7-13.

Index